Halliburton
Edgar Allan Poe: a
phenomenological view

Edgar Allan Poe

A PHENOMENOLOGICAL VIEW

Edgar Allan Poe

A PHENOMENOLOGICAL VIEW

DAVID HALLIBURTON

PRINCETON UNIVERSITY PRESS

L.C. Card: 72-4042
ISBN: 0-691-06237-4

This book has been composed in Linotype Times Roman

Printed in the United States of America
by Princeton University Press,
Princeton, New Jersey

FOR

Mary Ann

Murphy

Susannah

AND

Jyllian

Acknowledgments

I am indebted to David Levin and Claude M. Simpson, Jr., who did much to improve the manuscript; to Herbert S. Lindenberger, whose advice was valuable at every stage of composition; and to Albert J. Guerard, Robert Polhemus, and Lucio Ruotolo, whose counsel was a source of encouragement.

To J. Hillis Miller I owe my thanks for a number of helpful criticisms and suggestions. Carol Orr, of Princeton University Press, was unfailing in her efforts to see the book into print, while R. Miriam Brokaw shepherded my pages through the press with courtesy and skill.

Finally, I owe a particular debt to the late Frederick J. Hoffman, who was largely responsible for turning me toward the scholarly life, and to Philip Wheelwright, who helped me to think about thought.

Table of Contents

Edgar Allan Poe

A PHENOMENOLOGICAL VIEW

“Es gilt, einen *Weg* zur Aufhellung der ontologischen Fundamentalfrage zu suchen und zu *gehen*. Ob er der *einzige* oder überhaupt der *rechte* ist, das kann erst *nach dem Gang* entschieden werden.”

[The point is, to find a *way* to the clarification of the fundamental ontological question, and to *go* it. Whether it is the *only* way, or generally the *right* one, can only be decided *after the going*.] —Martin Heidegger

“By the very nature of things, as England is not all the world, much of the best that is known and thought in the world cannot be of English growth, must be foreign. . . . The English critic of literature, therefore, must dwell much on foreign thought. . . . Again, judging is often spoken of as the critic's one business, and so in some sense it is; but the judgment which almost insensibly forms itself in a fair and clear mind, along with fresh knowledge . . . must be the critic's great concern for himself. And it is by communicating fresh knowledge, and letting his own judgment pass along with it,—but insensibly, and in the second place, not the first, as a sort of companion and clue, not as an abstract lawgiver,—that the critic will generally do most good to his readers.”

—Matthew Arnold

1

FOREWORD

THE READER WILL have gathered, from the epigraphs that head this study, that its orientation is mainly European and phenomenological. The study derives, however, from American and traditional sources as well, and is therefore, in another sense, a work of synthesis. Each point deserves to be amplified, and the best way to do this, it seems to me, is to take them up one at a time. I have accordingly divided the preliminary section of the book into two parts: a methodological introduction, which clarifies phenomenological assumptions and procedures, and this foreword, which will attempt to explain the background of the study, my intellectual debts, and the relation of my commentary to existing scholarly work.

Poe's hard-won status as a major writer seems secure, though it is also true that he remains, as F. O. Matthiessen pointed out in 1946, the most controversial "of the major American authors of the nineteenth century."[1] In the words of Sarah Helen Whitman, whose defense of Poe appeared in 1860, "There are persons whom nature has made non-conductors to this sort of electricity."[2] Time has shown that there are just as many persons, or more, who conduct it very well. In 1848, the year before Poe's death, James Russell Lowell could offer, in his "Fable for Critics," the celebrated doublet

> "Here comes Poe with his Raven, like Barnaby Rudge—
> Three-fifths of him genius, and two-fifths sheer fudge."

If he were alive today Lowell might want to lower the fraction of fudge, for Poe has grown in stature to a degree that Lowell could not have foreseen. Jay B. Hubbell has traced this

[1] F. O. Matthiessen, "Edgar Allan Poe," *Literary History of the United States*, ed. Robert E. Spiller et al., 3rd ed., rev. (New York, 1963), p. 321.

[2] Sarah Helen Whitman, *Edgar Poe and His Critics* (New York, 1860), p. 39.

growth, showing, in an amusing account, the changing attitudes of the New England academic establishment, especially those of the critic Barrett Wendell, who began by burying Poe and who ended, like so many of his contemporaries and successors, by praising him.[3] After a quarter century, Matthiessen's summary view of Poe's status remains valid: "Poe wrote at a time when America was producing more real and alleged transcendental geniuses than maturely wrought poems or stories. In opposition to the romantic stress on the expression of personality, he insisted on the importance, not of the artist, but of the created work of art. He stands as one of the very few great innovators in American literature."[4]

In the placing and revaluation of Poe, foreign interpreters have played a crucial role. Hamilton Wright Mabie, introducing a volume of the Virginia edition of Poe's works, recalls Matthew Arnold's view "that contemporary foreign opinion of a writer is probably the nearest approach which can be made to the judgment of posterity. The judgment of English, French, and German critics has been, on the whole, unanimous in accepting Poe at a much higher valuation than has been placed upon him at home, where Lowell's touch-and-go reference in the 'Fable for Critics' has too often been accepted as an authoritative and final opinion from the highest literary tribunal." Donning the same prophetic mantle that Poe so often wore, Mabie goes on to predict that "As literary interests broaden in this country, and the provincial point of view gives place to the national, the American estimate of Poe will approach more nearly the foreign estimate."[5] The prediction has long since come true, partly through the "international diplomacy" of mediators like Edmund Wilson, partly through the labors of such commentators (less known today but influential in their own time) as Arthur Ransome, and

[3] Jay B. Hubbell, *The South in American Literature: 1607-1900* (Durham, N.C., 1954), pp. 548-549.

[4] "Edgar Allan Poe," *Literary History of the United States*, p. 342.

[5] "Poe's Place in American Literature," in *The Complete Works of Edgar Allan Poe*, the "Virginia Edition," ed. James A. Harrison (New York, 1902), II, xxiv-xxv.

partly through the efforts of Patrick F. Quinn, who has presented the French conception of Poe with exemplary thoroughness and care.[6]

The present study emphasizes what, as Matthiessen said, Poe himself chose to emphasize: the importance, not of the artist, but of the created work of art. My concern, in other words, is with the reading and understanding of texts. What this means in specific terms will emerge from the study itself. Here I can only suggest the background from which such an orientation derives, pointing out the extent to which it differs from, and the extent to which it resembles, the orientation of earlier workers in the field.

First, as to differences. This study does not deal directly with biographical materials, although it has benefited from works that do. Arthur Hobson Quinn's *Edgar Allan Poe: A Critical Biography* (New York, 1941) and N. Bryllion Fagin, *The Histrionic Mr. Poe* (Baltimore, 1949), both of which explore the relation between life and text, have been particularly useful. Fagin, whose book is not strictly biographical, offers a valuable cautionary remark about the relative weighting of an author's writings and an author's life. After citing Jacques Barzun's observation that Romantic artists are looked at primarily from a biographical perspective, Fagin observes: "It is wholesome to be reminded that what the man did in his work is a greater—if not the sole—justification for adding another volume to the overstocked shelves of the world than his merely having been a boy, a man, a husband, a lover, a pessimist, an optimist, a neurotic, a kindly soul, a boor, or a gentleman."[7]

This book has less in common with those psychoanalytically oriented works which tend to regard the text as a clin-

[6] Edmund Wilson, *Axel's Castle: A Study in the Imaginative Literature of 1870-1930* (New York and London, 1948), esp. pp. 12-19; Arthur Ransome, "Postscript: The French View of Poe," in *Edgar Allan Poe: A Critical Study* (London, 1910), pp. 219-237; Patrick F. Quinn, *The French Face of Edgar Poe* (Carbondale, Ill., 1957).

[7] N. Bryllion Fagin, *The Histrionic Mr. Poe* (Baltimore, 1949), pp. 16-17.

ical phenomenon. I have in mind Joseph Wood Krutch, *Edgar Allan Poe: A Study in Genius* (New York, 1926); Marie Bonaparte, *The Life and Works of Edgar Allan Poe,* trans. John Rodker (London, 1949); and some other commentators whose contributions are discussed in Philip Young's article, "The Earlier Psychologists and Poe."[8] These critics are worth reading, nonetheless, and their analyses have played an important historical role in the development of Poe criticism.[9] On Poe's legitimate merits as a psychologist I shall have, at the appropriate time, some comments of my own. There are, however, two differences between the way I use psychology and the way it is employed by the critics referred to above. The first difference is that my interpretations derive from the phenomenological and existential tradition, represented by such European figures as Jean-Paul Sartre, Eugène Minkowski, Ludwig Binswanger, Jacques Lacan, J. H. Van den Berg, and Roland Kuhn, and such American or Americanized figures as Erwin Straus and Rollo May. The second difference is that I attempt, on the few occasions when I try my hand at this type of analysis, to explore not the life of the author, but the life of particular works.

There were once two schools of thought about the relation between these works and the everyday world. One school held in effect that there *was* no relation, because Poe's imagination belonged to no particular time or place. The opposing school, now ascendant, argued that Poe was preeminently a man of his time: a nineteenth-century American who carried Southern values into Yankee country, and whose life was interwoven with the life of his national and regional culture. If we turn again to Mabie's comments in the Virginia edition, we find an interesting tension between the two views. Mabie first argues that Poe's "creative work baffles all attempts to

[8] Philip Young, "The Earlier Psychologists and Poe," *American Literature*, 22 (1950), pp. 442-454.

[9] See, for example, Roy P. Basler, "The Interpretation of 'Ligeia,'" *College English*, 5 (1944), pp. 363-372, and Robert Shulman, "Poe and the Powers of the Mind," *ELH*, 37 (1970), pp. 245-262.

relate it historically to antecedent conditions; that it detached itself almost completely from the time and place in which it made its appearance, and sprang suddenly and mysteriously from a soil which had never borne its like before."[10] Mabie then goes on, however, to recognize the influence on Poe of Byron, Moore, and Coleridge, and to suggest that the ideality in Poe is itself a peculiarly American characteristic. He argues further that Poe, like Hawthorne, was driven inward by his culture, which was too busy with practical affairs to spare time for art; then generalizes at length about the difficulties of being an artist in the United States. In these arguments Mabie foreshadows the line of critical development that has focussed on the connections between Poe and his milieu, a line gaining much of its momentum from the work of Killis Campbell, whose essays, "The Mind of Poe," "The Backgrounds of Poe," and "The Origins of Poe," have been supplemented but never supplanted, and Margaret Alterton, whose monograph on the origins of Poe's critical theory[11] remains the starting point for background studies of that apparently inexhaustible subject. In *The World of Washington Irving* Van Wyck Brooks argues that "Poe was bathed in the air of his time, and he was a man of a time when people were living 'Gothically' all about him . . . ," while Jay B. Hubbell demonstrates the Southern background that helped to form Poe and that, despite his Northern years, never ceased to influence him.[12] The political side of Poe is explored in several works, including a lively essay on political satire by William Whipple.[13] The bearing on Poe's work of science, philosophy,

[10] "Poe's Place in American Literature," in *The Complete Works of Edgar Allan Poe*, II, xiv.

[11] Killis Campbell, *The Mind of Poe and Other Studies* (Cambridge, Mass., 1933); Margaret Alterton, *Origins of Poe's Critical Theory* (Iowa City, 1925).

[12] Van Wyck Brooks, *The World of Washington Irving* (New York, 1944), pp. 277-278; Jay B. Hubbell, *The South in American Literature: 1607-1900*, pp. 528-550.

[13] William Whipple, "Poe's Political Satire," *Univ. of Texas Studies in English*, 35 (1956), pp. 81-95.

and *Zeitgeist* is shown in more scholarly writings than I have the space to list,[14] though I must mention a particular debt to I. M. Walker, "The 'Legitimate' Sources of Terror in 'The Fall of the House of Usher,'" *Modern Language Review*, 41 (1966), pp. 585-592. Poe's involvement with literary circles and his journalistic skirmishes, the significance of which was long underestimated, were taken up by Perry Miller in *The Raven and the Whale* (New York, 1956) and at closer range by Sidney P. Moss in *Poe's Literary Battles: The Critic in the Context of His Literary Milieu* (Durham, N.C., 1963). John Walsh's study, *Poe the Detective: The Curious Circumstances Behind "The Mystery of Marie Roget"* (New Brunswick, N.J., 1967), shows how changing circumstances and publishing pressures affected Poe's fictionalization of the Mary Rogers case.

While there is no precise equivalent in my study to researches of this type, I have attempted to relate Poe to several contexts. In the literary sphere I have compared certain of his practices to those of some English Romantics. In the sphere of the history of ideas I have tried to show the relevance, looking backward, of such thinkers as Leibniz, Pascal, and Schopenhauer, and the relevance, looking forward, of Sartre, Martin Heidegger, C. S. Peirce, and Paul Ricoeur. I have endeavored to trace connections between Poe's thought and the problem of the man-made or "technological" environment. If my efforts in such areas are modest, this is for three reasons. First, because previous investigators have done so much; secondly, because this study has a different focus, which I have not wanted to lose; and thirdly, because of cer-

[14] Of more than usual interest are Edward Hungerford, "Poe and Phrenology," *American Literature*, 2 (1930), pp. 209-231; Sidney E. Lind, "Poe and Mesmerism," *PMLA*, 61 (1947), pp. 1,077-1,094; Margaret Kane, "Edgar Allan Poe and Architecture," *Sewanee Review*, 40 (1932), pp. 149-160; George Kelley, "Poe's Theory of Unity," *Philological Quarterly*, 37 (1958), pp. 34-44; Floyd Stovall, "Poe's Debt to Coleridge," *Univ. of Texas Studies in English*, 10 (1930), pp. 70-127; Albert J. Lubell, "Poe and A. W. Schlegel," *Journal of English and Germanic Philology*, 52 (1953), pp. 1-12, and Robert D. Jacobs, *Poe: Journalist and Critic* (Baton Rouge, 1969).

tain disadvantages attaching to the very researches mentioned at the start of this sentence. I refer to the fact that contextual studies, as they increase in density and volume, can deter understanding (if they are not handled with discrimination) nearly as much as they advance it. Excessive concentration on source-hunting, for example, has meant, in the case of "The City in the Sea," neglect of the text, and plain misinterpretation. The phenomena of a work, I am suggesting, are not necessarily accounted for as soon as one discovers what the author had read—or, more often, might have read. The aim of exegesis is to explain, not to explain away. More distracting, and older, is the practice of concealing the work beneath layers of censure or, what is sometimes worse, of appreciation. Of "The Fall of the House of Usher" G. E. Woodberry declares: "Not a few would rank this tale more high than 'Ligeia'; for, if that be more distinguished by ideality, this is more excellent in the second virtue in Poe's scale, unity of design. In artistic construction it does not come short of absolute perfection. The adaptation of the related parts and their union in the total effect are a triumph of literary craft; the intricate details, as it were mellowing and reflecting one ground tone, have the definiteness and precision of inlaid mosaic, or, like premonitions and echoes of the theme in music, they are so exactly calculated as to secure their end with the certainty of harmonic law itself."[15] Woodberry expresses the feelings of a genteel age that, faced by an "impossibly unaesthetic whirl of social conditions,"[16] enshrined the Ideal and had a Walter Pater to show that a pedestal of enduring criticism could be set up on a base of firm appreciation. But if Pater was unique, Woodberry was typical, meaning that the critic had done his job if he had exhibited sundry literary "beauties." The trouble was that the critic put so much into the defense of his man, and into the enrich-

[15] G. E. Woodberry, *The Life of Edgar Allan Poe, Personal and Literary, with His Chief Correspondence with Men of Letters* (Boston, 1909), I, 229.

[16] Larzer Ziff, *The American 1890s: Life and Times of a Lost Generation* (New York, 1966), p. 22.

ment of his own prose, that he had nothing left for the texts. That is an exaggeration, but the essential point can be verified, I believe, by even a casual reading of criticism in the period. The result, often, is that the critic does not have the time to follow up his own insight. Thus Woodberry offers the startling suggestion that the plot of "The Fall of the House of Usher" is identical with the plot of "Berenice," but drops the issue in order to expatiate, in the passage quoted above, on music and mosaic.

The easy moralizing of the "Genteel Age" (which continued its influence long after periodization declared it dead) merges imperceptibly with the easy psychologizing of a later day. This is less paradoxical than may first appear, for the psychological investigator relies upon a sense of the abnormal that is not far removed from a sense of wrong. Deviation is error, and the psychologist's job, like the moralist's, is to amend it. The Marxist quarrel with "psychologism" is based not upon its solipsistic tendencies but upon the fact that its identification with prevailing morality perpetuates the status quo, diverting energy from collective channels to channels that are essentially private. The phenomenologist quarrels, too, and would ask the curer of souls to suspend his normative assumptions, the better to identify with the being he is trying to understand, and the better, through understanding, to help him.

Having mentioned some tendencies to which the present study offers a rejoinder, I should now like to indicate the kinds of work, within the limits that space allows, to which it is directly indebted or from which it indirectly derives. I have been greatly helped (to confine myself for now to the American scene) by Allen Tate's essays, "Our Cousin, Mr. Poe" and "The Angelic Imagination,"[17] which clarified the metaphysical questions raised by Poe's philosophical or angelic dialogues, and by the introduction W. H. Auden wrote for an edition of Poe's works.[18] I have learned much from in-

[17] The two essays, variously reprinted, are presently available in Allen Tate, *The Man of Letters in the Modern World: Selected Essays, 1928-1955* (New York, 1955), pp. 113-145.

[18] W. H. Auden, "Introduction" to *Edgar Allan Poe: Selected*

dividual essays, especially Leo Spitzer, "A Reinterpretation of 'The Fall of the House of Usher' "; Maurice Beebe, "The Universe of Roderick Usher"; and several essays (recently collected) by Floyd Stovall.[19] I am conscious of a special debt to Edward H. Davidson's *Edgar Allan Poe*, which proceeds "according to two critical theorems: one is the general premises of . . . 'Romantic idealism' from Wordsworth and Coleridge in England through Emerson and Poe himself in America; the other is a nineteenth- and a twentieth-century philosophy of aesthetics and symbolism which, from Emerson, Horace Bushnell, Peirce, and William James, down through Whitehead, Cassirer, and their followers . . . has suggested that works of art are not at the mercy of psychology and 'psychologism' but have meanings quite beyond anything material or temporary. So conceived, art is regarded as having a specific and autonomous function, both a part of and yet beyond the time and place in which it is formed; it is a way—for Poe the primal way—of man's knowing the world."[20] I shall often differ with Davidson in the pages that follow—especially with the unacknowledged psychologism that is evident, ironically, in his own approach—but always with the sense of invigoration that comes from contact with a lively mind.

I have also gained much from studies that deal with Poe in relation to other writers, or in relation to an overarching theme, such as Roy Harvey Pearce, *The Continuity of American Poetry* (Princeton, 1961), and William Carlos Williams, *In the American Grain* (New York, 1925). The sections on

---

Prose and Poetry (New York, 1950), reprinted in *The Recognition of Edgar Allan Poe: Selected Criticism since 1829*, ed. Eric W. Carlson (Ann Arbor, 1966).

19 Leo Spitzer, "A Reinterpretation of 'The Fall of the House of Usher,' " in his *Essays in English and American Literature*, ed. Anna Hatcher (Princeton, 1962), pp. 51-66; Maurice Beebe, "The Universe of Roderick Usher," *Personalist*, 37 (1956), pp. 147-160; and Floyd Stovall, *Edgar Poe the Poet: Essays New and Old on the Man and his Work* (Charlottesville, Va., 1969).

20 Edward H. Davidson, *Edgar Allan Poe: A Critical Study* (Cambridge, Mass., 1957), p. viii.

Poe in Robert Martin Adams, *Nil: Episodes in the Literary Conquest of Void during the Nineteenth Century* (New York, 1966), and Edwin Fussell, *Frontier: American Literature and the American West* (Princeton, 1965), were both instructive. It is also interesting to see, in retrospect, how one's analyses are influenced by works that are unsympathetic to one's subject. This was the case with the essay, "Edgar Allan Poe: A Crisis in the History of American Obscurantism," in Yvor Winters' *In Defense of Reason* (Denver and New York, 1947), a critique that by its very thoroughness and severity helped me to come to terms with the full meaning of Poe's art. Winters, as it happens, was the writer who awoke me to the possibilities of literary analysis, though the final effect of this influence may be more apparent to the author of these pages than to their reader. It may also be worth noting, in passing, that Winters' approach to Poe, stressing the agreement between his theory and his practice, paradoxically served to spread the idea, now generally held, that Poe's imaginative productions form a coherent whole.

Henry Bamford Parkes, while confessing his doubts about Poe's greatness, submits the following valuable generalization: "While Emerson, Thoreau, and Whitman are concerned with what America ought to be, Poe, Hawthorne, and Melville indicated what America actually was. These three writers, so different from each other in all their personal qualities, were alike in their basic preoccupations. Each of them saw life in terms of a battle between the will of man and his environment; for each of them there was nothing higher than the individual will, so that man, instead of subordinating himself to some ideal order or harmony, was tempted to strive for omnipotence. . . ." Parkes then draws a parallel between Coleridge and Poe. Coleridge, he suggests, "takes his bearings from the social order, and he may either rebel against it (like Coleridge in his youth) or idealize it and submit to it (like Coleridge in his old age). But Poe found himself in a void and could seek to make himself secure only by means of a fantastic exaggeration of the drive to power. He became pure will seeking omnipotence."[21] I shall try to show in my study that what Parkes calls a will to power is finally indistinguishable from a will—evident throughout Poe's writings —to affirmation. Thus a leading goal of Poe's imaginative works is transcendence or "going beyond"—the making of a bad situation into a good one, the reworking of an adequate poem into a better one, the conquest of decay and death through a theory of indestructible life. The pursuit of the goal is lifelong, and accounts, in substantial measure, I believe, for the "full design" of his works. This design has been seen from a variety of perspectives by a variety of critics, to many of whom, in different degrees, I am indebted. I have found value, for example, in a recent article by Joseph Moldenhauer, who argues that Poe "pursued a unity theory of metaphysics, nature, art, and the human mind," and that, although his works display "polar modes of imagination," one can discern behind them "a center of meaning or a unified design. . . ."[22]

If the present study is fed by all of the main currents described above (to borrow V. L. Parrington's metaphor) it is nourished to an even greater degree by the work of European or European-born philosophers and interpreters, and of American thinkers with similar views. The chief tutelary spirits of my book are Jean-Paul Sartre, Martin Heidegger, Gaston Bachelard, and Georges Poulet, the *Philologen* Leo Spitzer and Erich Auerbach, and the Americans, C. S. Peirce and Kenneth Burke. Only the pages that follow can demonstrate the extent to which I have profited from acquaintance with these minds. I should like, however, to borrow a few

[21] Henry Bamford Parkes, *The American Experience: An Interpretation of the History and Civilization of the American People* (1947; reprinted, New York, 1959), pp. 204, 205.

[22] Joseph Moldenhauer, "Murder as a Fine Art: Basic Connections between Poe's Aesthetics, Psychology, and Moral Vision," *PMLA*, 83 (1968), pp. 284-297. Also concerned with design, *inter alia*, are, G. W. Peck, "Mere Music," *The Literary World*, 50 (1850), pp. 225-226; Davidson, *Edgar Allan Poe: A Critical Study*, esp. pp. 75, 134, 158, and Stephen L. Mooney, "Poe's Grand Design: A Study of Theme and Unity in the Tales," Diss. Tennessee, 1961, and Jacobs, *Poe: Journalist and Critic*.

words from Kenneth Burke, who has shaped my thinking as much, perhaps, as anyone, and who has suggested some of the principles on which the present book is framed. In an article on Poe's "The Philosophy of Composition" Burke expresses his reservations about the biographical, the historical, and the "temporally 'genetic' account of a work's development." Such analyses, he says, "do provide us with a high-class kind of gossip that is often worth the effort. My point is not that such pursuits should be neglected, but simply that they do not replace the 'principle' involved in Poe's essay. And our problem is to see what can be said for that principle.

"We come closer when we consider a second kind of derivation, the kind that has to do with the poem as a finished public product, an 'art object,' the formal commodity for which you pay your good money. Regardless of where the poet started, of how many revisions he made, of what he added or left out, etc., etc., here is a self-consistent symbol-system, a structure with beginning, middle, and end, a whole with internally related parts. And the critic's job is to *appreciate* this production.

"The problem of derivation here primarily involves a close step-by-step analysis of the particular text, with the attempt to show how the various elements in the work require one another in the course of shaping and guiding and exploiting the expectations of the reader."[23]

My work, too, is oriented in the direction Burke indicates, though it is for the reader to decide whether my efforts are a success. In any case, a study such as mine is possible only because American predecessors have already, by introducing and in a sense domesticating vital foreign sources, helped to bring about a more receptive intellectual climate. I have in mind Charles Feidelson, Jr., whose *Symbolism and American Literature* (Chicago, 1953), draws analogies between nineteenth-century American literary practice and that of certain modern French authors, including Gide; Paul Brodtkorb, Jr.,

[23] Kenneth Burke, "The Principle of Composition," *Poetry*, 99 (1961), pp. 48-49.

who showed, in *Ishmael's White World: A Phenomenological Reading of "Moby Dick"* (New Haven, 1965), that phenomenological procedures are well-suited to the study of American texts; E. D. Hirsch, Jr., whose *Validity in Interpretation* (New Haven, 1967), is the first general treatment in the United States of literary hermeneutics; and Richard E. Palmer, who emphasizes, in *Hermeneutics: Interpretation Theory in Schleiermacher, Dilthey, Heidegger, and Gadamer* (Evanston, 1969), the European development of interpretative philosophies and procedures. Nothing has done more to prepare the way for new developments in native literary thought, finally, than J. Hillis Miller's two influential studies, *The Disappearance of God: Five Nineteenth-Century Writers* (Cambridge, Mass., 1963), and *Poets of Reality: Six Twentieth-Century Writers* (Cambridge, Mass., 1965). A statement by Miller in his preface to a new edition of the earlier work summarizes better than anything I can say the hope that animates my own endeavours: "Now it appears possible that European ways of doing criticism, whether that of the so-called 'Geneva School,' or that of the more recent structuralist critics in Paris, may present themselves to Americans as alternatives to the new criticism or archetypal criticism. The happiest result would be the creation of another indigenous criticism, one assimilating the advances of European criticism in the past twenty years but reshaping these to our peculiarly American experience of literature and its powers."[24]

It is to such assimilation and such reshaping that I have dedicated my energies in the present work.

[24] J. Hillis Miller, *The Disappearance of God: Five Nineteenth-Century Writers* (1963; reprinted, New York, 1965), p. vii.

2

METHODOLOGICAL INTRODUCTION: ASSUMPTIONS AND PROCEDURES

THIS BOOK IS, I believe, the first general interpretation of an American author from a phenomenological point of view.

It will be clear from my remarks in the Foreword that the book is about the writings of Poe and not about phenomenology. That is to say that I am more concerned with the reading of texts than with the illustration of method. What that reading reveals, or fails to reveal, only the book itself can show. I have promised, however, to discuss assumptions and procedures, and to do this I must temporarily reverse this emphasis and talk about phenomenology rather than about Poe. In this way, hopefully, the reader can become acquainted with an interpretative method that, although increasingly discussed, remains unfamiliar to many.

When Santayana observed that "each sort of net drawn through the same sea catches a different sort of fish,"[1] he was suggesting that every method of interpretation has its peculiar assumptions. One of the peculiar assumptions of much current criticism is that the literary work is a discrete object, a kind of inert and neutral "thing," which we can study exactly as we would study any other object in the world. According to this assumption, the critic need not worry about intentions, either the author's or his own. This approach posits, in effect, a "being in itself," called the text, which is totally disconnected both from the consciousness that creates it and from the consciousness that interprets it. The phenomenologist holds a different view. Without denying that the work has, in some sense, a life of its own, the phenomenologist believes that the work cannot be cut off from the intentionality that made it or from the intentionality that experiences it after it is made. If the work does not arise from *some* act of consciousness, how does it come to be? If the work is not interpreted by

[1] George Santayana, *The German Mind: A Philosophical Diagnosis* (New York, 1968), p. 40. Originally published under the title, *Egotism in German Philosophy*.

some act of consciousness, how does criticism come to be? To the phenomenologist the idea of a text-itself is a mystification arising from an historical situation in which criticism, in order to compete with more privileged disciplines, has tried to assimilate the literary work to scientific models. The phenomenologist questions the relevance of such models, much as he questions the "objectivity" that is sometimes claimed by critics whose procedures are based on the unexamined assumptions of nineteenth-century positivism. Writing might be described as an act in which a subjectivity passes into an objectivity without surrendering its own identity. When the author lays down his pen there are words on the page that were not there before. The author has created something apart from himself, an entity at once concrete, accessible to others, and reproducible. Yet this new thing preserves the intentional acts through which it came into being. The final product of the creative act is, then, a fusion in which both elements, the subjective and the objective, merge. An interpreter who attempts to construe the meaning of a text without regard to its intentional aspects limits himself unnecessarily. He denies precisely that aspect of the work which makes it something other than a laboratory paramecium, a speck of sand, or a molecule. In doing this he denies at the same time the subjective, intentional element in himself, surrendering thereby his most natural means of access to the text. The phenomenologist acknowledges this means and uses it, believing as he does that he can best approach a work through the capacities that he shares with its creator.

The intentionality he seeks out is not in the author but in the text. This is not to deny the value of, for example, biographical sources, such as letters and diaries, that are indispensable if one's emphasis falls on the life of the writer rather than on his works and that can be helpful in testing hypotheses that the interpreter develops in his reading. I have employed such sources, indeed, in the present study. But the best source for the analyst who is interested mainly in the word on the page *is* the word on the page. That word and that page, however, are precisely what many readers, including university students of literature, are unwilling to face. Nothing produces more anxiety in such a student than a confrontation with the actual workings of a sentence—its grammar and syntax, its diction, its structures and tensions. The anxiety only increases when it becomes necessary to relate one sentence to another, to discern the unfolding of a complex pattern, or to express, in any but the vaguest terms, the relation between the sentences and the author's presentation of character, class, money, God, or sex. The student develops defensive strategies that vary considerably but that always involve a shift away from the text toward something tidier and, frequently, more abstract. How do we discover the meaning of four consecutive sentences of paragraph seven on page 25? We invoke an "ism"—Romanticism, Naturalism, Impressionism. Or we reconsider the arguments for and against the view that the author drank. Or we turn to a "real" source, an entry in a daybook, for example, or a letter to a cousin. That such a letter may express an intention different from the one in the text under study is a possibility we would prefer not to contemplate.

The phenomenologist, on the other hand, tries, with the Russian Formalists, to meet the text, and to stick with it. This involves a willingness to put aside, for a time at least, considerations of value, personal taste, or ideology. The alternative (to take an extreme case) is the kind of misinterpretation that Boris Tomashevsky complains about in his essay "Thematics." Ostrovsky wrote a novel, *The Bankrupt*, about a character whom critics, because of the ideological commitment, found objectionable: "Such a misinterpretation of a work of art because of its ideology may create a completely insurmountable wall between the reader and the work if the reader begins to evaluate the emotions generated within the work in terms of his everyday personal or political feelings. To read, one must be innocent, must catch the signs the author gives."[2] In other words, to get hold of the text the interpreter must first, in a sense, let go. This letting go represents the passive side of interpretation which is often thought of, onesidedly, as an active, muscular, all-conquering enterprise. So it is for those critics whose principal concern is a knightly championing of causes. That is not the concern of the interpreter who would rather see what is in front of him and never judge it, than judge it and never see it. This does not mean the interpreter denies himself the option of deciding when something is good or bad, but only that he exercises the option, if at all, after his analysis is complete. The interpreter responds, in Descartes' words, to "what presents itself spontaneously to our senses. . . ." In the words of Count Yorck von Wartenburg, the interpreter must wait and listen: ". . . if you are still you will hear, that is, understand (wenn ihr stille seid so werdet ihr vernehmen das heisst verstehen)."[3] For Leo Spitzer understanding begins with a long, slow look. Reflecting on his experience as a philologist, he recalls: "how often, with all the theoretical experience of method accumulated in me over the years, have I stared blankly, quite similar to my beginning students, at a page that would not yield its magic. The only way leading out of this state of unproductivity is to read and reread, patiently and confidently, in an endeavour to become, as it were, soaked through and through with the atmosphere of the work. And suddenly, one word, one line, stands out, and we realize that, now, a relationship has been established between the poem and us. . . . And looking back on this process (whose end, of course, marks only the conclusion of the *preliminary* stage of analysis), how can we say when exactly it began? (Even the 'first step' was preconditioned.) We see, indeed, that to read is to have read, to understand is equivalent to having understood."[4]

[2] In *Russian Formalist Criticism: Four Essays*, trans. and with an introduction by Lee T. Lemon and Marion J. Reis (Lincoln, Neb., 1965), p. 90.

[3] Martin Heidegger, *Sein und Zeit*, 11th ed., unchanged (Tübingen, 1967), p. 401.

[4] *Linguistics and Literary History: Essays in Stylistics* (Princeton, 1948), pp. 26-27.

Peirce likens the phenomenologist to the artist who breaks through preconceived categories to see things in the world that have always been there but that have simply been overlooked. Peirce goes on to suggest (in a variation on Spitzer's analogy) that the phenomenologist sees "what stares one in the face, just as it presents itself, unreplaced by any interpretation, unsophisticated by any allowance for this or that supposed modifying circumstance."[5] Phenomenology does not distinguish between "good and bad in any sense whatever, but just contemplates phenomena as they are, simply opens its eyes and describes what it sees; not what it sees in the real as distinguished from figment—not regarding any such dichotomy—but simply describing the object, as a phenomenon, and stating what it finds in all phenomena alike."[6]

Literary phenomena differ from natural phenomena because they arise from human consciousness and human being. In Sartre's terms, verbal statements have signification while things, material things, have meaning: "Things signify nothing. Yet each of them has a meaning. By *signification* I mean a certain conventional relationship which makes a present object the substitute of an absent object; by *meaning* I denote the participation of the being of a present reality in the being of other realities, whether present or absent, visible or invisible, and, eventually, in the universe. Signification is conferred upon the object from without by a signifying intention; meaning is a natural quality of things. The former is a transcendent relationship between one object and another; the latter, a transcendence that has fallen into immanence."[7] The literary interpreter attempts to discover this signifying intention, and to identify with it sufficiently to determine "where it goes"—to ascertain, in other words, its aim and final purpose.

"Literature," writes J. Hillis Miller, "is a form of con-

[5] *The Collected Papers of Charles Sanders Peirce*, ed. Charles Hartshorne and Paul Weiss (Cambridge, Mass., 1931-1935), v, para. 42.

[6] Peirce, v, para. 37.

[7] *Saint Genet: Actor and Martyr* (New York, 1964), p. 332.

sciousness, and literary criticism is the analysis of this form in all its varieties. Though literature is made of words, these words embody states of mind and make them available to others. The comprehension of literature is a process of what Gabriel Marcel calls 'intersubjectivity.' Criticism demands above all that gift of participation, that power to put oneself within the life of another person, which Keats called negative capability. If literature is a form of consciousness the task of the critic is to identify himself with the subjectivity expressed in the words, to relive that life from the inside, and to constitute it anew in his criticism."[8]

Now the intentionality in the work evidently differs from other kinds of intentionality. There is, for example, the "pure" intentionality sought after by a systematic philosopher such as Husserl. On another level there is the aggregate of intentional acts that occur during the course of composition. And finally there is the intentionality expressed in the work. The phenomenological interpreter draws extensively on the theoretical foundations provided by Husserl, but endeavors to go beyond them by showing, as Husserl never chose to do, the complex role of intentionality in literary art.[9] The interpreter does not explore the second type of intentionality simply because it is nowhere to be found. During the writing process the creating consciousness intends many things that never reach the stage of final expression (i.e., the stage at which the words are placed on the page and allowed to remain). They do not reach this stage because they are negated in favor of other intentions, which is to say that certain intentions disappear into other intentions, which may persist or which may in turn disappear into still others. The totality of surviving intentions is the literary work; and it is with

[8] *The Disappearance of God: Five Nineteenth-Century Writers*, p. ix.

[9] Husserl recognized, however, that the work of art had its own peculiar mode of being, as indicated by his remark that "auch die Fiktionen ihre Seinsart haben." See Roman Ingarden, *Das Literarische Kunstwerk: Mit einem Anhang von den Funktionen der Sprache im Theaterschauspiel*, 3rd ed., rev. (Tübingen, 1965), p. xv.

this that the interpreter is primarily concerned. To summarize: the intention caught in the work is no longer purely subjective, though it arises from an intending subjectivity. Through the act of writing, subjectivity passes into objectivity, but without losing its subjective aspect. The work therefore can neither be equated with the subjectivity from which it emanates, nor divorced from it. The subjectivity is still "there," but is there in a unique way that is at once free and bound—free from the author in that he is not identical with what he makes, and bound to him in that he made it. The interpreter does not seek an intention independent of the work (for example, a letter written by the author before or after he started composing or even during composition), for these would merely be the expression of *those* intentions. The interpreter seeks, by definition, that which is in the work, and he makes his discovery—or discoveries, since a work is a series of surviving intentional acts—by standing open to the work; by taking what comes as it comes; by submitting himself to what Beckett calls "the spray of phenomena."

When I employ the first-person in my analyses of Poe, I am attempting to put myself in a situation that the text presents. Typically, a situation involves a character, a discrete consciousness within the work. I say discrete because the character is not to be equated with the creating consciousness that made him. On the contrary, he is the product of that consciousness, and has a subjectivity of his own. At the same time, he cannot be divorced from the creating consciousness that made him. The subjectivity of a character, in other words, is one of the objective elements in a work. The character belongs to the work and does not exist outside it. When I interpret I identify with this character, not in order to burden him with my consciousness, but to assume the weight of his, with the result that he shifts, as it were, toward the interpreter—only toward, for there is an inevitable distance between two subjectivities. *Inter*subjectivity is a relation between, not a condition of, complete identity. "I" am never completely "thou," whether "thou" be another person or a literary work. The process of identification might better be termed an alignment or a coming-near-to. At one point, before the process begins, the character is at a certain distance from me. During the process he comes nearer, hopefully very near, and later, when I turn again to the work of which he is a part, he recedes. My relation to the character is the corollary of the relation between the text and the philological interpreter, who moves, as Spitzer says, "to-and-fro," now scrutinizing an element in the text, now moving toward the whole, now back again to a detail within that whole.

Some readers will object that everything I say, while aligned with a character and while speaking in the first-person, must be subjective. Raw subjectivity is indeed what experience trains us to expect in the "I" of ordinary discourse, whether spoken or written. But "I" or "we" are not necessarily subjective any more than are "he" or "they" necessarily objective. The supposedly neutral, tasteless, and transparent "we" of the critic may mask a visceral, agitated "I" that knows better than to show its face. The aim of the phenomenologically situated "I" is not to extend my subjectivity but to reach the subjectivity of the character in the work. To render the situation of another is to stand outside of myself, and to draw the subjectivity of the other toward a kind of objectivity.

Phenomenology would dissolve the boundaries between subject and object, in order to return a sense of the unity of existence in its day-to-day, lived reality. When a phenomenologist turns toward literature he finds texts, however, in which the split between subject and object is at issue, as in the works of many Romantics, or in which a subjectivity is a central phenomenon, as in many first-person fictions. In this discussion I have been supposing that the hypothetical text was of the latter type, and have concentrated accordingly on a kind of being, that of a character or personage, within a text. But there are other kinds of texts and other kinds of being. A work may present (as in Poe and many Romantic authors) moods, feelings, states. Moreover, a work—any work, including those with characters—is itself a being. It exists as a whole and in its own way. What Max Scheler says of life in general is equally true of those human activities, such as literary creation, that are a part of life: "The physiological and psychic processes of life are strictly identical in an ontological sense. They differ only as phenomena. But even as phenomena they are strictly identical in their structural laws and in the rhythm of their processes. Both processes are nonmechanical, the physiological as well as the psychic. Both are oriented toward a goal and toward wholeness (teleoclitic and holistic)."[10] The work of art, too, is teleoclitic and holistic; it goes somewhere, and it is a whole. The interpreter, if he is to understand the work, must "soak" himself, as Spitzer would say, in this directedness and wholeness. If he does, his interpretation will share some of the qualities that Georges Poulet describes in the writings of Jean Rousset:

"There is not in his eyes any system of the work without a principle of systematization which operates in correlation with that work and which is even included in it. In short, there is no spider-web without a center which is the spider. On the other hand, it is not a question of going from the work to the psychology of the author, but of going back, within the sphere of the work, from the objective elements systematically arranged, to a certain power of organization, inherent in the work itself, as if the latter showed itself to be an intentional consciousness determining its arrangements and solving its problems. So that it would scarcely be an abuse of terms to say that it speaks, by means of its structural elements, an authentic language, thanks to which it discloses itself and means nothing but itself. Such then is the critical enterprise of Jean Rousset. It sets itself to use the objective elements of the work in order to attain, beyond them, a reality not formal, nor objective, written down how-

[10] *Man's Place in Nature*, trans. Hans Meyerhoff (Boston, 1961), p. 74.

ever in forms and expressing itself by means of them. As Focillon demonstrated from the point of view of art history, there is a 'life of forms' perceptible not only in the historic development which they display from epoch to epoch, but within each single work, in the movement by which forms tend therein sometimes to stabilize and become static, and sometimes to change into one another. Thus the two contradictory forces which are always at work in any literary writing, the will to stability and the protean impulse, help us to perceive by their interplay how much forms are dependent on what Coleridge called a shaping power which determines them, replaces them and transcends them."[11]

I have been deliberately shuttling back and forth between the two poles of the subjective and objective in order to show their interdependence, and to suggest that the interpreter must reckon with them when they cross or merge, and not merely when they appear in isolation. In this respect my argument bodies forth the to-and-fro hermeneutic procedure that I previously sketched in the abstract. I do this in the hope of bringing the reader along with me through the processes being described. I "show my cards" at this point, secondly, as a way of demonstrating that I, too, intend; that I intend the perspectives that I have both talked about and embodied; and that I know that I intend. I would now like to pass to-and-fro once more, this time between the poles of "science" and "non-science," with the aim of illustrating one more feature of the phenomenological approach to literature.

My concern here is with the argument that phenomenology can or cannot become truly scientific. Much depends, of course, on what one means by science. If the quantitative sciences are meant, the prospects for a scientific method of interpretation do not appear bright. Consciousness, intentionability, verbal meanings, and nuances are not measurable in the same way as a chemical compound. Neither are they pre-

[11] "The Phenomenology of Reading," *New Literary History: A Journal of Theory and Interpretation*, 1 (1969), pp. 66-67.

dictable. When a monolingual author sits down to write we know that he will write in the one language he knows, and we know that his words and sentences will conform to the system of that language, but we cannot predict with certainty what words he will choose, nor how his sentences will order them. If interpretation aspires to the status of a science, it must be scientific in the ways that are peculiarly suitable for the study of human utterances. Nothing could be more fundamentally scientific than such an approach, for every science, including the so-called exact ones, adapts itself to its subject. At the same time, if to a lesser degree, it adapts its subject to itself, as scientists have come to recognize, inasmuch as the investigator is himself implicated in the field he explores. The literary interpreter, too, must take himself into account—he must become critically self-conscious. He must above all respect the conscious, intentional, human nature of the object he investigates, and develop those methods and procedures which are suited to that object. The chief of these, according to E. D. Hirsch, Jr., is a "logic of validation." The interpreter achieves validation by appealing, not to a principle of quantitative measure, but to a principle of consensus: "A good many disciplines do not pretend to certainty, and the more sophisticated the methodology of the disciplines, the less likely that its goal will be defined as certainty of knowledge. Since genuine interpretation is impossible, the aim of the discipline must be to reach a consensus, on the basis of what is known, that correct understanding has *probably* been achieved."[12] There is nothing immutable about such a consensus; new considerations may cause it to be altered or even replaced: "In order to avoid giving the false impression that there is anything permanent about an interpretive validation or the consensus it aims to achieve, I now prefer the term 'validation' to the more definitive-sounding word 'verification.' To verify is to show that a conclusion is true; to validate is to show that a conclusion is probably true on the

[12] *Validity in Interpretation* (New Haven and London, 1967), p. 17.

basis of what is known. From the nature of the case, the goal of interpretation as a discipline must be the modest one of achieving validations so defined."[13]

The literary work is essentially a game, or a playing (*Spiel*), to borrow the concept of Hans-Georg Gadamer, who, with Roman Ingarden, has helped to provide a fuller theoretical basis for an ontology of art.[14] Art, for Gadamer, is not a means of securing pleasure, but a revelation of being. The work is a phenomenon through which we come to know the world. To call it a *Spiel* is not to reduce the work to a hedonistic pastime. For Gadamer as for Schiller, playing is a high and serious act: "A game is only a game as it comes to pass, yet while it is being played it is master. The fascination of the game casts a spell over us and draws us into it; it is truly the master over the player. The game has its own special spirit. The player chooses which game he will give himself to, but once he chooses he enters a closed world in which the game comes to take place in and through the players. In a sense the game has its own momentum and pushes itself forward; it wills to be played out."[15]

The literary text lives in a *con*text. For the work always exists in association with something other than, but related to, itself. This other, related thing forms a horizon for the work—it is something "against" which the work is experienced. There are, needless to say, several such horizons. In relation to a given work there is the horizon formed by other texts of a similar type, or a different type, by the same author; or by other texts, similar or dissimilar, by other authors. If these other writers are contemporaries, the horizon becomes a period, or a movement, or a *Zeitgeist.* If they are

[13] *Ibid.*, pp. 170-171.

[14] Hans-Georg Gadamer, *Wahrheit und Methode: Grundzüge einer philosophischen Hermeneutik* (Tübingen, 1960). Ingarden's principal writings on literary aesthetics are *Das Literarische Kunstwerk* (see note 9) and *Vom Erkennen des literarischen Kunstwerks* (Tübingen, 1968).

[15] Richard E. Palmer, *Hermeneutics: Interpretation Theory in Schleiermacher, Dilthey, Heidegger, and Gadamer* (Evanston, 1969), p. 172. Cf. Gadamer, *Wahrheit und Methode*, pp. 97ff.

remote in time, the horizon becomes a tradition, a continuity, an evolution. There are political, social, economic, and biographical horizons as well. There is even a horizon within the text—our sense that the text is a whole of a certain type and has certain limits that, when perceived as such by the reader, help him to understand and relate, one to the other, its individual parts. There is, above all, the horizon of life. For the work lives, and speaks truly and beautifully to the living. The act of reading is a process through which the work comes to pass. We are accustomed to calling that process linguistic and psychological. And so it is. But it is also ontological. When someone reads a work, a being experiences a being; and what it experiences is being. When we talk about the "language" of a work, we are talking about one aspect of its being: all our discussions, all our definitions, are implicitly ontological, because they are attempts to bring out, to our own satisfaction, what something *is*. Some critics will view such an idea skeptically. But no one was more cautious in his generalizations about language than Ludwig Wittgenstein, and it was Wittgenstein who said: "*Essence* is expressed in grammar (Das *Wesen* ist in der Grammatik ausgesprochen)."[16] That is why, in this book, I concentrate not only upon language, but upon being, space, and time. For it has seemed to me that there are three kinds of things one can always say about a phenomenon in the work or in the world: that it exists; that it exists somewhere; that it exists sometime. The interpretations that follow are merely attempts to learn what certain works have to say about these things, and how they go about saying them.

I have chosen to discuss Poe because he is an important writer who poses some interesting challenges. Any good writer can be challenging; Poe is unusual in that he seems to stand apart from other American authors. He is "obscure," "obsessive," "metaphysical." His works are little windowless cells; there is passion in them, but they are deficient in

[16] *Philosophical Investigations*, 3rd ed., trans. G.E.M. Anscombe (New York, 1958), p. 116, para. 371.

meaning. The challenge was to discover whether such generalizations are valid, or whether there were other generalizations with which they might be replaced. Is a given work obscure? If not, then what specifically does its language say? Is there a metaphysical element in the work? If so, what does it mean and how does it fit into the author's works as a whole? These are some of the questions I have attempted to answer.

Any interpreter must select a horizon, or horizons, on which to concentrate. I have selected two. One is oriented toward the work, and the things that are in it; the other is oriented toward the world and its relation to those things. The one is concerned primarily with the internal dynamics of works singly and collectively, and with the patterns, unique and common, that they reveal. The other is concerned with the world, by which I mean existence as it is normally experienced by human beings. This is not to say that "historical" contexts are not as valid as "existential" contexts. One could write a valuable study placing Poe, for example, in the context of Romanticism, whether American, English, or Continental, or in the tradition of American pastoralism; and I have offered such perspectives, after my own fashion, when the situation would appear to warrant them. But my chief concern is with the existential situation of the work—the way it stands against the horizon of interrelated phenomena that we call life. I am not speaking of some mystic spirit or *Geist*, but of everyday things: of consciousness, identity, process, body, love, fear, struggle, the material world. Phenomenology, as a philosophical discipline, has investigated these things, and, within its powers, has described and analyzed their operations and structures. "Literary phenomenology," in its own way, must, I believe, try to do the same. What this can mean in practical terms is one of the things, I trust, that the present study will show. To explicate every work that *someone* may consider important is beyond the scope of any interpreter who values economy of argument. I have therefore confined myself wherever possible to works that are well known, and that the reader would reasonably expect a commentator to take up. To keep the study within manageable length, I have focussed on imaginative writings—poems, tales, dialogues, the novel, and *Eureka*—though the criticism and the marginalia enter consideration whenever they can shed some light.

I have kept the organization of the book as simple as possible. Some grouping of texts was obviously necessary; the thing to avoid, it seemed to me, was a grouping that would "lead" the interpretation unduly. It occurred to me that the works already grouped themselves in terms of genre: some were poems, some were dialogues, and so on. Here was a minimal grouping constituted by the intention of the author and accepted by his audience (i.e., readers agree that a poem is not the same literary type as a dialogue). If it was desirable to leave the works *in situ* so far as genre was concerned, it seemed no less desirable to leave them untouched in respect to their order in time. There seemed to be no reason *not* to proceed chronologically within the genres, reading the works in the order in which they were written. I have varied this pattern only where this would cause needless confusion, or where another arrangement—a sub-grouping, as it were—suggested itself within a genre. This was the case with the ratiocinative or detective tales, with the tales and poems devoted to women, and with the "descriptive" or landscape sketches, the determination of type being based, again, on common, self-evident features on which readers are agreed. The chapter on poems begins with the earliest major works and continues chronologically from there, then turns to the poems about women, which are also considered in chronological order. The chapter on the tales takes up the stories about women, the detective stories, a larger group of stories that do not lend themselves to convenient classification, and the landscape tales. With minor exceptions, the ordering remains chronological. The tales about women are discussed first, just after the poems about women, in the belief that this juxtaposition might provide a useful continuity for the reader.

The dialogues are discussed in order in the next chapter, and *Eureka*, Poe's last work, is taken up last. I have adopted this strategy, finally, in the hope of preserving the sense of process that informs every literary work. This is not to deny the merits of the structural approach that has proved so valuable for humane studies in Europe and more recently in the United States. An analyst like Roland Barthes, whose work has influenced my own, can reveal important things by cutting across individual texts, distinguishing their elements, and then regrouping them so as to demonstrate the ways in which they are different or the same. The virtue of reading one work at a time, on the other hand (as Barthes himself does in the second part of his book on Racine),[17] is that you get to know *that* work, and that you can build on this foundation when you encounter other works. The process of "reading along" through one work and into another is an effective way, I believe, of experiencing the dynamic of a work in its line-by-line unfolding. Such an approach serves, finally, as a safeguard against the impulse to premature discriminations and judgments. Each work has its own way of going. One of my jobs as an interpreter is to find this way and go along with it, experiencing the process of the work *as* a process. Another of my jobs is to discover how this way of going relates to the way of going in other works. If I do both jobs successfully, the work survives both as an individual phenomenon and as a part of a whole.

All writing, all interpretation, all language is a naming. When I name, as an interpreter, I offer a creation in response to a creation offered me. I do this because it is only through my making that I can approach the making of another. I will never possess, in all its fullness, that other making—that word, that phrase, that mood, that text. It will always transcend me insofar as I am unable to exhaust it in my experience of it. My experience is not the less real for being limited, nor is the knowledge that results less concrete. It will not be, perhaps, the type of knowledge favored by a reader

[17] *On Racine*, trans. Richard Howard (New York, 1964).

who comes from a different critical tradition; but it is available to him if he will go a little way with me. This involves, on his part, a willingness to let me speak, or rather to let my tradition speak through me, in its own way. That means some unfamiliar ideas derived from modern European philosophy, and some unfamiliar words, including compounds that I will occasionally "make up." The use of neologisms and hyphenated words, though unappealing in some respects to Anglo-Saxon habits of mind, has a long and honorable history that endures to our own day in the writings of Heidegger and Sartre and Kenneth Burke. The interpreter uses such words to designate something that confronts him and for which there is no available term. Heidegger speaks of *In-der-Welt-sein* because he has found such a phenomenon in life, because he is an interpreter, and because an interpreter, to communicate, must name. By naming something that is there, but that has never been designated, the interpreter makes it accessible to understanding. "*Gesang ist Dasein*," says Rilke, and interpretation, too, is being. Like all other types of being, it has its peculiar responsibilities and privileges—not the least of which is the right to speak in its own authentic voice.

3

POEMS

A POEM, for Edgar Allan Poe, is a way of giving presence, or "bodying-forth." Through the meaning and music of words something is brought into being that had not existed before. The phenomenon so rendered may be a man, as in "Tamerlane" or "Israfel," or a thing: a city, for example, as in "The Doomed City" and "The City in the Sea," or an edifice, as in "The Haunted Palace." If the poetic utterance seems "out of Space—out of Time," this is because the experiences Poe selects have something autonomous about them, as if they do not quite depend on the laws of the physical world, or of conventional psychology, or even of poetic verisimilitude. It is as if Poe were asking us to consider each experience, and each poem, as a little world in itself. Yet when we look at the poems all together we see that they are not so hermetic after all, for within the fluctuations in tone, in point of view, in diction, there is always—as steady and organic as a heartbeat—an insistence on a few basic concerns. Without attempting at this stage a full typology, we can say that these include an interest in power and powerlessness; in states of being; in one-to-one relationships and confrontations, especially with mysterious presences; in memory and mourning; in victimization; in dehumanization and its cure; in the relation of body to soul; and, above all, in the need for transcendence and affirmation.

"Tamerlane" depicts a hero who has conquered the known world, while "Al Aaraaf," Poe's longest effort in verse, enters extra-terrestrial space to explore a variety of existences, mortal, angelic, and divine. Yet the plight of the central figures in these works is essentially the same. Tamerlane has never been the master of the force he wields, but its minion; all his life he has performed, like an automaton, the role determined by a malevolent external power. Similarly, in the longer poem the lovers Angelo and Ianthe fall to perdition because a superior power issues a summons to which they do not, or cannot, respond. This fascination with power, which stayed with Poe throughout his career, was shared by many of his precursors. From Blake, with his awe of energy, to Coleridge, with his stress on the shaping spirit of imagination, the Romantic effort is substantially an effort to come to terms with one or another type of power—to gauge its meanings and its magnitude, and, should the occasion arise, to deplore its loss. Wordsworth extols in *The Prelude*, and in other poems so familiar that it would be idle to list them here, the power of nature, the power of human imagination, and the power of God. Shelley's "Hymn to Intellectual Beauty" praises that mysterious "unseen Power" of the ideal that visits every human heart, reinforces the point, more discursively, in "A Defence of Poetry," and offers, in *Prometheus Unbound*, the drama of a defiant, human power struggling against the tyranny of a "Power, which seems omnipotent." Comparable struggles break out repeatedly in Byron, most memorably perhaps, in *Manfred*, a work that influenced Poe, and one that I will discuss in my remarks on "Tamerlane." In thinking long on power, especially the power of imagination, the Romantic poet worried about the consequences should he lose it, giving rise in the process to a tradition of laments over the state of powerlessness. Coleridge's "Dejection: an Ode" belongs obviously to that tradition, as do Shelley's "Stanzas Written in Dejection, near Naples," Byron's "Farewell to the Muse," and, *mutatis mutandis*, Keats's "Ode on Melancholy." On turning to Poe we find what might be described as a merger of two of these strains: a sense of struggle with great powers, as in Shelley's depiction of Prometheus, and a sense of loss and powerlessness, as in the tradition of the dejection ode. But the merger can also be thought of as a transformation in that Poe intensifies the heritage (and, arguably, narrows it as well) by insuring that the human participant in a power struggle does not have a chance to win. Tamerlane may be a world conqueror in history, but in Poe he is a born loser. (The Prometheus with whom Poe would sympathize, I am convinced, is not the defiant being described by Shelley, but the sufferer of the Hesiodic *Theogony*, chained to a rock, and exposed—like the propped-up sailor in *The Narrative of A. Gordon Pym*—to the beak of a hungry bird.)

Power, as defined by Poe, can be an absolute, arbitrary ascendancy that one being enjoys over another. The source of this ascendancy is unknown, if not unknowable; what interests Poe are the lived consequences—the nature of the victimization that ensues when one being submits to the will of another. Yet in certain poems the "bad" power relationship is recast into a "good" one. This is accomplished by shifting the victimization away from the poem's implied speaker toward some other agency: thus, in the sleeper poems and "Lenore," I remember to honor the departed while others forget. The reason for placing such value on the capacity to remember is not far to seek; it is simply that a man would rather have his beloved alive than dead, and the closest one can come to accomplishing this (short of turning to the supernatural, as sometimes happens in the tales) is to preserve her through mourning. Consequently, a leading presence in the poetry is the *guardian or mourner*,[1] whose duty is to watch over and protect (as in the sleeper poems), or to remember the departed one, while giving fresh voice to sorrow (as in "Ulalume").

To honor the dead is for Poe an imaginative, a poetic, act. It is not surprising, therefore, that he can claim, in one famous statement, that the death of a beautiful woman is the most poetic of subjects, and in another—less well known but not less significant—that the highest genius "is but the result of generally large mental power existing in a state of *abso-*

[1] In his article "Poe's 'The Conqueror Worm,'" *American Literature*, 39 (1967), pp. 375-379, Klaus Lubbers remarks: "God's power, but not his justice, is taken over by 'formless things' and 'a crawling shape.' . . . The angels retain their customary seats but lose their guardian functions" (p. 378). Lubbers' idea of guardianship (which he does not develop) seems close to mine; his discussion of the phenomenon is the only one of which I am aware.

lute proportion. . . ."[2] In the context we have been examining, that notion of power sounds Romantic, but the stress on proportion has an eighteenth-century ring. This is so, I think, because Poe wants very much to strike a balance—to find a just adaptation of pressures and needs; in a word, a decorum. He can find this balance, he seems to feel, by playing off an "old-fashioned" sense of propriety and right conduct against a "modern" sense of abandon. Thus we have, in "Lenore," what amounts to an argument over how a bereaved person ought to behave, and what kind of poetic utterance he ought to make. As often as not, the balance is never found, either because one fails to remember or to guard, or because one is in the spell of powers that compel one to do their will.

The guardian assumes a particularly heavy burden. He must, if he is to live with honor, watch over and protect, serving frequently an an intermediate agent capable of interceding between victimizer and victim. But his own powers are very limited. If he succeeds in his mission, the object of his care is not pulled back into normal life but is maintained in a kind of indeterminate state—on "the porch of spirits lingering," as Wallace Stevens would say. If he fails, the departed is no longer represented on earth, and slips irretrievably into the otherworldly state that the guardian can contemplate but never know. Guardian no longer, there is nothing for him to do but take up mourning, a kind of guardianship performed too late. It is a tautology to say that the mourner must remember, for mourning is by definition a function of memory; conversely, forgetting is close to killing. What this means in specific cases must be left for our discussion of "Berenice" and related works, in which I will offer some general remarks on the function in Poe of memory and being. It will suffice to say here that a number of the poems group themselves according to the success or failure of the guardian, a poem like "The Sleeper" exemplifying success-

[2] All citations from the prose are to *The Complete Works of Edgar Allan Poe*, the "Virginia Edition," ed. James A. Harrison, 17 Vols. (New York, 1902), hereafter cited by volume and page number.

ful performance, "Ulalume," as I have already implied, exemplifying failure. This is not to suggest that one finds in these verses, even when the failure is abject, the brutalities that are fairly commonplace in the prose: actions that are overt in the fiction are at best veiled or implied in the poems. Thus Tamerlane never acts openly against Ada, he merely leaves her; yet the end of her life coincides exactly with his departure. Similarly, the first-person of "Ulalume" never had a bad conscious thought about his lover; but for practical purposes he has—until he is suddenly brought back to memory—erased her from his life. Certain of these poems render, in other words, a human being who has made himself less than human; a being in the hands of a malevolent power that bars him from the performance of his proper role; a being, in short, who is alienated from the world and from himself. It is on the basis of such patterns as these that Allen Tate speaks of Poe's vision of dehumanized man,[3] a subject on which I will also have more to say below.

The object of the guardian's or the mourner's care is commonly the *sleeper*, a figure whose prototype may be found in Coleridge's "Frost at Midnight" and "Phantom or Fact," in Wordsworth's "Lucy" poems, in the "Thyrza" poems of Byron ("To Thyrza," "Away, Away, Ye Notes of Woe!" and "One Struggle More, and I Am Free"), and in Shelley's "The Magnetic Lady to her Patient." The difference between Poe's approach and, for example, Wordsworth's, is that the situation Poe selects is essentially, if in a very subdued way, dramatic. The sleeper is not an abiding spirit but a material presence on the threshold between life and death. This creates a feeling of suspense that is not to everyone's taste. About Haydn there is a story according to which the composer slept during the performance of a piano composition in another part of his house. The player failed, however, to strike the final chord, whereupon Haydn, unable to bear

[3] See "Our Cousin, Mr. Poe" and "The Angelic Imagination," in *The Man of Letters in the Modern World* (New York, 1955), pp. 113-145.

the irresolution, awoke, hurried to the keyboard, and sounded it himself. Readers of Poe, who can find no such release, must conclude that in Poe's case the composition is indeterminate by design.

The confrontations one encounters in Poe's verse are relations of one to one. This is as true of poems involving positive confrontations, such as "To Helen" and the other poems to women, as of problematic or negative ones, such as "Israfel" or "Ulalume"; and it is true as well of the great majority of the tales and the dialogues. These confrontations are charged pauses, intense moments of arrest in which consciousness comes face to face with something different from, and normally superior to, itself. This superiority, as we have seen, can be experienced as a bad thing or a good; as something that threatens and controls me, or as something I adore. The constant element is the necessity of relating to something larger than oneself. The relationship takes many forms: I can be within the sphere of the other's influence ("To Helen"); I can be brought up short by some reminder of my failure ("Ulalume"); I can see the other as an ominous presence forcing me to suffer through recollection ("The Raven"); I can watch over the other, guardian-fashion, while she sleeps (the sleeper poems), or reversing the situation, sleep while she watches over me ("For Annie"); I can be brought face to face with my past, and my powerlessness, through the mediation of an auditor ("Tamerlane" and, in a sense, "The Raven" as well). In other works, such as the city poems, or "The Haunted Palace," the rendered phenomenon is given, for lack of a better term, objectively. That is to say, it is no longer mediated by an implied speaker or central consciousness, but is "just there." In these poems we are looking at the experience, as it were, from the outside, as the external manifestation of a representative human state.[4]

[4] As in the case of power there is substantial precedent in literature and the history of ideas for a preoccupation with states of being. The problem fascinated Rousseau, whose reflections on the subject in the fifth promenade of *Les Rêveries du promeneur solitaire* is a high point of that work. Wilhelm von Humboldt returns again and again

We may distinguish a state from an act by observing that the former denotes a condition—the way a thing "is"—while the latter points to an event—what a thing "does." That is the bare outline of a definition that we can begin to fill out not by further abstractions but by looking at specific texts. Let us turn back again for a moment to "Tamerlane" and "Al Aaraaf." Looking at both works we notice more "action" than we are used to seeing in Poe's verse: "Al Aaraaf" has a complicated plot, and "Tamerlane" is about a man who conquered the known world. Yet there is something static about both poems. When we put "Al Aaraaf" down we think less about the narrative we have read (which is in any case hard to disentangle) than about isolated things: the beauty of Nesace or the music of her speech; the power and the majesty of God; the love and helplessness of Angelo and Ianthe. When we look at "Tamerlane" we see, ostensibly, an historical figure, a significant actor on the world scene. Yet in Poe's

---

to the problem of the ontological state [*Zustand*], not only in his writings on literature and aesthetics, but in his analysis of sexual differentiation and its influence in organic nature. More immediately relevant, perhaps, is the notion of states in Wordsworth's preface to the second edition of *Lyrical Ballads*, where it is argued that poetry involves "a selection of the real language of men in a state of vivid sensation," and the elucidation of the laws of human nature "chiefly, as far as regards the manner in which we associate ideas in a state of excitement." Poe's own interest in psychological and ontological states has drawn the notice of several commentators. Dostoievsky praised the American author for describing "the inner state" of a protagonist with "acumen and amazing realism" (Vladimir Astrov, "Dostoievsky on Edgar Allan Poe," *American Literature*, 14 [1942], p. 73). Sarah Helen Whitman makes a similar observation in *Edgar Poe and His Critics*, p. 45. In *The Continuity of American Poetry* Pearce argues that Poe attempts in the poem "Dreams" "to locate in the real world a place, or a state, in which one can conceive of the possibility of going beyond and above it" (p. 150; see also, pp. 151, 181). There are useful discussions as well in Geoffrey Rans, *Edgar Allan Poe* (Edinburgh and London, 1965), esp. pp. 82, 83, 87, where Rans appears to widen his original perspective so as to include, not merely psychological states or "states of mind," but states of being as well; in E. Arthur Robinson, "Order and Sentience in 'The Fall of the House of Usher,'" *PMLA*, 76 (1961), pp. 68-81, and in W. H. Auden, *The Recognition of Edgar Allan Poe*, p. 223.

treatment the man is neither very historical nor very active.[5] History, for Poe, is not a poetic subject, but a species of crude allegory: an "Inferior kind of Poetry," as Blake said, "formed by the daughters of Memory." Tamerlane as Poe sees him is an actor who has ceased to act; who in reality never acted on his own even in the past, but served merely as the instrument of a higher power; and who is now held immobile by the sheer inertial weight of his lifelong servitude. Even repentance, the one possibility theoretically left to him, is beyond his power. Therefore, if "Tamerlane" tells a story, it also spells out, like "Al Aaraaf" and the great majority of the other poems, a fixed and predestined condition. Poe's "religion" is a kind of Calvinism, but without the belief. Man suffers, in Poe, because he must.

I would like to conclude with a further look at the process of dehumanization referred to above, and to suggest what Poe offers as an alternative to it. Dehumanization can take different forms. I have already indicated some of them. In the doomed-city poems, and in "The Haunted Palace," the form is architectural. Human being is reified, transformed into an eerie, thinglike entity. This entity suffers nonetheless in human terms, and from the same gratuitous victimization that is the plight of its human counterparts. "The Conqueror Worm," though closer to allegory, enacts a similar process in theatrical terms. The tragedy being played, we are told at the end, is entitled "Man," and its hero is mortality, personified by the worm. "The Raven" employs two speakers (the bird and the human sufferer) to enact a double victimization. The mourner is reminded, through the mediation of his midnight visitor, of his loss; then uses this mediator to intensify his consciousness of the loss, and thereby his suffering. But in Poe every state has its complement, and (to come now to my main point) the complement of dehumanization

[5] For a discussion of Poe's sources (which in all probability did *not* include Marlowe's *Tamburlaine*, a work little known in Poe's day), see *Collected Works of Edgar Allan Poe*, ed. Thomas Ollive Mabbott. Volume One: *Poems* (Cambridge, Mass., 1969), pp. 23-24.

is *re*humanization. Here the aim is to transcend somehow the self-negating, self-baffling circularity in which Poe's central figure typically finds himself. The aim is realized by developing situations in which, though the other has an ascendancy I lack, this ascendancy is perceived affirmatively, as a good to which I am only too anxious to turn my gaze. This process takes place in that whole series of love poems that starts with "To Helen" and ends with "Annabel Lee." These poems form a group that is like an affirmative echo of the negative statement represented by the darker poems that surround them. "To Helen" depicts a confrontation with a lover representing pure beauty and ideality—in effect, a noumenal center drawing the first-person ever deeper into its sphere of soothing influence. In "To Helen [Whitman]" the woman is again the transcendent, vital, living figure; in "To Marie Louise" she is literally the only thing the first-person is able, in the end, to perceive. "Lenore," a monologue with an implied auditor who serves as an antagonist, returns to the problem of guardianship and remembrance, but, as I have already hinted, with a difference. The issue here is what form remembrance should take. Poe manages at the same time, through the construction of the "argument," to turn attention inward upon the nature, not merely of Lenore the person, but "Lenore" the poem. The distinctive feature of the poem "For Annie" is that the lover is able, for the first time, to enjoy the other side of the familiar guardian-sleeper relationship. Here, I become the sleeper, and she the guardian. Moreover (and here again we see Poe's desire to make these experiences as affirmative as possible) the guardianship is flawless; this woman's caring gaze is like a mother's, the repose of the sleeper like that of her child. In "Annabel Lee," finally, there is something like a balance between the situation of the first-person and the ascendancy of the other. "I" becomes "we"; the sustaining force is not my love or hers, but "ours": one experiences, at last, a kind of mutuality of being, as if vital power, for once, were capable of being balanced, understood, and shared.

CHAPTER 3

"Tamerlane" and Other Poems

Let us begin at the beginning, with the opening lines of "Tamerlane," the title poem of the 1827 volume with which Poe first offered himself to the public as a maker of verse:

> I have sent for thee, holy friar;
> But 'twas not with the drunken hope,
> Which is but agony of desire
> To shun the fate, with which to cope
> Is more than crime may dare to dream,
> That I have call'd thee at this hour:
> Such father is not my theme—
> Nor am I mad, to deem that power
> Of earth may shrive me of the sin
> Unearthly pride hath revell'd in—
>
> (ll. 1-10)[6]

Tamerlane has offended; the poem is his confession. It is also his testimonial to a kind of nagging bafflement, an inability to reconcile deed and desire. When he is here, his thoughts are there; when he is there, his thoughts are here: his being slides from pole to pole. With Ada, to whom he is bound by a supposedly idyllic love, he can think only of distant conquests:

> There—in that hour—a thought came o'er
> My mind, it had not known before—
> To leave her while we both were young—
>
> (ll. 234-236)

In Samarkand, the capital of his empire, Tamerlane can think only of Ada and of home:

> My eyes were still on pomp and power,
> My wilder'd heart was far away,

[6] Citations from the poetry are to *Collected Works of Edgar Allan Poe* (see note 5 above), hereafter cited as *CW*.

In vallies of the wild Taglay,
In mine own Ada's matted bow'r.
(ll. 355-358)

If I may take a Heideggerian liberty with a Heideggerian idea, Tamerlane has sacrificed "being-there" for "being-elsewhere." He is the man who exists where he is not.

This sense of alienation and the ensuing bafflement may account, at least in part, for the many negations in the poem; for the complex and confounded syntax; and for the fact that Poe wrote the poem, in all, four different ways. In sixteen of the seventeen stanzas that make up this, the original version of the poem, there is at least one negative construction; in the first stanza alone there are five: the principal means of establishing what anything is, is to suggest what it is not.[7] To some extent this is a matter of "high" style, a way of suggesting certain things without stooping to the vulgarity of bald statement. At the same time one satisfies the need for vagueness and indefiniteness, those familiar desiderata of Poe's criticism. But the negatives are more than that. They are of the very essence of a poem, for "Tamerlane" is the history of a being that negates itself. Tamerlane speaks as he lives, in terms of "not." Instead of explaining to the confessor what the confessor can do for him, the emperor explains what he cannot do. Tamerlane has *not* sent for him in a spirit of hope; he is *not* mad enough to think of an earthly power can shrive him; but he would *not* berate the priest because the priest does *not* have the gift of hope. After the extreme involution of the hypotaxis (especially in lines 2-5), and after all the negative constructions, the final two lines are relatively straightforward:

[7] In his *Edgar Allan Poe,* Rans observes that "The use [in "Tamerlane"] . . . of negatives, comparatives, and of diction suggesting vagueness, gives an effect of deliberate withdrawal from the object, of the difficulty of recalling a blessed time, which for the poem's sake must remain indefinite" (p. 47). Of "Ligeia" he remarks that "negatives and superlatives abound; allusions are used profusely to dull the edges of any too precise a physical detail. . . . his use of Miltonic negative similes is entirely fitting at this point" (p. 88).

> "If I *can* hope (O God! I can)
> It falls from an eternal shrine."
> (ll. 13-14)

The confessor, a presence, is deprived of efficacy in favor of an absence, God. The being of Tamerlane, oriented as it is toward this distant, transcendental power, remains a being-elsewhere.

This relation of Tamerlane to deity governs the immediate present and the whole of the future: according to the judgment of deity Tamerlane will be saved or damned. The past is governed, on the other hand, by a shadowy and gratuitous heredity. Tamerlane does not earn the power he wields; power descends through him, much as frailness descends through the Ushers. It is a kind of family or racial taint determining every attribute and every achievement—the conquests no less than the crimes:

> Shame said'st thou?
> Aye I did inherit
> That hated portion, with the fame . . .
> Aye—the same heritage hath giv'n
> Rome to the Caesar—this to me;
> The heirdom of a kingly mind—
> And a proud spirit, which hath striv'n
> Triumphantly with human kind.
> (ll. 24-37)

> . . . (believe me at this time,
> When falsehood were a ten-fold crime,
> There *is* a power in the high spirit
> To *know* the fate it will inherit)
> (ll. 189-192)

A more paradoxical type of power can hardly be imagined. The high spirit, having no freedom, cannot determine itself; it can only receive a determination from a spirit that is higher still. There is nothing left, within the authority of the receiver, but the ability *to be conscious of receiving.* To have power is to be in the power of another; and to know it.

Does the ultimate, transcendent power never descend to immanence? It appears to, and precisely by a type of physical descent:

> In mountain air I first drew life;
> The mists of the Taglay have shed
> Nightly their dews on my young head;
> And my brain drank their venom then,
> When after day of perilous strife
> With chamois, I would seize his den
> And slumber, in my pride of power,
> The infant monarch of the hour—
> For, with the mountain dew by night,
> My soul imbib'd unhallow'd feeling;
> And I would feel its essence stealing
> In dreams upon me— (ll. 38-49)

The dew-shedding mists are the early manifestation of a concern, throughout the poetry, with crucial downward movements, descending influences, advents-from-above. In its most material form (dewdrops, rain, and the like) the descending influence is a kind of "nucta, or magic drop that comes from the moon,"[8] and is capable, in literary tradition, of working either good effects or bad. In the mountains of Taglay the magic drop becomes a kind of evil intellectual milk, ingested through the mind. A mixture of venom and unhallowed feeling, this dewy nourishment preys upon the high spirit in concert with a light-diffusing cloud and a storm in which Tamerlane's future is prefigured. The episode initiates what is called, in the tales and the criticism, a condition of "novelty":

> The storm had ceas'd—and I awoke—
> Its spirit cradled me to sleep,
> And as it pass'd me by, there broke
> Strange light upon me, tho' it were

[8] *CW*, p. 181.

My soul in mystery to steep:
For I was not as I had been;
The child of Nature, without care,
Or thought, save of the passing scene.
(ll. 70-77)

The changeful moment is like the moment of religious revelation, except that it is evil. The imbibing of feeling is like the experience of the Wordsworthian Romantic, except that the feeling is unhallowed, and the dews of nature are venomous. The changing is like Gide's *acte gratuit*, except that the actor is the end of the act and not its source.

This moment consequently is not quite like any other moment in literature, nor is the power that brings it about quite like any other power. There are, in fact, three powers in "Tamerlane." In order of appearance these are the prideful power of the youthful hunter (ll. 41 ff.), the power of consciousness or prefigurative knowledge (ll. 179-194), and the capitalized Power that "Its venom secretly imparts" (l. 345), transforming Tamerlane into a being who possesses nothing in common "with human hearts" (l. 346).

The power that enables the hunter to "seize the den" of the chamois is evidently innate; it is perhaps little more than the capacity that any man has to force his will upon the material world. What sets this exertion apart is its relation to the attribute—also, apparently, innate—of pride. It is not power alone that distinguishes Tamerlane from other hunters, but *pride* of power. Alone in the mountains, slumbering like an "infant monarch" (l. 45), Tamerlane watches his future glory expand across the firmament in a vision that is pride's visual projection. Morally speaking, Tamerlane sins by putting himself above all others—thus his feelings of guilt. He is as much sinned-against as sinning, however, in that he is himself the chief victim of his pride. Pride-of-power is not something Tamerlane freely wields; it is something by which he is bound: *Tamerlane is in the power of pride-of-power.* Like the power of knowing the fate that he will inherit, pride-of-power expresses a subservient relation; it is at once a bondage and a fate. Tamerlane receives "The heirdom of a kingly mind / And a proud spirit" (ll. 35-36), experiences the corrupting influence of the dews and the storms, and finds himself no longer the child of nature.

Having suggested some of the concerns of the poem, we may find it helpful to broaden our perspective by comparing Tamerlane with his antecedents in Byron, "the favourite poet of all the Virginia young men," and, as has often been remarked, of Poe himself.[9] The relevant prototypes, for our purposes, are to be found in *Lara: A Tale* (1814), and *Manfred: A Dramatic Poem* (1817).

Tamerlane shares with Lara a consciousness of wasted powers, and a sense that he has been misused by forces beyond his control:

> His early dreams of good outstripp'd the truth,
> And troubled manhood follow'd baffled youth;
> With thought of years in phantom chase misspent,
> And wasted powers for better purpose lent.
> (Canto I, st. XVIII, ll. 11-14)

Unable to accept responsibility for his squandered years, Lara, like the fox in one of Blake's *Proverbs of Hell*, "condemns the trap, not himself":

> But haughty still, and loth himself to blame,
> He call'd on Nature's self to share the shame,
> And charged all faults upon the fleshly form
> She gave to clog the soul, and feast the worm;
> Till he at last confounded good and ill,
> And half mistook for fate the acts of will:

[9] Brooks, *The World of Washington Irving*, p. 265. Poe's debt to Byron is discussed in Campbell's introduction to *Poems of Edgar Allan Poe*, pp. xliv-xlv, and *The Mind of Poe and Other Studies*, pp. 150-152; Arthur Hobson Quinn, *Edgar Allan Poe: A Critical Biography*, pp. 12 ff.; Roy P. Basler, "Byronism in Poe's 'To One in Paradise,'" *American Literature*, 9 (1937), pp. 232-236; and *CW*, pp. xxvii, 4, 76, 540, *et passim*.

Too high for common selfishness, he could
At times resign his own for others' good,
But not in pity, not because he ought,
But in some strange perversity of thought,
That sway'd him onward with a secret pride
To do what few or none would do beside.
(Canto I, st. XVIII, ll. 19-30)

Byron here makes overt the problem of seemingly motiveless behavior, anticipating the notion of "Perverseness" that Poe will develop at length in "The Black Cat" and "The Imp of the Perverse"—a topic to which we shall return below. What is interesting about Byron's attitude is its hyperconsciousness; Byron recognizes the perverseness in his heroes and wants his readers to recognize it as well. In this too he anticipates the practice of Poe. There is a difference, however, between Byron's treatment of the self-fascinated, alienated hero and the treatment we find in Poe. Byron, despite our willingness to identify him with the protagonists of his "Tales," tends to keep them at a distance. He favors the third-person for narrative purposes, and normally employs the first only in dramatic characterizations, as in *Manfred*, *The Deformed Transformed* (1824), or *Werner: A Tragedy* (1823), or in shorter works, such as the lyrics, in which the first-person is a traditional *persona*. The third-person techniques of the story-poems enable the poet to frame his character—to generalize about his behavior and, above all, to judge it: thus the overtly evaluative nature (so unlike anything in the verses of Poe) of the lines from *Lara* quoted above. Furthermore, Byron situates his protagonists in such a way that we see them in interpersonal and social contexts, loving, fighting, dying, and, not infrequently, posing. By illuminating him in this way from different angles and different sides, Byron "relativizes" his hero, while at the same time keeping him, as it were, on center stage. Poe, by contrast, stresses the consciousness of his hero. We do not see the speaker so much as we hear him; he is a presence and a voice but not, in the Byronic sense, a figure. As a result, we lack the sort of perspective that Byron provides. We experience Tamerlane's world with and as Tamerlane experiences it, and feel the victimization he feels. The result is a work that, if it looks back to Byron in certain ways, looks forward as well to the dramatic monologues of Robert Browning. The apostrophes to the friar already suggest, it seems to me, the Browning manner. The difference between the two monologists is that Browning seems capable of slipping into an infinite variety of masks while Poe tries on very few. It is not surprising, therefore, that Browning turns so readily to the stage, whereas the American author makes, in *Politian*, only one attempt at writing a play, and an uncertain one at that.

The nearest relative of Poe's Tamerlane is Byron's Manfred. Both men are at home in the wilderness, especially in the mountains. Tamerlane grows up in mountainous heights, and it is to the mountains that Manfred repairs when, near the end of Act I, he has sunk into hopelessness. But the experiences the two men undergo are by no means identical. Unable to find meaning in his past life, Manfred wants to kill himself, and is saved by the intervention of the Chamois Hunter. Tamerlane has no such impulse. Unlike Manfred, who yearns to forget, Poe's hero yearns to remember. Tamerlane transgressed while Ada was alive by putting her out of his mind—a failure of guardianship. He transgressed after her demise by continuing to dwell on other things—a failure to assume the burden of mourning. Now, in the confession, he goes to the other extreme, forcing himself to remember, stretching out his victimization (with the same self-devouring consciousness that we will see in Roderick Usher) until existence comes to its preordained end. We see Poe's hero, furthermore, at an earlier stage than Byron's. Tamerlane presents his memory of heights, for example, at a time when, though the mists were already taking their effect on him, he was unaware of any evil influence.

In *Manfred* Byron presents two characters, a vocational hunter and an existential one: a man in quest of game, and a man in quest of meaning in life. Poe joins the first role to the second, fashioning a character who is both a hunter in a practical sense, like Byron's Chamois Hunter, and a man on the ontological heights, like Manfred. Poe modifies, at the same time, the second role, for Tamerlane does not ascend in order to find oblivion—at this point in his life he has no notion there is anything he might want to escape. He ascends as a matter of course, because it is the normal thing for one of his calling to do. Only later does he comprehend that his immersion in nature was, in effect, drugging him; that nature, through its potion-like influences, was turning him into an active leader of men, but a secret somnambulist.

In Byron's poem there is a real test of powers: on the one hand Manfred's, which enables him to command many spirits, and on the other, the demonic powers that array themselves against him in an attempt to quell his rebellious spirit. But, like Shelley's Prometheus, he is simply too defiant to be beaten down. Only one power is stronger than Manfred: on the cliffs he is tempted to fall to his death, but "There is a power upon me which withholds, / And makes it my fatality to live" (Act I, sc. II, ll. 23-24). Manfred, in other words, is held by a fate that makes him continue living but does not determine the nature of his being, which is his own proud creation. Tamerlane, however, is radically bound. When Edward H. Davidson assumes that "this mind is wholly self-directional, and nature has no power to move it any way other than the one it is determined to take,"[10] he forgets that it is nature, working through both body and mind, that has furnished the direction in the first place. It is not merely the obligation to live that is forced upon Tamerlane, as in the case of Byron's hero, but his very mode of being. There is no alternative for him but to do as the higher power dictates, to be as it ordains he must be.

The clearest Byronic echoes in "Tamerlane" come from Manfred's speech to the Abbot, in which he declares:

[10] *Poe: A Critical Study* (Cambridge, Mass., 1957), pp. 7-8.

Old man! there is no power in holy men,
Nor charm in prayer, nor purifying form
Of penitence, nor outward look, nor fast,
Nor agony . . . can exorcise
From out the unbounded spirit the quick sense
Of its own sins, wrongs, sufferance, and revenge
Upon itself; there is no future pang
Can deal that justice on the self-condemn'd
He deals on his own soul.

(Act III, sc. I, ll. 66-78)

Poe, had he written *Manfred,* would have started here. Indeed, this speech, which occurs when three-quarters of the drama has already been played out, anticipates, both in tone and substance, Tamerlane's opening statement to the friar. This very fact draws our attention to difficulties in Poe's work that do not arise in Byron's. The confrontation in Manfred is a dramatic moment. We want to see how defiant this hero really is. There is nothing very dramatic, however, in the verses of Poe. This is not merely because "Tamerlane" falls outside of the dramatic genre in the formal sense, but because there is no real struggle in it. By having Tamerlane speak to a virtual auditor, Poe gives his hero a certain vocal palpability, but he never develops a conflict, as Byron does, between the transgressor's point of view and that of the holy man. Nor does he show that Tamerlane ever had a chance to alter the pattern of his life. Tamerlane's story, as I have already suggested, is merely a confession. But just for this reason Poe creates a problem for himself for which there is no counterpart in Byron. The Abbot forces himself upon Manfred, giving the latter a chance to show, dramatically, that he has no desire to confess. Tamerlane, on the other hand, wants to do nothing *but* confess, and reverses the situation in "Manfred" by summoning the friar. He must then admit that he does not believe the priest can help him, and therefore, paradoxically, he cannot plausibly confess. There are, then, two sources for the grammatical anguish and the many negations at the beginning of the poem—one, as it were, ontological, the other formal. The first is that Tamerlane is by nature a self-baffling man, a being who defines himself, as I have said, in negative terms. The second or formal source is the situation Poe creates by presenting an ostensibly dramatic speech in a context from which dramatic potential has ironically been removed.

Tamerlane is the victim not of his free will, but of his "servile will." The paradox of the servile will, which Paul Ricoeur finds in all cultures, arises from a desire for self-enslavement. The guilty soul, yearning for release from its sin, wills to become possessed—to be taken over by some demonic power—in order that later, through supplication and divine intercession, the possession may be taken away. The servile will—as the name indicates—is a mixture of the passive and the active. A being with such a will "is at the same time *act* and *state*; that is to say, a sinful being in whom the very act of self-enslavement suppresses itself as 'act' and relapses into a 'state.' . . . In the language of St. Paul, the *act* is the 'yielding' of the body to servitude (as you have yielded your members as servant), the state is the reign (let not sin therefore reign in your mortal bodies). A 'yielding' *of* myself that is at the same time a 'reign' *over* myself—there is the enigma of the servile will, of the will that makes itself a slave."[11]

The second tendency of the servile will, as it appears in the religious myths with which Ricoeur is concerned, is less characteristic of Tamerlane. This is the tendency to externalize—to project one's evil into an external object that then becomes a source of temptation. Lara does this. In Tamerlane's case, however, the evil is really "out there," for the relation between the dreamer and his environment is a reciprocity. In order for him to drink a venom there must *be* a venom. Similarly, he can only imbibe unhallowed feeling because unhallowed feeling comes into him "with the moun-

[11] *The Symbolism of Evil*, trans. Emerson Buchanan (New York, 1967), p. 154.

tain dew by night" (l. 46). We finish, then, confronting the same two givens with which we began: the given of hereditary pride, which predisposes the inheritor to self-aggrandizement; the given of a corrupting natural environment, which feeds the pride until it outgrows and envelops its ostensible master.

Nothing, not even foreknowledge, can prevent the advent of the envenoming Power (l. 344) into which the lesser powers appear ultimately to be subsumed. Indeed, to possess the power of foreknowledge is to be conscious of one's essential powerlessness:

> The passionate spirit which hath known
> And deeply felt the silent tone
> Of its own self supremacy,—
> (I speak thus openly to thee,
> 'Twere folly *now* to veil a thought
> With which this aching breast is fraught)
> The soul which feels its innate right—
> The mystic empire and high power
> Giv'n by the energetic might
> Of Genius, at its natal hour;
> Which knows (believe me at this time,
> When falsehood were a ten-fold crime,
> There is a power in the high spirit
> To *know* the fate it will inherit)
> The soul, which knows such power, will still
> Find *Pride* the ruler of its will.
>
> (ll. 179-194)

Animated by "Genius," the ambitious dreamer leaves his lover in order to pursue his fortune in the world. This is the Manfred pattern. When the Witch asks him how he destroyed his lover, Manfred replies: "Not with my hand, but heart, which broke her heart. / It gazed on mine, and wither'd" (Act II, sc. II, ll. 118-119). Tamerlane's specific crime is an extreme form of the failure to watch over and to mourn: in a word, desertion. In this he anticipates, as we shall see, the pattern of some later poems where culpability attaches itself to various forms of neglect. There is nothing patently criminal in such failure. Tamerlane never suggests, for example, that Ada threatens him, or that he would like to be rid of her. But he is clearly alienated from her; and, faced by the choice between woman and dream, he chooses the dream, or rather, the dream chooses and he cannot resist. As in "Berenice," the woman and the dream contend until the woman is all but obscured. The principal difference between Berenice's lover and Tamerlane is that Egaeus turns *against* while Tamerlane turns *away*. Tamerlane leaves Ada in slumber, depriving her of life by depriving her of that for which she lives. The sleep in which he leaves her becomes, in effect, a sleep of death: the Tamerlane who returns to the matted bower when he is *still young* (l. 353) discovers that the woman who had loved him is *long dead* (l. 403). The absence of life in the sleeper thus effectively coincides with the absence of the guardian who betrayed his trust. The only possible atonement for such sin is fidelity at the subsequent stage, when guardianship gives way to mourning. Tamerlane's confession, then, is his attempt to compensate, an attempt to balance a plenitude of sorrow in the present against a lack of caring in the past.

It is not that Tamerlane despises Ada. He says often enough that he loves her. Moreover, love has a better chance of succeeding in a poem than in the more "fallen" world of the tales. Indeed, the satisfying love relationship can occur only in a remote and idealized sphere: the pairing of Annabel Lee and her lover orginates in an indeterminate "kingdom by the sea" ("Annabel Lee"); Angelo meets and falls in love with Ianthe in an afterlife on a God-directed star after their own seeming annihilation ("Al Aaraaf"); Pym and Dirk Peters live their alliance as they drift through a seascape of purer and purer novelty (*The Narrative of A. Gordon Pym*). Tamerlane's problem is not that he does not love, but that he does not love enough. "The fear of not loving enough is the purest and worst of fears. It is the fear that the saints know, the fear that love itself begets. And because man never loves enough, it is not possible that the fear of not being loved enough in return should be abolished. Only *perfect* love casts out fear."[12] Alienated from the object of his natural desire, Tamerlane leaves his true place in life for a false one. This withdrawal, this flight from authentic being, appears to be single but is in fact double: for when Tamerlane deprives the other of fulfillment in love, he deprives himself equally; the story of Tamerlane is the story of a victimizer who becomes, inevitably, a victim.

The full meaning of his loss emerges in stanza XIV:

> I went from out the matted bow'r,
> And hurried madly on my way:
> And felt, with ev'ry flying hour,
> That bore me from my home, more gay;
> There is of earth an agony
> Which, ideal, still may be
> The worst ill of mortality,
> 'Tis bliss, in its own reality,
> Too real, to *his* breast who lives
> Not within himself but gives
> A portion of his willing soul
> To God, and to the great whole—
> To him, whose loving spirit will dwell
> With Nature, in her wild paths; tell
> Of her wond'rous ways, and telling bless
> Her overpow'ring loveliness!
> A more than agony to him
> Whose failing sight will grow dim
> With its own living gaze upon
> That loveliness around: the sun—
> The blue sky—the misty light
> Of the pale cloud therein, whose hue
> Is grace to its heav'nly bed of blue;
> Dim! tho' looking on all bright!

[12] *The Symbolism of Evil*, p. 45.

O God! when the thoughts that may not pass
Will burst upon him, and alas!
For the flight on Earth to Fancy giv'n,
There are no words—unless of Heav'n.
(ll. 299-326)

In this sequence Tamerlane acts out his alienation, literally, in space, the physical flight figuring the ontological flight that is its origin. He presents at the same time, through a shift in grammatical persons, a perspective on the event. Within the first sentence, "I" becomes "he." Or more precisely, "my" becomes "his." If the passage is confusing (again, we are faced with a syntax as matted as the bower Tamerlane seeks to escape), this is because there is not a single third-person but two; and because their roles do not appear, at first sight, to be perfectly congruent with their assignment to sentences. The first syntactical caesura comes between lines 302 and 303, where first-person narrative gives way to general statement ("There is of earth an agony . . ."). The second caesura, even more abrupt, falls between lines 305 and 306, where the absence of a semicolon (which would be orthodox punctuation) creates a run-on effect. The lack of separation tends to suggest a parallelism between the first-person, with whom the sentence begins, and the third-person who now appears, and with whom the sentence ends. But the real governing principle is contrast. The "he" who gives a portion of his soul to God and the great whole is the dialectical complement of the "I" who flees the matted bower. The third-person, remaining with nature, can tell of her wondrous ways, thereby blessing her overpowering loveliness; but this is precisely what the first-person cannot do. The first-person, whose plight is detailed between line 315 and the end, finds himself condemned, in the midst of supernal brilliance, to dimness (indicative throughout the poetry of the fallen condition). The structure of the sequence, as regards grammatical and ontological persons, thus presents an "I" who is the alienated Tamerlane; a "he" who is not alienated; and a second "he" who is. The last of these third-persons, then, is synonymous with Tamerlane. The shift from a specifically identified "I" to a more generalized "him whose failing sight will grow dim" has another effect; it makes the situation less personal and at the same time less limited; the "I" becomes a "he" who becomes in turn a virtual type of the agonized being. The process diminishes Tamerlane's relation to earthly ties while increasing his relation to the power above. He emerges as a victim on a grand scale, a man who has lost not only his lover—the object of his natural desires—but nature itself.

"Tamerlane," like so many other of Poe's works, was much revised. The original version of 1827 has 406 lines; the second, which seems to have been composed the following year, and which exists in an incomplete state, has 346; the third version (1827-1831), has 252 lines; and the fourth (1827-1828/1845) has 243. As the poem shrinks, so does the narrative interest, Tamerlane becoming less a narrator of his own actions than a speaker of general truths. Stanza XVI of the original version embodies the loss of the sun, and thus of nature, alluded to two stanzas before. There the victim had appeared only in the third-person; here the victim appears in that manifestation and in the first-person as well. By arriving at sundown, Tamerlane experiences the literalization of loss suggested earlier in abstract terms:

> By sunset did its [Taglay's] mountains rise
> In dusky grandeur to my eyes;
> But as I wander'd on the way
> My heart sunk with the sun's rays.
> To him, who still would gaze upon
> The glory of the summer sun,
> There comes, when that sun will from him part,
> A sullen hopelessness of heart.
>
> (ll. 362-369)

This element is not, of course, new. Some of the lines occur in the version of 1827-1831; and power remains an issue.

But the emphasis has changed, as the next-to-last stanza makes particularly clear:

> Father, I firmly do believe—
> I *know*—for death, who comes for me
> From regions of the blest afar,
> Where there is nothing to deceive,
> Hath left his iron gate ajar,
> And rays of truth you cannot see,
> Are flashing thro' eternity:
> I do believe that Eblis hath
> A snare in every human path—
> Else how when in the holy grove,
> I wander'd of the idol, Love,
> . . . .
> How was it that Ambition crept,
> Unseen amid the revels there,
> Till growing bold, he laugh'd and leapt
> In the tangles of Love's very hair?
> (ll. 217-238)

With the assignment of a major role to love, "venom" and "unhallow'd feeling" disappear. Whereas the 1827 text presents Tamerlane's strife with the chamois (p. 28, l. 42) and with the "ill demon" who seems to have lent and then reclaimed a kind of corrupting eidetic power (p. 32, ll. 172-174), the second version offers a "strife of nations" (p. 43, l. 238). In versions three and four the strife is even less terrestrial:

> And I believe the winged strife
> And tumult of the headlong air
> Hath nestled in my very hair.
> (p. 46, ll. 42-44; cf. p. 55, ll. 38-40)

In the concluding stanza of the original version Tamerlane arrives, in the first-person, at his former home, where he meets a mountain hunter. When Tamerlane recognizes the other but is not himself recognized, his alienation is confirmed. In the homeland Tamerlane no longer exists; the place where he belongs has become the place where he cannot be. When the hunter tells him that Ada is long dead, his loss is complete: "What was there left me *now*? despair / A kingdom for a broken heart" (ll. 405-406). In contrast with this situation, in which the despair is dramatically earned, despair enters the third version as a personification:

> Despair, the fabled vampire-bat,
> Hath long upon my bosom sat,
> And I would rave, but that he flings
> A calm from his unearthly wings.
> (p. 46, ll. 27-30)

Similarly, hope appears as an eagle (p. 51, l. 193), while the agency that directs Tamerlane's fate takes the form of the Mohammedan-mythological figure, Eblis, the highest of wicked supernatural beings. The direct, physical imbibing of evil influence (such as we find in the venom episode of the original version) gives way to an implied cause-effect relationship between Eblis and Ambition (if Eblis does not set snares in every human path, how is it that Ambition overpowered Love?). In the third version of the poem, the personification of Ambition (stanza XXIII) complements a conclusion (stanza XXIV) in which Tamerlane, as in the original version, acts in his own person. Standing on the shore of some unnamed sea, he holds "particles of sand" (l. 246) that slip through his fingers into the watery depths. The situation images both his powerlessness and his mortality; future poems will offer many such moments of stasis and arrest. But in the final version "Tamerlane" lacks even this residual element of the "personal story." The author eliminates the final stanza, allowing the poem to end with the personified Ambition laughing and leaping in the hair of the equally personified Love.

If Ambition's surreptitious entry "amid the revels there" (l. 241) anticipates the entry of the mummer in "The Masque of the Red Death," Love recalls Tamerlane himself through the parallelism established between what happens in the hair of each. In stanza IV the mists of the Taglay shed their dews upon Tamerlane's head and the strife and tumult of the air nestle in his very hair; the process continues through the dew and rain of the next two stanzas, and concludes with the crucial and permanent change of stanza VIII. When Tamerlane speculates on the fateful assault of ambition, he is, in one sense, recapitulating: the process described has already occurred; this is simply another, and more etherealized, perspective on it. In another sense he is establishing, to borrow a favorite term of Poe's, a ratio: strife of air is to the hair of Tamerlane as Ambition is to the hair of Love. This heightens and dignifies the process, as I have already suggested, while establishing a parallelism between Love and Tamerlane—between, in other words, Love and the lover. Clearly this is a partial and not a complete identification. And that is the point. Complete identification is no more feasible between these two beings than between the two human lovers. The story of Tamerlane is the story of "near and yet so far," the narrative of a man who has everything in his grasp but has no grasp. The function of personification is not to specify unity, but unity-with-separation, or nearness. The related mode of allegory, depending on the perspective from which you examine it, implies either too little unity or too much. It implies too much if you hold that the allegorical figure (the signifier) is essentially identified with the thing it "means" (the signified); otherwise the significance of the fable is unintelligible. It implies too little if you hold (as Poe does in his reviews) that allegory depends upon two currents of meaning, an upper and a lower, which are necessarily separate. The personification in the later versions of "Tamerlane," by contrast, constitutes the signifier and signified as interchangeable yet discrete: we see them there together, bound in apposition, but we do not forget that things in apposition, however intimately they may be related, are never one.

"Tamerlane" is a narrative poem trying to become a lyric. The more it is rewritten, the more the contingent gives way to the idealized, the more acts are assimilated to states. With its intensity of feeling and concentration of form, the lyric is a genre well suited to the presentation of relatively pure states—as distinguished, for example, from discursive prose, which relies on exposition and argument, or plays, which present a great variety of states and depend on complex networks of incidents. The lyric tends to constitute a first-person, an "I," who talks but does not "do anything." Many of Poe's fictions are about such first-persons; and to this extent it may be said that they also aspire to the condition of the lyric. For Tamerlane is only the first of Poe's characters who can say, with Charles Du Bos, "I am no longer anyone, but merely the locale of my states" (*Je ne suis plus une personne, mais le lieu de mes états*).[13] The shift in "Tamerlane" from "I" to "it"—from a concrete human focus to one that is abstract and depersonalized—becomes fully meaningful, however, only when examined in the context of the advent from above. Envenoming power comes down onto the head; Ambition operates not in the heart but in the hair. Essence is placed, in effect, *outside*, as something already constituted, material and discrete. The pattern is evident throughout the poems. In "Lenore," for example, we read of "The life upon her yellow hair, but not within her eyes / The life still there upon her hair, the death upon her eyes" (p. 337, ll. 18-19).

"The Happiest Day," another poem about the loss of pride and power, is a kind of "Tamerlane" without Tamerlane. The speaker, a nameless "I," has never possessed real pride or power, but only the hope of them; and now even that hope has flown. But he is as much a victim as Tamerlane, and the instrumentality of victimization is the same:

> And, pride, what have I now with thee?
> Another brow may ev'n inherit
> The venom thou hast pour'd on me—
> Be still my spirit.
>
> (p. 81, ll. 9-12)

[13] Quoted in *Les Chemins actuels de la critique*, ed. Georges Poulet (Paris, 1968), p. 11.

This first-person, like the "high spirit" of "Tamerlane," has foreknowledge of his fate, but can do nothing to stay it. It comes upon him, as in the case of Tamerlane, from above: which is to say it literally comes *upon* him.

But were that hope of pride and power
  Now offer'd, with the pain
Ev'n *then* I felt—that brightest hour
  I would not live again:

For on its wing was dark alloy
  And as it flutter'd—fell
An essence—powerful to destroy
  A soul that knew it well.
(p. 82, ll. 17-24)

What is unique about the essence described in these verses is the compounding of materiality, separateness, and exteriority. Essence comes down moistly from above, in the manner of rain, but also in the manner of a living thing that wants to enshroud and possess. Consider, as a final example, the nucta in "The Sleeper":

An opiate vapour, dewy, dim,
Exhales from out her golden rim,
And, softly dripping, drop by drop,
Upon the quiet mountain top,
Steals drowsily and musically
Into the universal valley.
The rosemary nods upon the grave;
The lily lolls upon the wave;
Wrapping the fog about its breast,
The ruin moulders into rest. (ll. 3-12)

Essence, then, is a peculiarly external thing that enters a person, animates and directs him—perhaps for life—but never quite belongs to him. It is a lent power over which the temporary recipient has no real control. Between existence and essence (to borrow the oversimplified polarity derived from

Sartre) there is, in other words, a fatal separation. It could be argued that this makes Tamerlane an existential hero striving in a disintegrating modern world to "earn" his essence. It could also be argued that Poe is drawing here upon a platonic theory of separation according to which one's existence in the everyday world is an impoverished version of an earlier state of being in the realm of the ideal. Neither argument, however, wholly fits the case. Poe's hero may feel, with the existentialist, that he has somehow been, as Heidegger says, thrown into being, and that he ought to do something about it. But he cannot do anything, and there is all the difference. Existential man, if limited in his options, is free; Poe's hero is bound. Nor does the separation he experiences represent a warmed-over platonism. Essence is not confined, according to Poe's conception, to some primordial and ideal realm: essence is with me here, right now, coming down into me from above. By punning on two senses of the word (essence as physical extract and essence as basic nature) Poe stresses that essence is material as well as spiritual, a reminder that victimization in Poe is a matter of the body as well as the soul.

The poem "Stanzas" is Poe's attempt to lift certain features of Tamerlane's plight to a higher and more universal plane. As the epigraph from Byron's *The Island* indicates, the poem examines the reciprocity of man and nature:

> In youth have I known one with whom the Earth
> In secret communing held—as he with it,
> In day light, and in beauty from his birth:
> Whose fervid, flick'ring torch of life was lit
> From the sun and stars, whence he had drawn forth
> A passionate light—such for his spirit was fit—
> And yet that spirit knew not—in the hour
> Of its own fervor—what had o'er it power.
>
> (ll. 1-8)

The means by which this third-person acquires his light is less passive than the means by which Tamerlane took in the influences of nature. And there is even (it may be argued) something faintly Promethean about the lighting of the torch. The final two lines imply, on the other hand, that this situation differs from Tamerlane's more by degree than by kind, for the spirit is wholly in the grasp of the natural power and, like the youthful Tamerlane, does not even know it. The truth is to be found between these two extremes of interpretation. The third-person of the opening stanza, and the first-person who gradually takes his place, are indeed subservient to power in nature. That power, however, is thought of here as basically good, and even—what is more important—potentially redemptive. It is as if a Tamerlane-in-the-making were being given a chance to make a free choice between salvation and ruin.

Nature in "Stanzas" has no wish to dominate. It attempts rather to prevent suffering by warning against a course that will prove self-destructive. Nature, in short, would prefer the role of guardian to the role of victimizer, though victimization could well occur if man does not heed the signs.

> Perhaps it may be that my mind is wrought
> To a ferver by the moon beam that hangs o'er,
> But I will half believe that wild light fraught
> With more of sov'reignty than ancient lore
> Hath ever told—or is it of a thought
> The unembodied essence, and no more
> That with a quick'ning spell doth o'er us pass
> As dew of the night-time, o'er the summer grass?
> (ll. 9-16)

Sovereignty spells strength and self-sufficiency and lawful title. In contrast with an upstart power, which can ascend only by usurpation, a sovereign power is ascendant by right, a consideration that takes on new meaning in the final stanza, where rebellion and self-serving lawlessness are described and all but prophesied. Such things bother Poe, who felt as strongly about the decay of order as about anything, except perhaps the efficacy of love and reason. Thus the tragedy of "The Haunted Palace" begins when the monarch Thought is suddenly and arbitrarily overthrown; similarly, in "Al Aaraaf" the tragedy of Angelo and Ianthe begins when they fail to perform their function in the divine order, thereby emulating the comets whose infidelity threatened the harmony of the spheres. Against such a background the unembodied essence of a thought matters enormously, as the speaker intuitively understands. Unfortunately, essence is hard to get at, and the best he can do is steal toward it by analogy:

> Doth o'er us pass, when, as th'expanding eye
> To the loved object—so the tear to the lid
> Will start, which lately slept in apathy?
>
> (ll. 17-19)

"Expanding" embraces at least three interrelated senses: extending in range, so as to take in more; going out in sympathy; and weeping. This is a characteristic spectrum for Poe. It indicates his general belief that one is the greater for loving and also—on the theory that one adores what one may lose or has already lost—the sadder. Its "local" service, as F. R. Leavis might say, is to introduce the idea of the loved object while maintaining the level of abstraction necessary in a poem that is not about an individual dilemma but the human condition.

With that aim in view, the speaker expands from the first-person singular to the first-person plural, constituting a kind of collective sleeper who has failed to perceive the loved object and whatever of divinity may be in it. The meaning of "object" should not be too strictly limited. It is more abstract than the expanding eye and more inclusive. It can refer to the natural world as a whole or to any part of it, or to living beings, human or not, with qualities in them that might be loved. There is nothing hidden about such an object. Like the purloined letter it is there in front of us, waiting to be seen. But first we must quit our state of sleep:

And yet it need not be—(that object) hid
From us in life—but common—which doth lie
Each hour before us—but *then* only bid
With a strange sound, as of a harp-string broken
T'awake us—'Tis a symbol and a token,

4

Of what in other worlds shall be—and giv'n
In beauty by our God, to those alone
Who otherwise would fall from life and Heav'n
Drawn by their heart's passion, and that tone,
That high tone of the spirit which hath striv'n
Tho' not with Faith—with godliness—whose throne
With desp'rate energy't hath beaten down;
Wearing its own deep feeling as a crown.

(ll. 20-32)

The strange sound alludes to an ancient tradition according to which a great statue near Thebes gave off a note like that of a breaking harp-string when struck by the morning sunlight. Though Poe drew upon the tradition again in "The Coliseum," as Mabbott points out in his notes, its role is more central here, where so much depends on whether you hear the note or whether you do not. In this respect the poem again anticipates Poe's treatment of Angelo and Ianthe, who fail to hear the warning sent to them by audible means from God. When we observe that they are preoccupied by the beating of their own hearts, we can understand that "high" in the present context denotes loftiness of aspiration and at the same time simple loudness. The breaking harp-string, then, is a sonic version of that unembodied essence of a thought rendered earlier, in terms of light. It is the guardian spirit's warning to the sleeper that he had better wake to the loved object, wherever it may be found, and to the divinity that shapes sleeper and object alike.

For those who wake and watch, there is the promise of future and higher worlds. Poe opens up this prospect by having the poem expand—like the eye of stanza three—to a wider and more cosmic perspective. He will employ the technique again in "To Helen," which ends with a new beginning, as human Helen yields to supernal Psyche, Greece and Rome to Holy-Land. The ending of "Stanzas" is not of course as affirmative as that. Indeed, the longer the concluding stanza goes on, the more it sounds as if the call must come too late. Like the lovers in "Al Aaraaf," the usurpers in stanza four seem too absorbed in their own "deep feeling" to hear that appeal from nature which is also a summons from God.

"Al Aaraaf"

The nature of the strange wandering star is established, as the nature of Tamerlane was established, by negative constructions:

> O! nothing earthly save the ray
> (Thrown back from flowers) of Beauty's eye . . .
> O! nothing earthly save the thrill
> Of melody in woodland rill . . .
> Oh, nothing of the dross of ours—
> Yet all the beauty—all the flowers
> That list our Love, and deck our bowers—
> Adorn yon world afar, afar—
> The wandering star.
>
> (Part I, ll. 1-15)[14]

The series "nothing/save, nothing/save, nothing/yet" describes a realm of being that incorporates the qualities of earthly experience while surpassing them; it is spatially and ontologically a world elsewhere. But the negativity has nothing to do with the distancing from being that afflicts the hero of the earlier long poem. Al Aaraaf is elsewhere only from

[14] My discussion of "Al Aaraaf," to say nothing of other poems, is indebted to Floyd Stovall, *Edgar Poe the Poet: Essays New and Old on the Man and his Work* (Charlottesville, 1969), pp. 102-125.

the vantage point of earth; in itself it is integral, harmonious, full. If Tamerlane is an emptiness seeking a plenitude it can never find, Al Aaraaf is that plentitude.

Al Aaraaf is, in relation to earth, a realm beyond. But where precisely is this "beyond" situated? Stanza one presents a remote object, seen from an earthly perspective: "yon world afar, afar— / The wandering star" (Part I, ll. 14-15). The second stanza establishes an interstellar space in which the earth is only one of several points of reference. For the wandering star (which is no longer, at the moment, wandering) exists less in relation to the planet earth, which is one of the "distant spheres" (Part I, l. 24) to which the spirit Nesace occasionally travels, than to the "four bright suns" (Part I, l. 18) which are near. By a circular process, the stanza reverses the earth-to-star perspective of stanza one. We see Nesace, first, in her usual celestial environment, then on a journey:

> To distant spheres, from time to time, she rode,
> And late to ours, the favour'd one of God—
> But, now, the ruler of an anchor'd realm,
> She throws aside the sceptre. . . .
>
> (Part I, ll. 24-27)

The perspective from earth-to-star has been replaced with a perspective from star-to-earth: for a moment we are as far from earth as, before, we had been far from Al Aaraaf. The process is circular inasmuch as the stanza concludes, where it had begun, with Nesace's presence in the "anchor'd realm" in which she had first been seen.

Stanza three situates the action once more in or near the star; now earth becomes "yon" (Part I, l. 30). Yet this very distancing of earth brings with it, by the same process of here-there shifting employed in the preceding stanza, a new nearness:

> Now happiest, loveliest in yon lovely Earth,
> Whence sprang the "Idea of Beauty" into birth,

(Falling in wreaths thro' many a startled star,
Like a woman's hair 'mid pearls, until, afar,
It lit on hills Achaian, and there dwelt)
She look'd into Infinity—and knelt.
(Part I, ll. 30-35)

This is the first time that earth has entered poem as anything more than a distant object or an implicit point of reference; now we are given a complete mythological account of the way in which the Idea of Beauty entered terrestrial experience. At the same time we are confronted with another here-there shifting, for the process takes place in an "elsewhere" space (the earth) and an "elsewhere" time (the past). To complicate matters, the consideration of beauty on earth is effected through Nesace, to whom the phrase "Now happiest, loveliest in yon lovely Earth" stands in apposition, although Nesace is not now, and as far as one can tell, never has been in the earth. The underlying relation, then, is one of potentiality: Nesace would be the happiest and loveliest if she were there. It does not matter whether she has ever been or will ever be situated there materially. It does not matter because we are dealing here with indeterminacy, a kind of pervasive fluidity that affects the function of space as well as the function of time. Accordingly a sentence such as the one with which we are dealing can, and does, shift about in a variety of ways. Digressions are permissible because they are not, finally, digressions, but movements to and fro, away and back. There can even be movements within the movements, both in syntax and in plot: thus the entire birth-of-beauty description, involving an elsewhere space and an elsewhere time, takes place parenthetically, in a clause that is dependent in the sense that it is subordinated to the structure of the sentence in which it occurs. The complete utterance, in effect, goes in two directions that it thereby tends to confound. If personification, as Poe conceives it, produces near-unity, this process creates near-merger. Everything—including at times the syntax itself—seems to flow into everything else, yet never quite does. Always, as in the personifications, a gap persists, and a sense of discrete identities. In extreme cases, such as the one before us, the shifts and subordinations place a heavy burden on the reader. He must understand that Nesace is not in the earth but would be happiest and loveliest if she were; must then experience the birth of beauty, which took place in an indeterminate past that no longer is; must follow that beauty, as it were, "until, afar, / It lit on hills Achaian" (Part I, ll. 33-34); then, still holding in his mind the parenthetic history, the appositions and the subordinations in their proper relationship, he must shift suddenly away from the terrestrial scene to the narrated present in Al Aaraaf whence Nesace sends him off in another direction by looking away into infinity. Beyond a certain point the process begins to annihilate what it creates, with the result that here and there become a not-here and a not-there; the reader finds himself simultaneously everywhere and nowhere, directionless in a space that is not the less indeterminate for being material.

The poem begins in an equally indeterminate time, a time in which, seemingly, things do not "happen" but merely "are." We do not see Al Aaraaf, for example, in the act of wandering. The star is defined for us, rather, as something that *by its nature* is a wandering thing. Showing the *act* of wandering would only reveal what Al Aaraaf was doing at a certain time. To name it "the wandering star," on the other hand, is to specify what it *always is*. The following stanza, by contrast, tells what it *sometimes does*. Only now, apparently, does an element of contingency and temporality arise; Al Aaraaf becomes "historical"—a thing that functions in real time. But in fact Al Aaraaf has never been entirely out of time any more than it has ever been entirely out of space. Al Aaraaf is precisely, to borrow a word from one of Poe's own footnotes to the poem, a "medium," a "place-between" through which deity attempts to influence the occupants of other spheres of being; and, in order to do this, the star must exist in time and space. What happens in the second stanza, then, is that the temporal and contingent aspects of Al Aaraaf (where it goes and what it does when it goes there) simply begin to emerge. For the first time in the poem something happens, or rather, it is given that things *have* happened; for the present, Nesace finds herself situated in a retrospective pause, a moment of arrest in which past acts are reviewed. Tamerlane, too, experienced a retrospective pause, though a longer and in several respects a very different one. For Tamerlane, everything has already been done; in order to tell all, he has merely to recapitulate the events of his life in chronological order. But it is impossible to tell all at this stage of "Al Aaraaf" because the series of events that the poem embraces is in progress. Nesace's rest, we are reminded, is "temporary" (Part I, l. 18).

In considering the time-scheme of the poem we may find it useful to distinguish between the poetic and the historical order of the things that occur. The poetic order is the series of events that unfold, line by line, in the verses as they are given. The historical order is the series of events in normal chronological sequence. The historical order (which must be reconstructed if the reader is to construe the meaning of the poetic order) is as follows: Angelo, a human being, dies of normal causes and proceeds in spirit toward some higher state. While Angelo is on his way, Al Aaraaf brings about a catastrophe that destroys the earth, transforming Angelo's flight into a fall. Much as the narrator of "MS. Found in a Bottle" passes from ship to ship, Angelo passes from planetary body to planetary body, ending on Al Aaraaf. On the wandering star he becomes, with all its other denizens, a servant of Nesace, and falls in love with Ianthe, who was transported to Al Aaraaf after her death on, presumably, another star. After the destruction of earth (though not necessarily immediately after), Nesace rests. God soon commands Nesace to warn other stars that they will fall, as comets have done, if they emulate the negligent ways of man. Nesace calls upon Ligeia to alert the occupants, of Al Aaraaf; Angelo and Ianthe, deafened by the sound of their own beating hearts, and perhaps to some extent by the conversation in which they are engaged, do not hear, and consequently fall.

The poetic order begins with Nesace's rest and follows the historical order up to the fall, except that the conversation, which explains the history of Angelo and Ianthe, is postponed until they have already fallen. Only then do we learn the sequence of events that have brought them to this juncture. The poetic order of "Al Aaraaf" reconstitutes, in other words, a more anterior and more human time. In her final speech Ianthe recreates the moment when the two lovers first gazed upon the wandering star: " 'We paus'd before the heritage of men, / And thy star trembled—as doth Beauty then!' " (Part II, ll. 259-260). The situation has a familiar look. Nesace also paused; Nesace also trembled before a higher power: to that extent the poem ends as it begins. But the distance between Nesace and the fallen couple is as great as the distance between the mediatrix of a higher power, which Nesace always is, and the victims of it, which Angelo and Ianthe become.

> What guilty spirit, in what shrubbery dim,
> Heard not the stirring summons of that hymn?
> But two: they fell: for Heaven no grace imparts
> To those who hear not for their beating hearts.
>
> (Part II, ll. 174-177)

In their transgression the lovers resemble Tamerlane, who could appreciate the ability to transcend self toward God but could never possess it. The situation of Angelo and Ianthe seems more tragic because they have doubly erred: first as members of the human race which, as we shall see below, has collectively sinned; then as beings of a higher order who fail to meet that single all-consuming obligation that is service to God. Tamerlane rises to power in the secular world, Angelo and Ianthe in the spiritual; how much greater, therefore, is their obligation, and how much lower their fall.

Of the two lovers, the male is the more culpable. Like Tamerlane, Angelo, who does most of the talking in the stanzas spoken by the pair, turns his imagination away from the here and now to a magnetic elsewhere. In the company of his lover, he finds his attention returning to earth: " 'And half I wish'd to be again of men' " (l. 226). Angelo's aspiration toward a lover, anterior condition is an inversion of Tamerlane's aspiration toward a higher condition in the future. Whatever differences there are between the two men, they both commit, in the final analysis, the double sin of alienation from nature (sexual love) and alienation from God.

Generic human sin—the sin of which all earthly beings are guilty—is nothing more than this self-preoccupation and self-aggrandizement on a collective scale. God commands Nesace to

> "Divulge the secrets of thy embassy
> To the proud orbs that twinkle—and so be
> To ev'ry heart a barrier and a ban
> Lest the stars totter in the guilt of man!"
>
> (Part I, ll. 147-150)

God is angry, because men, in the words of Nesace, " 'Have dream'd for thy Infinity / A model of their own' " (Part I, ll. 104-105). A model, in "Al Aaraaf," is a kind of derived type, a representation in low form of something high:

> Rich clouds, for canopies, about her [Nesace] curled—
> Fit emblems of the model of her world—
> Seen but in beauty—not impeding sight
> Of other beauty glittering thro' the light—
> A wreath that twined each starry form around,
> And all the opal'd air in color bound.
>
> (Part I, ll. 36-41)

Such a model is a direct and natural literalization—a carrying out into matter—of a spiritual state. The syntax, if one so construes it, can misleadingly suggest three discrete entities where there are only two. The relation can best be distinguished through the two prepositions that, though they appear the same, have two different meanings. The model *of* her world signifies the copy or representation of it; the sense is "derived or coming from" (as one would speak of a reproduction of an art object). On the other hand, the "of" that connects "emblems" with "model" denotes belonging-to. Thus the model of Nesace's world has emblems, which are clouds. Or: the world of Nesace is modelled in emblematic clouds.

On a slightly lower scale is the modelling of which Nesace speaks in Part II:

> "The sound of the rain
>   Which leaps down to the flower,
>
> . . . .
>
>   The murmur that springs
> From the growing of grass
> Are the music of things—
>   But are modell'd, alas!"
>
> (ll. 120-127)

Nesace suggests that a certain sadness attaches itself to any secondary creation—any creation, that is to say, which is not immediately constituted by God. From the sublunary vantage point that Ellison will assume in "The Domain of Arnheim," this secondary state is relished precisely because of its mediate position:

"Now let us suppose this sense of the Almighty design to be *one step depressed*—to be brought into something like harmony or consistency with the sense of human art—to form an intermedium between the two:—let us imagine, for example, a landscape . . . whose united beauty, magnificence, and *strangeness*, shall convey the idea of care, or culture, or superintendence, on the part of beings superior, yet akin to humanity—then the sentiment of *interest* is preserved, while the art intervolved is made to assume the air of an intermediate or secondary nature—a nature which is not God, nor an emanation from God, but which still is nature in the sense of the handiwork of the angels that hover between man and God." (VI, 187-188)

What would an angel think of such a creation? Nesace's comments imply that the angelic imagination would test secondary against primary, and find the secondary wanting. But for all their inadequacies, these models are not the result of culpable action. They are *innocently* inferior. Only the model created by man (Part I, ll. 102-105) manages to be both inferior and sinful. The clouds that surround Nesace represent circumscription of space, harmonious intimacy, and self-completeness. Equally important, they are non-interfering: being transparent (only their beauty is opaque and therefore visible), they allow other phenomena to pass through them. But the model with which mankind supplants deity does interfere, because it is derived from the wrong original. The model of infinity that man has created is based, not on infinity, but on the finite, not on God, but on man. The residents of earth sequestered themselves, like Prince Prospero's guests in "The Masque of the Red Death" or the company in "Silence. A Fable," in a private mirror-world that no ordinary power could induce them voluntarily to quit. So God, the extraordinary power, destroyed them. For the same sin of pride the comets, too, were punished. And the remaining stars? Their fate presumably depends, as Angelo's and Ianthe's depended, on their ability to hear. Whether they have that ability is not clear. Hearing, supposedly, is a given. But so are those beating hearts that *prevent* hearing. The only certainty is that existence is lived beneath the perpetual gaze of an all-powerful other.

These early poems thus establish a situation that will recur throughout the canon, namely, subjection to a higher power. The negative form of this subjection normally involves a confrontation and an attitude of helplessness or unfulfilled yearning. The positive form can also involve confrontation, in the sense that the other is given before me, in an arresting presentment; but here the prevailing attitude is adoration, fascinated attachment, devotion. We shall see the latter type further on in this section, when we come to the love lyrics or elegies; we shall see the former type both sooner and later—sooner because it appears in the poems we will be considering next, and later because it appears in the tales as well.

"Israfel"

The poem presents an eight-part structure. The first four stanzas are an account, in the third-person, of the famed singing angel. The next three stanzas (five through seven) contain a direct address to Israfel in the second-person, further description in the third-person, and a contrast, reminiscent of the opening lines of "Al Aaraaf," between "our" earthly world and the world above. Finally, in the concluding stanzas, Israfel is spoken of by a first-person. The aim of this 4-3-1 pattern—according to which the angel is alternately the one-who-is-spoken-of or the one-who-is-spoken-to, while the speaker emerges only in stanza eight—is to hold Israfel before the reader while allowing the speaker gradually to establish his own identity and presence. Little by little we see that the speaker and Israfel have moved toward a kind of subdued confrontation that will allow the former to challenge—or to be more precise, to talk about challenging—the angel's power. The low were set against the high in "Al Aaraaf" as well; the comets erred in the sight of God and fell, and the lovers followed in their wake; in "The Haunted Palace" the power figure is overthrown by "evil things" who will presumably reign forever; and in the tale "Hop-Frog" the title character, long brutalized by king and court, takes an appropriately brutal revenge. Poe was interested, then, in both sides of a power relation, and was willing to try out different ways in which power might be, so to speak, distributed. His emphasis nonetheless is on static situations, and on the ability of certain beings to dominate others. In this sense "Israfel" is more characteristic than the other works I have just mentioned, for the relative positions of the high and low, despite the speaker's wish for change, is the same at the end of the poem as at the beginning.

In "Irenë," another poem in the same 1831 volume, Poe adopted a similar strategy, holding back the first-person until near the end. Later he shifted the speaker forward to the opening lines in order to establish guardianship as a central feature of the poem (which he had by then retitled "The Sleeper"). The speaker keeps his original position in "Israfel," by contrast, for any shifting would upset the balance of power and weaken the crucial separation between angel and man. The human presence must therefore emerge just enough to be credible, but not enough to pose a real threat to the angelic order. To this end, the first-person intervolves himself (to use a word Poe liked) with Israfel long before he expresses his yearning to change places with him. Thus, although his presence is not fully realized until the concluding stanza, it is implied as early as stanza four of text A through the imperative: "Stay! turn thine eyes afar!" (l. 21). In the long apostrophe of the following three stanzas I address Israfel directly in the second-person, while the first-person plural of stanza seven ("ours") establishes my place in a broad earthly milieu. In text G, a new imperative in stanza five ("Merrily live, and long!" l. 34) replaces the imperative deleted from the preceding stanza.

Even before he emerges, the first-person is at work "humanizing" heaven by stressing the passional nature of poetry there, and indeed the passional nature of heaven itself: when Israfel sings "the giddy stars are mute" (l. 5) and "The enamoured moon / Blushes with love" (ll. 8-9). The Heavens are

Where Love is a grown god—
Where Houri glances are—
—Stay! turn thine eyes afar!
(ll. 19-21)

One musical instrument provides Israfel with "fire" (l. 14), another has "fervor" (l. 32), therefore Israfel despises "an unimpassion'd song" (l. 26).

Poe is very clear throughout his writings about the incompatibility of poetry and criticism. From early in his career until late he accepts Coleridge's insistence on the primacy of imagination. By saying, in effect, the opposite, the first-person of the poem makes it possible to infer that, since I am more earthly than Israfel and consequently more passionate, I will perform more forcefully than he if only I could gain access to his sphere. Israfel, being less passionate, would also perform less well here on earth.

Had the poem been written from the standpoint of Israfel, I would have suffered what amounts to a more rarefied version of victimization: the other, by singing more passionately, would have surpassed me in the very function through which I have my being. The poem as it exists approaches the problem the other way round, presenting an I who aspires to surpass:

> If I did dwell where Israfel
> Hath dwelt, and he where I,
> He would not sing one half as well—
> One half as passionately,
> And a stormier note than this would swell
> From my lyre within the sky.
>
> (ll. 39-44)

But I only aspire; I do not achieve. Israfel and the other heavenly beings function, until the concluding stanza, in the present tense, where he joins me in my tense—the conditional. The transfer which I desire depends upon an unrealizable proviso—an exchange of places with an angel. This is impossible for two reasons. First, because the angel and the man are literally separated from each other in space, the man being here on earth, the angel up there in heaven. The speaker himself never forgets this separation; and if he shares Tamerlane's fascination with "being-elsewhere," it is with the knowledge that his place as a man is ontologically fixed. Tamerlane's ambition is of the earth, earthly, but ambition like that in "Israfel" could be realized only in some extra-terrestrial, extrahuman space. It is well to remember, on this point, that "Israfel" is one of many works by Poe in which the setting is not a specific locale, or even the world, but the universe itself: if there is a lyrical element in Poe's cosmogony, *Eureka*, one may fairly say that there is a cosmogonic element in his lyrics, which show a marked tendency to expand, as here, into the infinite reaches of space. The second reason why Israfel's rival cannot change places is precisely the fact—which he has himself so carefully spelled out—that he is a human being and Israfel is not. By his own definition, and by the added force of our traditional ways of envisioning them, the two realms of being are spatially and ontologically separate. It is only when a thing is away from me that I can desire to have it.

Consequently, as the poem is revised, the concluding stanza, in which the speaker expresses his very human wish to be superhuman, is toned-down:

> If I could dwell
> Where Israfel
>   Hath dwelt, and he where I,
> He might not sing so wildly well
>   A mortal melody,
> While a bolder note than this might swell
>   From my lyre within the sky.
>
> (ll. 45-51)

By abandoning the suggestion that Israfel could not sing one half as passionately, I deprive myself of the one capacity on which the possibility of a transfer was predicated. My sphere is no longer that of the passions, but that of mortality. The probability of a successful transfer is even further diminished —my original "could," already sufficiently qualified, becomes a "might." I am left, in the end, with my desire and the possibility, at best, of its fulfillment. My superior power is contingent; to exercise it I must exist elsewhere, which I am unable to do. That is the reason for my original caution, and for the muting of my claim in the final version; and it is the reason that, from first version to last, my final, critical utterance begins with an "if," from which and on which everything depends.

Mabbott writes: "It has become customary to identify Poe with his angel; the name is the title of Hervey Allen's biography. The practice probably began with Mrs. Osgood's 'Echo Song,' published in the *Broadway Journal* of September 6, 1845. The transfer of name, however, is unfortunate, since it disregards the main point made in the poem, the excellence of Man."[15] The application of Israfel's name and identity to Poe is indeed a transfer, and one for which there is no basis whatever in the text. But the poem has to do, as well, with the things a human being cannot do: it is about man's limited excellence, and the necessary separation (first explored in "Tamerlane") between superhuman power and the power of men.

"Irenë" and "The Sleeper"

The moon, speaking, describes

> . . . winged visions [that] love to lie
> Lazily upon beauty's eye,
> Or worse—upon her brow to dance
> In panoply of old romance,
> Till thoughts and locks are left, alas!
> A ne'er-to-be untangled mass.
>
> (ll. 3-8)

As in "Tamerlane" the advent-from-above threatens. Again as in "Tamerlane," the power descends upon the victim in the form of an endangering nucta:

> An influence dewy, drowsy, dim,
> Is dripping from that golden rim;
> Grey towers are mouldering into rest.
>
> (ll. 9-11)

[15] *CW*, p. 173.

Here the distant perspective on the moon ("that golden rim") indicates a shift away from the moon-as-speaker to the moon-as-object-of-sight. Some indeterminate consciousness or voice is watching the process by which the influence induces sleep throughout the natural world: the lake takes "A conscious slumber" (l. 14), and even the flowers are no longer awake. Yet the attitude expressed toward the process merely continues the attitude of the moon, which was itself concerned with the imminent danger to what is twice referred to as beauty (ll. 4, 22). The sequence establishes that the moon is conscious of some danger from above, and that the danger comes to some degree from the moon itself. In the following stanza, the third, the moon takes on the guardianship for which its early solicitude has already prepared the way, and speaks directly to the sleeper, warning of the " 'wanton airs' " that " 'Laughingly thro' the lattice drop' " (ll. 33-34). And finally:

> "Lady, awake! lady awake!
> For the holy Jesus' sake!
> For strangely—fearfully in this hall
> My tinted shadows rise and fall!"
>
> (ll. 37-40)

This is an unashamedly anthropomorphic nature. The moon possesses consciousness, talks, and worries about its human counterparts. And in an equally human way it has only limited knowledge (it cannot perceive the source of the threat) and limited power (it cannot arouse the sleeper to a sense of danger). Its consciousness, too, is limited, for the moon fails to recognize that it is its own influence that has lulled the sleeper into her present state, and thus exposed her to the power of the wanton airs.

With the revelation that the lady has died, emphasis shifts in the fourth stanza from a concern for the future, expressed in warning, to a concern for the past, expressed in remembrance. The indeterminate first-person, once more replacing the moon, warns that the living quickly forget those who have died. As predicted, those who mourn for the sleeper immediately following her death are soon indulging in a "light laughter [which] chokes the sigh" of grief (l. 46). Only when this obvious parallel with the laughing "wanton airs" occurs does the departed spirit actually depart:

> Indignant from the tomb [the spirit] doth take
> Its way to some remember'd lake,
> Where oft—in life—with friends—it went
> To bathe in the pure element,
> And there, from the untrodden grass,
> Wreathing for its transparent brow
> Those flowers that say (ah hear them now!)
> To the night-winds as they pass,
> "Ai! ai! alas!—alas!"
> Pores for a moment, ere it go,
> On the clear waters there that flow,
> Then sinks within (weigh'd down by wo)
> Th'uncertain, shadowy heaven below.
>
> (ll. 47-59)

The stanza presents the failure of human remembrance. Only the flowers—endowed, like the moon, with intelligible speech—express regret, and even this sentiment is little more than a generalized melancholy. If Poe's tales often describe dehumanization—the reification or "thinging" of human beings—poems such as "Al Aaraaf" or "Irenë" offer a compensatory humanization of the inanimate. In neither of these poems, however, does the material world displace the human. "Al Aaraaf" becomes increasingly, as it approaches its conclusion, a human-oriented creation. "Irenë" also ends, not where we have temporarily left it, but with a *re*humanization. After the break that separates the last two stanzas from the sections we have been examining, the indeterminate consciousness or voice emerges in the identity of a guardian:

> I pray to God that she may lie
> Forever with as calm an eye,

That chamber chang'd for one more holy—
That bed for one more melancholy.
(ll. 63-66)

This use of the first-person comes as something of a surprise. For sixty-two lines of its seventy-four lines the poem had contented itself with the third-person. All the while, apparently, the guardian "I" has been standing in the shadows, letting the moon do the work. That is not fine conduct in a guardian, which may explain the changes Poe made in the subsequent version of the poem, called "The Sleeper." Here, words spoken in the earlier poem by the moon are uttered by the human speaker, whose presence, instead of being held over for the last stanza, is established in the first: "At midnight, in the month of June, / I stand beneath the mystic moon" (ll. 1-2). Putting the guardian under the moon in that way makes it sound as if he too is exposed to influences from above; yet when the poem concludes, she is dead, or dying, and he is untouched. William B. Hunter speculates that the man who prays for her eternal rest may also be responsible for drawing down the vapours from above, but decides that the poem "neither supports nor denies such an interpretation."[16] The suspicion presumably arises from the attitude of the guardian, in whom the critic seems to detect an ambivalence. The guardian, however, is simply ineffective, a quality shared by many of Poe's guardians, for whom failure is a kind of career. Poe's aim in "The Sleeper" is to "elevate" the earlier work in two ways. The first way is to reverse the tendency to let nature take the place of a human presence: this is arranged by allowing the role of the human figure (the guardian) to expand and the role of the natural figure (the moon) to contract. Second, the demise of the sleeper, gratuitous in "Irenë," is placed against what may be called, for lack of a better word, a religious background. Thus, in addition to keeping the direct plea to God, the speaker declares, "Heaven have her in

[16] "Poe's 'The Sleeper' and *Macbeth*," *American Literature*, 20 (1948), pp. 55-57.

its sacred keep!" (l. 39), and calls the sleeper, near the end, "poor child of sin!" (l. 59). This is all very makeshift in the eyes of Allen Tate, who looks skeptically at Poe's unorthodox metaphysics, but it represents Poe's serious attempt to make his work a little purer, a little more "holy" and sublime.

"The Valley of Unrest"

The power to which the valley is subjected reveals itself indirectly, through a failure of guardianship:

> *Once* it smiled a silent dell
> Where the people did not dwell;
> They had gone unto the wars,
> Trusting to the mild-eyed stars,
> Nightly, from their azure towers,
> To keep watch above the flowers.
> (ll. 1-6)

There is thus for the valley, as for the sleeper, a brief period of time before the implied threat becomes reality. The city in the sea, in the poem of the same name, also experiences this *interval-before.* In all three poems, then, the initial premise is that the worst is yet to come, and it does, but never through an overt act. At one moment the lady is imperilled; at another she is dead. At one time the valley smiled in contented trust; at another it becomes violently agitated:

> *Now* each visiter [sic] shall confess
> The sad valley's restlessness.
> Nothing there is motionless.
> Nothing save the airs that brood
> Over the magic solitude.
> Ah, by no wind are stirred those trees
> That palpitate like the chill seas
> Around the misty Hebrides!

Ah, by no wind those clouds are driven
That rustle through the unquiet Heaven
Uneasily, from morn till even.

(ll. 9-19)

Between the past, when one condition prevailed, and the present, where a radically different condition has come about, there is nothing—no transition, no intermediate steps, no acts. The first section of the poem declares, "The worst is yet to come." The second section declares, "The worst is already here." But there is no section that explains the process by which the earlier state gives way to the later. The reason is that the act that results in the change is scarcely an act at all: the alteration comes about solely through a failure to prevent. In their forgetfulness the stars thus resemble the forgetful survivors of the dead sleeper. But they resemble even more the wanton airs who stole dangerously through the lady's negligently opened window, the difference being that the stars behave even more indirectly.

This muting or subtilizing of behavior is part of the rarefying process that the poem undergoes in its evolution from a form in which concrete circumstances and details play a prominent role:

It is called the Valley Nis.
And a Syriac tale there is
Thereabout which Time hath said
Shall not be interpreted.
Something about Satan's dart—
Something about angel wings—
Much about unhappy things:
But "the valley Nis" at best
Means "the valley of unrest."

(ll. 7-16)

Poe sometimes tried to make his poems better by making them longer. "The Bells," which expanded to more than six times its original size, is a case in point. He usually preferred, however, to shorten, as though to reach the essential by a process of stripping away; and when, as in "Tamerlane," a poem exists in two states of varying length, he normally settles at last on the shorter. Poe is following a characteristic pattern, therefore, when he converts the relatively long and detailed "The Valley Nis" (from which I have just quoted) into the relatively short and vague "The Valley of Unrest." This is accomplished in part by leaving things out: the naming of the valley and the allusion to the Syriac tale simply disappear. There is, at the same time, an increasing reliance on negative constructions: *did not dwell*, *Nothing is*, *nothing save*, *no wind*, *no wind*. Even the modifiers—and for that matter the title itself—are implicitly negative: motion*less*, *un*quiet, *un*easily; the valley of *un*rest. The poet tries at the same time, as Killis Campbell says, to "curtail the personal,"[17] by dropping a reference that seems to point too obviously to the occasional aspect of the poem. Thus the flowers in the lines "Helen, like thy human eye / There th'uneasy violets lie" (p. 192, ll. 29-30) become "the violets there that lie / In myriad types of the human eye" (p. 196, ll. 20-21).

The first-person who figured so significantly in "Irenë" and "The Sleeper" is missing from both versions of the poem. As if to complement this absence of a human speaker there is absence of speech in nature: these flowers, lacking the correspondent breeze that inspires the flowers in the works just mentioned, do *not* make utterances. They have a kind of power, as do the trees and clouds that move despite the lack of wind, but it is an immanent power. This is not surprising, for the world of "The Valley of Unrest" is strangely interiorized. One watches its agitations much as the first-person of "The Fall of the House of Usher" watches the agitations of Usher and his house. The valley of unrest, in a way, is even more hermetic, and more dehumanized. The type of dehu-

[17] Introduction to *The Poems of Edgar Allan Poe* (Boston, 1917), p. xxxvii. Poe's emphasis on detachment is examined by Stephen L. Mooney, "Poe's Gothic Wasteland," *Sewanee Review*, 70 (1962), pp. 278ff., and by James W. Gargano, "The Question of Poe's Narrators," *College English*, 25 (1963), pp. 177-181.

manization that Allen Tate discovered in Poe exhibits people losing their humanness, becoming "thingish" and inanimate. The type of dehumanization we are studying here is more like depopulation: a landscape is suddenly deprived of human beings, producing an obscure but intense feeling of loss. In the place of the departed human beings (a collective version of the departed spirit in "Irenë), there are guardians—flowers, clouds, trees—which remember. The problem is that their remembrance cannot be articulated because the one animating agency that the guardians share—the wind—no longer blows. The flowers, clouds, and trees, consequently, fall back upon themselves: the trees palpitate, the clouds rustle through Heaven, the flowers wave and weep, independent of external impulse. This newly manifested, immanent, interiorized caring is the equivalent, in inanimate nature, of the caring I who emerges at the end of "The Sleeper" and "Irenë." In all three poems some betrayal from above is compensated for by an earthly, more humanized agency that remembers. There is little enough that such an agency can do. The first-person of "The Sleeper" and "Irenë" utters a prayer while the violets and the lilies of "The Valley of Unrest," lacking speech, wave and weep. The gestural character reveals more clearly perhaps than the words of the human speaker the ritualistic nature of all these endings. The last sections of the poems are not contributions to evolving acts but signatures, beautiful but ineffectual, of completed states.

"The Doomed City" and "The City in the Sea"

In both of these works the interval-before emerges later than in "The Valley of Unrest" and the sleeper poems. The sleeper, we remember, is threatened, succumbs, and is mourned; the valley becomes deserted and is briefly contented before remembrance manifests itself in the material world. In each case the absent one still claims some earthly ties. But the condemned city is already beyond such clinging.

Its earthly life being effectively completed, nothing remains but the perfecting of the state to which it has been condemned. The hopelessness of the situation results neither in calmness nor resignation. On the contrary, the poem bulges with exclamations (there are nine in "The Doomed City" and five in "The City in the Sea") from beginning to end:

> Lo! Death hath rear'd himself a throne
> In a strange city, all alone,
> Far down within the dim west—
>
> . . . .
>
> There shrines, and palaces, and towers
> Are—not like any thing of ours—
> O! no—O! no—*ours* never loom
> To heaven with that ungodly gloom!
> Time-eaten towers that tremble not!
>
> (ll. 6-10)
>
> But there! that everlasting pall!
> It would be mockery to call
> Such dreariness a heaven at all.
>
> (ll. 17-19)
>
> For no ripples curl, alas!
> Along that wilderness of glass.
>
> (ll. 37-38)
>
> But lo! a stir is in the air!
> The wave! there is a ripple there!
>
> (ll. 45-56)

The city, like the House of Usher, is in a condition of extreme suspense, a condition that can be relieved only by that submergence which, as the poem ends, is just beginning to occur. Each poem prophesies this submergence, ending with a hint that the process has already begun, but, despite many claims to the contrary, neither city is submerged when the poem begins. Killis Campbell and Louise Pound, and others after them, have endeavored to trace Poe's sources in the belief that he was adhering to ancient and modern legends about sunken cities that were a popular literary topic in his time. Widely used collections of Poe's work, such as Campbell's edition of the poems, have given the assumption wide currency, and it has continued, as by a process of inertia, to go virtually unchallenged. Unfortunately, there is nothing in either poem to suggest that the assumption is correct, as at least two commentators have pointed out. Montgomery Belgion observes in "The Mystery of Poe's Poetry" that the city is "surrounded by the sea" rather than being sunken in it.[18] In a more detailed analysis, " 'The City in the Sea': A Reexamination," Frederick T. Keefer points out that nothing in the text supports the conventional reading, and that the preposition in the title means "bounded by," as in "island in the sea."[19] Both commentators appear to regard the prophetic nature of the poems as self-evident, as do I, and they do not directly engage the text. This I will now attempt to do. Because the lines bearing on the location of the city are virtually identical in both versions, we may concentrate on the later and more familiar one, "The City in the Sea."

The opening stanza places the city, not within the sea, but more vaguely "within the dim West" (l. 3). We are then told:

> There shrines and palaces and towers
> (Time-eaten towers that tremble not!)
> Resemble nothing that is ours.
>
> (ll. 6-8)

The paradox of decrepit architecture that continues to stand when it ought to fall is another anticipation of the House of Usher, which despite its obvious decay has managed, at the time the narrator first sees it, to survive. That the architecture resembles nothing of ours echoes the description in "Al Aaraaf," where it is said that "nothing of the dross of ours"

[18] *Essays in Criticism*, 1 (1951), p. 54.
[19] *College English*, 25 (1964), p. 437.

can be found in the wandering star—an indication that the city is not to be identified too closely with ostensible earthly counterparts.

The first mention of water shows that the sea *surrounds* the city:

> Around, by lifting winds forgot,
> Resignedly beneath the sky
> The melancholy waters lie.
>
> (ll. 9-11)

The later phrase "that wilderness of glass" (l. 37) confirms that the sea is being contemplated here as a flat surface, like a mirror, or like the tarn in which the House of Usher, in more than one sense, is reflected. The city's elevation above the level of the waters is indicated by the manner in which the light from the sea comes up to illuminate it:

> But light from out the lurid sea
> Streams up the turrets silently—
> Gleams up the pinnacles far and free
> Up domes—up spires—up kingly halls—
> Up fanes—up Babylon-like walls—
>
> . . . .
>
> Up many and many a marvellous shrine
> Whose wreathéd friezes intertwine
> The viol, the violet, and the vine.
>
> (ll. 14-23)

If the city were submerged in the sea, it would not be necessary, it would indeed be impossible, for the illumination to come *out* of the sea in order to reach it.

The city and the sea that surround it are both related to the sky. It is twice averred that the waters lie beneath the sky. Later we read that "No rays from the holy heaven come down" (l. 12) on the city's night, and that the turrets and shadows of the city, like the columns in Part II of "Al Aaraaf," appear blended and "pendulous in air" (l. 27). The city sits there, in other words, encircled above by the atmosphere, and below—at what would elsewhere be described as ground level—by the flat sea. Mabbott would reply "that the ruins of the Cities of the Plain are close to the surface at ordinary times, and in very dry weather the tops of walls and columns may be seen above the water."[20] But Poe's architecture looms much higher than that, and there is no indication that the area has been suffering from drought.

> There open fanes and gaping graves
> Yawn level with the luminous waves;
> But not the riches there that lie
> In each idol's diamond eye—
> Not the gaily-jewelled dead
> Tempt the waters from their bed.
> (ll. 30-35)

The picture seems clear enough. Overhead are the looming turrets and shadows blending in the air, lower are the halls and fanes and bowers, and, lower still, on line with the water, the graves. If the city were sunken altogether—if the city were even substantially submerged, as Mabbott has it—it would be impossible for these burial sites to be on the same level as the waves. In his effort to tie Poe to a conventional interest in the sunken cities of legend, Mabbott has forgotten his usual position on such matters, which is that Poe combined his sources, altered them at will, and often went far beyond them.

The idea in both poems is that the city is doomed to sink, like the House of Usher, into the watery depths, and that, as the poems near their conclusion, this process has already begun. I mention the House of Usher again in order to suggest that the poems can be understood if one pays at least as much attention to related patterns in other works by Poe as to conventional models that the author may or may not have known and may or may not have used. The behavior of the light in these poems may not be a convention in works Poe

[20] *CW*, p. 97. Cf. Louise Pound, "On Poe's 'The City in the Sea,'" *American Literature*, 6 (1934), pp. 22-27.

read, but it is a convention in works he wrote. In his article "Infernal Illumination in Poe," Oliver Evans demonstrates Poe's fascination with a "subterranean (or sub-aqueous) illumination" proceeding upward from what Evans calls "infernal regions."[21] The phenomenon occurs in *The Narrative of A. Gordon Pym*, where "A sullen darkness now hovered above us—but from out the milky depths of the ocean a luminous glare arose. . ." (III, 241). In "The Pit and the Pendulum" a "sulphurous light" emanating from a fissure illumines the prisoner's underground room (v, 84), while from the graves envisioned in "The Premature Burial" there arises "the faint phosphoric radiance of decay . . ." (v, 267). Evans concludes his survey with "The Fall of the House of Usher," in which light from the setting sun streams through a fissure at an angle that is arguably more horizontal than upward. The pattern, nonetheless, is clear, and begins, as Evans indicates, at least as early as "The Doomed City," in which the pattern develops in stanza four, only to be advanced, in the later version, to stanza two.

> The waves have now a redder glow—
> The hours are breathing faint and low—
> And when, amid no earthly moans,
> Down, down that town shall settle hence,
> Hell, rising from a thousand thrones,
> Shall do it reverence.
>
> (ll. 48-53)

The prophetic intention (emphasized in the C text, which bears the subtitle "A Prophecy") is signalled by the change in tense. Stanza one begins in the present perfect, while the next three stanzas (with the exception of a dependent clause in l. 40) are in the present. The final stanza, beginning also in the present, ends however in the future tense, pointing to the fate to which the doomed city will submit. The future tense is the province of the prophetic mode in which Poe, a Bible reader and a reviewer of religious books, experimented

[21] *Modern Language Notes*, 75 (1960), p. 295.

in works like "Shadow. A Parable," "The Colloquy of Monos and Una," and his commentary on Stephens' *Arabia Petraea* (x, 1-25). Were the pursuit of the contexts to be turned in this direction, one might be able to determine not merely Poe's exploitation of sources, but his place in the tradition of secular prophecy that, as Albert La Valley has shown, starts with Blake and proceeds through a notable line of thinkers and writers including Carlyle, Nietzsche, and Marx.[22]

The eschatological nature of the city's last moments are underlined by references to "eternal rest," "ungodly gloom," and the absence of "holy rays." Earthly ties begin to drop; ahead lies mystery, the unknown. Powerless to act, one can only indulge in a kind of desperate vocal gesturing—an inconsequential expression of terror. That is what Usher does when he shouts that his sister stands outside the door. It is what the narrator of "MS. Found in a Bottle" does when he cries, "the ship is quivering—oh God! and—going down!" and it is what the passive guardian does in the doomed-city poems when he exclaims, "Lo!" and "alas!" What one sees is inexpressible, with the result, again, that negative constructions proliferate: *not like any thing of ours, O! no, ungodly, doth not contemn, no holy rays, not the riches* and *not the dead, no ripples, no swellings, no earthly moans.* There is a tendency to define the city negatively as well, for if it is not quite a recognizable town neither is it a recognizable man. The human element in the city, such as it is, has been reified, or rather architecturalized, in the "sculptur'd ivy and stone flowers" and the "entablatures of the many melancholy shrines." There is no opposition in this sphere between man and his environment because he has become merged with it. That is the first difference between the role of environment here and in the tales. The second difference is that in the tales the environment—the chamber, for example—is normally experienced through the interiority of a victim ("The

[22] *Carlyle and the Idea of the Modern: Studies in Carlyle's Prophetic Literature and Its Relation to Blake, Nietzsche, Marx, and Others* (New Haven and London, 1968).

Pit and the Pendulum") or a victimizer ("The Cask of Amontillado"). But "The Doomed City" and "The City in the Sea" present an exteriorized experience. We are not asked to regard the city as the mere projection of the guardian's fancy, but as a phenomenon existing in its own right. Being outsiders, as it were, we must watch for visible signs and cues that will express the state that is being developed before us: the appearance of light on this or that architectural component, changes in the behavior of the water, and so on. The third difference is that in these poems man is victimized in his architecture in a different and more extreme way. If the tales present man imprisoned in architectural space, these poems present man made consubstantial with it. The prose is concerned, among other things, with "man in architecture," the poetry with "architecture-man"—again, dehumanization. But that is not why there is emotion in the poem. There is emotion in the poem because the speaker still experiences the human element in this new hyphenated being. The city, for him, is precisely the *man*-city: "thingish" in appearance, but human in essence. That is why the impending engulfment is worth exclaiming about, and why the city (in still another of those final ritualistic moments) still merits solicitude:

> And when, amid no earthly moans,
> Down, down that town shall settle hence,
> Hell, rising from a thousand thrones,
> Shall do it reverence.
>
> (ll. 50-54)

"The Coliseum"

The manner of this poem is established by the apostrophe and invocations of the opening stanzas:

> Type of the antique Rome! Rich reliquary
> Of lofty contemplation left to Time
> By buried centuries of pomp and power!
>
> (ll. 1-3)

Vastness! and Age! and Memories of Eld!
Silence! and Desolation! and dim Night!
(ll. 10-11)

There is an obvious difference between these utterances and the ones we find in "Tamerlane" or the doomed-city poems, which are full of crisis and anguished emotion. There is emotion in "The Coliseum," too, but of a controlled and practiced kind. It is public emotion, and the voice that bears it does not exclaim so much as declaim. The voice in "Tamerlane" and "Stanzas" has a certain intimacy as befits, in the first place, confession to an imagined auditor, and, in the second, a mood of reflection. In subsequent works, such as the sleeper and doomed-city poems, there is an increase in what might be called vocal urgency, as if the speaker were lifting himself to a more intense occasion. Yet "The Coliseum" depends more than any of these on the oral attributes of verse: on the ability of the reader to hear the poem as oral projection.

Francis Berry, himself a poet, insists on the essentially oral nature of poetry, even when the sounded words are heard only, as in reading, within the head: "Speech is significant vibration of the air produced by mind and body, though I dare say that behind mind and body, compelling their joint action, is a third factor, an X, for which the English word used to be 'soul.' But the 'I' that speaks usually means to be heard, and the speaker's voice will vary not only according as to *what* it says but also according to *whom* it says it, and even *where* it has to say it. (The voice, where 'intention' and the 'soul' are in doubt, has a certain autonomy best indicated by 'it.') That is, the manner of a voice at any one moment is controlled by the listeners and the surroundings as well as by the speaker—unless indeed the speaker is, as the idiom forcibly has it, 'beside himself,' speaking 'without regard to person, time or place,' and as though not within his body but from outside."

Berry goes on to describe the functioning of voice in various auditory spaces, a consideration not irrelevant to

Poe, who lived in the age of the lyceum, and who spent many hours at the lectern, from which, in his mild Southern accent, he intoned his poetic cadences. "I am not forgetting, of course, that it is not only the size, shape and acoustic properties of the room which modify or control the voice of a poet. That voice will also be controlled by the audience in that room, its size and constitution. It will also be controlled by the poet's relation towards that audience. He has one relation when he tells a story (*Beowulf*); another relation when, speaking through actors, he shows them a drama; another relation when he declaims *at* them—speaking to his audience as 'you' or 'ye' (*Childe Harold*), etc., etc. I mention actual audiences, but I do not forget that most poets since 1820, or even before then, in default of an actual audience, have simply assumed one. But even then—when an audience is merely assumed—the poet has had to adopt an attitude to it and that attitude has controlled his voice."[23]

The poet achieves his effects (Berry continues) partly through register, defined as "the range of pitch possible to a voice when the larynx is in one position rather than another. . . . if one sings (or whispers) the lowest note in the scale that one can manage and then ascends, there comes the point at which one must draw fresh breath and alter the position of the larynx before continuing the scale upwards. . . . One may liken the operation to a driver changing gears from fourth to third as his car encounters an increasing gradient." This means that if someone says a line of verse that is light and lyrical, requiring a resonance in the mouth, "he will find that he cannot immediately follow it with a line requiring a full chest-resonance without first changing gear, i.e. effect a physiological adjustment of the larynx. . . ."[24] Berry outlines three main registers, a top, for singing the higher notes of the poetic scale; a middle, for normal or conversational speech and verse; and a low register, for sounding the bass tones of poetry that is monumental or grand, as in much of *Paradise Lost*.

[23] *Poetry and the Physical Voice* (London, 1962), pp. 19, 25.
[24] *Poetry and the Physical Voice*, p. 18.

Low register in Poe is uncommon, and can be found in those places where he is being more or less consciously Miltonic or "sublime," as in the speech of God in "Al Aaraaf," or at the end of "Shadow. A Parable," where the mysterious presence declares: " 'I am SHADOW, and my dwelling is near to the Catacombs of Ptolemais, and hard by those dim plains of Helusion which border upon the foul Charonian canal' " (II, 150). Poe confines himself for the most part to the top and middle registers. Sounds fall differently on different ears, but I believe that many of the poems, like "Tamerlane," "Stanzas," "The Happiest Day," "Israfel," "To Helen," and the other verses to women, are within the normal range of speech, and that if they move away in either direction it is up rather than down. The voice in these works is quiet, hushed, and intense, as if the speaker were exploiting full breath and energy within certain restraints. On the basis of subject matter, one might expect the lower register in the doomed-city poems, "The Valley of Unrest," and "The Haunted Palace," but these poems are elegies—expressions of that perennial sense of loss so characteristic of Poe—and lend themselves to the effect of mournful intoning best achieved by a pitch slightly higher than normal or, at the limit, "voiced" from the head. That leaves the highest or top register, which one hears in a number of works. It is audible for the first time in the rhetorical "Oh, Tempora! Oh, Mores!" an early poem in which the youthful author tries on the jacket of eighteenth-century wit, only to find it too tight for his taste. It is audible throughout *Politian* in the many declamations, cries, and oaths the characters hurl at one another, and in "The Coliseum," which was designed, if ever a poem by this author was, to be heard at the back of the auditorium. And it is audible in that unabashed *tour de force*, "The Bells." In short, the upper register lends itself in Poe, as in many authors, to a kind of Ciceronian or rhetorical mode that is more or less self-consciously public. It can be heard at the same time in poems that are rhetorical only in part: "The Conqueror Worm," "Lenore," "Ulalume," and, of course, "The Raven." You have to get your breath up, if you want to read these poems aloud, for they are very intense, and in all but the first there are people in them—characters—who shout. Nor is the first the exception it appears, for here too there are cries, a command ("But see . . . A crawling shape intrude!"), and an entire cast of wildly dramatic characters. If the number of exclamations is a fair sign of the top register, even better, as I have just implied, is evidence of dramatic intent, which can be signalled conspicuously as in "The Conqueror Worm," where the setting is theatrical, but can be expressed as well in the tensions between two characters, or between two states. This is the case in both "The Raven" and "Ulalume," which depict a confrontation between personages (The Raven and the mourner, Psyche and the mourner) and the equally important struggle (brought to a climax by the tensions between the personages) between forgetfulness and remembrance.

"The Coliseum," to which we may now return, is an attempt to body forth the spirit of classical antiquity, and can be thought of to this extent as a companion poem to the more celebrated lyric "To Helen," which communicates that spirit through the visible presence of an adored woman. An explication of the latter poem will be offered when we are in a position to consider the poems to women as a group; here we need only observe that the admirer of the Coliseum, like the admirer of Helen, is a returning wanderer, and that the concluding words of the following description echo the famous lines about the glory that was Greece, the grandeur that was Rome:

> At length—at length—after so many days
> Of weary pilgrimage and burning thirst,
> (Thirst for the springs of lore that in thee lie,)
> I kneel, an altered and an humble man,
> Amid thy shadows, and so drink within
> My very soul thy grandeur, gloom, and glory!
> (ll. 4-9)

Other sections of the poem look forward rather than back. The lolling monarch of stanza three, who has been overthrown by time, anticipates the monarch Thought in "The Haunted Palace," whose position is usurped by a mob of "evil things," while the "corrosive Hours," which the speaker fears will be his only legacy of the Roman past, foreshadow Monos' account of the aftermath of life in "The Colloquy of Monos and Una." Poe is also characteristic here in his use of architecture. "The Haunted Palace" is an architecturalized version of a human head or brain, and we have just seen, in the doomed-city poem, the architecturalization of the collective human condition. What "The Coliseum" architecturalizes, of course, is the past, and here again "To Helen" is apposite. In both poems the past is viewed as something both far from me and near, and as something good. It is a remote thing insofar as I can contemplate and revere it but never be one with it; and it is near insofar as I can feel the almost tangible presence. It is, finally, a good thing, insofar as it affirms its own continuing identity and its ability to transcend the ravages of time. Now it may be, as Mabbott argues in his introduction to the poem, that Poe is brightening the gloomy picture of the Coliseum drawn by Byron in *Childe Harold* and *Manfred*. But we are probably nearer the truth if we recognize that Poe is, as usual, answering himself, and that "The Coliseum" stands in the same relation to the doomed-city poems as "Stanzas" to "Tamerlane." In both sequences the poet offers a vision that is essentially negative followed by a vision that is essentially affirmative. The thesis of "The Coliseum" is that this piece of architecture is *not* doomed, and that this victim is *not* powerless:

> These stones—alas! these gray stones—are they all—
> All of the famed, and the colossal left
> By the corrosive Hours to Fate and me?
>
> "Not all"—the Echoes answer me—"not all!
> Prophetic sounds and loud, arise forever
> From us, and from all Ruin, unto the wise,
> As melody from Memnon to the Sun.
> We rule the hearts of mightiest men—we rule

With a despotic sway all giant minds.
We are not impotent—we pallid stones.
Not all our power is gone—not all our fame—
Not all the magic of our high renown—
Not all the wonder that encircles us—
Not all the mysteries that in us lie—
Not all the memories that hang upon
And cling around about us as a garment,
Clothing us in a robe of more than glory."
(ll. 30-46)

The negations are neither those of a philosopher, who cancels out aspects of the phenomenon he wants to define, nor those of a "contradictory" Tamerlane, who explains why his situation is not suitable for the confession he chooses to voice. The "Nots" in "The Coliseum" are rhetorical negations, put forward in reply to the question posed by the first-person. The drift of that question, its argument, is that the Coliseum is an empty ruin, powerless and defunct. The ensuing negations contradict this view. The attributes in the catalogue (power, magic, wonder, mysteries, memories) are in no sense denied; what is denied is the argument that they have been lost; the "Nots" are those of the debater who defends an object by refuting the claims against it. In short, although this is one of the largest clusters of negations in Poe, it is also one of the most affirmative.

The justification for the top register is the very nature of the topic, which is a matter of public knowledge and interest. "Resolved: That the Roman past, and by implication history in general, has nothing to say to modern man." To which the Echoes, adopting the "con" position, answer, "No: the past (embodied in the Coliseum) is not dead, and has much to say."

Poe remembered that prophecy is traditionally an oral mode—that the future can be predicted, and men controlled, by the inspired word. The Echoes accordingly produce "prophetic sounds and loud" that through their innate power control the destinies of men throughout all time.

"The Haunted Palace"

The poem, writes Davidson, "is about some mind or psyche seen from the inside the mind itself and describing not only its present state of being but how that state came to exist."[25] Poe's architecturalizing produces, on the contrary, an inside seen from an outside:

> Wanderers in that happy valley,
> Through two luminous windows, saw
> Spirits moving musically.
> (ll. 17-19)

This is not a subjectivity experiencing in and through itself. If I am a palace, then my windows are openings through which to look out, not, as here, openings through which others look in at me. Further on we read:

> And travellers, now, within that valley,
> Through the encrimsoned windows see
> Vast forms that move fantastically
> To a discordant melody,
> While, like a ghastly rapid river,
> Through the pale door
> A hideous throng rush out forever
> And laugh—but smile no more.
> (ll. 41-48)

Again, the notion of a psychological experience viewed from the inside does not suit the case. If I were a palace, and a throng were to rush out of my inner space, I would experience this in an inner way: as a going-away-from-me, or a

[25] *Poe: A Critical Study*, p. 79. Davidson is nearer the mark it seems to me, when he states that "Poe's poems of this genre were what might be termed a 'picturesque of consciousness'; that is, he sought to investigate and present conditions of mental awareness . . . by means of a series of topographical descriptions or apocalyptic visions which . . . would transcend the world of the commonplace and reach toward the infinite and the eternal" (p. 83). Cf. Pearce, *The Continuity of American Poetry*, note 4 above.

voiding of my interior volume. But movement is experienced here from the outside, as a coming-out-toward, or a coming-out-and-going-by, in relation to a viewpoint that is external (first the wanderers, and then the travellers).

Consciousness, a process, has been made into a thing, a container variously filled and emptied, like a chamber people enter and leave. It is not the sort of chamber one finds in, say, "Berenice," where a surrounding space is known only from the inside. We get closer to the effect of "The Haunted Palace" by imagining that the brain of someone like Egaeus (the narrator of "Berenice") has been made *into* a chamber. Having done this, we move outside it in order to look back in, whereupon the experience becomes, as I have said, an inside seen from outside. It is typical of Poe that this container should be seen always in relation to a larger one, for, despite his interest in isolation, insularity, and subjective experience, he likes to set things in perspective. It is not that he does not describe, say, states of psychic disturbance, for example, or extreme hypersensitivity. He does the one in "Berenice" and the other in "The Fall of the House of Usher." The perspective can be physical, as in *The Narrative of A. Gordon Pym*, where Pym is contained in the hold of a ship in the sea, a container within a container within a container. The perspective can be on a very large scale, as in *Eureka*, which we shall examine more closely below, or in "Al Aaraaf," where lesser planetary bodies are placed in relation to greater, localized sites in relation to vast spaces, human existence in relation to the angelic and the divine. The desire, throughout, is to see one phenomenon in relation to, and often literally within, another. The framing perspective in "The Haunted Palace" is dual, on the one hand spatial and concrete, on the other abstract. The first container in the poem (and it is literally the first, for Poe mentions it in the opening line) is the valley in which the palace stands, a spatial entity surrounding the edifice and providing a medium through which the wanderers and travellers can approach and observe the situation within. The victimization in the poem is reflected in the adjectives applied to this valley, which is "the greenest" in the opening line, "happy" in stanza two (where again it is mentioned initially), only to be reduced, in the last stanza, with the bare modifier, "that," to a place without redeeming qualities. A second "within" connects the palace with the abstraction, "the monarch Thought's dominion" (l. 5), which is only vaguely spatial, and does not appeal to the eye in the same way as the valley.

Nothing is more apposite to such concerns than grammatical constructions stressing relation. Any construction, to be sure, can be relational in some sense. Even the shortest sentences, such as "Go," posit connection between the point of origin and some more remote site. But the positing is inferential. It is something one supplies from an implicit context as distinguished from something actually given in the concrete utterance. In the sentence, "Go to him," on the other hand, relation is stipulated. The preposition locates the other word in a context which is its *own* situation. The peculiar virtues of this part of speech are nowhere more evident than in "The Haunted Palace," where the prepositional phrase is a dominant construction:

In the greenest of our valleys
  By good angels tenanted . . .
In the monarch Thought's dominion . . .
  Over fabric half so fair . . .
  On its roof . . .
  (. . . in the olden
  Time long ago) . . .
  In that sweet day,
Along the ramparts . . .
. . . in that happy valley,
  Through two luminous windows . . .
  To a lute's well-tuned law,
Round about a throne . . .
In state . . .
  The ruler of the realm was seen.

And all with pearl and ruby glowing
   Was the fair palace door,
Through which . . .
A troop of Echoes . . .
In voice of surpassing beauty,
   The wit and wisdom of their king.
. . . in robes of sorrow,
. . . for never morrow
Shall dawn upon him . . .
And round about his home . . .
Of the old-time entombed.
. . . within that valley,
   Through the encrimsoned windows . . .
   To a discordant melody . . .
   Through the pale door . . .

The three phrases that deal directly with time affirm two periods: one, an ancient time long outlived ("in the olden / Time long ago," "In that sweet day," "Of the old-time entombed") and an equally remote time in the future ("for never morrow / Shall dawn upon him"). Between these distant temporal realms there is only, in the concluding stanza, a "now" (l. 41). But the time this word expresses has no more to do with the spontaneous, the momentary, and the unrepeatable than do the words in the other phrases. "Now" refers not to something that briefly transpires, but to something that happens always. It is the new, permanent condition in which the haunted palace finally exists. The process by which the alteration comes about remains obscure. As in the sleeper poems and the city poems, there is an anterior time in which things were one way, and a later time in which they are another. The historical moment—the period in which the change comes about—occupies only two lines: "But evil things, in robes of sorrow, / Assailed the monarch's high estate" (ll. 33-34). When precisely did this happen? When everything happens—in an indeterminate sometime. To specify more would assimilate the process to the tyranny of cause and effect, which in turn would adversely affect the privileged role of the ontological state. The event is so self-fulfilling that there is no point in spelling it out. No sooner do the evil things assail than we are already bewailing the alteration that has yet to be specified, and looking sadly upon the fact that it is obviously permanent: "(Ah, let us mourn!—for never morrow / Shall dawn upon him, desolate!)" The remaining lines of the stanza present a contingent and ephemeral past ("the glory / That blushed and bloomed," ll. 37-38) that has given way to a new present: now the glory "Is but a dim-remembered story / Of the old-time entombed" (ll. 39-40).

All the time words in the poem evidently express permanence. The "once" of line 3, like the "now" of the last stanza, denotes the olden time long ago, and is no more momentary and contingent than the "never" of line 7. The troop of echoes "which came flowing, flowing, flowing, / And sparkling evermore" (ll. 27-28) seem also to be unending, but only, paradoxically, for a time. For this "evermore" is no more permanent (as its dictionary meaning would apparently require it to be) than the "now" of the concluding stanza is momentary and contingent:

> And travellers, now, within that valley,
>   Through the encrimsoned windows see
> Vast forms that move fantastically
>   To a discordant melody,
> While, like a ghastly rapid river,
>   Through the pale door
> A hideous throng rush out forever
>   And laugh—but smile no more.
>
> (ll. 41-48)

What happens here is that the permanence that the previous stanza seemed to create only now becomes a reality. That the action described is rapid should not be allowed to obscure its true temporal nature. For the hideous throng is condemned to an *eternal* rushing. The travellers are observing something that is *presently taking place for all time.*

Functions assigned in other works to a single figure are here distributed to three types of being. The most obvious guardians are the good angels who tenant the valley, but do little else. By the time the evil things appear the good angels have slipped out of sight, and the monarch's high estate falls without a struggle. A second function is performed by the wanderers and the travellers, who observe without themselves becoming involved. And there is, finally, the first-person plural, this anonymous collectivity which expresses a kind of sympathetic identification with the victimizing of the palace. The relation between this collective personage and the world of the palace is suggested in the first line by the phrase "our valleys," a word with possessive overtones in keeping with the use of words like "tenanted" and "dominion," all implying a condition of lawful occupancy and due relation between levels of authority. Finally, with the end of the monarch's lawful reign, we emerge ("Ah, let us mourn!") in the identity of the mourners. Scattering the functions in this way, instead of assigning them to a single guardian, makes it possible to concentrate on the palace itself. Poe wants to hold the palace in front of us as an object interesting in itself, not pictorially but three-dimensionally, with the full modelling of a building that is also a brain.

The powerlessness that characterizes the observers, the angels and the first-person plural (it is the one thing they have in common) characterizes as well the hideous throng that, as has often been suggested, represents vocalized thoughts or feelings of the victim. If we cannot comprehend this speech it is not because we lack access to its hidden content. Concealment implies an absence within a presence: there is something that I contact directly, but in my experience of it there is a gap. In addition to what I confront here, something exists there, away from me, in a secret place from which I am barred. To reveal this hidden thing, I must draw it forth from its hiding place, or remove whatever it is that separates me from it. But the throng that rushes out conceals nothing; there is no secret message, no hidden intentionality, either "behind" or "in" it. The throng is an outside without an inside, a surface without a depth.

In considering why speech has here been given material form, we will find it helpful to remember that the poem is not merely about a mind but about an entire bodily head. Poe seems to hint at the material basis of the poem when he tells Rufus Wilmot Griswold, in his letter of May 29, 1841, that the piece concerns a mind *or a brain.*[26] In any event, the poem offers the complete physical object—cranium, hair, eyes, mouth, teeth, and lips—that rests atop the normal human neck. The relation of mind to matter or body to soul was a preoccupation with Poe throughout his life. He was especially interested in the head—how things got into it and how they got out, and how the head, as the seat of reason and imagination, relates to the physical environment. In "Tamerlane" evil influences work upon the individual through his head and hair; in "The Fall of the House of Usher" the head of Roderick Usher is related metonymically to the edifice in which he lives; in "A Predicament. The Scythe of Time" the burlesque character Psyche Zenobia is decapitated as she sticks her head out through the dial plate of a gigantic clock; in "Ligeia" the identity of the figure at the end is not known until "she let fall from her head, unloosened, the ghastly cerements which had confined it, and there streamed forth, into the rushing atmosphere of the chamber, huge masses of long and dishevelled hair . . ." (II, 268). And finally, on a more rationalistic level, there is Poe's long interest in phrenology, with its claims to scientific authority and its unitary theory (inevitably attractive to a monist like Poe) of mental and spiritual operations. The point I want to make here is that "The Haunted Palace,"

[26] *CW*, p. 312. There are interesting discussions of "head symbolism" in Lafcadio Hearn, *Interpretations of Literature* (New York, 1926), II, 161, and Richard Wilbur, "The House of Poe," in *Poe: A Collection of Critical Essays*, ed. Robert Regan (Englewood Cliffs, N.J., 1967), pp. 98-120.

like many another work of Poe, has as much to do with the corporeal as with the spiritual or mental. Poe may have worked up the "higher" side of man in parts of his theory and criticism, but in his imaginative productions he was concerned to explore both sides, in themselves and in their interrelations. Yearning to recover a state of primal wholeness, he tried in works like the tales about women to show the eternality of identity and being, and in works like the dialogues and *Eureka* to take man as near to Aidenn as the power of words could carry him. But in the meantime he was following a second line through the world as it is in its present state, and the realities of such a world were separation, victimization, guilt, dehumanization, and loss. In showing them he revealed his affinities with what is sometimes called the Gothic mode. "The Gothic in fiction," says Stephen L. Mooney, "may be defined as a Gestalt of psychic states produced from architectural images, including the grotesque. Gothic is heightening of sense perception, sublimity of mind; secrecy; terror of soul. It is Cartesian and Biblical: the physical as container for the spiritual, but separated from it—the soul in the body, the spirit in the temple, the Ghost in the Machine, The Family in the House."[27] Too much separation spells a particular danger. Cut off consciousness, for example, and you fall prey to the will of another who can control you by controlling your person (as in "The Pit and the Pendulum") or, as in "The Haunted Palace," to an automatism that is like a seizure that does not pass. When this happens, *psyche* is, in effect, in the power of *soma*, and words stream forth from the palace like so much material substance with no more claim to real meaning than a galvanized corpse has claim to real life.

The cause of this reduction is not the overthrow of the palace alone, but something much worse. The cause, as the text makes clear, is the overthrow of the very estate of Thought, the entire dominion encompassing the palace. What

[27] "Poe's Gothic Wasteland," 261.

happens to the order of the palace amounts to a repetition-in-little of what has happened to the order of the universe since that time long ago when primal wholeness gave way to separation. The "legal" language of stanza one, with its overtones of justness and decorum, is eroded; the last fragment of it is the word "estate," seen just at the moment when it is being destroyed. Harmony too is lost. The spirits that once moved musically to the "well-tunéd law," recalling Poe's references to the music of the spheres in "Al Aaraaf," are replaced by the vast forms that move "To a discordant melody." The poem, in other words, is not about a particular loss of reason, but a general loss of Reason felt through a particular case. This fear of loss need not be traced to a specific origin, for it is in accord with Poe's whole sense of his time, which was being ruined, in his eyes, by democracy, industrialism, social ostentation, and a body of scientific thought opposed to the imaginativeness which was for him the highest thought.

"Sonnet—Silence," written some eight months later, explores on a higher level of abstraction an even more terrible form of separation and dispossession:

There are some qualities—some incorporate things,
  That have a double life, which thus is made
A type of that twin entity which springs
  From matter and light, evinced in solid and shade.
There is a two-fold *Silence*—sea and shore—
  Body and Soul. One dwells in lonely places,
  Newly with grass o'ergrown; some solemn graces,
  Some human memories and tearful lore,
Render him terrorless: his name's "No more."
He is the corporate Silence: dread him not!
  No power hath he of evil in himself:
But should some urgent fate (untimely lot!)
  Bring thee to meet his shadow (nameless elf,
That haunteth the lone regions where hath trod
No foot of man,) commend thyself to God!

The corporate or bodily silence, whose description begins in line 6 and continues through line 11, is the aftermath of death in the ordinary sense. This is the silence of the mourner, who is safe from the scourge of terror so long as he faithfully carries out the expected services: performing graces, remembering, and expressing his loss in the traditional way. Although this entity has the potential to harm, his power is restricted, as may be seen by the relative ease with which the mourning rites render him powerless. The ultimate source of the restriction is the arbitrary will of that higher power which has made the corporate silence its instrument. That higher power, who is presumably God Himself, has made a kind of loan: the corporate silence will be allowed the power to terrorize, but subject to cancellation when confronted with true mourning.

Loss of reason involves, as shown by "The Haunted Palace," a separation in being, a radical sundering of part from part that leaves behind an empty form—a body without a soul. That is bad enough, but it is not so bad as a confrontation with something that has no form at all. The difference between this and the confrontation with the less-frightening corporate silence is, as Richard Wilbur explains, the difference between two kinds of death, the lesser silence implying the death of the body and the great silence the death of the soul. In the first case it is not being that is lost but only its material form. Just as the mourner has recourse to an indemnifying rite, so the deceased has recourse to some higher realm—some state beyond death in which one can continue to exist. But in the second case, being itself is lost. To meet the bodiless silence is to encounter non-being.[28] Here is a phenomenon separated not from part of its own being but from being itself. Separation can go no further.

Poe may have lacked moral vision, as is often said, but these are not the poems on which to build a case. There are angels in "The Haunted Palace" and they are called good.

[28] Richard Wilbur, *Poe: Complete Poems* (New York, 1959), pp. 141-142.

There are evil powers in that work and in "Sonnet—Silence," and they are called by the name of evil. Admittedly Poe has no "solutions," and the afflicted are not to apply to him for programs of self-improvement. But neither is he inclined to drop the weighty issues he has raised, nor to suggest that he has said the last word on them. Between "The Haunted Palace" and "Sonnet—Silence" he publishes "The Fall of the House of Usher," which incorporates the text of the first poem and may be thought of as its elaboration. Later, in "The Power of Words," he will turn again to the problem of a speech that is also, strangely, a substance, and later still, in *Eureka*, to a reconsideration of the entire relation of the material and spiritual worlds.

"The Conqueror Worm"

An angel throng, bewinged, bedight
  In veils, and drowned in tears,
Sit in a theatre, to see
  A play of hopes and fears,
While the orchestra breathes fitfully
  The music of the spheres.[29]

(ll. 3-8)

In this variation on the *topos* of the world-theatre, everything happens in a perpetual present very similar to the present with which "The Haunted Palace" concludes. The second stanza, in which the mimes do the bidding of the "vast formless things" (l. 13), is also in the present tense, as are the fourth and fifth in which, respectively, a shape intrudes to devour the mimes, and the angels affirm "That the play is the tragedy, 'Man,' / And its hero the Conqueror Worm" (ll. 39-40). The perpetual nature of the play is underlined by a shift in the middle or central stanza. For the first and only time, present tense gives way to future, as we are told

[29] I have been helped by the commentaries of Klaus Lubbers (see note 1 above) and Fagin, *The Histrionic Mr. Poe*, pp. 150-151.

that the play will have a permanent effect. But this permanence is indissociable from the process that is going on right now; accordingly, the statement returns immediately to the present tense (it is clear from the syntax that the exclamation point occurs not as an end-stop but as enforcing punctuation within the sentence):

> That motley drama—oh, be sure
> It shall not be forgot!
> With its Phantom chased for evermore,
> By a crowd that seize it not,
> Through a circle that ever returneth in
> To the self-same spot,
> And much of Madness, and more of Sin,
> And Horror the soul of the plot.
>
> (ll. 17-24)

The title suggests that the poem concerns human mortality. So does the final stanza. One looks, consequently, for the human element, but one can scarcely find it. Instead, there are "Mimes, in the form of God on high" (l. 9), mere puppet-creatures whose actions are directed by

> . . . vast formless things
> That shift the scenery to and fro,
> Flapping from out their Condor wings
> Invisible Wo!
>
> (ll. 13-16)

Two extremes of being are represented here, both of them bad: the things that have the wrong form, and the things that have no form at all. The mimes, which have the wrong form, are like the idolatrous models in "Al Aaraaf" that supplant the deity they are supposed to embody—absurd creations that can only "Mutter and mumble low, / And hither and thither fly" (ll. 10-11). Being powerless, these low creations are subservient, as man himself is subservient, to great forces that manipulate life but can never be anthropomorphically embodied. The quasi-personification they enjoy (condor wings) puts them in a class with those other evil influences who operate on their unwitting human victims from some inaccessible "above."

> But see, amid the mimic rout
>   A crawling shape intrude!
> A blood-red thing that writhes from out
>   The scenic solitude!
> It writhes!—it writhes!—with mortal pangs
>   The mimes become its food,
> And seraphs sob at vermin fangs
>   In human gore imbued.
>
> (ll. 25-32)

Only in victimization does the human element clearly emerge: the human is that which is devoured by something more powerful. Here the guilt is, if anything, even greater than the guilt in "Al Aaraaf." In that poem the culpable beings only dreamed a model of their own; in "The Conqueror Worm" they *are* models. Yet there is no suggestion that greater guilt emanates from greater freedom of will. Indeed, these beings are even less free than Angelo and Ianthe. If there was ever a time when they could have chosen to be anything but mimes, that time is not presented. As given, they are the purest bondsmen, bound to do what they are told, and bound to be destroyed for doing it.

> Out—out are the lights—out all!
>   And, over each quivering form,
> The curtain, a funeral pall,
>   Comes down with the rush of a storm,
> While the angels, all pallid and wan,
>   Uprising, unveiling, affirm
> That the play is the tragedy, "Man,"
>   And its hero the Conqueror Worm.
>
> (ll. 33-40)

The combined effect of velocity and passivity results—as it does in the tales or at the end of "The Haunted Palace"—in a peculiarly charged stasis, a kind of oxymoronic motion-no motion. The purport of all this activity is to reveal a pre-existing, irreversible, permanent condition.

As there is no real change, neither is there any real agon. An agon requires two active agents, and here, typically, only the destructive beings (the vast formless things, the crawling shape) are active. The angels, like the good angels in "The Haunted Palace" or the guardians of the sleeper poems, are passive and helpless. They can do what the survivor does in the sleeper poems, what nature does in the doomed-city poems, what the angels do in the dialogues: they can witness, sympathize, and testify, but they can neither alter nor prevent. Their speech, like that which ends "The Haunted Palace," has no praxis: it *changes* nothing. Neither is it particularly revealing. The earlier stanzas, through mood as well as overt statement, have made the nature of the action and its outcome very clear. Furthermore, the veils the angels drop conceal nothing. The unveiling of the angels, like their affirming, is essentially ceremonial. The angels declare that the endless circle is still endless and still circular. They name what was, what is, and what will be. Nothing has changed, because nothing can.

"The Raven"

Once upon a midnight dreary, while I pondered, weak
  and weary,
Over many a quaint and curious volume of forgotten
  lore—
While I nodded, nearly napping, suddenly there came
  a tapping,
As of some one gently rapping, rapping at my chamber
  door—
" 'Tis some visiter," I muttered, "tapping at my chamber
  door—
    Only this and nothing more."

(ll. 1-6)

The celebrated opening stanza presents a time that, while not strictly historical, situates an event in a distinct circumstantial framework that the following stanza supplements by placing the interruption in December, and by identifying the first-person as the mourner of a dead woman. Yet a sense of mystery attends the event. This is in part because it is not fully an event: tapping is a prelude to an entry that has not yet occurred. The waiting and the mood of expectancy operate continuously through six stanzas; only in the seventh does the raven make its long-delayed appearance. The suspense thus furnished by the plot has already been adumbrated by the suspensive syntax of the very first stanza, where a series of grammatically dependent statements requires the reader to wait until the middle of the third line before reaching the governing predicate. There are, indeed, no less than six prefatory word groupings before the "resolution" of the independent clause: three predominantly temporal ("once . . . while . . . while"), one predominantly spatial ("over . . ."), and two in apposition to the dependent verbs ("weak and weary," "nearly napping"). The first-person is presented, throughout this first section of the poem, in time:

> So that now . . . I stood repeating. (l. 15)

> Presently my soul grew stronger; hesitating then no
> longer. (l. 19)

> Deep into that darkness peering, long I stood there
> wondering, fearing. (l. 25)

> Soon again I heard a tapping. . . . (l. 32)

Some spatial element adheres, to be sure, to any temporal phenomenon. I am speaking here of *relative* emphasis. Even in the third quotation above, where the spatial component seems the most evident, the emphasis falls on expectancy, which is a time orientation:

Deep into that darkness peering, long I stood there wondering, fearing,
Doubting, dreaming dreams no mortal ever dared to dream before;
But the silence was unbroken, and the stillness gave no token,
And the only word there spoken was the whispered word, "Lenore?"
This I whispered, and an echo mumured back the word, "Lenore!"
Merely this and nothing more. (ll. 25-30)

The unprecedented dreams are, of course, another form of novelty, in Poe's special sense of the word. Generally speaking, novelty can be thought of in either spatial or temporal terms. It is spatial to the extent that it suggests an experience that has never happened before. The temporal emphasis is much the more common in Poe, and this passage is no exception: the dreams are novel because they are occurring for the first time. If there is spatial novelty here, it is in the darkness, that awful blankness from which nothing clear emerges. This darkness is perceived, however, in aural rather than visual terms, being merged with the unbroken silence in which there is something of the awe that attends the mourner's encounter with the bodiless "shadow" in "Sonnet—Silence."

Only with the arrival of the raven does space begin to crowd in on time:

Open here I flung the shutter, when, with many a flirt and flutter,
In there stepped a stately Raven of the saintly days of yore;
Not the least obeisance made he; not a minute stopped or stayed he;
But, with mien of lord or lady, perched above my chamber door—

Perched upon a bust of Pallas just above my chamber door—
Perched, and sat, and nothing more.
(ll. 37-42)

In this heavily prepositional stanza the first phase of suspense comes to an end; the bird supplants, with his bodily presence, the emptiness of the darkness outside. The poem becomes a confrontation: I must face the creature, literally and figuratively, and interpret its word. My chamber has become a monadic world unto itself. I will never leave it; I will not even go again to the window or the door. The chamber door no longer exists for me as an opening-out, a possibility of movement; it exists only in relation to the immobile bird. I will never again speak of the door without speaking of the raven, and will never regard the door as anything but that which the bird is upon or above.

As the confrontation gets underway, and as the mourner begins to view the bird as a speaker, the poem enters a second phase of suspense. If the first phase answers the question, "Who is there?" the second phase answers the question, "Will I rejoin the loved one after death?" In this poem of refrains and repetitions there is, then, a fundamental repetition in the very structure. The similarity between the two phases is underlined by the two interrogations, both of which hinged upon the issue of Lenore's presence: in the first instance (when I listen in the stillness after opening the door) I say, "Lenore?" In the second I say, " 'Tell this soul with sorrow laden, if within the distant Aidenn, / It shall clasp a sainted maiden whom the angels name Lenore—' " (ll. 93-94).

It is not merely the raven that confronts the interrogator, but the *word* the raven speaks. "Nevermore" meets the speaker's consciousness wherever he turns, baffles him with a thereness, an opacity, he cannot penetrate. Poe is full of such confrontations. In "Silence. A Fable" the rock seen by the demon first bears the inscription "DESOLATION" which expresses the first state of the human being he victimizes, and later, "SILENCE," which expresses the final condition which the victim must face. In "MS. Found in a Bottle" the narrator confronts himself indirectly with his own word by daubing the furled canvas idly with a tar-brush, and only later discovering—ironically—that he has written the word "DISCOVERY." The confrontation assumes an oral, low-register form when, at the end of "Shadow. A Parable," the motionless presence which has taken possession of the chamber declares, " 'I am SHADOW, and my dwelling is near to the Catacombs of Ptolemais, and hard by those dim plains of Helusion which border upon the foul Charonian canal' " (II, 150). Finally, there is the kind of vocal pointing that occurs at the end of "Ligeia," when the helpless first-person can do nothing but name the presence that overwhelms him: " 'Here then, at least,' " I shrieked aloud, " 'can I never—can I never be mistaken—these are the full, and the black, and the wild eyes—of my lost love—of the Lady—of the LADY LIGEIA' " (II, 268). The confrontation in "The Raven" is more complex than any of these. For one thing, it is more extended, involving as it does a series of repeated utterances that have an overlapping, cumulative effect. For another, the word comes at the first-person in two directions, whereas in the tales it comes in only one. In the tales the word is either presented to me, by some outside agency ("Shadow," "Silence"), or I present it to myself ("Ligeia," "MS. Found in a Bottle"). In "The Raven" both things happen. The raven articulates the word *to me*, and I articulate the word *to myself.* Ask someone to recall who utters the "Nevermore" in the poem and he is likely to reply, "The Raven." But in fact the human speaker uses the word nearly as often as the bird—five times to the raven's six. One easily remembers the first time the raven speaks, just after the interrogator has asked him his name: "Quoth the Raven 'Nevermore' " (l. 48). One tends to forget that the first-person then picks up the word:

> Much I marvelled this ungainly fowl to hear discourse so plainly,

Though its answer little meaning—little relevancy bore;
For we cannot help agreeing that no living human being
Ever yet was blessed with seeing bird above his chamber door—
Bird or beast upon the sculptured bust above his chamber door,
With such name as "Nevermore."
(ll. 49-54)

The relation between the two speakers is a reciprocity. The raven speaks the crucial word, I take it up, the raven says it again, I take it up, and so on. Thus, in the next stanza, the bird declares "Nevermore" after the mourner expresses aloud his expectation that the raven will leave as other friends and hopes have left. The pattern is as follows: Raven / I / Raven / I / I / I / Raven / Raven / Raven / Raven / I. The pivotal section is that grouping of three stanzas in which the "Nevermore" is spoken by the first-person. On the basis of the first four stanzas, the poem headed toward a regular, back-and-forth rhythm: Raven / I / Raven / I. This changes when the first-person, instead of deferring once more to the raven, continues the thinking process that culminates in each of his three "Nevermores." The cue is already present in the stanza immediately following the one in which I first take up the "name" of the bird:

But the Raven, sitting lonely on the placid bust, spoke only
That one word, as if his soul in that one word he did outpour.
Nothing farther then he uttered—not a feather then he fluttered—
Till I scarcely more than muttered "Other friends have flown before—
On the morrow *he* will leave me, as my Hopes have flown before."
Then the bird said "Nevermore."
(ll. 55-60)

The exchange is crucial, for the dialogue has no way of proceeding further unless the raven has something to which it can respond. The mourner, at this point, has nothing to say to the bird directly: he asked the creature its name, and it has already replied. If the confrontation is to continue, then, the first-person must somehow address the bird without directly addressing it. This he accomplishes by thinking aloud. The next three stanzas are pivotal because it is here that he goes through processes of consciousness that assimilate him to a "Nevermore" way of thinking and feeling:

> Startled at the stillness broken by reply so aptly spoken,
> "Doubtless," said I, "what it utters is its only stock and store
> Caught from some unhappy master whom unmerciful Disaster
> Followed fast and followed faster till his songs one burden bore—
> Till the dirges of his Hope that melancholy burden bore
> Of 'Never—nevermore.' "
>
> But the Raven still beguiling my sad fancy into smiling,
> Straight I wheeled a cushioned seat in front of bird, and bust and door;
> Then, upon the velvet sinking, I betook myself to linking
> Fancy unto fancy, thinking what this ominous bird of yore—
> What this grim, ungainly, ghastly, gaunt, and ominous bird of yore
> Meant in croaking "Nevermore."
>
> This I sat engaged in guessing, but no syllable expressing
> To the fowl whose fiery eyes now burned into my bosom's core;
> This and more I sat divining, with my head at ease reclining
> On the cushion's velvet lining that the lamp-light gloated o'er,

But whose velvet-violet lining with the lamp-light gloating o'er,
She shall press, ah, nevermore!
(ll. 61-78)

This interpreter is no Dupin. The French detective does some of his best thinking on the move (as when he divines his companion's thoughts in "Murders in the Rue Morgue"); moreover, he investigates, and, above all, he analyzes. The first-person of "The Raven," however, analyzes as little as he moves. As his stationary, Usher-like posture indicates, it is not the solution of a riddle that he awaits, but the fulfillment of his victimization. Consequently, although he is ostensibly preoccupied with the mystery of the raven, his thoughts turn at last to their original object, the lost Lenore.

The raven is a mediator, a means through which my victimization may be brought about. The raven has the capacity to block off futurity, to bar me from any reconciliation with the one for whom I grieve. This capacity has been conferred upon the bird; I did not give it to him. But only I can activate it. This I did when I asked the creature its name, and again when I thought aloud within its hearing. The obstacle to thinking aloud again is that I have been sunk for so long in reverie; there is no occasion now to address the bird; furthermore, I have just avowed that I am not presently talking to it at all. I need, then, an instrumentality—frankly, an "excuse"—that will allow me again to address the raven without appearing to do so. This could be achieved if I addressed *myself*. How can this be accomplished? By *deus ex machina*, by some hitherto non-existent agency that induces me to address myself?

In a manner of speaking, yes, except for one proviso. The stanzas have been presenting consciousness in process. This interceding agency, to be consistent, should make its gratuitous advent, too, through the good offices of consciousness. The solution, then, is an address-to-myself precipitated by a sudden presence that I *think* I perceive:

Then, methought, the air grew denser, perfumed from an unseen censer
Swung by seraphim whose foot-falls tinkled on the tufted floor.
"Wretch," I cried, "thy God hath lent thee—by these angels he hath sent thee
Respite—respite and nepenthe from my memories of Lenore;
Quaff, oh quaff this kind nepenthe and forget this lost Lenore!"
Quoth the Raven "Nevermore."
(ll. 79-84)

This form, the exclamatory address, is easily transferable, and becomes the basic form of the next three stanzas in which the first-person puts forward two questions and a command to which the raven replies with his inevitable "Nevermore." Is there balm in Gilead? Nevermore. Shall I embrace Lenore in the afterlife? Nevermore. " 'Be that word our sign of parting, bird or friend!' I shrieked, upstarting— / 'Get thee back into the tempest and the Night's Plutonian shore!' " (ll. 97-98). Nevermore. The change in posture does not alter the process of victimization, but confirms it. The stance is as helpless and as passive as the speech that accompanies it. The narrator of "Ligeia" also shrieks at the peak of his helplessness, and Roderick Usher, like the speaker here, both rises and shrieks: " 'MADMAN!'—here he sprang furiously to his feet, and shrieked out his syllables, as if in the effort he were giving up his soul— 'MADMAN! I TELL YOU THAT SHE NOW STANDS WITHOUT THE DOOR!' " (III, 296). To the command as to the questions, the raven responds with a "Nevermore" as inevitable as the rhythm of the stanza. The four consecutive stanzas ending with the line "Quoth the Raven 'Nevermore' " establish the irreversible dominance of the bird and, equally important, the irreversible condition to which the victim has been reduced. The time sense in the last stanza is, accordingly, a world away from the time sense in the opening stanza:

> And the Raven, never flitting, still is sitting, *still* is sitting
> On the pallid bust of Pallas just above my chamber door;
> And his eyes have all the seeming of a demon's that is
>   dreaming,
> And the lamp-light o'er him streaming throws his shad-
>   ow on the floor;
> And my soul from out that shadow that lies floating on
>   the floor
>   Shall be lifted—nevermore!   (ll. 103-108)

The effect of an unchanging condition is created in part by the shift from the contingencies of "once," "while," and "suddenly" to the more permanent "still" and the endless "nevermore," and in part by the use of the present participle. In the first stanza and through most of the poem, as you will recall, this verbal form plays a subordinate role to the preterite. At the end of the poem, as at the end of "MS. Found in a Bottle," the present participle becomes, in the first two lines, the dominant tense, indicating that the confrontation is going on even now. The present tense in the three following lines reinforces this, while the shift to the future in the concluding line confirms that the inability to end the victimization is as absolute as the inability to prevent it from starting.

"The central drama of 'The Raven,' " concludes Geoffrey Rans, "is the poet's fear that he will fail in the function characterized in 'The Poetic Principle,' and symbolized in the poem by the dead Lenore."[30] If we look to the piece of criti-

[30] *Edgar Allan Poe*, p. 28. Davidson remarks: "But as the drama proceeds and the terror increases, the question of the student's existence or Being itself dominates: he asks whether or not there is any sensitivity or perception in life which is beyond the barriers of ignorance we must endure in this existence. The replies, though in the croaking voice of the Raven, are really from the innnermost consciousness and even subconsciousness of the student . . ." (p. 89).

cism most directly concerned with "The Raven," we find Poe saying something rather different. "The Philosophy of Composition" suggests that the central issue, for Poe, was just the one that we have been examining. After offering the famous proposition that " 'the death, then, of a beautiful woman is, unquestionably, the most poetical topic in the world' " (XIV, 201), Poe goes on to describe the strategy he employed in order to give the topic suitable aesthetic form. The fulcrum, as I have many times suggested, is the experience of loss felt by a "bereaved lover," against whose presence Poe balances the presence of the bird:

"I had now to combine the two ideas, of a lover lamenting his deceased mistress and a Raven continuously repeating the word 'Nevermore.'—I had to combine these, bearing in mind my design of varying, at every turn, the *application* of the word repeated; but the only intelligible mode of such combination is that of imagining the Raven employing the word in answer to the queries of the lover. And here it was that I saw at once the opportunity afforded for the effect on which I had been depending—that is to say, the effect of *variation of application.* I saw that I could make the first query propounded by the lover—the first query to which the Raven should reply 'Nevermore'—that I could make this first query a commonplace one—the second less so—the third still less, and so on—until at length the lover, startled from his original *nonchalance* by the melancholy character of the word itself—by its frequent repetition—and by a consideration of the ominous reputation of the fowl that uttered it—is at length excited to superstition, and wildly propounds queries of a far different character—queries whose solution he has passionately at heart—propounds them half in superstition and half in that species of despair which delights in self-torture—propounds them not altogether because he believes in the prophetic or demoniac character of the bird (which, reason assures him, is merely repeating a lesson learned by rote) but because he experiences a phrenzied pleasure in so modeling his questions as to receive from the *expected* 'Nevermore' the most delicious because the most intolerable of sorrow." (XIV, 201-202)

When Rans argues that Poe's imaginative writings are themselves comments on the function of art, he makes a useful point. If criticism is a metalanguage (a language about language) so too is much art, including at times the art of Poe, as illustrated by those sections of "The Raven" where certain words relate the mourner's situation to overt forms of artistic expression. Thus you find, in line 49, a word like "discourse," and two stanzas later, a whole cluster of similar terms from "songs" to "dirges" to "burden" (ll. 64-65). Nor does the process end there, for while the art is imitating the criticism (in the sense that it is conscious of its own operations, and remarks on them), the criticism is imitating the art. To show how he arrived at his proposition about beauty in death, Poe emulates his own procedure in "The Raven," setting up an imaginary dialogue in which he argues himself into the view he finally espouses—the proposition is in double quotation marks above because it is already a quote in the essay, where Poe records his thoughts as speaker. "The Philosophy of Composition," is not, however, a mere gloss on the poem, nor a chronological account of its genesis. The essay, as Kenneth Burke has said, is about the principle of poetic making, and deals with the logical rather than the temporal priorities of composition.[31] The doctrine of effect holds that the artist must keep his mind on his audience, especially on the points of impact where the work is recorded on the reader's consciousness. To know the means he should use, the poet must also know the ends he wants the means to achieve. Again, the relation is not temporal: the poet need not sit down, decide on an effect, then think how best to produce it (as Poe would have us believe); it is more likely that the end is already implicit in the means, and that every well-chosen means points as by instinct to the end, or effect, that it will eventually achieve.

The impact of "The Raven" on its original audience is

[31] "The Principle of Composition," *Poetry*, 99 (1961), p. 89.

well-documented, though some effort of historical imagination is required to make that impact come to life. From remarks collected by Mrs. Whitman one can begin to approximate the way the poem was received by poetry lovers who, if they belonged to what was already a print culture, were probably more aurally attuned than their twentieth-century counterparts. Elizabeth Barrett Browning declares: "This vivid writing—*this power which is felt*—has produced a sensation here in England. Some of my friends are taken by the fear of it, and some by the music. I hear of persons who are haunted by the 'Nevermore,' and an acquaintance of mine who has the misfortune of possessing a bust of Pallas, cannot bear to look at it in the twilight." An anonymous Poe admirer, rushing to the scene of a blaze, compares the sound of the alarm bells with Poe's descriptions in "The Bells" and concludes, "how truly the poem reproduced the sense of danger which the sound of the bells, and the glare and mad ascension of the flames, and the pallor of the moonlight conveyed."[32] Some ninety years later Montgomery Belgion, in trying to account for what he calls the "mystery" of Poe's poetry, decides that, despite their faults, the lines "run enchantingly in the head,"[33] suggesting by that prepositional phrase that we are less likely than our ancestors to read the poem aloud, but that it is still in some sense heard. To say practically *how* it is heard would require a full phenomenology of reading. The essay by Georges Poulet, quoted in the methodological introduction to this study, suggests one way of approaching such a task; Roman Ingarden's treatises, *Das literarische Kunstwerk* (Tübingen, 1965), and *Vom Erkennen des literarischen Kunstwerks* (Tübingen, 1968), suggest another way, and the writings of Kenneth Burke, with their concern for authorial strategy and sense of audience, suggest still a third.

What remains unfinished is the hard work of describing (even more concretely and exhaustively than Ingarden has done) the ways in which sequences of words, in all their

[32] Sarah Helen Whitman, *Edgar Poe and His Critics*, pp. 22, 38.
[33] "The Mystery of Poe's Poetry," p. 60.

dynamics, are experienced by the mind. We need to know how the reader himself contributes to the grouping of words into patterns; how he bridges the gaps between words and phrases; how he makes up for false starts, wrong associations, or mispronunciation. We might also ask precisely how the reader hears poetic voice. Is it an idealized voice that he hears, or merely his own; or a variety of voices modelled on those he encounters in everyday life? The best one can do, until such questions receive the full theoretical and practical consideration they deserve, is to steer a frankly speculative course guided by such bearings as one can take from phenomena that are more certainly known. On the basis of the theory developed in my discussion of "The Coliseum," one can say, for example, that "The Raven," to which we may now return, is in a middle register, tending up, as the poem goes on, or at any rate getting more intense. We also recognize that the poem is mainly in one voice, despite the fact that it has two "speakers." One would not read the poem aloud, for instance, in the same way that one would read aloud a passage from Dickens, who was also—to use Fagin's word—histrionic. A good sayer of Dickens (such as Emlyn Williams or Philip Collins) does characters in a complete vocal sense, rendering their respective timbres and pitch, their accents and dialects, their malapropisms and lisps. But the transfer of the same arts to "The Raven" would be fatal. A literal, Stanislavskian imitation of a raven stands a better chance of tumbling the auditors into the aisles than of rivetting them in their seats, and the same caution applies when one reads the poem to oneself. The ludicrous enters the poem, we remember, for contrast, a subject to which Poe devotes, in "The Philosophy of Composition," the bulk of three consecutive paragraphs, concluding with the observation that "I have availed myself of the force of contrast, with a view of deepening the ultimate impression. For example, an air of the fantastic—approaching as nearly to the ludicrous as was admissible—is given to the Raven's entrance" (XIV, 205). In an earlier book review Poe had argued that the only type of humor that blends with the ideal is " '*archness*'—a trait with which popular feeling, which is unfailingly poetic, has invested, for example, the whole character of the fairy" (XI, 24). Every other sort of humor, Poe insists, is incompatible with the spirit of the ideal that reigns over any poem worthy of the name. Humor is admissible in "The Raven" solely because it intensifies the central effect (XIV, 199) of a sorrow the more exquisite for being all but intolerable (XIV, 202).

Poe's objection to the raven in *Barnaby Rudge* was that Dickens confined his treatment to the merely amusing aspects of the bird. Poe toys with an alternative handling that would have brought out—just as he was to do in "The Raven"—the resemblance of the two speakers. The character of the bird, he says, "might have performed, in regard to that of the idiot, much the same part as does, in music, the accompaniment in respect to the air. Each might have been distinct. Each might have differed remarkably from the other. Yet between them there might have been wrought an analogical resemblance, and although each might have existed apart, they might have formed together a whole which would have been imperfect in the absence of either" (XI, 63). Thus in his poem it is not the squawking of a bird we are meant to hear but the merging of its utterance with the utterance of the human speaker through whose voice the story evolves. The effect of the speaking bird in *Barnaby Rudge*, on the other hand, depends precisely on the incongruity of the things it says and the raspy way it says them. Again, someone who reads the relevant scenes aloud will impersonate the creature with all the vocal resources at his command. To this extent Dickens is, indeed, as his readers and critics have long felt, theatrical. The same cannot be said of Poe, who has a different set of aesthetic principles. If we call "The Raven" a "dramatic" poem we understand the adjective in a special sense. We do not have in mind the full differentiation of roles and voices we find in a play, but the fact that the poem somehow realizes a scene, a conflict, and, in the manner defined above, speakers, while yet maintaining its generic identity as a poem. "The Raven" might more accurately be described as a kind of play-within-a-poem, meaning that its most dramatic component—the exchange between the two speakers—is situated "inside" a larger form, which is a narrative ballad in the first-person. Here again Poe locates a given phenomenon within a greater, the speaker's relation with the bird being circumscribed, as it were, by his relation to Lenore.

If we describe the poem as "narrative" we mean that it tells a tale—again without, in the generic sense, being one. What the poem has and the tale has not is rhyme, meter and, above all, refrain. Refrain in "The Raven" serves at least three interrelated aims. First, it suggests an underlying sameness or identity of experience from beginning to end. Second, it intensifies the "monotone" effect of "Nevermore," an effect built up by the "variation of application." Third, it creates a sense of inevitability by returning the first-person again and again to the original confrontation with the victimizing word.

From a theoretical point of view the relation between variation and identity has a parallel in the relation between the unexpected and the expected. "What, in rhyme, first and principally pleases, may be referred to the human sense or appreciation of *equality*—the common element, as might be easily shown, of all the gratification we derive from music in its most extended sense—very especially in its modifications of metre and rhythm" (XVI, 84). Like identity, equality can be achieved only, as Milton would say, by trial of what is opposite, in this case "unexpectedness," which Poe equates with novelty and strangeness. Poe illustrates the effect of the unexpected with the line "*Thrilled* me, *filled* me with fantastic terrors never felt before," the unexpectedness arising from the fact that the reader's ear has become attuned to the prospect of a rhyme at the end. Another type of unexpectedness operates visually rather than aurally. After quoting the line, "And the silken, sad, uncertain rustling of each purple curtain," Poe remarks: "What there is of the element unexpectedness, is addressed, in fact, to the eye only—for the ear divides the verse into two ordinary lines, thus—

> And the silken, sad, uncertain
> Rustling of each purple curtain."
>
> (XVI, 86)

Poe's discussion thus has the added interest of tying together his sense of the poem as something seen and as something heard. We find him, as ever, defining the phenomenon not in absolute terms but in relative ones, by a kind of dialectic that is more dance than struggle: as soon as one thing comes into prominence, you can be sure that a different thing will soon come along to join hands with it. We do not mistake the one for the other, for each has its separate identity, but we get used to seeing them together, and we accept the idea that when one is before us the other is never far away. Thus an essay like "The Philosophy of Composition" depends as much on the things that are out of sight (because taken for granted) as on the things brought openly into view. What Poe talks about, in his paragraphs on the refrain, is the fairly technical business of varied application; what he takes for granted is that the effect does after all serve the traditional purpose of reinforcing and confirming an underlying identity. Similarly, his discussion of unexpectedness reflects the assumption that the poem must above all satisfy the expectation it creates. The aim of his little surprises in rhyme is to heighten the inevitability that alone bespeaks full authorial control and full realization of design. The poem has become a prophecy of itself: something that comes true on the terms that it has itself laid down. Poe speaks throughout his *Barnaby Rudge* essay about design, which he equates with intention:

". . . *the intention once known*, the *traces* of the design can be found upon every page." (XI, 49)

"The design of *mystery*, however, being once determined upon by an author, it becomes imperative, first, that no undue or inartistical means be employed to conceal the secret of the plot; and, secondly, that the secret be well kept." (XI, 51)

". . . our author discovered, when too late, that *he had anticipated, and thus rendered valueless, his chief effect.* This will be readily understood. The particulars of the assassination being withheld, the strength of the narrator is put forth, in the beginning of the story, to *whet curiosity* in respect to these particulars; and, so far, he is but in proper pursuance of his main design. But from this intention he unwittingly passes into the error of *exaggerating anticipaiton.*" (XI, 57)

Realization of design is closely analogous, for Poe, with the fulfilling of prophecy. In the essay Poe applies both words, design and prophecy, to himself as well as to the Dickens book. There is, for instance, the design he has in mind as he interprets the text (XIV, 40, 63), and the prophecy he voices precisely through this interpretation. In amplification of the second point we will find it useful to recall that the essay has nearly as much to do with Poe's predictions about the way the book would end as with the book itself. At one juncture Poe suggests that he prophesied better than Dickens wrote: "We may therefore say of our supposition as Talleyrand said of some cockney's bad French—*que s'il n'est pas Français, assurément donc il le doit être*—that if we did not rightly prophesy, yet, at least, our prophecy *should have been* right" (XI, 53).

More significant still is the realization of prophetic design within the text: "The raven, too, intensely amusing as it is, might have been made, more than we now see it, a portion of the conception of the fantastic Barnaby. Its croakings might have been *prophetically* heard in the course of the drama" (XI, 63). How Dickens might have accomplished this Poe does not say, but we can see readily enough the steps he took in his own poem. About the word "Nevermore" itself we have perhaps already heard enough; here we need only recall that the word produces a kind of echoic confrontation wherein the mourner finds himself faced with a vocal embodiment of loss, and that this vocal embodiment is indissociable from the literal embodiment—the actual physical presence—of the mysterious bird. The raven's prophetic nature is developed in two ways. First, the relation of the raven to the mourner in the initial phase of the poem prefigures and determines the relation at the end. Everything that happens is a variation on the opening confrontation in which the bird utters his single word in response to the mourner. The entire poem—to develop a point on which I have already touched—thus acquires the structure of an overarching refrain, of which the variable element is the question being put and the invariable element is the reply. Gradually the first-person takes onto himself the burden of the word first spoken by the raven until, in the end, it becomes his word, too. This can occur only because he is already, when the bird arrives, in a state conducive to victimization. To that extent the poem is about that "X" behind the voice that, as Francis Berry reminded us, was once called soul. But the poem is also about the material world—about an actual bird that bodily enters a room and produces sounds that make waves in the air. Take away that bird, that material presence, and you have no confrontation, no "Nevermore," no consciousness of loss, no victimization, and for that matter no title. Indeed, the poem depends for much of its effect on the way in which material things are felt and blended. Thus, the absence of Lenore, who no longer exists corporeally, is reflected tactilely:

> This and more I sat divining, with my head at ease reclining
> On the cushion's velvet lining that the lamp-light gloated o'er
> But whose velvet-violet lining with the lamp-light gloating o'er,
> *She* shall press, ah, nevermore!
>
> (ll. 75-78)

The materialization of angelic presence (which occurs in a stanza we have already discussed in another connection) will take us toward my second point about the raven's prophetic character:

Then, methought, the air grew denser, perfumed from
  an unseen censer
Swung by seraphim whose foot-falls tinkled on the tufted
  floor.
"Wretch," I cried, "thy God hath lent thee—by these
  angels he hath sent thee
Respite—respite and nepenthe from thy memories of
  Lenore.
Quaff, oh quaff this kind nepenthe and forget this lost
  Lenore!"
    Quoth the Raven "Nevermore."

(ll. 79-84)

The passage rings with echoes and anticipations: the tangible influences in the atmosphere of "Tamerlane" and "Stanzas," the palpability of sound in "Al Aaraaf," the bodily materialization of Ligeia in the atmosphere of Rowena's chamber. In another and perhaps more important respect the lines foreshadow "Ulalume," which also has to do with a mourner who feels, or thinks he feels, the power of a superhuman presence. The trouble is that neither man has any way of validating his interpretation, which looks suspiciously like wishful thinking. Irony results, for there is a gap or separation between the perceiver and the perceived, and irony is good at tracing the consequences to which such separation inevitably gives rise. One consequence can be seen in the following lines:

"Prophet!" said I, "thing of evil!—prophet still, if bird
  or devil—

. . . .

Is there—*is* there balm in Gilead?—tell me—tell me,
  I implore!"
    Quoth the Raven "Nevermore."

"Prophet!" said I, "thing of evil!—prophet still, if bird
  or devil!

By that Heaven that bends above us—by that God we
both adore—
Tell this soul with sorrow laden if, within the distant
Aidenn,
It shall clasp a sainted maiden whom the angels name
Lenore—
Clasp a rare and radiant maiden whom the angels name
Lenore."
Quoth the Raven "Nevermore."
(ll. 85-96)

The words are ironic because the bird *is* prophetic after all, but not in the way that the speaker thinks. He is prophetic in the way that Poe would have had Dickens' raven be prophetic—not by saying what will come to pass, but *by providing the very instrumentality through which the future can come to be.* If such prophecy is self-fulfilling, it is largely because the mourner himself cooperates to bring it about. It does not in the least matter whether the bird is right in its "predictions" about Gilead or about anything else. All that matters, in terms of the poem, is that the prophecy is believed.

In no other work since "Tamerlane" does Poe offer a fuller representation of that servile will that seeks perfection in the purity of a bondage that can never end.

"Ulalume—A Ballad"

Here, instead of sitting, the mourner walks, living his experience in a woodland instead of a chamber. But he is no freer than his predecessor in "The Raven." He is, indeed, doubly constrained, first by the circumscription of space (he moves with Psyche "through an alley Titanic, / Of cypress," ll. 10-11), and secondly by the confrontation that awaits him, at the end of their path, in the form of his dead lover's tomb. The landscape he traverses, and its relation to influences from above, has a familiar look. In the sleeper poems, a dim and drowsy influence lulls the landscape into a dangerous sleep. The valley of unrest, responding to the infidelity of the stars, palpitates with borrowed human affectivity. In "Fairy-Land" one moon among many buries the landscape "In a labyrinth of light" (l. 26) that causes unconsciousness, while "Dream-Land," that realm existing "out of Space—out of Time" (l. 8), exhibits a nervous agitation reminiscent of the restless valley:

> Mountains toppling evermore
> Into seas without a shore;
> Seas that restlessly aspire,
> Surging, unto skies of fire;
> Lakes that endlessly outspread
> Their lone waters—lone and dead,—
> Their still waters—still and chilly
> With the snows of the lolling lily.
>
> (ll. 13-20)

The landscape of "Ulalume" is relatively lifeless:

> The skies they were ashen and sober;
>   The leaves they were crispéd and sere—
>   The leaves they were withering and sere:
> It was night, in the lonesome October
>   Of my most immemorial year.
>
> (ll. 1-5)

The mourner, by contrast, is passionately alive:

> These were days when my heart was volcanic
>   As the scoriac rivers that roll—
>   As the lavas that restlessly roll
> Their sulphurous currents down Yaanek.
>
> (ll. 13-16)

Surrounded by lifelessness, though himself alive, the first-person recalls the mourning survivor of the sleeper poems. He recalls as well the narrator of "The Raven," the principal difference being that he could not forget, while the first-person of "Ulalume" cannot remember:

> We noted not the dim lake of Auber,
> (Though once we had journeyed down here)
> We remembered not the dank tarn of Auber,
> Nor the ghoul-haunted woodland of Weir.
> (ll. 26-29)

In "The Valley of Unrest" the stars fail their trust. In the sleeper poems it is the others who fail, and I alone who remember. But here, as in "The Raven," it is the mourner himself who fails. What happens as a result may be compared with what often happens in the tales. In "Ligeia" and "Eleonora" the survivor turns to a second woman only to discover that she is the inescapable first. Similarly, in "Morella," the original Morella bears in upon the survivor through the second, in this case a pseudo-daughter instead of a pseudo-bride. The deceased in all three works is determined to continue existing, and through this determination the survivor is compelled, not merely to remember, but to confront, bodily, a revivified presence. "Ulalume" also deals with confrontation and remembrance, but in a different way. The reincarnation tales are built on triads: the man who tells the story, the woman who dies and returns to life, and the woman through whose existence the return is effected. The second woman serves, in other words, as a mediator for the first, a kind of body made available to a dispossessed soul. "Ulalume" is also built on a triad with a mediator, except that here the mediating agency is non-human. We have seen non-human mediators in other poems: the valley in "The Valley of Unrest," the bird in "The Raven," and so on. Even nearer the present case are those "overhead" or planetary influences depicted in works like "Tamerlane," "Fairy-Land," the sleeper poems, and, on a grander scale, "Al Aaraaf." "Astarte's bediamonded crescent" (l. 37), the mediator in "Ulalume," is also a suddenly appearing star, and here too are depicted human guilt and human punishment. The difference is that guilt and punishment are very far-reaching, almost cosmic, in the earlier poem, whereas they are earthlier, more individualized, in the later. The mourner in "Ulalume" must figure things out for himself in much the same way as his counterpart in "The Raven." His effort at interpretation closely resembles the latter's first effort in "The Raven," where the intercession of the agency is explained away as the chance appearance of an ordinary visitor. On observing the star, the mourner of "Ulalume" surmises that she " 'has come past the stars of the Lion, / To point us the path to the skies' " (ll. 44-45). The ensuing exchange with Psyche amounts to a struggle between two versions of prophetic interpretation: my optimistic, "wishful-thinking" forecast versus the doubting and fearful reading offered by Psyche:

> But Psyche, uplifting her finger,
>   Said—"Sadly this star I mistrust—
>   Her pallor I strangely mistrust—
> Ah, hasten!—ah, let us not linger!
>   Ah, fly!—let us fly!—for we must."
>
> (ll. 51-55)

The blithe affirmativeness of tone with which the first-person replies enforces the irony that this most neglectful of beings, this man who has entirely forgotten his beloved—let alone the fact that tonight marks the anniversary of her entombment—proceeds wholly on trust:

> "Ah, we safely may trust to its gleaming
>   And be sure it will lead us aright—
> We surely may trust to a gleaming
>   That cannot but guide us aright
> Since it flickers up to Heaven through the
>   night."
>
> (ll. 67-71)

Psyche herself is far from blameless. She was a guardian. Her task, as representative of the higher side of man's nature, was to preserve the ennobling relationship between the mourner and the spirit of his beloved. But this she failed to do, and must therefore share in the guilt:

> Our talk had been serious and sober,
> But our thoughts they were palsied and sere—
> Our memories were treacherous and sere;
> For we knew not the month was October,
> And we marked not the night of the year.
> (ll. 20-24)

"Treacherous" is a strong word, reminiscent of the harsh language employed in the initial version of "Tamerlane." It is strong because the transgression is great and must be faced, as it is, in the end, in a physical confrontation that is also a confrontation with a word:

> And we passed to the end of the vista—
> But were stopped by the door of a tomb—
> By the door of a legended tomb:
> And I said—"What is written, sweet sister,
> On the door of this legended tomb?"
> She replied—"Ulalume—Ulalume!—
> 'Tis the vault of thy lost Ulalume!"
> (ll. 75-81)

It is neither Psyche nor the ghouls who have brought the speaker here, but the speaker himself. Only his perseverance in the face of obstacles, only his wishful misinterpretation, brings him to the tomb and his victimizing remembrance.

Ulalume never assumes bodily form. The speaker confronts her as a name, much as the mourner of "The Raven," and other protagonists, confront some baffling, overpowering word: *discovery, silence, nevermore.* "Ulalume," in this sense, is a further experiment with the idea that a piece of language functions not only in time but—whether spoken, as in "The Raven," or whether spoken and seen, as in the passage we have just examined—in space as well. If the poem also implies that a name can be nearly as powerful as the phenomenon it identifies, it does this, too, in a spatial way, giving the deceased, in addition to an onomastic presence, an architectural one. It is neither the tomb nor the inscription discretely, but both, the piece of architecture and the piece of language, that bring Ulalume back to life in the mourner's consciousness and the mourner's time and space.

Finally, the poem is an experiment in irony, for the mourner brings his victimization about through the one agency expressly designed to prevent it. It is not the will to suffering that distinguishes this mourner from a Tamerlane, but the discrepancy between his being and (to borrow a word from "The Raven") his seeming. Here is a man whose memory is treacherous and who can yet believe that the star appears because " 'She has seen that the tears are not dry on / These cheeks where the worm never dies' " (ll. 42-43). The discrepancy cannot be traced to the difference between the way the man looks to us and the way he looks to himself, as is often the case with ironic narratives, for we see only what the speaker sees, and only as he see it. It is the speaker himself who describes the tears on his cheeks, and it is he who lodges the claim of treachery. The central experience of the poem, we remember, is presented by him retrospectively, as something he can look back on, as from a distance, and "frame." What is framed, as in "The Raven," is a play-within-a-poem, a dramatic exchange within what is basically a monologue. Like the opening of the other poem, the opening of "Ulalume" establishes a setting in time and space leading to the delineation of the two speakers, and the unfolding of the familiar "once-now" pattern: once I roamed with Psyche, now in our path a star appeared, and so on. The chief structural difference is that the first-person of "The Raven" returns to the fore after the exchange, whereas "Ulalume" breaks off, so that the last words spoken in the poem as a whole are also the last words spoken in the exchange.

According to J. E. Miller, Jr., the experience of the poem is given "in symbolic terms as it is related to the pervading intelligence of the narrator—an intelligence in a suspended state, in static conflict with itself."[34] For Eric W. Carlson "the speaker's grief is located in the obscurity of the subconscious: 'misty mid region' and 'ghoul-haunted woodland' imply the archetypal image of the dark forest, symbolizing the buried self, where inhibitions, complexes, and rationalizations abound."[35] One can agree that "Ulalume" is "mental" in a way that "The Raven" is not. For one thing, the "The Raven" transpires in a plausible room with a door and windows and furnishings, "Ulalume" in a space with imaginary features. For another, the raven is an actual bird, whereas Psyche is a personification like Love in "Tamerlane" or Thought in "The Haunted Palace." If we rush too quickly after subconscious archetypes, however, we are liable to lose our focus on the text, which has interesting things to say about the relation between the two speakers, the protagonist's relation to nature, and the role of language in creating the poem's singular landscape.

Poe follows the pattern of traditional body-soul dialogues to the extent that he identifies Psyche with soul and Astarte (a surrogate of Venus) with the body. He departs from convention by replacing Astarte with another speaker, while letting her stay on as indirect participant. Being visible but silent, like most of the other stars in Poe, she must be interpreted, which is the protagonist's invitation to see what he wants to see. Accordingly, Astarte appears " 'warmer than Dian' " (l. 39), and the mourner marches hopefully and obliviously on. The pleadings of Psyche do not affect him, any more than the whispers of conscience affect a man who is bent on evil, or the whisperings of temptation a man who is bent on good. They do not affect him because, like the victim in "The Haunted Palace," he has become separated from his higher part. He is all turbulence and passion now, a being

[34] " 'Ulalume' Resurrected," *Philological Quarterly*, 34 (1955), p. 205.

[35] "Symbol and Sense in Poe's 'Ulalume,' " *American Literature*, 35 (1963), pp. 22-37. For a different account of Poe's topography see J. O. Bailey, "The Geography of Poe's 'Dreamland' and 'Ulalume,' " *Studies in Philology*, 45 (1948), pp. 512-523.

caught in a kind of instinctual undertow drawing him irresistibly to an end he cannot consciously foresee. Yet there is something in him that foresees it, some almost bodily magnetism that attracts him toward that confrontation, both material and spiritual, which will enable him to regain his lost identity as a faithful mourner. The struggle of Psyche and I is thus in a fuller-than-usual sense of the word "psychosomatic," a conflict between what once would have been called the spirit and the flesh. The goal of this struggle is to recover a state of wholeness—to put an end to separation and, by restoring a mourner to harmony with himself, so restore him to harmony with the deceased. When the two characters, whose spoken remarks have been confined to the first-person singular, give voice in the first-person plural, the end is in sight:

> Said we, then—the two, then—"Ah, can it
>   Have been that the woodlandish ghouls—
>   The pitiful, the merciful ghouls,
> To bar up our way and to ban it
>   From the secret that lies in these wolds
>   From the thing that lies hidden in these wolds—
> Have drawn up the spectre of a planet
>   From the limbo of lunary souls—
> This sinfully scintillant planet
>   From the Hell of the planetary souls?"
>
> (ll. 95-104)

As the question mark indicates, there is something problematic about the role of the ghouls, to whose intention the mourner has no immediate access. In "The Raven," too, there is a problematic element, inasmuch as the mourner cannot be sure whether the bird comes on its own or on the instructions of a higher power. But this is not to say that the interpretation with which "Ulalume" concludes is wrong. In the first place, it is not shown to contradict the facts, and in light of what became of the first interpretation, that is something in itself. In the second place, some credibility attaches to the last words in the poem just because they are the last words—an inference supported by Poe's frequent willingness to end works on a note of implied revelation or disclosure. In the third place, the interpretation is whole in a way that his earlier one was not. In lieu of two separate perspectives on the star, there is one, suggesting that the mourner, who was for a time "beside himself," has regained his focus. Finally, the mourner acknowledges the problematic element in his interpretation. He offers his analysis as *probably* true. He knows, in short, what he does not know, which is a way of saying that the poem is about a man regaining consciousness, a man learning to remember and to recognize.

This raises questions about the relation between the mourner and the world around him, and about the language through which it is conveyed. It is a strange world, as reflected in the vocabulary, with its *boreal* and *scoriac*, its *Auber*, *Yaanek*, and *Weir*, to say nothing of *Ulalume*. The derivation of Auber and Weir is known with reasonable certainty, Daniel-François-Esprit Auber being the name of a contemporary French composer and Robert Walter Weir the name of a well-known painter of the Hudson River School. For those of his readers who were *au courant*, Poe's references have had something of the "Aestheticist" overtone one hears when Baudelaire speaks of nature as a temple with columns, or when Oscar Wilde says that nature imitates art. Those readers who had never heard of either Auber or Weir were perhaps, on the other hand, even more fortunately placed, because to them (and to any present-day reader who has not done his scholarly homework) the names were sounds, mysterious, and of unknown origin and meaning. That is still the case with "Yaanek," for which Mabbott lists seven possible derivations, none entirely convincing. But again this may be an advantage, for it forces one to listen to the sound more than the sense—and no one should have to be reminded of Poe's interest in the musicality of words. Neither is it difficult to see that the one feature uniting all these old usages is precisely their novelty, that literary effect which for Poe was second in importance only to unity or design. According to one story Poe was asked, after reciting "Ulalume," why he did not write poems that everyone could understand, to which he replied, "Madam, I write so that *every* body can *not* understand them."[36] However apocryphal, the answer accords with Poe's emphasis on the poetic merits of indefiniteness and mystery, and helps to explain how he could reconcile adjectives from contemporary science and exploration, like "boreal" and "scoriac," with names drawn from the arts, like Auber and Weir, and an invented name based, arguably, on the Latin verb *ululare*, to wail, and the substantive, *lumen*, a light (or alternatively, the English verb "to loom").[37] They could be reconciled because they were all—the way he used them—novel.

Given such an underlying unity to fall back on, Poe could introduce as much variety—as much "variation of application," to borrow again from "The Philosophy of Composition" —as he saw fit. Thus we find the latinate, harshly consonantal "scoriac" consorting with the vowel-rich Anglo-Saxon "Weir," the trochaic, awesome "'Yaanek" with the anapestic, doleful "Ulalume." In view of the obvious oral characteristics of the poem it is not surprising that we owe the occasion for it to the author of a book called *Elocution, or Mental and Vocal Philosophy*, who entreated Poe "to write something suitable for recitation embodying thoughts that would admit of vocal variety and expression."[38] A comparison between stanza five, with its heavy proportion of high, forward vowels, and the eighth or "confrontative" stanza, with its heavy proportion of low, back vowels, will testify to Poe's care in exploiting different sounds for different effects.

This is not to suggest that the poem is merely an exercise. It is much more than that. It is a symbolic landscape in which an individual comes to terms with himself and with his past. Discussing "The Island of the Fay" Geoffrey Rans writes: "This imagined landscape is one of many; the Fays are like

[36] *CW*, p. 415. [37] *CW*, p. 419.
[38] *CW*, p. 410.

the function of art in a fallen world, the finding of 'an exemption from the ordinary cases of humanity.' "[39] The observation applies equally to "Ulalume," which describes the process by which a man is brought face to face with his own sinfulness. A significant step on this journey to self-recognition is the one through which the mourner transcends the facile identification with nature that led him to regard the spectre-star as a guiding light. The breakthrough is the penultimate stanza: "Then my heart it grew ashen and sober / As the leaves that were crispéd and sere" (ll. 82-83). The "as" signals the end of the speaker's impulse to displace his own feelings to nature. No longer does nature palpitate with hot throbs transferred from his own volcanic heart. This man has learned his place with respect to nature just as he has learned his place with respect to the deceased.

As a true mourner, as one who has experienced that good victimization which furnishes "the most delicious because the most intolerable of sorrow" (XIV, 202), the mourner is not persuaded by the ghoul's beneficent intentions. However generous their aim, the orb they created posed the greatest danger of all. Had it succeeded, it could only have perpetuated the speaker's obliviousness, enabling him to continue, treacherously forgetful, in a state of sin.

"To Helen"

Helen, thy beauty is to me
  Like those Nicéan barks of yore,
That gently, o'er a perfumed sea,
  The weary, way-worn wanderer bore
  To his own native shore.

(ll. 1-5)

The first orientation in the poem is provided by an apostrophe, a literary type directing a speaker "at" or in the direction

[39] *Edgar Allan Poe*, p. 84.

of some object of consciousness. The object addressed in this amiable confrontation is both a name and an attribute, the name recalling Greek Helen and the attribute of beauty affirming the identification. As the poem goes on to show, beauty is indeed the only quality at issue, for no other attributes are mentioned, and it is the beauty of Helen, delineated in stanza two, which brings the speaker home. Beauty, in other words, is not a mere attribute after all, but the essence of this being. Everything depends on this essence, which enjoys an extraordinary power of attraction, a power sufficient to draw homeward the archetypal wanderer in the opening stanza, and his predecessor, the speaker, in the stanza that follows. Helen, we note, has no predicate. She is an object of address, the being toward whom the speaker is, as it were, faced. The subject of the opening statement is beauty—the grammatical center of interest and the thing the statement is "about." Only through the mediation of beauty is the attractive force of Helen expressed.

This beauty does not act. The single event in the opening stanza is undertaken by the Nicéan barks, but this is only by analogy: as Poe carefully indicates by leading off with the word, Helenic beauty is "like" those barks; it is not identical with them.

The statement aims, through this parallel, to suggest the relation between the speaker and the object of the apostrophe, which, as already stated, is the relation between the attractive power and the thing attracted. Beauty exists on the same terms as the quality of genius that, Poe argues in "The Philosophy of Composition," fulfills its high office just by being. Beauty does not act, but *is*. By concentrating on the identity of the wanderer, as many critics have done, it is possible to forget that the line in which he appears, like the line that follows it and the two that precede it, is grammatically dependent on the opening statement: "Helen, thy beauty is to me. . . ." The role of the wanderer, whoever he may be, is to frame and foreshadow the first-person who begins to emerge in the middle of stanza two. The opening stanza offers precisely what the nexus "is to me" implies: a type of being who exists in a relation to me analogous to the relation existing between the Nicéan barks and the weary, wayworn wanderer.

The Helen of stanza two is less abstract than the Helen of stanza one, and more active:

> On desperate seas long wont to roam,
>   Thy hyacinth hair, thy classic face,
> Thy Naiad airs have brought me home
>   To the glory that was Greece,
> And the grandeur that was Rome.
>
> (ll. 6-10)

Hair, face, airs: Helen starts to sound less like an idea and more like a woman. She becomes more physical than before, more present in the scene, and more active. Heretofore I was the object of a prepositional phrase ("to me"). I am now the object of the predicate: something has happened to me, and Helen has made it happen. Something has been going on in the temporal sphere as well. The opening stanza describes far-off days, a remote and indefinite time of "yore" connected analogically with the present by our associations with Helen and the Miltonic or classical allusions that cloak the wanderer. Thus the stanza exhibits a present tense ("is") and a past ("bore") made proximate by the linking word "like." The time of stanza two, by contrast, is the present perfect, which links a situation experienced now with the things that brought it about: there is an unbroken continuity between Helen's attracting presence and the fact that the speaker is now again at home. The past tense in the grammatically dependent concluding lines ("was") evolves smoothly from the present perfect, which brings the first-person home not to a specific geographical site but to that blended legacy of a past both Roman and Greek.

The last stanza presents a double shift:

Lo! in yon brilliant window-niche
  How statue-like I see thee stand,
  The agate lamp within thy hand!
Ah, Psyche, from the regions which
  Are Holy-Land!

(ll. 11-15)

Everything moves toward this present moment in which I contemplate the other more vividly, more physically, than ever before. It is a moment not only in time but in space as well: if I am "here now," then I am both now and *here*. The mediating Helen, similarly, performs a double function. She is a go-between both in time, connecting present to past (this moment to Greece and Rome), and in space, connecting this near place to that far one (my position before the window to Holy-Land). The poem presents this function in an affirmative light, stressing the dominance of the lady's presence rather than the passivity of the speaker's. Helen is a guardian: she offers escape from desperate seas, the gratification of homecoming, and a vision of things beyond. Her function is underlined by the agate lamp she holds, the term agate deriving from the appelation *fidus Achates* in reference to "the *faithful* friend of Aeneas in Vergil."[40] The first-person plays the complementary role: to speak of my predecessor as weary and way-worn is to make of him, in effect, a sleeper, and by analogy to make myself a sleeper as well. What the sleeper receives from the watchful lady—whose attitude is that of a beacon—is a vision of restorative presence that is also a vision of restorative time. In the words of Edward H. Davidson, the poem describes "the way the mind can move toward the past and, in some such symbol as the indefinable beauty of woman, is able to comprehend a world and culture long vanished from this earth. The woman as tangible form actually passes out of existence: her 'hyacinth hair,' her 'classic face,' her 'Naiad airs' are means and incentives for the poet

[40] *CW*, p. 171, note to ll. 11-14.

to make the imaginary journey backward in time to an almost tactile, physical sense of the glory of Greece and the grandeur of Rome. The poem is, in short, the Idea of antiquity gained through a virtual sensing of physical forms, just as Roman Catholics obtain a 'sense' of God in the worship of the Virgin Mary."[41] The critic nicely catches again what the poet had caught: the peculiar way in which the lady's presence, built up line by line throughout the poem, is suddenly turned into a kind of transparency, a medium through which we glimpse that even remote and higher sphere which is Holy-Land.

The woman confronted in the final stanza is more than reassuring, she is numinous: thus, in a poem that has so far known nothing but full stops and commas, there are three exclamations. Now it may be that Poe had Jane Stith Stanard in mind when he began the poem; but from the very first word—or rather, the very first name—she is famous, classical, supernal Helen. This onomastic way of lifting the women in his life to a higher power is a well-known habit of Poe, and, more to the point, is evident within the poem as well, for Helen is elevated in turn to the name and identity of Psyche. Even that, apparently, was not enough, for just as Helen gives way to Psyche, Greece and Rome give way to Holy-Land. Mabbott says: "Greece is the Holy Land of art, Richmond the Holy Land of the poet's heart. Poe possibly also knew of the association of Bacchus with Palestine. One of the many places called Nysa where Bacchus was especially revered is in that land, although it is not a seaport."[42] Possibly Poe did not know that reference, or possibly it does not matter, for it is no more satisfactory to equate Holy-Land with one of these than to equate Helen with one of the women the author admired when he was a child. As Mabbott himself insists elsewhere, Poe's forte is the imaginary landscape—the restless valley, the doomed city or (to mention a poem written before "To Helen" and one written after) "Fairy-Land" and "Dream-Land." Holy-Land, I suggest, is one of these places, but, as the first word indicates, it is loftier than the others.

[41] *Poe: A Critical Study*, p. 33. [42] *CW*, p. 171, note to l. 15.

Its excellence is that it represents what is highest and best in the past: it "contains" Greece and Rome, but is greater because more ideal. This is an important variation on the theme of the imaginary land, which Poe tends to set up in opposition to everyday or historical reality. Here the higher place is higher precisely because it is able to expand and elevate the timeless legacy of the human past.

"Lenore"

There are in Poe's verse several varieties of speech and speaking situations, most of them in some sense negative or incomplete. Tamerlane, for example, offers his confession in circumstances that, by his own definition, do not lend themselves to confession. At critical junctures of "Al Aaraaf" and "Irenë" everything hinges on a speech that those to whom it is addressed are unable to hear. "The Haunted Palace" presents words that anyone can hear (or to be more precise, watch) but no one can understand. In "The Raven" we encounter a dialogue in which only one speaker, the mourner, has the capacity for articulate expression as we normally understand it, for the bird produces a pseudo-speech made possible by a peculiarity in its physical make-up: its words lack that intentionality that marks the utterance of a human being. There is a want of reciprocity in "Lenore" as well. Between the two speakers—the first-person and Guy de Vere—there is simply no demonstrable exchange: I address De Vere; De Vere addresses the collectivity (those who exploited Lenore); I address De Vere; De Vere addresses the world at large. Nonetheless, the poem is a debate, the issue being the proper mode of remembrance for the dead Lenore. Shall her passing be mourned, as a sign of her loss and as a reminder to those who misused her, or shall it be celebrated, as a sign of her passage to a happier realm?

Paralleling this debate is a running tension between emotion and will, which explains why the poem is largely made up, on the one hand, of exclamations, and on the other, of imperatives:

> Ah, broken is the golden bowl!—the spirit flown for-
> ever!
> Let the bell toll!—a saintly soul floats on the Stygian
> river:—
> And, Guy de Vere, hast *thou* no tear?—weep now or
> never more!
> See! on yon drear and rigid bier low lies thy love,
> Lenore!
>
> (ll. 1-4)

The first line expresses my feeling of loss; the second explains what I desire (a traditional funeral rite); and the third, with its accusatory overtone, challenges De Vere to meet his responsibility as mourner. Instead of answering directly, De Vere darts an even more pointed accusation against the collectivity:

> "Wretches! ye loved her for her wealth and ye hated her
> for her pride;
> And, when she fell in feeble health, ye blessed her—that
> she died:—
> How *shall* the ritual then be read—the requiem how be
> sung
> By you—by yours, the evil eye—by yours the slander-
> ous tongue
> That did to death the innocence that died and died so
> young?"
>
> (ll. 8-12)

De Vere does not ignore the question put to him; he merely redirects it. The appropriateness of this strategy becomes clear in the following stanza when the first-person identifies himself (whether in the ceremonial role of scapegoat or because he really belongs there is uncertain) with the collectivity: "*Peccavimus*:—yet rave not thus! but let a Sabbath song / Go up to God so solemnly the dead may feel no wrong!" (ll. 13-14). Taking the guilt upon myself in behalf of the others, I turn again quickly to the imperative, challenging De Vere to show as much devotion toward the dead as hostility toward the living. In this way, by admitting and then challenging, I effectively answer De Vere's accusation. My next step is to work on De Vere's feelings. Accordingly, instead of exclaiming and commanding, I attempt to invoke the presence of the dead Lenore through a poignant description:

For her, the fair and debonair, that now so lowly lies,
The life upon her yellow hair, but not within her eyes—
The life still there upon her hair, the death upon her
eyes.
(ll. 17-19)

De Vere answers, again indirectly, with an address at large:

"Avaunt!—avaunt! to friends from fiends the indignant
ghost is riven—
From Hell unto a high estate within the utmost
Heaven—
From moan and groan to a golden throne beside the
King of Heaven:—
Let *no* bell toll, then, lest her soul, amid its hallowed
mirth
Should catch the note as it doth float up from the
damnéd Earth!
And I—tonight my heart is light:—no dirge will I
upraise,
But waft the angel on her flight with a Paean of old
days!"
(ll. 20-26)

I am answered: De Vere refrains from demonstrating his grief in the traditional way, as I had demanded, for fear of staying Lenore's ascent. At the same time he affirms his faithfulness by offering another and more joyous song in her memory.

The lack of direct reciprocity between the two speakers comes about because De Vere, like Usher, does not acknowledge what he hears. He hears, as it were, remotely; but he does hear and, accordingly, he answers the challenge put to him, then agrees to a song. That it is a different type of song from the one proposed (a paean as against a Sabbath or funereal song) becomes the more significant if we consider that the debate has to do not only with death but with poetry. *To decide what kind of song shall be offered is also to determine what kind of poem this shall be.* If "Lenore" deals with Lenore, it also deals with "Lenore": it is at least in part, in other words, a poem about itself, which may explain why Poe had more difficulty with it than with any other.

"There is an interesting explanation of what Poe was trying to accomplish, written at about the time when he recast the poem for the second time. In his 'Marginalia,' number 103, printed in the *Democratic Review*, December 1844, he has a long critique of a poem by Amelia Welby called 'The Departed.' He discusses several attitudes appropriate in elegiac poems, and concludes, 'Better still, they should utter the notes of triumph. I have endeavored to carry out the latter idea in some verses which I have called "Lenore." ' "[43]

The actual poem is not in fact a wholly triumphant elegy so much as a kind of elegiac dialectic which concludes that triumph is the appropriate attitude for an elegy *which has yet to be sung*. For the "Paean of old days" never occurs in the poem; it is something that *will* occur. The actual poem thus arrives at the threshold of becoming the type of poem the author's critical pronouncement authorizes. That in itself is a kind of victory. The second, more obvious victory in the poem is that of Lenore herself—her release from earthly ties (aided by De Vere's decision not to sing a conventional song) and her ascent to heaven. This power of transcendence is a unique capacity. It is what women possess and men do not. All of the poems to women, especially in their endings, con-

[43] *CW*, pp. 330-331.

vey this sense. We saw the pattern in "To Helen"; we see it again here, and we shall encounter it in the poems that follow.

Poems to Marie Louise Shew

The declamatory manner of "To M.L.S.—," the first of the three poems to the woman who nursed Poe's wife and Poe himself, recalls the manner of "The Coliseum," but the relationship described is closer in structure and feeling to the relationship in "To Helen." The speaker, a helpless sufferer, expresses his gratitude to the guardian figure who has quite literally saved him:

> Of all who hail thy presence as the morning—
> Of all to whom thine absence is the night—
> The blotting utterly from out high heaven
> The sacred sun—of all who, weeping, bless thee
> Hourly for hope—for life—ah! above all,
> For the resurrection of deep-buried faith
> In Truth—in Virtue—in Humanity—
> . . . .
> Of all who owe thee most—whose gratitude
> Nearest resembles worship—oh, remember
> The truest—the most fervently devoted,
> And think that these weak lines are written by him—
> By him who, as he pens them, thrills to think
> His spirit is communing with an angel's.
> (ll. 1-18)

The speaker may be said to borrow a public manner for a private occasion. Through the use of rhetorical inversions and by delaying the predicate as long as possible (until line 14 in the case of "remember," line 16 in the case of "think"), he holds his imagined audience much as the orator holds the attention of an assembly. Yet the situation being presented is intimate, involving as it does two closely linked characters, the speaker, who has been restored, and the lady, to whom he expresses his debt. The reason for the rhetorical nature of the piece lies in the speaker's self-consciousness, by which I mean that awareness of himself as poet revealed by the term "hail" in the opening line, and by the picture of himself composing which he offers in lines 16 and 17. As in "Lenore," the first-person thus has his mind partly on the woman he is writing about, and partly on his situation as writer. There is a sense, too, that he is pressing his gratitude on the lady in much the same way that he is pressing high-register language on a low-register situation; we are not surprised that the dominant verbs in the poem are in the imperative.

But the real aim of establishing himself in this way is to establish the other. Thus the imperative—by enjoining the lady to think that he considers her angelic—turns the poem back toward her. When we consider that the direct object of the initial verb "hail" is the lady's *presence*, we can see that the poem works circularly, setting up a phenomenon at the start and coming back to it in the end. The virtue of circular form in this case is that it matches the service performed by the lady, who offers a return in consciousness to realities that were once known—who offers, in a word, memory. When we consider, finally, that the speaker's imperatives are "remember" and "think," we again come full circle, for he is asking of her essentially what she has asked of him.

"The Beloved Physician," which survives only in fragments, takes a slightly different approach:

The pulse beats ten and intermits.
God nerve the soul that ne'er forgets
In calm or storm, by night or day,
Its steady toil, its loyalty. [. . .]

* * *

The pulse beats ten and intermits.
God shield the soul that ne'er forgets. [. . .]

* * *

The pulse beats ten and intermits.
God guide the soul that ne'er forgets. [. . .]
IX
[. . .] so tired, so weary,
The soft head bows, the sweet eyes close;
The faithful heart yields to repose.

The poem is reminiscent of Shelley's "The Magnetic Lady to her Patient," which also concerns feminine powers of restoration, but approaches the nurse-patient relationship from the standpoint of the lady rather than that of the man she cures. Poe's patient is, again, a variation on the figure of the sleeper, just as the lady is a variation on the figure of the guardian. The difference is that the first-person now expands the field of the poem in two directions. One direction is toward God. In "To M.L.S.—" the religious overtones are confined to the lady herself, or rather to the speaker's vision of her. It is she who offers "resurrection of deep-buried faith." But "The Beloved Physician" expands to include God Himself, for enough of the poem survives to show the speaker turning again and again to the mediation of deity: *God nerve, God shield, God guide.* The reward for fidelity in the earlier poem is merely a form of consciousness—a recognition that the speaker has a certain elevating view of the lady. But the reward for fidelity in "The Beloved Physician" is the prospect, or at least the hope, of divine intercession.

At the same time that the poem expands in a spiritual sense it expands in a physical sense as well. In contrast to the first-person of the other verses, where affliction is kept on a high level of abstraction, this speaker has a specific bodily complaint—a heart that beats with dangerous irregularity.[44] The juxtaposition of the bodily affliction in the first line with the entreaty to God in the second conveys a familiar message. It says that this break in rhythm is a threat to the unity of life itself, and that its victim can be saved only by a being who remembers, or, as Poe says in his characteristically negative

[44] *CW*, pp. 401-402.

way, who "ne'er forgets." As her reward, the lady is allowed to rest: we see her physically there, her head going down, her eyes closing, and if we cannot see her heart, it is certain that it too achieves its well-earned repose. The lady becomes a sleeper but not—and now we can see the intention behind the reiterated appeals to God—a victim. She is not a victim because she has come under the protection of that higher power, the guardianship of deity itself, which the speaker had sought from the opening stanza.

The third poem, "To Marie Louise," reverts to the pattern of "To M.L.S.—" in the sense that the presence of the lady is constituted through the presence of the speaker, who is, as before, self-conscious about his identity as poet:

> Not long ago, the writer of these lines,
> In the mad pride of intellectuality,
> Maintained the "Power of Words"—denied that ever
> A thought arose within the human brain
> Beyond the utterance of the human tongue:
> And now, as if in mockery of that boast,
> Two words—two foreign, soft dissyllables—
> . . . .
> Have stirred from out the abysses of his heart
> Unthought-like thoughts—scarcely the shades of
>   thought—
> Bewildering fantasies—far richer visions
> Than even the seraph harper, Israfel,
> Who "had the sweetest voice of all God's creatures,"
> Would hope to utter. . . .
>
> (ll. 1-16)

Line 3 alludes, as Mabbott says, to Poe's remark in the "Marginalia" that he sometimes thinks it possible "to embody even the evanescence of fancies" normally considered beyond the powers of human expression.[45] When the speaker confesses to that belief, it may appear that he is about to re-

[45] *CW*, p. 408.

pudiate the efficacy of language itself, but that is not at all what he does. What he denies is that the capacity to say all necessarily lies within his own powers, or even within the powers of poetry in general. There yet remains—as ever in Poe—a higher power, a speech beyond normal speech. In the dialogue, "The Power of Words," it takes a peculiarly material form, as one of the speakers literally embodies, in space, the thing he speaks. In "To Marie Louise," the power is in the name itself, much as power is in the name of Ulalume or Lenore, or those other confrontative names and words we have been examining. A little later in the poem the first-person furnishes some further details of his powerlessness:

All pride—all thought of power—all hope of fame—
All wish for Heaven—is merged forevermore
Beneath the palpitating tide of passion
Heaped o'er my soul by thee. Its spells are broken—
The pen falls powerless from my shivering hand—
With that dear name as text I *cannot* write—
I cannot speak—I cannot even think—
Alas! I cannot feel; for 'tis *not* feeling—
This standing motionless upon the golden
Threshold of the wide-open gate of Dreams,
Gazing, entranced, adown the gorgeous vista,
And thrilling as I see upon the right—
Upon the left—all the way along,
Amid the clouds of glory, far away
To where the prospect terminates—*thee only.*
(ll. 18-32)

Seen from the outside, I am the classic victim who lives a fearful series of deprivations: first I cannot write, then I cannot even speak. Within my subjectivity, on the other hand, the deprivations have an affirmative side. My inability to write or speak confirms my sense of a novel realm of expression beyond my reach; the proof is precisely the fact that I cannot attain it. The two other losses, the loss of the power of thinking and feeling, have the identical effect, for they prove the existence of realms of experience that are beyond me and therefore transcendent.

The poem, with its long suspense leading to the words "thee only," creates an interval-before the advent of a numinous presence, an interval that comes to an end, indeed, only with those same words. In contrast to the conclusion of "To Helen," which it otherwise so closely resembles, the confrontative presence does not open suddenly away from me, but gradually before and around me. "To Helen" begins, as it were, where "To Marie Louise" ends. In the earlier poem, Helen is given before me from the outset, even prior to my own emergence. From this placement she shifts at the end into a relationship with a new, deep background that places her not only beyond me but beyond herself. In "To Marie Louise," by contrast, the first-person emerges long before the other: there is an "I" before there is a "thee." Indeed, there is *everything* before thee, the dénouement of the poem being simply that Marie Louise is finally, as Helen was initially, *there.* The spatial field in which Marie Louise appears is less a background than a foreground, an area-before which is the spatial corollary of the interval-before. Thus, prior to her literal presence in the last line, she is a virtual presence along the line of vision down which I progress toward her. She is even more than that: she is a presence around me, a ubiquitous diffusion, like an atmosphere. The result is not claustration, for claustration bespeaks a sense of intense material confinement, whereas this confinement verges on the immaterial. The encompassing presence is a gentle, mediating influence that, far from forcing me in upon my self, guides me toward a noumen. For if "thee" is something around me (on the right and the left) it is also something, as I have already indicated, before me (threshold, gate, vista, prospect): the second-person at the end of the poem is all that I see and all there is.

In general, all three poems preserve the sleeper-guardian relationship from the earlier poems while reversing the point of view. Here it becomes the sleeper who speaks (in contrast to, say, "Irenë" and "The Sleeper") and the guardian who is spoken-to. All three works are thus in character with the other odes to women, the aim of which is to purify, rarefy, and etherealize the familiar situation of helplessness and incapacity—to constitute a good, even a saving, victimization.

"To Helen [Whitman]"

In the previous poem I arrived at a moment in which I saw the loved one; here I begin with such a moment viewed, as in "Ulalume," from a perspective of intervening time: "I saw thee once—once only—years ago" (l. 1). The lady reclines, as in the sleeper poems, beneath the influence of a moon from which

> There fell a silvery-silken veil of light,
> With quietude, and sultriness, and slumber,
> Upon the upturn'd faces of a thousand
> Roses that grew in an enchanted garden.
> (ll. 6-9)

Unlike the nucta-producing orb of the sleeper poems, this moon appears to have undergone the same purifying process that lifts the other odes to women to a high level of ideality. Thus the death that the lunar influence brings is experienced by nature rather than the lady; secondly, it is a kind of *Liebestod.* The light

> Fell on the upturn'd faces of these roses
> That gave out, in return for the love-light,
> Their odorous souls in an ecstatic death—
> Fell on the upturn'd faces of these roses
> That smiled and died in this parterre, enchanted
> By thee, and by the poetry of thy presence.
> (ll. 11-16)

To have presence in this way is to exist in the scene more palpably than thee only, who is at once diffused and remote.

Helen is closer; I actually confront her there in the garden for an extended time. Yet she, too, undergoes that diminution of vitality that Poe's women, if only for a time, so frequently undergo:

> Clad all in white, upon a violet bank
> I saw thee half reclining; while the moon
> Fell on the upturn'd faces of the roses,
> And on thine own, upturn'd—alas, in sorrow!
> (ll. 17-20)

That is an almost funereal tableau, so strong is the association, here and elsewhere in the poem, between the loving and the lifeless. There is a similar lifelessness in the natural milieu during the first moments of the confrontation:

> And in an instant all things disappeared.
> (Ah, bear in mind this garden was enchanted!)
> The pearly lustre of the moon went out:
> The mossy banks and the meandering paths,
> The happy flowers and the repining trees,
> Were seen no more: the very roses' odors
> Died in the arms of the adoring airs.
> (ll. 29-35)

Is there nothing that can survive the annihilating capacity of such a love? The answer, of course, is the same for this poem as for the others: woman. Woman transcends. She is, was, and will be; I "am" only in relation to her. As in the earlier "To Helen," where the presence of the beloved is first invoked through her attributes, or as in "Ligeia," where the heroine is identified with her eyes and her hair, so in this poem the woman is presented materially, but in something less than her full corporeal self. Through a process of what might be called essentialization, Helen *becomes* her eyes.

> . . . *Only thine eyes remained.*
> They *would not* go—they never yet have gone.
> Lighting my lonely pathway home that night,
> *They* have not left me (as my hopes have) since.

They follow me—they lead me through the
  years.
They are my ministers—yet I their slave.
(ll. 51-56)

Helen's eyes are a rarefied version of Berenice's teeth: "They—they alone were present to the mental eye, and they, in their sole individuality, became the essence of my mental life. I held them in every light. I turned them in every attitude. I surveyed their characteristics. I dwelt upon their peculiarities. . . . I shuddered as I assigned to them in imagination a sensitive and sentient power, and even when unassisted by the lips, a capability of moral expression" (II, 24). Egaeus distinguishes himself from the first-person of "To Helen [Whitman]" commencing with the second sentence, where he begins to reveal that he is nearly as interested in his own behavior toward the object of his attention as in the object himself. Whereas Egaeus talks about his preoccupation, the speaker in this poem is literally preoccupied. The difference between the two situations is reflected in the grammar, the "Berenice" passage relying heavily on the first-person, the passage in "To Helen [Whitman]" relying on the third-person plural (eyes). This concentration elevates the woman to a novel state of being by conferring upon her an ontological power which then operates reciprocally on the worshipper:

Their office is to illumine and enkindle—
My duty, *to be saved* by their bright light,
And purified in their electric fire,
And sanctified in their elysian fire.
(ll. 57-60)

In persisting before me the eyes confirm the woman's continuing transcendence while obliging me to play a subordinate role. Consequently my final situation, as in the other odes, is devotional and passive: I kneel to the stars (eyes); I contemplate them; I exclaim over the indestructibility of their light (ll. 61-66).

CHAPTER 3

"For Annie"

The sleeper reappears in these verses, but not as an object of contemplation or as the target of an impending threat. In this poem the first-person becomes, as in the poems to Marie Louise Shew, a sleeper:

> And ah! let it never
>   Be foolishly said
> That my room it is gloomy
>   And narrow my bed;
> For man never slept
>   In a different bed—
> And, to *sleep*, you must slumber
>   In just such a bed.
>
> (ll. 45-52)

I universalize my situation by envisaging my bed as a type, the representative resting place for all those who truly sleep. Although some may take this as an allusion to death, that is precisely the connection I have tried to prevent by opposing any idea of gloominess or narrowness. I am not in death any more than the sleeper was when she was being presented *as sleeper*. Death, for the sleeper, was something yet to come; for the present sleeper it is something that has already been surpassed:

> And I rest so composedly,
>   Now, in my bed,
> That any beholder
>   Might fancy me dead—
> Might start at beholding me,
>   Thinking me dead.
>
> (ll. 13-18)

Truly to sleep is to rest in an intermediate condition in which I am safe both from annihilation and from "the fever called 'Living'" (ll. 5, 29). Others may think the sleeper is lifeless, but he is merely experiencing a different state of being.

I have entered (as the lake seems to do in the sleeper poems) a conscious slumber in which I enjoy the best of both worlds, that of peaceful oblivion and that of knowing awareness. As in "Irenë" and "Lenore," there is a special relationship between the one who is threatened and the one who fulfills an office of trust, in this case Annie. From this relationship all others are excluded. In "Lenore" the outsiders are a faceless "they"; here they are "any beholder" (l. 15) and "you." These persons cannot know the continuing guardianship of Annie—that quality which is called, in "To Helen [Whitman]," "the poetry of thy presence." I first knew this presence in the past, when Annie kissed me, caressed me, lulled me to sleep, and protected me through prayer from harm. But the presence endures: I experience it even now though I am contemplated by an outsider who does not:

> And I lie so composedly,
>   Now, in my bed,
> (Knowing her love)
>   That you fancy me dead—
>
> . . . .
>
> That you shudder to look at me,
>   Thinking me dead:—
> But my heart it is brighter
>   Than all of the many
> Stars in the sky,
>   For it sparkles with Annie—
> It glows with the light
>   Of the love of my Annie—
> With the thought of the light
>   Of the eyes of my Annie.
>
> (ll. 85-102)

As in "To Helen [Whitman]," my role is entirely passive: *I know, I am shorn, no muscle I move as I lie, I am better, I rest, I have drank, I fell to sleep, I lie, I rest.* As the one who is saved, I am reduced to the same physical position—recumbency—as the most helpless victims in any of the tales. If I were not, Annie could not perform her angelic role, the role of the mediatrix who elicits a display of saving beneficence from above. Of these eyes I can say, as in "To Helen [Whitman]," "Their office is to illumine and enkindle— / My duty, *to be saved* by their bright light."

"Annabel Lee"

In this last of Poe's poems to women I am again temporarily victimized and finally saved.

> *I* was a child and *she* was a child,
> In this kingdom by the sea;
> But we loved with a love that was more than love—
> I and my Annabel Lee—
> With a love that the wingéd seraphs in Heaven
> Coveted her and me.
>
> (ll. 7-12)

These envious angels prey upon Annabel Lee much as the wanton airs preyed upon the victim in the sleeper poems, or the breath of moons on the starlight in "Fairy-Land." Indeed, it is through the air that her annihilation comes about: "A wind blew out of cloud, chilling / My beautiful Annabel Lee" (ll. 15-16). Though ostensibly annihilated by this destructive influence from above, the loved one transcends death, her capacity to accomplish this arising from the very superiority (similar to the human singer's supposed superiority over Israfel) which inspired angelic envy:

> But our love it was stronger by far than the love
> Of those who were older than we—
> Of many far wiser than we—
> And neither the angels in Heaven above,
> Nor the demons down under the sea,
> Can ever dissever my soul from the soul
> Of the beautiful Annabel Lee.
>
> (ll. 27-33)

What is unusual about this poem, and what makes it in some ways more ambitious than the other poems to women, is that here love is shared. In contrast to the split between first- and third-persons in the other works (I as worshipper, she as the worshipped), "Annabel Lee" presents, as these quotations show, a credible first-person plural. The problem is that "we" are confined to a past that has ceased to exist. "Our" realm was the past, "my" realm is the present. Yet even though I am obliged to speak in the first-person of another, that other is not absent. She is rather, like the second Helen and Marie Louise, a continuing presence. Through that extraordinary power of survival that only women possess, she has transcended death:

> And the stars never rise, but I feel the bright eyes
> Of the beautiful Annabel Lee;—
> And so, all the night-tide, I lie down by the side
> Of my darling—my darling—my life and my bride,
> In her sepulchre there by the sea—
> In her tomb by the sounding sea.
>
> (ll. 36-41)

Alive in death, she exists for me as a real being: I lie down with her as in the nuptial bed we were heretofore denied. Now that is perhaps as overt an act as any man ever performs in these works. Yet it is, at the same time, a passive act, and one that some readers may wish to regard as another *Liebestod.* The difference between this and a true *Liebestod* is that the lovers are not consumed in the act of union. This is specifically a union *after* death, a union that shows the nothingness of death but does not reintegrate the lovers as a true couple. The concluding moment of the poem is a merger in which the loved one is both lost and recovered, both gone from me and with me. That is why I no longer speak of "we" but of "I" and "my bride."

Like all these poems to women, "Annabel Lee" ends in a present tense suggestive of a timeless realm. The past having been outlived, nothing remains but an eternal now in which my continuing salvation depends upon a guardianship that protects me from the threat of victimization to which every man is prey.

Concluding Remarks

Milton, who influenced Poe's theories about verbal melody as well as his poems,[46] marched through the genres one after another, conquering all. Byron, an even stronger presence in the writings of Poe, also mastered a variety of forms, from ballad to satire, from parliamentary oration to closet drama. Although the same cannot be said of Poe, whose patterns of thought and expression became fairly settled at an early stage, neither can it be said that he always did exactly the same thing, or that he spoke in exactly the same way. Like these predecessors, if to a lesser degree, he experimented and explored, even after he had developed his own peculiar voice. Perhaps the truest observation about his poetic career is that it has the effect of a refrain, an expressive technique that he relied on in practice and defended in theory, mainly for its ability to convey a sense of identity within variation. The point will be clarified if we briefly review some of the high points of his poetic *oeuvre.*

Looking back over the poems, we see the young Poe striving to free himself from the shadows of influence—Byron's in "Tamerlane," Milton's and Thomas Moore's in "Al Aaraaf," and so on. He attempts in the latter poem to be epic in a four-beat measure, and in "Stanzas" to be philosophical in iambic pentameter. An elegiac mood appears in the sleeper poems and, in a modified fashion, in "The Valley of Unrest," where he is already working in the "objective" mode of the doomed-city poems. In these two works, and

[46] See, for example, Poe's remarks on the melodiousness of *Comus* (xvi, 26). Works with clear Miltonic echoes include "Tamerlane," "Al Aaraaf," "Israfel," "Lenore," "The Raven" and "Annabel Lee" (*CW*, p. xxvi, *et passim*).

to some extent in "The Haunted Palace," the poet constitutes an experience that is "just there," presenting a typical human situation rather than a particular one, and one that is viewed for the most part from the outside. The approach is a little different in "The Haunted Palace," where, as in "The Conqueror Worm," Poe leans in the direction of allegory; or in "Sonnet—Silence," which is philosophical in the manner of "Stanzas," but more experimental in form (being a fifteen-line sonnet), and again, like the other works of this period, more allegorical. "Israfel" and "Lenore" both deal, in a broad sense, with the problem of poetry itself, the former describing the singer's limits and aspirations, the latter describing his efforts to find an appropriate mode in which to memorialize another. "The Raven" and "Ulalume" are narrative ballads in which one speaker, through a more or less dramatic exchange with a second speaker, rises to a new consciousness of loss. Finally, the poems to women, stretching from the early "To Helen" to the late "Annabel Lee," present a speaker faced with a redeeming female presence to whom he dedicates his being and his words.

There are the variations. But there too are the continuity and identity, for one is never very far at any moment from the same few basic patterns. Here is a poetic world divided into those who have power and those who have it not, with the emphasis falling heavily on the latter. Here are the guardians or mourners, who victimize the other through forgetfulness and feel guilty about it, or who atone for failure after the other is finally "gone"; and here are the sleepers, helpless beneath the gaze of those other beings who are charged to remember but so often forget.

Everywhere one sees some new confrontation or victimization, the shape of a poem often depending on whether it is perceived as a good thing or a bad. There is in the air itself a heaviness that causes things to descend—nucta, dews, a city, a man in space ("Al Aaraaf"), the wings of Psyche—and that takes the form in the mourner of helplessness, immobility or sleep:

"To the mourner, everything seems deserted and empty, as though seen through a veil; the eye stares into space, the voice is muffled, feet move with caution. All thoughts are always with the dead; the eye seeks him and wants to retain him as long as possible; time and again, the steps would turn toward the body. . . . What actually takes place in the mourning effect was described by M. Heidegger with unexcelled clarity: 'The "deceased," who in contrast to the "dead" has been torn away from the "bereaved" [*den 'Hinterbliebenen'*], becomes an object of "care"—by way of the funeral rite, the burial, the grave-cult. And this occurs because the deceased, in his way of being, is "still more" than just some "stuff at hand," in the environment [*ein nur besorgbares umweltlich zuhandenes Zeug*]. In their mournful-commemorative remaining with him, the survivors *are with him* in a mode of honoring care. The relation to the being of the dead must, therefore, not be understood as a mere dealing with something at hand. In such being-together with the dead, the deceased himself is in fact no longer "there." But being-together always means being together in the same world. The deceased has left and relinquished our world: Only out of it [*aus ihr her,*] i.e., in relation to it can the remaining ones still be with him.' "[47]

Death cannot be directly known, Heidegger goes on to say, by those who remain behind. For these, death is something that happens to the other, a mystery they can witness but that, because it does not possess them as it possesses the deceased, they cannot fully penetrate. Death—as Poe understood—is separation, and it is precisely to overcome this separation that the mourner submits himself to the forms of burial rites or lamentation or elegiac verse. The mourner is struck by the contrast between his own state and that of the being he loves. Here he stands, feeling the rhythm of life in

[47] Roland Kuhn, "The Attempted Murder of a Prostitute," trans. Ernest Angel, in *Existence: A New Dimension in Psychiatry and Psychology*, eds. Rollo May, Ernest Angel, and Henri F. Ellenberger (New York, 1958), p. 406.

heart and breath; there she lies, inert; the world has become a place of contrast and arbitrary change. Thus the lack of transition within a given work from one depicted state to another (as in "The Haunted Palace"). Thus the tendency to find the image of sorrow, by inversion, in things that are healthily alive, and the tendency (as in "The Raven," with its rustling curtains) to suggest the lifelessness of the departed through the immediate experience of motion.

There is, of course, a complementary relationship that is very different in effect. I refer to those situations (as in the poems to women) in which one faces a presence perceived as soothing or redemptive. The structure is essentially the same: one "side" is all power and attraction, the other all helplessness and responsive passivity; but the latter no longer feels so achingly remote, and can contemplate the prospect of increasing closeness or even reunion. For that matter, all confrontations are good insofar as facing the other means an end to separation.

Contrast may also be found in a temporal pattern that is evident in many poems. This is the "once-now" structure that presents a situation at two separate stages without trying to account for the differences between them. The structure is explicit in "The Valley of Unrest":

> *Once* it smiled a silent dell
> Where the people did not dwell;
> . . . .
> *Now* each visiter shall confess
> The sad valley's restlessness.
>
> (ll. 1-10)

It is also explicit in "The Haunted Palace," where Poe decides to do without the italics:

> Once a fair and stately palace—
> Radiant palace—reared its head.
>
> (ll. 3-4)

And travellers, now, within that valley,
  Through the encrimsoned windows see
Vast forms that move fantastically.
(ll. 41-43)

"Once" is equally explicit in the opening line of "The Raven," while "now" is understood in the concluding stanza, which applies the present participle to the speaker's relationship with the bird. Other poems in which we find the same structure, with the temporal shift understood rather than stated, include "Tamerlane," "Al Aaraaf," the sleeper poems, and "The Conqueror Worm." In each case a situation that appeared to be in some sense affirmative is shown in a later and less attractive light. This "once-now" sequence is, in a word, the temporal structure of victimization.

It is, however, the temporal structure of the opposite condition as well, as may be seen in "To Helen [Whitman]," which begins with the words "I saw thee once—once only—years ago" and ends with a recollective "now" (l. 48) in which the poet describes those eyes to which in the present he continues to kneel, and which he continues to see (ll. 62-66). As in the more negative works, Poe removes the obvious time words and allows the temporal shift to be inferred. This is the case in "Annabel Lee," which begins in a "once upon a time" of harmony, passes through an intermediate phase of loss, and ends in a kind of eternal present that allows the speaker not only to see his lover's eyes, as in "To Helen [Whitman]," but to lie with her. All of this indicates again the pattern of refrain, in that the poet achieves a variation of effects through an identity of means. What is more important, it shows that there is always, for Poe, even in the face of intense and seemingly universal suffering, the possibility of affirmation. It can appear in different forms, but will always suggest a vision—as in "To Helen"—of expanding perspectives and rising hopes. If something exists, Poe implies, it exists in relation to something other than itself and to something greater than itself—greater in power and possibly in goodness as well.

In Poe's poetic voice one can detect the same pattern of identity within variation. Here, we may be helped by an analogy with his handwriting, which in his youth "was generally rather large and flowing. Later, in the early thirties, he wrote pieces meant for publication in an imitation of print (it would now be called 'script'), and then he turned to a plain hand which, as the years advanced, became more and more designedly calligraphic."[48] More will be said in the next chapter about the significance of handwriting and manuscripts in Poe's imaginative world. Here one need only notice a parallel between Poe's hand and Poe's voice. The early handwriting is that of an author who is penning words for himself, but, as the years go by, his hand turns increasingly public. The reasons are not far to seek. Poe regularly sees his ideas go from the handwritten to the printed page, and is increasingly conscious of the public eye. He is conscious at the same time, as the essay on "Anastatic Printing" will testify, of the direct relation between posterity and print:

"A printed book, *now*, is more sightly, and more legible, than any MS. and for some years the idea will not be overthrown that this state of things is one of necessity. But by degrees it will be remembered that, while MS. was a *necessity*, men wrote after such fashion that no books printed in modern times have surpassed their MSS. either in accuracy or in beauty. This consideration will lead to the cultivation of a neat and distinct style of handwriting—for authors will perceive the immense advantage of giving their own manuscripts directly to the public without the expensive interference of the type-setter, and the often ruinous intervention of the publisher. All that a man of letters need do, will be to pay some attention to legibility of MS., arrange his pages to suit himself, and stereotype them instantaneously, as arranged." (XIV, 157)

However inaccurate the statement may have been as prophecy, it reveals the extent to which Poe thought of his writing in relation to an immediately accessible audience of

[48] *CW*, p. xx.

readers. That he thought of it also as an audience of listeners is suggested by the oral and declamatory features in such works as "The Coliseum," "The Raven," and "Ulalume." These poems ask to be sounded, and lend themselves to the practice of elocutionary arts. Since the first of the three is relatively early and the last is late, it does not seem that Poe's poetic voice underwent any more change in these works than in the less "public" verses—despite Francis Berry's argument that a poet's voice necessarily changes with age. The essential identity of voice from poem to poem is confirmed by several considerations. First, the elegiac strain of the more intimate poems is audible in the more public ones as well. Second, the experiences depicted in the latter are complementary to the experiences depicted in the former: it is only the manner of presenting them that has changed, and even that change is a variation rather than a break. Third, Poe moves easily back and forth between the two types: significantly, "To Helen," which sets the tone for all the poems to women, precedes the "public" verses noted above, while works like "To Helen [Whitman]," "For Annie," and "Annabel Lee" follow them, indicating that Poe was always at home in both spheres, and could wander between and within them at will.

Having considered the refrain as a metaphor for the pattern of Poe's poetic career, we may find it in order to offer a few remarks on the refrain as a specific technique. Anthony Caputi has shown that Poe "used the refrain much more extensively in his later work than in his early work. Only two of the poems published in *Tamerlane and Other Poems* (1827) have refrains. Fourteen poems with refrains were included in Griswold's edition in 1850; and though that number included the two of the 1827 volume and at least one other early poem, 'To One in Paradise,' the evidence favors the conclusion that the remaining eleven were completed within the last five or six years of the poet's life. . . . His use of the refrain in the final years of his life almost amounted to a dependence."[49] The tendency shows, to begin within, Poe's increasing interest in the musical and incantatory powers of poetic cadence. The interest is always there in Poe's verses; it simply increases over the years. There is some truth in Fagin's remark that "Poe was above all a lyrist in the ancient sense of oral tradition. If his poems, for some of us, fail to come alive it is because we have lost the art of uttering poetry."[50] The generalization needs, however, to be qualified, as I have already implied, by respect for Poe's awareness of the printed medium and his day-to-day involvement in publication; and by the fact that, as Francis Berry argues, poetry can be sounded with an inner voice as one reads it to oneself, and not only with an outer voice as one recites it for others. There is merit as well in the view of Arthur Ransome, who says that Poe emphasized the lyrical because "he had recognized, like Croce in our own day, the lyrical nature of all art. He perceived that the essential quality of all art, whether drama, poem, statue, melody or picture, is the same lyricism that was once attributed only to poems of a certain brevity."[51]

Such an argument, if carried through, would make Poe a bard, not in the epic tradition, but in the tradition of ballad and "primitive" song. Lafcadio Hearn goes nearly this far. In his discussion of "Ulalume" he defines the repetend (a traditional device that Poe often employs) as "the artistic repetition of lines or phrases, partly with a view to the intensification of some new fancy. Yet the repetend is not exactly repetition: it is repetition with modification. The line is repeated almost in its first form, but not quite so, and the slight change deepens the effect." Hearn then goes on to

[49] "The Refrain in Poe's Poetry," *American Literature*, 25 (1953), p. 171. Caputi suggests "that Poe was interested in the kind of circular form that can be achieved through a judicious use of refrain, a form wherein the latter part of the poem comes back upon the beginning" (p. 174).

[50] *The Histrionic Mr. Poe*, p. 148.

[51] *Edgar Allan Poe: A Critical Study* (New York, 1910), p. 126.

conclude that Poe's is a more complex and sophisticated version of the technique, which occurs in the Finnish epic, the *Kalevala*.[52] Given Poe's relative ignorance of older national traditions, it seems unlikely that he should be placed very directly in such a bardic line. On the other hand he knew Romantic literature very well, and had some grounding in classical authors, suggesting that it is through such comparatively ready and familiar channels that he learned to "sing" in old, or old-sounding, ways. The pivotal word in Hearn's analysis in any case is intensification, which emphasizes that Poe's main concern, even when he is developing plots and dramatic confrontations, is the increasing of certain already established effects, chiefly that of sorrow. One consequence, over the long term, is an effort to achieve an ever more chastened lyric mode. It is not that he gives up arresting situations or the chance to tell a story; on the contrary, some of the ballads are in their own ways (as we have seen, and as Fagin reminds us) histrionic. What happens, as the years go by, is that the impulse to narrate and dramatize becomes indistinguishable from the impulse to sing.

Poe's own remarks on the refrain are precisely an argument for the merits of intensification: "As commonly used, the *refrain*, or burden, not only is limited to lyric verse, but depends for its impression upon the force of monotone—both in sound and thought. The pleasure is deduced solely from the sense of identity—of repetition. I resolved to diversify, and so heighten, the effect, by adhering, in general, to the monotone of sound, while I continually varied that of thought: that is to say, I determined to produce continuously novel effects, by the variation *of the application* of the *refrain* —the *refrain* itself remaining, for the most part, unvaried." (XIV, 199)

Poe continues on the following page: "The sound of the *refrain* being thus determined, it became necessary to select a word embodying this sound . . ." (XIV, 200), while in "The

52 *Interpretations of Literature* (New York, 1915), II, 151-152.

Rationale of Verse" he speaks both of "the body or interior of a word" and "the body of a line" (XIV, 228, 229). Poe is here expressing as critic the same interest in corporeality which he expresses in the poems. Tamerlane declares:

> The world with all its train of bright
> And happy beauty (for to me
> All was an undefin'd delight)
> The world—its joy—its share of pain
> Which I felt not—its bodied forms
> Of varied being, which contain
> The bodiless spirits of the storms.
>
> (ll. 160-166)

Poe offers here a useful reminder that the imaginative world the poet fashions never, for all its ideality, entirely forsakes the material world. Arthur Hobson Quinn bore this in mind when he observed: "His verse form in 'Tamerlane' is his favorite four-stress measure. He did not know, of course, of Dr. Holmes' later experiments [in the *Physiology of Versification*] which proved that the four-stress line coincides in time interval with human breathing, and that since there are four heart beats to each breath, it is the natural line."[53] In his own theories Poe tends to restrain the more impulsive or instinctual—one might almost say the more bodily—elements in his more purely imaginative works. He might therefore have replied that a theory like Holmes' paid too little attention to Psyche's role in poetic composition, which aspires to the sort of purity we associate with mathematics and music. Yet Poe sees words and lines of verse as bodies: "This effect would be extended so as to embrace repetitions both of vowels and of consonants, in the bodies as well as in the beginings of words; and, at a later period, would be made to infringe on the province of rhyme, by the introduction of general similarity of sound between whole feet occurring in the body of a line . . ." (XIV, 228-229).

[53] *Edgar Allan Poe: A Critical Biography*, p. 126.

The idea of body employed here suggests several familiar ideas: the materiality of entities, their separateness from one another, and the fact that they have an inside of their own while occupying a position inside something else. If these "bodies" are in one sense vital, in another they are manipulable, like parts of a machine. The aim is to shift the notion of language as substance to a level that, in Poe's eyes if not in ours, is higher and more purely "functional." It is as if Poe is hovering between the poles of the organic and the mechanical that M. H. Abrams has documented in *The Mirror and the Lamp.* If the idea of a quasi-mechanical manipulation of words sounds odd in a "Romantic," it is well to remember that Poe shared Hume's skepticism about creativity, holding that the artist makes nothing new, but merely puts together things that already exist. Elsewhere Poe takes the body still further, expanding it, as it were, into the very atmosphere. There is a hint of this in the way Nesace moves through the atmosphere:

From the wild energy of wanton haste
  Her cheeks were flushing, and her lips apart;
And zone that clung around her gentle waist
  Had burst beneath the heaving of her heart.
Within the centre of that hall to breathe
  She paus'd and panted, Zanthe! . . .
(Part II, ll. 52-57)

This amounts to a sexualization of the atmosphere, that ether-like medium that is a peculiar mixture, in Poe, of airy nothingness and almost tangible substance. A sense of the corporeal also attaches itself to Angelo and Ianthe, who fall because of the beating of their hearts, and to the speaker of "The Raven," whose very heart, he feels, is pierced by the raven's beak, and the curtains of whose room undergo the nervous vitalization that we have already observed. "Ulalume," we saw, is a dialogue between one "side" of being, representing the spirit, and another, representing the emotional and the corporeal. In the poems to women, finally, we observe a sleeper whose spirit drowns almost physically "in a bath / Of the tresses of Annie" (ll. 71-72), and in another work ("The Beloved Physician") is ministered to in body as well as spirit. All of this is not to suggest that Poe dwells on the bodily. It is to suggest that he sees man as a whole, a soul *and* a body, and that he believes an inclusive vision ought to take both aspects into poetic account.

Poe figures the relationship between matter and spirit (to continue our review) in several ways. One is slumber, the state in which the soul, released from its fleshly anchor, may for a time drift free. Another is the more or less automatic functioning of the heart, which has a will of its own, more forceful at times than that of the soul itself. Another, more pervasive than these, is the breath and related phenomena, which, like so many other things in Poe, are seen in both a negative and an affirmative light. There are, for example, the abstractedly destructive "breath / Of science" referred to in "Al Aaraaf" (Part II, ll. 163-164), and in a more whimsical vein, the exhalations of the moons in "Fairy-Land" which "put out the star-light / With the breath from their pale faces" (ll. 9-10). The personified "hours" of "The City in the Sea," described as "breathing faint and low" just before the city's submergence, are also threatening, but in a manner that is more prophetic and more sublime. In two of the texts of "Tamerlane" the idea of sublimity, passion, vitality, and potential destructiveness merge when "The wild, the terrible, conspire / With their own breath to fan its [ambition's] fire" (p. 51, ll. 175-176; p. 58, ll. 163-164). By Poe's peculiar dialectical logic a breath that can do such things finds its complement—its affirmative answer, as it were—in a breath that purely animates. The word is employed in "Tamerlane" to signal the very fact of existence (p. 51, ll. 177-178). Elsewhere in the same poem we encounter "the breath / Of young life" (p. 39, ll. 381-382), while there are two references to the basic process by which the breath is gathered in (p. 52, l. 211; p. 60, l. 205). The loftiest breath, inevitably, is that of the universe or of deity itself. "The Conqueror Worm," in a manner reminiscent of the low breathing hours in "The City in the Sea," presents its play-within-a-poem "While the orchestra breathes fitfully / The music of the spheres" (ll. 7-8), while "The Spirits of the Dead" concludes:

> The breeze—the breath of God—is still—
> And the mist upon the hill
> Shadowy—shadowy—yet unbroken,
> Is a symbol and a token—
> How it hangs upon the trees,
> A mystery of mysteries!
>
> (ll. 23-28)

It is not by chance that line 26 repeats almost verbatim line 24 of "Stanzas," for the symbol and token delineated here are merely more substantial forms of that unembodied essence described in the other poem. Nothing could be clearer throughout the canon than Poe's readiness to merge the properties and functions of all "aerial" phenomena: breathings, breezes, mists, odors, ethers, perfumes, and a variety of sounds, from voices to whispers and sighs. In a word, Poe fancies atmosphere (as "The Fall of the House of Usher" will confirm) not as mood only but as an almost tangible medium, a kind of all-embracing, circumscribing entity that contains human beings while being itself contained within that great breathing apparatus, the slowly expanding, slowly contracting universe.

Hawthorne, whose tales Poe reviewed and admired, was similarly inclined, and portrayed the workings of the imagination in a nocturnal atmosphere that was an almost palpable transmitter of images and visions. He also tended—independently of Poe's theoretical musings about circumscribed space—to place the imaginer in a condition of material confinement, the better to illustrate the ability of spirit to transcend its earthly restrictions. We see this, for example, in "The Haunted Mind," where consciousness becomes all but co-extensive with the room that contains it (a phenomenon that assumes a more extreme form, as we shall see, in Poe's

"Berenice"). In "The Artist of the Beautiful" a man who combines imagination with manual skill attempts "the spiritualization of matter"; and as for the minister's black veil or the scarlet letter, it is difficult to say whether Hawthorne is asking us to witness the spiritualization of matter or the materialization of spirit. The affinities did not escape Poe, who was impressed with the way Hawthorne embodied the merger of the physical and the spiritual, the circumscription of space, and the notion of medium in "The Hollow of the Three Hills":

"The subject is commonplace. A witch subjects the Distant and the Past to the view of a mourner. It has been the fashion to describe, in such cases, a mirror in which the images of the absent appear; or a cloud of smoke is made to arise, and thence the figures are gradually unfolded. Mr. Hawthorne has wonderfully heightened his effect by making the ear, in place of the eye, the medium by which the fantasy is conveyed. The head of the mourner is enveloped in the cloak of the witch, and within its magic folds there arise sounds which have an all-sufficient intelligence." (XI, 112)

Poe tends, like any critic, to understand the text in his own terms, and designates the woman who has the visions as the mourner, whereas another author might have called her the sinner. But nonetheless he does understand, and does recognize Hawthorne's ability to exploit the sense of hearing (through the literal "embodiment" of imagined phenomena), and to suggest that the situation of the woman's body cannot be dissociated from the situation of her soul. It had been less than three years since Poe had presented, in "The Fall of the House of Usher," his own version of the suffering experienced by a mourner confined within a limited space, plagued with guilt, and afflicted with an agonizingly acute sense of hearing. Without anticipating unduly our consideration of that story below, it may be pointed out that the House is contained by the medium of its own peculiar atmosphere; that the hair of its chief occupant is likened to this atmosphere; that Usher is tortured by sounds that force their way to his hearing, despite material obstruction (Lady Madeline's noises coinciding with the crude physical assaults of the knight in the story Usher reads aloud), and that the physical return of Lady Madeline, who had presumably ceased to breathe, is heralded by a great wind. By a similar logic "The Haunted Palace," as we have seen, shows what happens when language assumes substantial form—when it becomes, in other words, so much matter. There is meanwhile, throughout the poetry, a tendency to identify breath with voice, sound with movement in space. These are common associations; what is uncommon is the degree to which Poe is willing to extend them:

> Sound loves to revel in a summer night:
> Witness the murmur of the grey twilight
> That stole upon the ear, in Eyraco,
> Of many a wild star-gazer long ago—
> That stealeth ever on the ear of him
> Who, musing, gazeth on the distance dim,
> And sees the darkness coming as a cloud—
> Is not its form—its voice most palpable and loud?
> ("Al Aaraaf," Part II, ll. 40-47)

In his footnote Poe remarks, "I have often thought I could distinctly hear the sound of the darkness as it stole over the horizon" (p. 107). Through the use of "thought" and the conditional tense, Poe draws a line between the everyday world, where such materialization remains a possibility, and the realm of poetry, where it actually occurs. The virtue of imagination, then, is that it provides a way of going further, a way of expanding on the one hand from the potential to the real, and on the other from the human to the cosmic.

> [Nesace] stirr'd not—breath'd not—for a voice was there
> How solemnly pervading the calm air!
> A sound of silence on the startled ear
> Which dreamy poets name "the music of the sphere."

Ours is a world of words: Quiet we call
"Silence"—which is the merest word of all.
All Nature speaks, and ev'n ideal things
Flap shadowy sounds from visionary wings—
But ah! not so when, thus, in realms on high
The eternal voice of God is passing by,
And the red winds are withering in the sky!
("Al Aaraaf," Part I, ll. 122-132)

More than anything else, perhaps, it is this inclination, this expansiveness, which distinguishes Poe from Hawthorne. It is not that Hawthorne holds us to a narrow frame. On the contrary, allegory invites the reader to go beyond its body, as it were, to its spirit. Poe differs from Hawthorne in the manner of his going-beyond, for, without being less spiritual than Hawthorne, he is somehow more material. It is scarcely an exaggeration to say that for Poe the body *is* the spirit. Poe's famous materialism is so thoroughgoing that when you think it through to the end, as Poe did in *Eureka*, "matter" tends to dissolve, since there is no sure way to distinguish it from spirit, and at the same time to triumph since, if there is no way of distinguishing between them, matter and spirit—like man and God—might as well be thought of as expressions of the same underlying identity.

Poe's materialism has proved bothersome to some critics, who see him as a kind of melancholy engineer, given to cold analysis and pointless tinkering.[54] It must be admitted that Poe is forever taking his poems apart and putting them back together again. His motives, however, are never trivial. Like any other self-respecting architect of verses, Poe works on a line to make it better. Indeed, the toughest editor Poe ever

[54] W. C. Brownell, *American Prose Masters: Cooper, Hawthorne, Emerson, Poe, Lowell, Henry James* (London, 1910), attributed to Poe "what might be called the technical temperament. . . . It is the temperament that delights in terminology, labels, little boxes and drawers, definitions, catalogues, categories, all ingeniously, that is to say mechanically, apposite and perfectly rigid" (p. 212). A similar point of view is advanced in Edward J. O'Brien, *The Advance of the American Short Story*, rev. ed. (New York, 1931), pp. 74-75.

faced was Poe, of whom it may fairly be said that if he was passionate about anything, it was revising. Witness Killis Campbell: "Six of the poems appeared in two different forms, thirteen in three different forms, nine in four different forms, eleven in five different forms, one (*Lenore*) in eight different forms, and one (*The Raven*) in fifteen different forms. . . . Twenty of the poems underwent a change of title, and five changed twice." One can even find, embodied in the revisions of some of the poems, that rhythm of expansion and contraction which is evident not only in breathing but in the material universe as understood by the science of Poe's time and, as *Eureka* shows, by Poe himself. We watch "Tamerlane," for example, go from 406 lines in 1827, to 243 lines in 1829, to 268 lines in 1831, to 243 lines in 1845. Other poems reveal the same pattern: from 21 to 66 and back to 21 in one case, from 46 to 64 and back to 46 in another.[55] In each case the return is to exactly the original number—a quantitative affirmation of identity and an embodiment of the repetitive impulse expressed within a poem by the refrain. If the resulting form is circular, as Caputi says, that is because the circle is the traditional figure for perfection, the qualitative expression of what we have just been seeing in terms of quantity. Discussing Poe's fascination with dead women, Kenneth Burke recalls "that, in *La Vita Nuova*, Dante tells how he dreamed of Beatrice as dead while she was still alive. Whatever the *psychological* motives for such a fantasy, and whether or not in some cases it is 'necrophile,' there is the purely *logological* fact that death is a species of *perfection* (that is, 'finishedness'). And however differently Dante and Poe may have conceived of poetry, both were concerned with *perfection* as a poetic motive."[56] To strive for perfection is to affirm:

[55] Campbell, *The Poems of Edgar Allan Poe*, p. xxxvi.

[56] "The Principle of Composition," p. 53. Arthur Ransome observes that Poe's aesthetic theory "brought him as near perfection as his nature would permit" (p. 80), a view concurred in by Joseph Moldenhauer (see "Foreword," note 22 above), who states that perfection, for Poe, "involves the reduction of all divided and opposed things into single wholes or unities" (p. 295).

to say yes, if not in thunder, at least with a certain insistence. Nothing shows more clearly this will to affirmation than the poems to women with which I conclude my discussion of Poe's verse. In these works the poet challenges himself, in effect, to answer darkness with light: to transform negative features into positive ones, as if to end his utterance on an uplifting note. Poe joins through this effort what Josephine Miles has called the "poetry of praise"[57] and Roy Harvey Pearce "the mode of assent." "In short," writes Pearce, "the power of American poetry from the beginning has derived from the poet's inability, or refusal, at some depth of consciousness wholly to accept his culture's system of values. By the nineteenth century that refusal, freed from its matrix in Puritan dogma, had been in effect transformed into its opposite, a mode of assent, and the American poet again and again imaged himself—in Emerson's and Whitman's word—as an Adam who, since he might well be one with God, was certainly one with all men." Pearce goes on to say:

"Whereas the Puritan community was made up of individuals whose sense of their individuality told them only that they were nothing except as God made them, so the 'Romantic' community was made up of individuals who could acknowledge God only to the degree that their idea of the godhead demonstrated that they were nothing except as their individuality made them so. In seventeenth-century New England, antinomianism was taken to threaten the existence of the community. In the nineteenth century, antinomianism was taken to make the community possible. We are so familiar with the latter formulation (contained, most notoriously, in Whitman's hymning at once the simple, separate person, yet democratic, en-masse) that we do not associate it with the first, which it inverts and so transforms. The transformative continuity of the first formulation into the second is, in fact, the great leap of the American spirit (*genus Americanus*) with which our poetry came into being: the paradox of

[57] In *Eras and Modes in English Poetry* (Berkeley and Los Angeles, 1964).

a Puritan faith at once reborn and transformed, its principle of negation transmuted into a principle of affirmation."[58]

Poe might be happier if we were to replace "individuality" with "identity," but the generalization says more about Poe than one would think probable after reading some of his critics. If I have not already done something to suggest this possibility, then it is too late to make the attempt now. I do not suggest, in any event, that the affirmative strain is the only one in Poe's verse, or even the dominant one. I wish merely to show that the strain is present (increasingly so in his later years) and that Poe takes on a different look if one examines him, for a change, in the light of it.

[58] *The Continuity of American Poetry*, pp. 5, 41-42. Cf. the chapters on Puritanism and Poe in John F. Lynen, *The Design of the Present: Essays on Time and Form in American Literature* (New Haven and London, 1969), which did not come to my attention until the present study was in press.

4

TALES

IT MAY BE useful to pause a moment on the threshold of the tales and look back at the course we have so far traced. This will enable us to keep our bearings, to relate the pages to come with those which precede, and to maintain, to a reasonable degree, an attitude of critical self-consciousness.

The foreword endeavored, as the reader will recall, to place the present study in the framework of existing scholarship, and to explain its principal sources and debts. The methodological introduction then sought to clarify the assumptions and procedures of phenomenological interpretation in general, while outlining the particular course envisaged here. An effort was made, at the start of the section on the verse, to identify dominant patterns within individual poems and within the poetry as a whole. A series of exegeses probed the workings of the poems one at a time; examined the similarities and differences between poems singly, in pairs, and in groups; and traced the appearance and development through Poe's poetic career of the patterns outlined at the beginning of the interpretation. Finally, the closing pages of the section recapitulated the high points of the preceding analysis, and placed his poetic *oeuvre* within a more general cultural context. It may therefore be assumed that the reader, at this point, has a clearer idea of what the present study is trying to do, and of what it can, or cannot, reveal to him about the writings of Edgar Allan Poe. If this is the case it will be permissible to hold these introductory remarks to a minimum, and to proceed more directly than before to the texts.

In the late essay, "Byron and Miss Chaworth," Poe argues that the most angelic love is expressed by a man who is both young and a poet: "The boyish poet-love is indisputably that one of the human sentiments which most nearly realizes our dreams of the chastened voluptuousness of heaven" (XIV, 150). Such love results in "blended fervor, delicacy, truthfulness and ethereality" (xiv, 150); in "a passion . . . of the most thoroughly romantic, shadowy, and imaginative character" (xiv, 151), and in a willingness to seek in a woman "the incarnation of the ideal" (xiv, 151). Although the list is drawn up for Byron, it is equally valid for Poe, who moulded himself in his early years so much on the Byronic pattern. Poe would probably have denied, on the other hand, that he was capable of "the gross earthliness" (xiv, 150) that he finds occasionally in Byron; and indeed such voluptuousness as we find in Poe is for the most part, to use his word, chastened. But there is at the same time—as in Byron and many English or European Romantics—a strain that has, at the very least, a potential for gross earthliness. The situation of the sleeper, for example, is one of imminent bodily harm; and if such lines as "vermin fangs / In human gore imbued" ("The Conqueror Worm," ll. 31-32) do not cross the border of the earthly, they certainly approach it. There can in any case be no doubt, when we come to the tales, that the border is crossed many times, and that the relative "grossness" of these works, with their violence and gore, can obscure our perception of those areas they have in common with the works in verse.

In "Berenice," the first of the tales that we shall be examining below, a man who is alienated from the real world and from knowledge of his own acts violates the tomb of his deceased lover and performs dental surgery on the corpse. Poe would never have allowed such behavior in a poem, and admitted, when discussing the matter by mail with Thomas W. White, publisher of the *Southern Literary Messenger*,[1] that such things were too unsavory even for prose. Hereafter, he resolved, his victimizers would not be allowed to prey on their women in such an overtly sadistic way. It is not that he banned the victimization of women in the tales; it was just that the villain would have to proceed in a more roundabout

[1] See Arthur Hobson Quinn, *Edgar Allan Poe: A Critical Biography*, p. 211, and Napier Wilt, "Poe's Attitude toward his Tales," *Modern Philology*, 25 (1927), pp. 101-105.

way, as in "The Fall of the House of Usher," where Usher allows his sister to remain buried though certain she is still alive, or in "The Black Cat," where the narrator, who seems virtually unaware of his wife, kills her almost incidentally, while preoccupied with the cat. All of this appears removed from anything we have encountered in the poems, with their stress on ideality and refined sentiment. Yet in at least one important respect the situation in these three tales is a familiar one, for each depicts a central consciousness that expresses itself in the first-person, and that finds itself confronted with and in some way challenged by the presence of a woman. This is not to say that Poe has taken the characteristic poetic relationship, in which the man worships the woman, and turned it inside out. On the contrary, he has simply learned how to realize in a variety of situations certain of the darker tendencies that are already present in the poems. The typical victimizer of women in a tale is not therefore the opposite of the neglectful guardian, but his logical development, just as the murder victim is the logical development of the sleeper.

The relative clarity of this "evolution" should not lead us, however, into oversimplifications. Poe's tales do not march in lock step along a single road of development; there are meanderings, detours, and (as in the case of a potboiler like *The Journal of Julius Rodman*) occasional dead ends, reflecting the fact that Poe found in prose an even greater opportunity for exploration and experiment than in verse. This is in large part because prose fiction by its very nature obliges the imagination to involve itself in the world, to record the connectedness of events in space and time, the tangled complexity of intersubjective life, and the varied texture of material existence itself. Consequently, things that could be underplayed or ignored in the verse—such as elaborate settings, physical adventure, or the push and pull of violent conflict—come into prominence in the prose. Poe, we remember, wanted to make his way as a poet, and only when it became clear that this was not to be did he become a "magazinist." That meant writing things that people would pay to read, which meant, in turn, learning how to tell a gripping yarn, how to be effectively melodramatic and at the same time plausible, and how to cultivate, in De Quincey's phrase, the fine art of murder. The unforeseen benefit of this forced labor was that Poe brought out into the open possibilities of experience that, in the more rarefied atmosphere of poetry, would never have occurred. One could now explore experiences that, if similar in kind, would be more varied in form and scope. Victimization could now be experienced within, say, the subjectivity of an unbalanced personality, as in "The Tell-Tale Heart," or within the material world itself, as in "MS. Found in a Bottle." This did not at all mean giving up the rational or the ideal. On the contrary, one could create the most rational of beings, the ratiocinative detective, and enmesh him in a network of intricate circumstance. Or one could talk—in "Ligeia," for example—about the immortality of the will, while showing how the ideal realm intersects with that of everyday reality. Similarly, one could incorporate contemporary scientific knowledge into a work without prejudice to its ability to invoke a sense of the romantic or the ideal. Thus, *The Narrative of Arthur Gordon Pym of Nantucket* (to give the full title of a work that it will henceforth be convenient to call *Pym*) is simultaneously a chronicle of exploration, the spelling-out in fictional form of theories about the polar zones, and a metaphysical adventure; while "The Fall of the House of Usher" is simultaneously a condensation of nineteenth-century notions about atmosphere and matter, a portrait of a supernaturally victimized family, and an account of psychophysical struggle and ontological despair. In short, prose fiction meant a chance to expand into new areas without quite leaving the old ones; and it was a chance that, as the stories testify, Poe was fully to exploit.

With these considerations in mind, we may turn to the first in our initial group of tales. As before, I shall attempt in my analyses to do equal justice to the specific features of each work, and to show how they relate to features in other writings, whether in verse or prose. This approach will, I hope, preserve the integrity of the individual work while allowing us to trace, as we move along, the continuing pattern that I have termed the full design.

Tales About Women

"*Berenice*"

"Misery is manifold. The wretchedness of earth is multiform. Overreaching the wide horizon as the rainbow, its hues are as various as the hues of that arch,—as distinct too, yet as intimately blended. Overreaching the wide horizon as the rainbow! How is it that from beauty I have derived a type of unloveliness?—from the covenant of peace a simile of sorrow? But as, in ethics, evil is a consequence of good, so, in fact, out of joy is sorrow born. Either the memory of past bliss is the anguish of to-day, or the agonies which *are* have their origin in the ecstasies which *might have been*." (II, 16)

The turning point in the paragraph comes immediately after the definitions presented by the first three sentences. Sentence four, unlike its predecessors, lacks a predicate, while in sentence five the "is" and "are" of the previous sentences give way to "have derived," indicating a shift away from a vague, universal present to an immediate, lived past. In lieu of a substantive we have, as a subject, a first-person, and instead of the declarative an exclamation followed by a double question. These changes reveal, first of all, an emergent identity: we watch someone coming toward us. Yet we do not see him in a physical way; he appears only through an act of consciousness. The exclamation of sentence four is an expression of mind catching itself unawares, declaring, "What have I said?"

Consciousness is, inevitably, consciousness *of*. And the thing consciousness is aware of here is not the external world but its own operations. Indeed, so long as it remains reflexive there can be no room in it for the external world; by the same reasoning, whenever it is oriented toward the external world there will be no room in it for reflexiveness. Different things can enter this consciousness, but they must enter one at a time. A being who possesses such consciousness is thus fundamentally discontinuous: whatever he does in the external world remains closed to him because he is unaware that he is doing it. He experiences, consequently, an inversion of the imaginary and the real: "The realities of the world affected me as visions, and as visions only, while the wild ideas of the land of dreams became, in turn,—not the material of my every-day existence—but in very deed that existence utterly and solely in itself" (II, 17). Reflexive consciousness, of the type we see here, is predicated upon a time lag: I cannot examine something in my mind until something is there; I cannot think about a thought until I have thought it. Being one step behind, the reflexive consciousness is always trying to catch up. That is what happens in sentences four and five when the narrator (who later identifies himself as "Egaeus") repeats with surprise his own statement about the rainbow, and when he asks how he could have arrived at it: he wants to know what has been happening inside his own head. At the same time he wants to know what has been happening in the world. But in both cases something surrounds him like a wall, shutting him away from the object of his curiosity. That something, that impenetrable medium, is his own consciousness. Egaeus cannot see through the welter of his consciousness into the world; but neither can he see through the welter into the depths of consciousness itself. This is because, though he is in one sense confined within his own consciousness, in another sense he is excluded from it. He occasionally notices what his consciousness is up to, but always tardily and always from a distance. It is as if he were not quite inside the mental space that he ostensibly occupies. To put it another way, he is an outside observer of an activity that takes place, paradoxically, inside himself.

The objective correlative of this consciousness is the chamber. In this chamber Egaeus was born, and here he has remained. Indeed, so far as he is aware, he has never left it;

he *cannot* leave it, consciously, because its boundaries are identical with consciousness. Egaeus himself recognizes the connection: "The shutting of a door disturbed me, and, looking up, I found that my cousin had departed from the chamber. But from the disordered chamber of my brain, had not, alas! departed, and would not be driven away, the white and ghastly *spectrum* of the teeth" (II, 23). In this chamber there is something of the intense hermetic fullness we experience in the theatre of Racine, whose highest personages exhaust their being in strict confinement. Unable to quit their tragic site, to borrow Roland Barthes' term,[2] they depend on mediators—messengers, servants, confidants—to bring them news of the outside world. Egaeus, in the same way, has no idea what has happened to Berenice until his manservant enters the chamber to enlighten him. The difference, of course, is that Racine's characters have done nothing in that exterior world offstage, while Egaeus has violated a tomb and grievously abused its occupant. That Egaeus is curious about his activities in the mysterious external world cannot be denied. But neither can it be denied that he is fascinated by the haunted palace of his own consciousness. He experiences that consciousness (as do, perhaps, many normal people) as a volume, as a space that can be empty but is usually filled. Egaeus differs from the rest of us in regarding this space as self-sufficient. For Egaeus, consciousness is an all-absorbing fullness—a plenitude in his own head. Through his attentive "monomania" (II, 19), as he calls it, he contemplates phenomena not because they interest him but because it is his nature to contemplate:

"To muse for long unwearied hours with my attention riveted to some frivolous device on the margin, or in the typography of a book; to become absorbed for the better part of a summer's day, in a quaint shadow falling aslant upon the tapestry, or upon the door; to lose myself for an entire night in watching the steady flame of a lamp, or the embers of a fire; to dream away whole days over the perfume of a flower;

[2] *On Racine*, pp. 3ff.

to repeat monotonously some common word, until the sound, by dint of frequent repetition, ceased to convey any idea whatever to the mind; to lose all sense of motion or physical existence . . . such were a few of the most common and least pernicious vagaries induced by a condition of the mental faculties, not, indeed, altogether unparalleled, but certainly bidding defiance to anything like analysis or explanation." (II, 19)

Egaeus recognizes that the objects are frivolous, and admits that he takes no pleasure in observing them. What he does not recognize is that his attentiveness to them prevents him from confronting the more significant, more threatening object, Berenice. Alienation such as Egaeus' involves a double process: replacing a true object of desire or fear with a surrogate object, and changing the true object into a more manageable form. The first, substitutive phase results in the preoccupation with frivolous things that we have just seen. The second, transforming phase converts the object, Berenice, into the object, teeth. If these "ivory-looking substances" (II, 26) bear a family resemblance to other lustrous objects, like the stars and moons that appear frequently in the verse, or like the eyes in "To Helen [Whitman]" or "Ligeia," it is because, as in the case of these other objects, a numinous power has been conferred upon them. With stars, moons, and eyes, the motive is the familiar desire to etherealize and rarefy; and this desire, as we shall see, is perceptible in the image of the teeth as well. But the main purpose of the teeth is to defend consciousness from something it cannot face: the teeth preserve the numinous attributes of the original object (the living Berenice) while purging it of its flesh; the protagonist, by concentrating on them, is able to forget the phenomenon from which they are detached so as to recapture it in a disguised and acceptable form. Roland Kuhn observes:

"A world-design which is phobically forgetful of the body could very well cause the sexual interest to shift to objects. Once the 'forgotten body' is recovered in form of a glittering object from the world of things, serious consequences for the further fate of the person will ensue. Experience has shown that he who has incorporated in himself the being of a beloved person is able to find again and love again that being in another person. But if the 'memory' of a beloved dead is split into two 'parts' which can no longer be fused because the object can never be one with the being it ought to be . . . then the path to love is completely blocked, both the existential mourning and the fetishist tendency remain, and along with them the special disposition to mourning affects."[3]

Forgetting, like neglect, becomes in such cases a form of passive aggression, a way of diminishing the other without acting openly against her. Kuhn goes on to suggest that "a phenomenological inspection of *forgetting* and *killing* would show up their close inner relations"; and the role of the guardian in some of the poems invites a similar pairing of *remembering* and *saving*. In "Berenice" there is a movement in both directions, for Egaeus desires to forget *and* to remember. First, he has very little to do with the woman while she is alive, and is only too glad to put her out of his mind when she is dead, even to the extent of remaining totally unaware of his contact with her in the tomb. This is the movement of forgetting, which aims to reduce the presence of the other. At the same time, however, he keeps a part of the body that is fleshless and imperishable: this is the movement of remembering, which aims to preserve the other in a form that is at once material and immutable. The teeth accomplish, therefore, a dual aim, serving simultaneously as a memento of life and a proof of death.

The danger in a living confrontation, for Egaeus as for other male lovers in Poe, is that the woman may get too close, may take up too much precious breathing space. This is precisely what occurs just prior to the impending marriage, which will compel Egaeus at last to face the full, living reality of the other: "An icy chill ran through my frame; a sense of insufferable anxiety oppressed me; a consuming curiosity

[3] "The Attempted Murder of a Prostitute," p. 425.

pervaded my soul; and sinking back upon the chair, I remained for some time breathless and motionless, with my eyes riveted upon her person" (II, 22-23). It is no accident that Egaeus falls into the chair *without breath* (anticipating the condition of another helpless male, the husband in the burlesque tale "Loss of Breath," published later in the year). In this self-limiting, hermetic world there is never enough vitality to go around, and there is nothing on which vitality more directly depends—as certain poems have already implied—than respiration: a man may go a long time without food or water, but deprived of breath he quickly dies.

It is at this point in his relationship with Berenice that Egaeus begins focussing on the teeth, or rather, through them, as if, though visible and palpable, they were also somehow transparent. Egaeus does not desire the thing so much as the thing-in-itself; not accidence but essence. Accordingly, under the beam of his attentive powers, the teeth all but shed their materiality: "Of Mad'selle Sallé it has been well said, '*que tous ses pas étaient des sentiments*,' and of Berenice I more seriously believed *que toutes ses dents étaient des idées. Des idées*!—ah here was the idiotic thought that destroyed me! *Des idées*! ah *therefore* it was that I coveted them so madly!" (II, 24).

Tamerlane is alienated away from the here and the now toward a future time and a distant space. Egaeus' alienation offers the same elements, but inverted. The distant space—the space "outside," in which he commits his atrocities—does not draw him irresistibly away from his present site, as in the case of Tamerlane; Egaeus is completely committed to his chamber. From a temporal point of view, Egaeus' preoccupation is not the future, as with Tamerlane, but the past. A man's *projet*, as Sartre defines it, is a forward-tending, future-oriented endeavor; it is something I do that makes me different from what I was and that also, to a greater or lesser degree, alters the world. Egaeus has a *projet*: he steals the teeth of his would-be lover. But he does not know he has it, not even after it is complete. His *projet*—unlike that of other men—has no interiority; he is never "inside" it as the rest of us are inside ours. Consequently, he has no sense of his own continuity in time: he is a man who does not know where he is going, a man without a future. He is also a man, as we have seen, without an immediate past, for the immediate past is too close to the time of the *projet.* When Egaeus undertakes his *projet* he does not know what he will do; as he performs it he does not know what he is doing; and when it is finished he does not know what he has done. Egaeus' memory leaps over the immediate past, which is identical with the last phase of the *projet*, as I have outlined it, to a remote past free of the impingements of the material world: "There is, however, a remembrance of aërial forms—of spiritual and meaning eyes—of sounds, musical yet sad—a remembrance which will not be excluded; a memory like a shadow, vague, variable, indefinite, unsteady . . ." (II, 17). This dreamlike memory, with its platonic overtones, stays with Egaeus throughout his life, a haunting reminder of a preexistence in which, could he recover it, he might again be happy and whole.

Egaeus' violation of the tomb and of Berenice gives rise in the last section of the tale to a second dreamlike memory, more shadowy than the first and more sinister: "It seemed that I had newly awakened from a confused and exciting dream" (II, 25). The period during which Egaeus was committing his offenses becomes itself a kind of preexistence, but one writ small and dark: "It was a fearful page in the record of my existence, written all over with dim, and hideous, and unintelligible recollections. I strived to decypher them, but in vain . . ." (II, 25). The literary analogy is apposite. If Egaeus is to understand what he has done, he must become an interpreter. The challenge is no different, fundamentally, from the challenge taken up by Dupin when he analyses the newspapers in "The Mystery of Marie Rogêt"; by Legrand when he decodes the pirate map in "The Gold-Bug"; or by Poe himself every time he writes a piece of criticism. The thing that they have and which Egaeus lacks is *access to intention.* Interpretation, in Poe, is nothing but the construing of intention. To understand a text the interpreter "reads the author's mind" as the detective, in "The Mystery of Marie Rogêt," reads the minds of both the murderer and his victim. But the one thing Egaeus can never grasp is what he intends. He knows nothing that is not in his consciousness and there is nothing in his consciousness but the shadowy play of sourceless, patternless acts. Unable to place himself in the context of the external world, he must rely on someone who can, a mediator free from the affliction of discontinuity. This role is performed at the end of the story by the servant who points to the mud and gore on the victimizer's clothes, shows him the imprint of the finger nails on his hand, and directs his attention to a spade leaning against the wall. Crying out, Egaeus leaps to the table, tries to open the box lying there, and drops it, whereupon dental tools and teeth come rolling out. Egaeus acts out his moment of recognition through physical movement but never once says that he remembers what he has done. If he did, we would know that he has become conscious at last of his relation to the external world. But that is not what we are given in the story. What we are given is an enclosed state of being in which consciousness is alienated from everything, including the intentionality of its own acts. The muteness of Egaeus preserves this hermetic state and prevents the boundaries of the story from extending beyond the boundaries of the consciousness through which it came to be.

"Ligeia"

Of the past nothing remains known, neither the origin of the lady nor of one's relations with her; "I cannot, for my soul, remember how, when, or even precisely where, I first became acquainted with the lady Ligeia" (II, 248). This forgetfulness is not to be equated with the forgetfulness of Egaeus. In comparison with the nameless narrator of "Ligeia," Egaeus retains some memory of the remote past. He recalls, for example, that he and Berenice grew up together "in my paternal halls" (II, 18), and that she strolled on hillsides while he remained enclosed within the haunted palace of his own chamber. What he cannot remember, as it were, is the present: thus his inattentiveness to Berenice here and now, when she is healthily alive. Only as she begins to decline physically does he begin to observe her "person." The pattern is characteristic of Poe, who gets close to the female body only as the female body gets close to death; the detailed descriptions in "The Murders in the Rue Morgue" and "The Mystery of Marie Rogêt" are, significantly, descriptions of corpses. Only when the body has ceased fully to live can consciousness dwell on it without fear: "A dead body," as Blake says, "revenges not injuries." In order to face the body in its living state, on the other hand, consciousness must, as in the poems, see vaguely and in spiritual light. Mortal flesh in "Ligeia" becomes therefore, typically, a kind of spiritual glow: "In beauty of face no maiden ever equalled her. It was the radiance of an opium-dream—an airy and spirit-lifting vision more wildly divine than the phantasies which hovered about the slumbering souls of the daughters of Delos" (II, 249-250). The lady dwells in the realm of epistemology, not of sex. She exists to be examined, as the choice of verbs testifies: *saw, perceived, felt, tried to detect* and *to trace, examined, looked, regarded, scrutinized, found, peered.* Consciousness moves from physical particular to spiritual essence, knitting together a covert argument that the body is what it stands for. The chin, the last of the body's parts to be described in the paragraph, becomes a shrine of qualities: gentleness, softness, fullness, spirituality. In the body's rivalry with its own materiality, the eyes (as in "To Helen [Whitman]") come closest to victory. The eyes of Ligeia do not look, they are looked at, for they are essentially objects of inquiry: "The expression of the eyes of Ligeia! How for long hours have I pondered upon it! How have I, through the whole of a midsummer night, struggled to fathom it! What was it—that something more profound than the well of Democritus—which lay far within the pupils of my beloved? What *was* it? I was possessed with a passion to discover. Those eyes! . . . they became to me twin stars of Leda, and I to them devoutest of astrologers" (II, 251-252).

Ligeia establishes early an omnipresence that Morella acquires only late. The lady *is* literally everywhere. Yet she is not there in quite the pantheistic way one might expect. She is there partly by mediation of the narrator. Nothing shows more clearly the interdependence between lady and lover than the mechanism by which she is, to use a term from *Eureka*, diffused:

"I mean to say that, subsequently to the period when Ligeia's beauty passed into my spirit, there dwelling as in a shrine, I derived, from many existences in the material world, a sentiment such as I felt always aroused within me by her large and luminous orbs. . . . I recognized it, let me repeat, sometimes in the survey of a rapidly-growing vine—in the contemplation of a moth, a butterfly, a chrysalis, a stream of running water. I have felt it in the ocean; in the falling of a meteor. I have felt it in the glances of unusually aged people. And there are one or two stars in heaven . . . in a telescopic scrutiny of which I have been made aware of the feeling. I have been filled with it by certain sounds from stringed instruments, and not unfrequently by passages from books." (II, 252)

The difference between this and the Baudelairean *correspondances* that it anticipates lies in just this focus upon mediation. The narrator declares, "Correspondences exist solely through the lady whose being I mediate. Without her they cannot be. *My* task is not so high. My task—my mediation—is merely to bring out, by perception, what is already there, the lady herself having conferred perceptual capacity upon me as a form of grace."

Ligeia is the personification of intellect and, above all, as we are reminded by the epigraph attributed to Glanvill, of will: "And the will therein lieth, which dieth not. Who knoweth the mysteries of the will, with its vigor? For God is but a great will pervading all things by nature of its intentness.

Man doth not yield him to the angels, nor unto death utterly, save only through the weakness of his feeble will." Glanvill establishes, in this formulation, the presence of God in the natural world, and the power of His will; Poe establishes, through his narrator's formulations, Ligeia's presence in the natural world, and the power of *her* will. He anticipates here, in other words, the idea, put forward in *Eureka*, of the essential identity of man and God, and the ultimate indestructibility of life. The story of "Ligeia" is the story of a being who, like the transcendent female figures in the poems, but with a more explicit consciousness, insists on staying alive:

"I would have soothed—I would have reasoned; but, in the intensity of her wild desire for life,—for life—*but* for life—solace and reason were alike the uttermost of folly." (II, 255)

"It is this wild longing—it is this eager vehemence of desire for life—*but* for life—that I have no power to portray—no utterance capable of expressing." (II, 256)

In his own way, Poe, as I have already suggested, was on the side of life, which is perhaps why he preferred "Ligeia" to his other works. It is the strongest testimonial he ever made, in story form, for the indestructibility of life. It is insistent, indeed, to the point of taking on a self-conscious and programmatic quality. But that is what the story is about: the fact that you have to bear down, if you want to survive, with all the vital and conscious force you have.

Man, according to one of Lawrence's definitions, is that being who strives to possess the secret of life with his consciousness. That is perhaps another reason why the narrator hangs upon every detail of the other's dissolution. But the narrator does not seek possession for its own sake; he would possess in order to transcend. His coming-to-knowledge brings him to the verge of what Lawrence calls a "death-process" but that is really, in Poe's terms, the flow of death back into life. To watch the lady die is to watch her going back to the sources of life that one can glimpse but never, until the moment of one's own passing, fully know. Final knowledge is not to be sought in futurity, but in memory: "in our endeavors to recall to memory something long forgotten, we often find ourselves *upon the very verge* of remembrance, without being able, in the end, to remember" (II, 252).

Victimization is more muted here than in other tales. Never does the narrator act openly against the lady; he simply fails effectively to resist. Everything points toward the time when he himself will be overtaken, when Ligeia will say in effect, "I am still here." By "dying," Ligeia delivers her lover to an awful freedom. For the first time the narrative contains something like ordinary action. The narrator wanders about, buys and decorates an old abbey, starts using opium, and takes a second wife. With Ligeia out of the way he indulges himself, decorating his habitat (in a manner that anticipates the efforts of Prospero in "The Masque of the Red Death") according to the dictates of a bizarre fancy: "The ceiling, of gloomy-looking oak, was excessively lofty, vaulted, and elaborately fretted with the wildest and most grotesque specimens of a semi-Gothic, semi-Druidical device. From out the most central recess of this melancholy vaulting, depended, by a single chain of gold with long links, a huge censer of the same metal, Saracenic in pattern, and with many perforations so contrived that there writhed in and out of them, as if endued with a serpent vitality, a continual succession of parti-colored fires" (II, 259-260). What is terrible about this freedom is its duplicity. The narrator resembles a prisoner who celebrates his release by building himself a new cell. The features of this typical Poe chamber are unmistakable: an enclosed, rectilinear space with a single window, metallised by its "leaden hue" and a suspended censer made of gold, and rendered kinetic by flickering fires. The furnishings, moreover, are largely black: there is an Indian couch of ebony, a sarcophagus of black granite, and a tapestry covered "with arabesque figures, about a foot in diameter, and wrought upon the cloth in patterns of the most jetty black" (II, 260).

The importance of the chamber's kinetic effects should not be overlooked. Its final appointment epitomizes the mutable:

"But these figures partook of the true character of the arabesque only when regarded from a single point of view. By a contrivance now common . . . they were made changeable in aspect. To one entering the room, they bore the appearance of simple monstrosities; but upon a farther advance, this appearance gradually departed; and step by step, as the visiter [sic] moved his station in the chamber, he saw himself surrounded by an endless succession of the ghastly forms which belong to the superstition of the Norman, or arise in the guilty slumbers of the monk. The phantasmagoric effect was vastly heightened by the artificial introduction of a strong continual current of wind behind the draperies—giving a hideous and uneasy animation to the whole." (II, 260-261)

The chamber, as in "Berenice," is the spatial complement of the narrator's consciousness, which, as he repeatedly informs us, is in a dreaming state. In the chamber, the first-person embodies his dreams. It becomes, like consciousness itself, the medium through which reality is seen. Here, as in "The Fall of the House of Usher," the medium is an atmosphere that is at once mental and physical—a kind of film the narrator sees through, and the playing-out into space of his conscious experience. The chamber is the arena in which are staged both of the central, and finally indistinguishable, struggles: the struggle of dream and reality, and the struggle of death and life. The effect of motion and changeability that the narrator creates in the chamber makes it not only the site of the activity that takes place, but the very mediator of that activity. With its "phantasmagoric influences" (II, 262) and its "atmosphere" (II, 263), the room is itself a participant in the "hideous drama of revification [sic]" (II, 266) that ensues.

The rhythm of the struggle, analogous to the rhythms of "The Tell-Tale Heart" and "The Pit and the Pendulum," is an attempt to heighten terror, on the theory that if the first attack appalls, the second, having the first to build on, appalls more. At the same time it gives the ordeal an intense, all-or-nothing quality, turning what might have been a series of clammy shivers into a conflict of primal forces. Accompanying this conflict is a second and more problematic series of events that transpires along that wandering boundary that separates pure psychic experience from physical space. There are sounds among the tapestries, then motions, then a synesthesia of sound and motion. To this succeeds an order of stimuli belonging to no particular sense but to all: the narrator feels an object pass (a tactile sensation), he sees a shadow on the carpet, he hears a footfall, then watches drops of a ruby-colored fluid falling, like a precipitate of the very atmosphere, into the goblet of the Lady Ligeia. But it is not the atmosphere alone that acts; it is a human existence operating in and with the atmosphere—it is the Lady Ligeia actualizing herself, by gradation, in the realm of the living. The narrator's recently acquired habit of opium-taking adds to the phantasmagoric quality of the experience but does not cause it. The quality exists in the chamber, which has become a kind of self-contained but shared sensorium. Not merely the narrator, but the Lady Rowena herself, experiences the mysterious phenomena in the chamber: "She partly arose, and spoke, in an earnest low whisper, of sounds which she *then* heard, but which I could not hear—of motions which she *then* saw, but which I could not perceive" (II, 262). The narrator's references to the opium he has been taking do not explain these events; they explain them away. Nothing would please this frightened man more than the assurance that the supernatural mystery to which his senses are increasingly attuned is only a dream. The problem, as Charles Feidelson, Jr. has said, is that a man who wants to be rational must face a reality that is entirely irrational.[4] The story is indeed "psychological," but not in the sense that Ligeia is returning only in the narrator's mind. The things that are happening in the

[4] *Symbolism and American Literature*, pp. 35-36.

room are really happening: the psychological interest is in the narrator's attempts to come to terms with them. Unlike certain twentieth-century critics,[5] earlier readers had no trouble accepting Ligeia's return as a literal fact, nor did Poe himself. As James A. Schroeter points out in "A Misreading of Poe's 'Ligeia,' "[6] Philip Pendleton Cooke takes it for granted, in his well-known letter to Poe, that Ligeia returns, and suggests that Rowena's body be retained as a receptacle for her in order to make the event more plausible. What is more important, Poe accepted the view, observing that it coincided with his original intention. "The lady Ligeia has so powerful an intelligence," concludes Robert Martin Adams, "that even after death it survives, and finally metamorphoses the corpse of the fair Rowena."[7]

Ligeia does return and does take over the body of Rowena. Yet from a rational point of view such things obviously cannot be. The mind shrinks from the reality and whispers, "It's only a dream." But the brute fact, as Peirce says, bears in. The narrator tries, like the narrator of "Ulalume," to rationalize. "Yet I cannot conceal it from my own perception that, immediately subsequent to the fall of the ruby-drops, a rapid change for the worse took place in the disorder of my wife . . ." (II, 264). In that admission, *I cannot conceal it from my own perception*, the reality of the revivification increases its pressure against the narrator's rationalistic holding-action. It will not break through, however, until the other struggle, the struggle between life and death, reaches its climax as well.

The return of Ligeia is signalled by those signs of presence which were established, in the beginning of the story, as peculiar to her. The narrator describes, very early, "the in-

[5] Basler, "The Interpretation of 'Ligeia,'" pp. 363-372; James W. Gargano, "Poe's 'Ligeia': Dream and Destruction," *College English*, 23 (1962), pp. 337-342.

[6] *PMLA*, 76 (1961), pp. 397-406. Cf. John Lauber, "'Ligeia' and Its Critics: A Plea for Literalism," *Studies in Short Fiction*, 4 (1966), pp. 28-32.

[7] *Nil*, p. 42. The same point of view is taken by Woodberry, *The Life of Edgar Allan Poe*, I, 228-229.

comprehensible lightness and elasticity of her footfall. She came and departed as a shadow" (II, 249). Later, he perceives on the chamber floor "a faint, indefinite shadow of angelic aspect" (II, 263), then "became distinctly aware of a gentle foot-fall upon the carpet, and near the couch . . ." (II, 263).

As life comes and goes in rhythmic pulsations, the narrator becomes increasingly the prisoner of the chamber he has created. He cannot leave, even for help; the only action-space left to him is his own consciousness: "It was necessary that some immediate exertion be made; yet the turret was altogether apart from the portion of the abbey tenanted by the servants—there were none within call . . . I therefore struggled alone in my endeavors to call back the spirit still hovering" (II, 265). But there are really two spirits, Rowena's and Ligeia's, and two struggles: on the one hand, the narrator's struggle to call back the spirit of Rowena, on the other, Ligeia's struggle—which the narrator never perceives as such—to revivify herself. Within the confines of the narrator's consciousness there is only room enough for one of these beings at a time; accordingly, if Ligeia is to appear, even as an image, Rowena must disappear: "In a short period it was certain, however, that a relapse had taken place; the color disappeared from both eyelid and cheek, leaving a wanness even more than that of marble; the lips became doubly shrivelled and pinched up in the ghastly expression of death . . . and all the usual rigorous stiffness immediately supervened. I fell back with a shudder upon the couch from which I had been so startlingly aroused, and again gave myself up to passionate waking visions of Ligeia" (II, 265). Volition plays no role in this pendulum swing of consciousness. I do not decide on the object, the object decides on me, alerting me through the agency of sound, holding me, letting me go, and calling me back:

"Suddenly, the color fled, the pulsation ceased, the lips resumed the expression of the dead, and, in an instant afterward, the whole body took upon itself the icy chilliness, the livid hue, the intense rigidity, the sunken outline, and all the loathsome peculiarities of that which has been, for many days, a tenant of the tomb.

"And again I sunk into visions of Ligeia—and again . . . *again* there reached my ears a low sob from the region of the ebony bed." (II, 266)

Contemplating the struggle but unable to intervene, the narrator loses, like the narrator of "The Raven," all power of motion: "I had long ceased to struggle or to move, and remained sitting rigidly upon the ottoman, a helpless prey to a whirl of violent emotions . . ." (II, 267). The returning presence, whose identity the narrator is not yet ready to face, uses up all the will and life-force that exist within the ontological confines of the chamber. To watch this being return to life is to become increasingly passive, increasingly like a corpse: "I trembled not—I stirred not—for a crowd of unutterable fancies connected with the air, the stature, the demeanor of the figure, rushing hurriedly through my brain, had paralyzed—had chilled me into stone" (II, 267).

The passage illustrates the contrast, throughout the final section of the story, between the narrator's growing powerlessness and immobility, and the motion-producing force of both the chamber and Lady Ligeia. Indeed at no point can the movements of the one be separated from the movements of the other. To perceive "a rapid change" in the condition of Rowena is to perceive the changeableness of the space that encloses her: "I gazed with unquiet eye upon the sarcophagi in the angles of the room, upon the varying figures of the drapery, and upon the writhing of the parti-colored fires in the censer overhead" (II, 264). For a moment repose seems assured. The shadow that had appeared on a previous night is gone and one can, literally, breathe easier. But the stasis is an illusion, a respite preparing the way for the renewal of terror; for consciousness is a victim not only of the kinetic chamber but of a kinetized and increasingly potent memory: "Then rushed upon me a thousand memories of Ligeia—and then came back upon my heart, with the turbulent violence of a flood, the whole of that unutterable wo with which I had regarded *her* thus enshrouded" (II, 264).

These passages have placed before us a further and even more climactic rhythm: the rhythm of stasis and motion. If the last part of the story is full of the narrator's immobility, it is equally full of velocity and suddenness, two of the properties commonly associated in Poe with terror: Lady Rowena changes rapidly for the worse, visions rush from memory, and later there is "I know not what of wild change in the personal appearance of the corpse" (II, 267). The true identity of this being is not yet fully recognized by the first-person, who still sees through the medium of dream, and who is still trying to explain the phenomenon away. There is, as a result, a to-and-fro quality in his perception. On the one hand, he tries to persuade himself that what he observes is only an imaginary being, an "apparition" (II, 267). On the other hand, the true nature of the transformation is all the while increasing its pressure on his consciousness. First he states that he "might have dreamed" that Rowena was triumphing over death, then that this idea could be doubted no longer when the creature begins to move forward in the room. The sentences that follow are witness to the perceptual struggle in both its aspects, the psychological and rational, which "explains" in terms of dream and opium, and the supernatural and mystical, which sees in terms of a gradually overpowering reality. Thus the revivified being moves both with the uncertainty of a ghostly creature, and the vigor of a living one: "and with the manner of one bewildered in a dream, the thing that was enshrouded advanced boldly and palpably into the middle of the apartment" (II, 267). Instead of a dream that might have been, the narrator experiences an actuality that is. In the moving figure that advances bodily through the chamber, the two discrete objects of consciousness are united: the vision of Ligeia has subsumed the body of Rowena; the indestructible identity of Ligeia, defeating death, has regained what the narrator said he could never forget—the living person. This identity is recognizable by the qualities through which it is actualized: by energy, first described in terms of her volition and the force of her words (II, 253), and by expansion, first revealed by the behavior of her eyes (II, 253). Energy returns as the hues of life itself, while expansion takes the form, first, of an increase in bodily size, and, second, of the unbinding of Ligeia's hair: "Shrinking from my touch, she let fall from her head, unloosened, the ghastly cerements which had confined it, and there streamed forth, into the rushing atmosphere of the chamber, huge masses of long and dishevelled hair; *it was blacker than the raven wings of the midnight!*" (II, 268).

There is for Poe, as we have seen, an almost numinous quality about the hair, and indeed about the head itself. The dews of "Tamerlane"—the precipitation of an atmosphere at once material and spiritual—come down upon the victim's hair, while in "The Fall of the House of Usher" the hair of Roderick Usher will be identified with the peculiar atmosphere pervading the house. In "Ligeia," the hair, as a sign of Ligeia's identity, vitality, and renewed physical presence, has, if not a more central role, at least a more climactic one. The kinetic energy is felt both in the expansion of the hair and in the atmosphere of the chamber, which is described as "rushing." There is energy in the air (as in the depiction of Nesace's rushing activity in extra-terrestrial space) because there is life—real life, overpowering life, indestructible life—in the room. It is not the life of the narrator, this man of servile will, but of the insistent, eternal, confrontative female presence. Once Ligeia has established continuity of life and supremacy of will, there is nothing for the first-person to do but confirm it. He has, as he says, "no power to portray" this passion for life. He possesses but one word, "that sweet word alone" (II, 249), the name Ligeia. There is nothing he can do but recognize the being before him, and repeat her name: " 'Here then, at least,' I shrieked aloud, 'can I never—can I never be mistaken—there are the full, and the black, and the wild eyes—of my lost love—of the lady—of the LADY LIGEIA' " (II, 268).

What Nietzsche says about Schopenhauer's notion of womanly beauty applies with equal force to Poe's: "Schopenhauer speaks of beauty with melancholy ardour,—why in sooth does he do this? Because in beauty he sees a bridge on which one can travel further, or which stimulates one's desire to travel further. According to him it constitutes a momentary emancipation from the 'will'—it lures to eternal salvation. He values it more particularly as a deliverance from the 'burning core of the will' which is sexuality,—in beauty he recognises the negation of the procreative instinct. Singular Saint! Some one contradicts thee; I fear it is Nature. Why is there beauty of tone, colour, aroma, and of rhythmic movement in Nature at all? What is it forces beauty to the fore? Fortunately, too, a certain philosopher contradicts him. No less an authority than the divine Plato himself (thus does Schopenhauer call him), upholds another proposition: that all beauty lures to procreation,—that this precisely is the chief characteristic of its effect, from the lowest sensuality to the highest spirituality."[8]

If Ligeia's soul-mate shrieks when she returns, it is because that return in one sense confirms his inferiority—makes him, in a word, a victim. This transcendent woman possesses all life and all power; takes up all the breathing space; reduces the man to a position of despair, or adoration. He could never, if he wanted to, be rid of her. But does he want to be? For this defeat is also a kind of triumph. To experience the return of the other, to watch her emerge victorious, is to experience vicariously the reality of transcendence. Woman has proved, through the force of her will, that life is everlasting. The achieving of this complex goal, this victory which is also a defeat, is at once a tribute to the continuity of personal identity, and a bridge to eternal salvation.

[8] *The Complete Works of Friedrich Nietzsche*, ed. Oscar Levy (Edinburgh, 1911), XVI, 77-78.

"*Morella*"

A time arrives in all of these "love stories" when the woman becomes a mere hostile pressure, an offensive touch, a suffocating presence. Effect in such a case does not articulate its cause; the change is gratuitous, uncertain in origin: "But, indeed, the time had now arrived when the mystery of my wife's manner oppressed me as a spell. I could no longer bear the touch of her wan fingers, nor the low tone of her musical language, nor the lustre of her melancholy eyes. And she knew all this, but did not upbraid; she seemed conscious of my folly, and, smiling, called it Fate" (II, 29). The woman shows her superiority. She sees more, understands more. Both Morella and Ligeia, for example, are women of superior erudition; above all they are creatures of powerful volition. To the inversion of dream and waking reality in "Berenice" Poe thus adds in the later stories the inversion of masculine and feminine roles, the woman displaying a volition that conquers time, the male representing a resistance that suffers defeat. There is no marriage in Poe in which male volition plays a significant role. Marriages just happen, either by drift or by fate. "Yet we met; and fate found us together at the altar . . ." (II, 27). Even his affection for the partner expresses fatedness: she is "a being whom destiny compelled me to adore . . ." (II, 32). So close is the association between the woman and the condition of fatedness that the former, in returning to assert her imperishability, absorbs the latter: "and the stars of my fate faded from heaven, and therefore the earth grew dark, and its figures passed by me, like flitting shadows, and among them all I beheld only—Morella" (II, 34). Morella does not *express* her partner's fate; she *is* his fate.

Without volition and incapable of positive action, one stands motionless amid change and discontinuity. Alterations are as sudden as they are gratuitous: "And then, hour after hour, would I linger by her side, and dwell upon the music of her voice—until, at length, its melody was tainted with terror,—and there fell a shadow upon my soul—and I grew pale, and shuddered inwardly at those too unearthly tones. And thus, joy suddenly faded into horror, and the most beautiful became the most hideous, as Hinnon became Ge-Henna" (II, 28). Beyond the mutability of body, which terrifies, shines the permanence of idea, which consoles. With the discussion of Schelling's and Locke's notions of identity the narrative reveals itself as a covert argument: "That identity which is termed personal, Mr. Locke, I think, truly defines to consist in the sameness[9] of a rational being. And since by person we understand an intelligent essence having reason, and since there is a consciousness that always accompanies thinking, it is this which makes us all to be that which we call *ourselves*—thereby distinguishing us from other beings that think, and giving us our personal identity" (II, 29). After hypothesis, proof, which brings us to that point of transition that we have already glanced at, and that is more a point in an argument than in an historical series: "But, indeed, the time had now arrived when the mystery of my wife's manner oppressed me as a spell" (II, 29).

In order to test the theory, one must negate the other's presence; but what can one do without acting? One can wish: "Shall I then say that I longed with an earnest and consuming desire for the moment of Morella's decease? I did . . ." (II, 30). The longer death delays, the more impatient the incipient murderer becomes: "I grew furious through delay, and, with the heart of a fiend, cursed the days, and the hours, and bitter moments, which seemed to lengthen and lengthen as her gentle life declined . . ." (II, 30). That she dies does not imply that the narrator has more force than he supposes, but quite the opposite. The point is that he *cannot* will her dead: the best he can attain is temporary absence, and even this is

[9] The Virginia edition text has "saneness," but the sense seems to require "sameness." The *Broadway Journal* text supports this emendation, as does the passage in Locke's *Essay Concerning Human Understanding* (Book II, chap. 27, sect. 9), from which Poe paraphrases. I am indebted for this suggestion to my colleague Claude M. Simpson, Jr.

apparently due to fate. Inevitably, she will return. Or does she ever depart? So confined is the ontological economy of the love stories that no more than two persons can be alive at one time. For the child to exist, the mother must cease to be: "Yet, as she had foretold, her child—to which in dying she had given birth, and which breathed not until the mother breathed no more—her child, a daughter, lived" (II, 31). The mother, consubstantial with her child, proves the permanence of identity by exerting the continuity of her conscious being. To do so, however, involves working in a kind of foreign medium. Morella enjoys complete autonomy in time. She prophesies her return and then accomplishes it. The changes she undergoes only confirm her immutability: she is the one who is constant in change, the perfect continuous being. But the narrator has stayed behind, immobile and trapped in a terrible paradox. It is this: *he would negate the one whose ability to survive his negation attests to the principle of life in which he believes.* The only possibility of victory thus lies, ironically, in defeat. He is trapped in a condition of helpless stasis in which he must watch change as the paradoxical expression of that immobility which he has not attained. As if to heighten his terror Morella increases in physical stature with great speed: "Strange indeed was her rapid increase in bodily size . . ." (II, 31). Like Egaeus, who loathed the idea of Berenice's "development," the lover is appalled by the swelling hegemony—the literal inflation—of the other's being. In addition to occupying more and more space (always a terror-producing situation in Poe) she quickly exhibits her dominance in time. With three words ("I am here") she demonstrates at once the continuity of her being, the force of her will, and her dominion over time.

Nothing remains for the languishing male but the possibility of acknowledgment, of saying that identity has been proved to be what he had expected; that, for a knowledge-oriented being, is something. But knowing is not the whole of being. In seeing the permanence of identity established in this way, one also sees one's own identity diminished. Morella's omnipotence in space and time is but the converse of the narrator's impotence. It is this impotence which is the source of the duplicity in which he finds himself. Lacking the power of life—the power to create a new existence by giving himself physically to another—he would negate the other whose presence reminds him of his weakness. He would, had he the capacity, become a fullness unto himself by clearing the other from his living space. Lacking the will to do this, he must wish her dead. But to wish her dead is dangerously close to wishing death. If she dies, death *is*; and, whatever his idiosyncrasies, this man is on the side of life. In order to exonerate life the narrator must desire a death that cannot be, reconciling himself to the fact that, since it cannot be, he must live, for the present, under the shadow of the other. Despite his insistence that Morella survives in person, he seems more conscious, in the end, of an absolute presence that is almost a presence of the absolute. Morella has transcended the condition of womanhood; she is an incantation, a primal and timeless rhythm, a name: it is with the enunciation of Morella's name that each of the last three sentences ends.

The importance of this, as of the role of sound throughout the story, cannot be overemphasized. It is through the sound of Morella's voice that the narrator first experiences the chill of terror (II, 28), and it is through the voice of Morella, who delivers the prophecy, that the narrator's fate is articulated. Finally, it is through sound (this time in an exchange between her spirit and the narrator) that Morella is revivified: "What demon urged me to breathe that sound. . . . What fiend spoke from the recesses of my soul, when, amid those dim aisles, and in the silence of the night, I whispered within the ears of the holy man the syllables—Morella? What more than fiend convulsed the features of my child, and overspread them with hues of death, as starting at that scarcely audible sound, she turned her glassy eyes from the earth to heaven, and, falling prostrate on the black slabs of our ancestral vault, responded—'I am here!'" (II, 33).

It is a timeless entity, if not indeed a god principle, that actualizes itself at will in time and space, echoing the words of God in the Old Testament: *I am here.* Morella cannot be defined in relative terms; like the eternal truth that Poe discusses in *Eureka* she is an "absolute Irrelation." For the narrator, life has remained a sphere of relativity. In the revivification of Morella he experiences the terror of merger, the process by which a phenomenon violates the natural order, passing out of its appointed place into the place of another. Like the victim of premature burial he is overtaken by time. There is of course an important distinction between the way in which the different zones of time merge. In premature burial the present actualizes a past. The constant in both situations is, in general, the domination of time, and more particularly, the merging of times in a way that the victim can neither control nor affect. Morella alone is above merger, a being to whose continuous presence the narrator can only call repeated attention. The final incantation of her name aims less at communication than at the articulation of sacred feeling. In so aiming it expresses, as the words reveal, high and absolute purpose with low and relative means. To see this we have only to contrast the volitional and active force of Morella's "I am here" with the open-mouthed, echoic "Morella" of the narrator. In the end the only "act" remaining is to recognize Morella as existing where she never really ceased to be.

"*Eleonora*"

The two lovers, Eleonora and her nameless, first-person cousin, live in a circumscribed space from which, for a time, earthly cares are excluded. The "Valley of the Many-Colored Grass" is an "encircled domain," closed in by "a range of giant hills that hung beetling around about it, shutting out the sunlight from its sweetest recesses. . . . Thus it was that we lived all alone, knowing nothing of the world without the valley . . ." (IV, 237). Egaeus, of course, was also enclosed; so were Ligeia and her lover. But there is a difference between that kind of enclosure, which verges on the claustrophobic, and the kind in "Eleonora," which is comfortable and secure. Poe's preoccupation with circumscribed spaces reveals what Sartre calls a "metastable" psychic structure. In a metastable condition one experiences sudden, seemingly gratuitous changes: something that was attractive a moment ago is now repulsive; something that I had just thought bad now seems good. Enclosure in Poe is metastable. It is bad in "The Pit and the Pendulum," "The Cask of Amontillado," or "The Premature Burial." It is good in "Eleonora" and in the landscape writings—"The Domain of Arnheim," "The Landscape Garden," "Landor's Cottage." It can also be, finally, a good thing that turns into a bad one, as in "The Masque of the Red Death" and "Shadow. A Parable," where people lock themselves in for protection only to realize that they have created their own tomb. The valley of "Eleonora," by contrast, is a beneficent container. When a mysterious cloud settles down over the valley like a great lid, the lovers experience what amounts to a "good" premature burial: "And now, too, a voluminous cloud, which we had long watched in the regions of Hesper, floated out thence, all gorgeous in crimson and gold, and settling in peace above us, sank, day by day, lower and lower, until its edges rested upon the tops of the mountains, turning all their dimness into magnificence, and shutting us up, as if forever, within a magic prisonhouse of grandeur and of glory" (IV, 239).

In the original version of "Eleonora" Poe embodies the metastable condition, with its quick transformations and sudden shifts, in the title character herself: "The grace of her motion was surely etherial [sic]. Her fantastic step left no impress upon the asphodel—and I could not but dream as I gazed, enrapt, upon her alternate moods of melancholy and of mirth, that two separate souls were enshrined within her. So radical were the changes of countenance, that at one instant I fancied her possessed by some spirit of smiles, at another by some demon of tears" (V, 314). If the description anticipates the analysis of doubleness in Dupin (who will be examined more closely in the following chapter) it also recalls the polar tensions in the earlier tales about women: the contrast between the healthy and the diseased Berenice, the to-and-fro dynamics of the atmosphere in "Ligeia," or the pendulum swings in that tale not only between the two contrasting ladies but between the contrasting forces of life and death. The difference is that the swings in "Eleonora" do not impinge on the freedom of the narrator. The contrariety in her is balanced and, like the valley itself, self-contained. This lady is in every way a rarefied version of the earlier ones. If Ligeia's step is light, Eleonora's is "fantastic," and all but immaterial. In these respects the later story is a heightened or exaggerated version of the stories that come before: the hermetic realm of "Eleonora" is a realm of extremes. There is also exaggeration, perhaps even a parodic overtone, in the Valley of the Many-Colored Grass, with its obvious allusion to Shelley's dome of many-colored glass. The problem of comic intention is, however, complex, and should be viewed in the kind of context I will try to supply when we return to the subject below.

Nature in "Eleonora" reveals an interiority, an "innerness," which is a quality not only of human existence but of its own existence as well:

"It was one evening at the close of the third lustrum of her life, and of the fourth of my own, that we sat, locked in each other's embrace, beneath the serpent-like trees, and looked down within the waters of the River of Silence at our images therein." (IV, 238-239)

"No guile disguised the fervor of love which animated her heart, and she examined with me its inmost recesses as we walked together in the Valley of the Many-Colored Grass, and discoursed of the mighty changes which had lately taken place therein." (IV, 240)

"Oh bright was the seraph Ermengarde! and in that knowledge I had room for none other.—Oh divine was the angel

Ermengarde! and as I looked down into the depths of her memorial eyes I thought only of them—and *of her*." (IV, 243)

Through such passages the narrative takes on a spatial quality. It is as if life were merely a self-sufficient container in space, an enclosure in which being can house itself in perfect confidence. But to believe this is to make the same error as the people who sequester themselves in "The Masque of the Red Death" and "Shadow. A Parable." It is to forget how thoroughgoing is the pattern through which one thing exists within another; it is to forget, furthermore, that the valley is on earth and that everything earthly is subject to time. Eleonora does not forget, and reminds her lover "of the last sad change which must befall Humanity" (IV, 240). The prospect does not frighten Eleonora, who knows that she will continue to exist in the afterlife. What she fears is that the narrator, falling prey to the weakness testified to in so many of the poems, will forget her. At this point we may ask: what kind of man is she speaking to; how equipped is he to carry the burden of remembrance?

He is a man to whom things happen. The first change, described above, is one of those things; the second change is another. There is nothing he can do about these changes, any more than he can do anything about his love of Eleonora, which also just happens to him: Eleonora is given; then she is taken away. Later, in lieu of Eleonora herself, her presence comes upon him, and this bestowal, too, is gratuitous: signs of her presence "were still given me in the silent hours of the night" (IV, 243). But that which is arbitrarily given can be just as arbitrarily taken away: "Suddenly, these manifestations they ceased; and the world grew dark before mine eyes . . ." (IV, 243).

If "Berenice" is oriented mainly toward the past, "Eleonora" is oriented mainly toward the future. When Eleonora implores her lover to remember her, she is playing the sleeper role; when the lover promises not to forget, he is playing the combined role of the survivor and the guardian. The difference is that this sleeper has not yet died and this survivor has not yet forgotten. What preoccupies Eleonora is the future path that her lover, given his nature, will be likely to follow. When she makes him pledge never to love another, she extends an influence over him that will be as enduring as it is complete. The behavior of nature, some years after Eleonora's passing, implies, however, that the survivor may be slipping into forgetfulness: in place of the asphodels that wither away, there spring up "ten by ten, dark eye-like violets that writhed uneasily and were ever encumbered with dew" (IV, 241-242). This obviously recalls the valley of unrest; and the eye motif suggests that the first-person is being watched. The prospects for remembrance look even dimmer when the narrator quits the pastoral environment for the city, with its "terrible temptations" (IV, 243). It is doubtless this movement which prompts Northrop Frye to group "Eleonora" with Johnson's *Rasselas* and Blake's *Book of Thel.* Such works "introduce us to a kind of prison-Paradise or unborn world from which the central characters long to escape to a lower world, and the same feeling of malaise and longing to enter a world of action recurs in the most exhaustive treatment of the phase in English literature, Keats's *Endymion.*"[10]

In the lower world of the city the narrator confronts a woman whose presence overpowers him. His surrender to her is not, as it appears, a violation of his pledge, for Ermengarde reincarnates Eleonora in much the same way that the Lady Rowena reincarnates the Lady Ligeia. The first-person is thus, paradoxically, a survivor who forgets, and at the same time is prevented from doing so: he becomes unfaithful by knowingly yielding to a woman he believes to be different from Eleonora; but he is prevented from becoming unfaithful by the fact—which he can neither know nor control—that the first and second lovers are actually the same. Why is he spared, despite his conscious failure? Because that is the way Eleonora wants it. She has left nothing to her partner's voli-

[10] *Anatomy of Criticism: Four Essays* (Princeton, 1957), p. 200.

tion—knowing in advance that he has none. She has left him only the illusion of a will. The only true will in the story is her own.

Eleonora is imperial, which means that she can reign anywhere; and she is immortal, which means that her empire extends throughout all time. The immortal facet of her existence is evidenced by the bodiless presence that attests to her uninterrupted existence; while the "imperialism" is indicated by the language with which she communicates:

"And once . . . there came through my lattice the soft sighs which had forsaken me; and they modelled themselves into familiar and sweet voice, saying:

" 'Sleep in peace!—for the Spirit of Love reigneth and ruleth, and, in taking to thy passionate heart her who is Ermengarde, thou art absolved, for reasons which shall be made known to thee in Heaven, of thy vows unto Eleonora.' " (IV, 243-244)

To summarize, each of these narratives devoted to the transcendent woman—"Morella," "Ligeia," and "Eleonora"—ends with a confrontation. Here is the man, helpless, and here is the woman, overpowering. The man has lost the contest in the sense that he tried to negate the woman, only to be himself negated. In the sense that the woman proves the continuity of being and identity, he achieves, on the other hand, a kind of victory. If the woman survives, he, being human, should survive as well. This is never, of course, a victory over the woman, but a victory *through* her. In these final confrontations the two roles of the woman as Poe sees them—the role of the victor and the role of the mediator—are blended into one.

STEPHEN MOONEY observes "that Poe, early and late, was not above satirizing ideas and topics that he appeared at times to take seriously"; one should therefore be warned that "behind all of Poe's doors lurks the ghost of the hoaxer. . . ."[11]

[11] "Poe's Gothic Wasteland," *Sewanee Review*, 70 (1962), pp. 267-268, 254.

It is this possibility which Rans has in mind when he suspects that "Ulalume," which he regards as a serious major work, contains also "a strain of self-mockery, [which is] certainly not alien to Poe's antic spirit," or when he says in discussing *Pym* (which is again in his eyes a predominantly serious work), that "at times it is difficult not to suspect that Poe, in his language, is mocking the kind of thing he is engaged in. . . ."[12] Similarly, it is possible, as noted above, that Poe's references to the "Valley of the Many-Colored Grass" contain a parodic overtone. Some readers may also feel that the landscape pictured in that work is too idyllic to be taken with perfect seriousness. In his reading of another of the tales about women, Clark Griffith goes much further. Griffith's premise is that a critic can get better results from "a chronological rather than a typal investigation." Since "Ligeia" was published closely in time to a tale of horror, "Silence. A Fable," and the Psyche Zenobia spoofs, it is to be read as a hybrid piece, part horror story and part burlesque.[13]

Now the mystifying tendencies in Poe are well-known. He enjoyed hoaxing the public, he was not above baffling his readers with exotic knowledge, and he was an active inventor of mysteries. Seen in this light, a story like "Mystification" is not only about the mystifying impulse in the Baron Ritzner Von Jung but the mystifying impulse in Poe himself. As a student of autography, Poe plays the same polar game, composing what James A. Harrison, the editor of the Virginia edition, calls a "double" (IV, X): on the one hand the serious studies of autographs, and on the other, the tongue-in-cheek "Autography." There is often, then, a risk in taking Poe too seriously, a risk that critics such as Griffith have sought to avoid by following up all possible ironic leads.

But there are risks in the other direction as well. The hunt for concealed ironic messages has a way of leading the critic indefatigably on—much like the hunt for concealed sex.

[12] *Edgar Allan Poe*, pp. 54, 92.

[13] "Poe's 'Ligeia' and the English Romantics," *University of Toronto Quarterly*, 24 (1954), p. 8.

Raise the suspicion that the author is pulling your leg, and it becomes difficult to take him seriously at any time. No reader wants to seem a fool by missing the joke; moreover, conventional wisdom holds that the true meaning of the text is often, if not the reverse of what it appears, at the very least hidden or disguised. In any event, recent critical efforts have more than compensated for the neglect that befell the "grotesques" of Poe because of changes in taste. The temptation today is to lean too far in the other direction—to infer comic intention where it does not in fact exist. This attitude alienates the serious work from its own identity, and, by obscuring the differences between the two types, alienates the comic work from its identity as well. What is needed, and what Mooney has largely provided, is a reliable basis for determining, with some hope of accuracy, what Poe had in mind. Mooney's criteria (supported by more examples than we need to consider here) are five. A story has significant comic intention if it presents: (1) ascending motifs—patterns in which, as in "The Balloon-Hoax," some central phenomenon in the work literally goes up; (2) group motion ("King Pest," "Lionizing," and so on); (3) "machine-motions, as of automata," physical deformity, artificial members, and the like ("Four Beasts in One;" "The Homo-Cameleopard," "The Man That Was Used Up," "Some Words with a Mummy"); (4) avoidance of proportion, which "may be taken to represent a deliberate imitation of 'ontological' deformity; non-sequitur constructions, ignorantio-elenchi constructions, and loosely episodic constructions are varieties of this type"; (5) the devil ("The Duc de L'Omelette," "Bon-Bon," "Never Bet the Devil Your Head").[14]

To this list might be added a sixth in acknowledgment of Poe's onomastic patterns, that is, the tendency to fashion names embodying the spirit of the work in which they occur. Comic works are characterized by names like Blunderbuzzard, Vondervotteimittis, Dubble L. Dee, Rumgudgeon,

[14] "Comic Intent in Poe's Tales: Five Criteria," *Modern Language Notes*, 76 (1961), pp. 432-434.

Lacko'breath, Tarr and Fether, Shuttleworthy, Rattleborough, Snap, Gruff, and Bag. In contrast, serious or arabesque works feature names such as Ligeia, Morella, Usher, Ellison, Monos, Una, Eiros, or Charmion. The presence of even the most absurd name does not guarantee that the work in which it appears is designed for an exclusively comic response. A fractured name like "Aries Tottle" in the first part of *Eureka* bespeaks a comic aim in the first part of *Eureka*, but not in the whole of the work. Indeed, it is because these pages are so ridiculous that the rest of the writing seems, by contrast, serious and even sublime. A similar caution applies to all of these criteria, which can claim heuristic value only if they are discriminatingly applied. Before deciding that the intention of a work is comic, it is well to ascertain not merely that the one or more criteria are met, but that they play a dominant role. If they do not—as in the case of *Eureka*—we may reasonably infer that the principal intention of the work is serious. When none of the criteria is present, the same inference applies with even greater force.

Between the extremes of the patently serious and the patently comic there are areas in which it is much easier to lose one's way. Consider, for example, the Valley of the Many-Colored Grass in "Eleonora," to which we may now briefly return. If we are looking for the ghost of the hoaxer we detect a parodic overtone: surely Poe meant the Shelleyan reference to be taken with tongue in cheek. If on the other hand we regard the story as the culmination of the "supernatural" tendencies in the other tales about women, we have a different reaction. We consider that Poe meant the allusion to epitomize those tendencies; and since the tale does not meet any of our other criteria, we proceed on the view—until our attention is drawn to something we have missed in the text—that the work is mainly serious in intention; that the allusion is at best a reinforcement of this intention and at worst intrusive (by virtue of the fact that it might prove distracting to, say, someone who dislikes Shelley, or someone who objects on principle to this type of allusiveness). In short,

"Eleonora"—according to this view, which is shared by the great majority of readers, including myself—extends patterns with which we are already familiar. In her concluding words to her lover, Eleonora effects the identical saving arrangement we saw in "For Annie": " 'Sleep in peace!—for the Spirit of Love reigneth and ruleth and, in taking to my passionate heart her who is Ermengarde, thou art absolved, for reasons which shall be made known to thee in Heaven, of thy vows unto Eleonora' " (IV, 244). The guardian is not only absolved of his forgetfulness, but is transformed into a sleeper, while the transcendent Eleonora assumes the functions of a guardian. "Eleonora" thus accomplishes, in relation to the earlier stories about women, what the later love lyrics accomplish in relation to the earlier poems: familiar, negative relationships are rendered affirmative, as the woman not only triumphs, but assuages and saves.

When the antic spirit does break out in Poe it is usually, as in the grotesques, obvious—too much so, often, for twentieth-century tastes. Another characteristic of this spirit is its sheer playfulness, which contributes to what Adams calls "a sort of freedom": "It is as if there were a slipping clutch between the world of things and the world of the person. This asks for a sort of freedom; De Quincey's type of psychic mobilization takes place readily in Poe. But also there is the reverse of this procedure; the mind, so swift to rally to its own fears, is parodied as glib and self-assured in making up rules which have nothing to do with any specific facts." Stories such as "Thou Art the Man," "Never Bet the Devil Your Head," and "Hop-Frog" are full of "off-balance, off-point generalizations" which "burlesque the mind's tendency to slip into and out of focus on what it accepts as the real world."[15]

Poe was in the habit, as we know, of playing one work off against its polar complement. This means parodying in one work matters that are treated seriously in another, as Mooney points out. It also means (a point that is often overlooked)

[15] *Nil*, pp. 48-49.

just the reverse: that is, taking seriously in one place what is treated lightly or satirically in another. "MS. Found in a Bottle" opens with the narrator's sober account of his tendency to "methodize." Seven years later, in the farcical tale "The Business Man," the narrator, Peter Pendulum, will unwittingly ridicule precisely this tendency in himself. Similarly, "A Predicament. The Scythe of Time" will furnish, as Auden, Davidson, and others have remarked, a comic version of the life-or-death predicament of the victim in "The Pit and the Pendulum," while at the same time parodying the stylistic abuses to be found in one of Poe's favorite satirical targets, *Blackwood's Magazine*. The business man's surname is itself an oblique reference to the crucial mechanism in "The Pit and the Pendulum," and an implicit suggestion that the methodical business man is a victim of his own clocklike regularity. Such works, says Davidson, "ridiculed what were later to be his most reasoned ideas of art. These grotesques and others were Poe's permission to make fun of himself. . . ."[16]

"Loss of Breath. A Tale Neither In nor Out of 'Blackwood,' " again, as the subtitle confirms, parodies the mannerisms of the Edinburgh publication, while offering a comic perspective on one of Poe's own preoccupations. Here is a representative case of a work that moves in a crisscross pattern. While tracing a comic design on serious material and a serious design on comic, it also moves temporally in two directions, pointing back to earlier things and forward to things that were still to come. The sufferings of the first-person are a comic *mélange* of the sufferings experienced in works like "Tamerlane," "The Raven," or the tales about women. The protagonist loses two crucial and interrelated powers: the power to breathe and the power to speak. He also expounds on that perversity in human nature which causes a man "to reject the obvious and the ready, for the far-distant and equivocal" (II, 153), thus anticipating the remarks on perversity in "The Black Cat" and "The Imp of the Perverse." Shortly

[16] *Poe: A Critical Study*, pp. 144-145.

thereafter the narrator undergoes a burlesque version of physical victimization in which, among other things, he experiences the sort of interment procedures that Poe elsewhere treats, especially in "The Premature Burial," with profound seriousness.

Parody is in one sense a determinate and in another sense an indeterminate mode. Parody must be like its model or we will miss the point. But while the parodist adopts the patterns and strategies of the model, he also, through exaggeration, surpasses them. His work must in a manner of speaking be more like the model than the model itself. Through this surpassing activity, parody has a way of releasing itself from its model, a way of taking free and sometimes, as in Melville's *Pierre*, dizzying flight. In parody the author can give freer rein than usual to the play instinct that, according to the classic theory developed by Schiller, and refined by F. J. J. Buytendijk, Johann Huizinga, and Hans-Georg Gadamer, informs all creative activity.[17] Once the playful juices start flowing, the author may move about imaginatively in a yawing way, now heading one direction, now another, now ridiculing a given phenomenon, now taking it seriously, and now forgetting about it altogether. All of these tendencies are evident in a work such as "The Unparalleled Adventure of One Hans Pfaall." The tale begins as a mock version of the balloon-ascension, moon-voyage genre then in vogue. The messenger from the moon who lands in Rotterdam at the opening is patently comic—a ball-like figure with enormous hands, a long, crooked nose, and gaudy dress. But as the reader enters the world of the manuscript composed by Pfaall and delivered by the little man, the story slips into a more serious phase. What happens to the author of the manuscript comes increasingly to resemble the things that happen to the author of "MS. Found in a Bottle," and *Pym*—another manuscript narrative about an extraordinary journey. The

[17] See the discussion in Gadamer, *Wahrheit und Methode*, especially in the section, "Spiel als Leitfaden der ontologischen Explication," pp. 97ff.

closer Pfaall comes to Poe's characteristic terror-producing situations, the more intense and serious the narrative becomes. Here, for example, is Pfaall's description of his loss of breath:

"I began to find great difficulty in drawing my breath. My head, too, was excessively painful; and, having felt for some time a moisture about my cheeks, I at length discovered it to be blood, which was oozing quite fast from the drums of my ears. . . . I was suddenly seized with a spasm which lasted for more than five minutes, and even when this, in a measure, ceased, I could catch my breath only at long intervals, and in a gasping manner,—bleeding all the while copiously at the nose and ears, and even slightly at the eyes. . . . I anticipated nothing less than death, and death in a few minutes. The physical suffering I underwent contributed also to render me nearly incapable of making any exertion for the preservation of my life. I had, indeed, little power of reflection left. . . ." (II, 70-71)

Notwithstanding the comic premise of the tale, the experiences Pfaall undergoes—loss of the power to breathe, loss of the power to reflect, or consciousness, and a lived sense of the intimate connection between the body and the mind—are the experiences of protagonists of the most serious works. At the same time Pfaall possesses precisely those ratiocinative faculties which are the dominant trait of Auguste Dupin, the hero of the detective tales to which we will shortly turn. Pfaall also shares the imaginativeness that in Dupin and other Poe characters is the necessary complement of reason. Indeed, some of the most sustained passages in the tale are those devoted to visions:

"Fancy revelled in the wild and dreamy regions of the moon. Imagination, feeling herself for once unshackled, roamed at will among the ever-changing wonders of a shadowy and unstable land. Now there were hoary and time-honored forests, and craggy precipices, and waterfalls tumbling with a loud noise into abysses without a bottom. . . . But fancies such as these were not the sole possessors of my brain. Horrors of a nature most stern and most appalling would too frequently obtrude themselves upon my mind, and shake the innermost depths of my soul with the bare supposition of their possibility." (II, 80-81)

The unshackling of imagination applies not only to Pfaall but to his creator as well. The deeper he involves himself in his character's dilemma, the more plausible it becomes: Poe begins to take the whole enterprise seriously; what had begun as a flight of comic fancy gradually assumes the shape of a metaphysical journey. Only as Pfaall makes his immediate approach to the moon, and as the manuscript nears its end, does the parodic intention come again to the fore. The parody, then, is a framework embracing a narrative that took, perhaps in an unanticipated way, a direction of its own.[18]

Even critics who are most alert to comic and satiric elements have recognized the necessity of relating these to Poe's serious aims. Discussing "MS. Found in a Bottle," Mooney remarks: "The fact that in this tale he may have been satirizing what he regarded as Gothic excess need not proscribe any interpretation of the tale for ultimately serious purposes. Indeed, the possibility of satiric intent opens up for explication another dimension of Kierkegaardian absurdity as a factor in the modern literary theme of anxiety."[19] In his chapter on Poe's comic fiction, "The Short Story as Grotesque," Davidson concludes that even the absurd stories "are indeed 'poems,' and Poe remained a poet even when he was contributing some of his most uninspired narratives to the periodicals. . . . Eventually the tales investigated some of the same themes which had been the province of the poems: the extent to which man can give idea and meaning to the farther range

[18] A similar view is advanced by Arthur Robson Quinn, *Edgar Allan Poe: A Critical Biography*, p. 215, and Edmund Reiss, "The Comic Setting of 'Hans Pfaall,'" *American Literature*, 29 (1957), pp. 306-309. For the view that the comic frame was added on the advice of a friend see J. O. Bailey, "Sources for Poe's *Arthur Gordon Pym*, 'Hans Pfaall,' and Other Pieces," *PMLA*, 57 (1942), pp. 531-532.

[19] "Poe's Gothic Wasteland," 265.

of experience beyond mere sense; the method of making known the variables of meaning itself—these symbolic tangents which the word and the image can establish in the human mind; and the tragic dislocation of man in a world which, however well that world assumes an order in the mind, nevertheless forbids any ultimate participation or sense of kinship."[20]

The tales about women express a similar aim; so, for that matter, do most of Poe's writings, whether early or late, whether in poetry or in prose. This is not by any means to deny the comic element in Poe, but merely to recommend caution in assessing it, and a willingness to see it within the predominantly serious design of his work as a whole.

Detective Tales

The circumscription of persons that we have seen in the poems and the tales about women is a given of the detective tales as well. Like the ladies and their lovers, Dupin and his companion live in cloistered intimacy: "Our seclusion was perfect. We admitted no visitors. . . . We existed within ourselves alone" (IV, 151). The pair create an atmosphere for dreaming, their main pastime during the day, by blocking out the sunlight and reading, writing, or talking until nightfall, when they go out into the city. These forays merely lengthen the dreaming period, for the two are alone together even in the streets, where their sole concern is "that infinity of mental excitement which quiet observation can afford" (IV, 152). The inner life in the shuttered house and the outer life in the busy city are thus, at the same time, polarities and complements. There is a similar doubleness in Dupin himself. Noticing how differently Dupin acts when possessed by one of his ratiocinative moods, the narrator speculates "upon the old philosophy of the Bi-Part Soul," and amuses himself "with the fancy of a double Dupin—the creative and the resolvent"

[20] *Poe: A Critical Study*, pp. 154-155.

(IV, 152). The pattern extends to Dupin's modes of detection as well. There are, on the one hand, "inductions" (IV, 172), corresponding respectively with the "*à posteriori*" [sic] approach (IV, 174) that Dupin mentions, and the *a priori* that he does not refer to by name but frequently employs. To the two "conditions" of "Eleonora" (IV, 236)—that of lucid reason, associated with the past, and that of shadow and doubt, associated with the present—"The Murders in the Rue Morgue" thus responds with a complete binary system:

inner	outer
dream	observation
deduction	induction
a priori	*a posteriori*
creative	resolvent

These pairs are not "hateful contraries" but rather, like Dupin and the narrator, coequal partners; the relationship is a reciprocity in which each member works with and for its complement. While reserving perfect reciprocity—in which cause and effect are completely interchangeable—for God, Poe recognized that a lower, more contingent reciprocity was characteristic of human life (VIII, 272). A thoroughgoing reciprocity, such as we find in "The Murders in the Rue Morgue," relates the paired elements so intimately to one another that they all but merge. This can be seen, for instance, in the pairing of dream and observation. The superiority of the analytical mind, says the narrator, "lies not so much in the validity of the inference as in the quality of the observation" (IV, 148). With Dupin, the greater intellect of the two, observation becomes " 'a species of necessity' " (IV, 155). This is not to equate Dupin with Berenice's Egaeus, who stares obsessively and intensely at objects of no interest. But there is in both men, Dupin and Egaeus, a strong imaginative element. Dupin's reflective moods are trances (IV, 152); at such times he is, for all practical purposes, a man possessed. The narrator, furthermore, cites imagination as one of Dupin's great virtues, and concludes "that the ingenious are always fanciful, and the *truly* imaginative never otherwise than analytic" (IV, 150). It is misleading to contend, as Davidson does, that "the ratiocinative exercise of the detective is simply an allegory of how the mind may impose its interior logic on exterior circumstances."[21] What the story demonstrates, on the contrary, is that "exterior circumstance" has a logic of its own that the human mind is able to comprehend. Dupin's mind operates *in* the world, not *on* it. Observation, far from being incompatible with imagination, works with it in a partnership as close as the partnership of the narrator and Dupin. For an investigator like Dupin there is no way to see facts but imaginatively. If he is a seer he is a seer of circumstance.

The second sight Dupin seems to possess is only a higher form of insight. To have *in*sight is literally to see in—to enter the interiority of another through an act of identification. Interpreters share this faculty with writers: "Indeed the author of Crusoe must have possessed, above all other faculties, what has been termed the faculty of *identification*—that dominion exercised by volition over imagination which enables the mind to lose its own, in a fictitious, individuality. This includes, in a very great degree, the power of abstraction . . ." (VIII, 170). The narrator of "The Murders in the Rue Morgue" illustrates the process by showing how the interpreter would play a game of draughts in which only four kings remain on the board: "It is obvious that here the victory can be decided (the players being at all equal) only by some *recherché* movement, the result of some strong exertion of the intellect. Deprived of ordinary resources, the analyst throws himself into the spirit of his opponent, identifies himself therewith, and not unfrequently sees thus, at a glance, the sole methods . . . by which he may seduce into error or hurry into miscalculation" (IV, 147-148). This process of analysis differs in no material way from the process by which an interpreter analyses a text. If it is a cipher-

[21] *Poe: A Critical Study*, p. 221. Cf. Robert Daniel, "Poe's Detective God," *Furioso*, 6 (1951), pp. 45-52, and Lynen, *The Design of the Present*, pp. 237ff.

text, as in "The Gold-Bug," the interpreter's first job is " 'to divide the sentence into the natural division intended by the cryptographist' " (v, 137). If it is a literary text (such as, for example, Dickens' *Barnaby Rudge*) the procedure remains the same: ". . . *the intention once known*, the *traces* of the design can be found upon every page" (xi, 49). Identification with the intention of a writer leads the interpreter back, full circle, to an even earlier identification: "While on this topic we may as well offer an ill-considered opinion of our own as to the *intention of the poet* in the delineation of the Dane. It must have been well known to Shakespeare, that a leading feature in certain more intense classes of intoxication . . . is an almost irresistible impulse to counterfeit a farther degree of excitement than actually exists. Analogy would lead any thoughtful person to suspect the same impulse in madness. . . . This, Shakespeare *felt*—not thought. He felt it through his marvellous power of *identification* with humanity at large . . ." (xii, 227). The power of identification, then, is something shared by the author and the interpreter, whether his "text" happens to be words on a page or events in the everyday world. In the exercise of this power the interpreter thus follows the lead of Friedrich Schleiermacher, the founder of modern hermeneutics, who held that we comprehend a text by going back into the consciousness that made it, in order to relive its signifying acts. There is no reason to believe that Poe read Schleiermacher, or that he had to. As a reader and a reviewer he was in contact with developments in the rising, related disciplines of Biblical and grammatical study, and could comment, in his review of Stephens' *Arabia Petraea*, on "the vast importance of critical and philological research in dissipating the obscurities and determining the exact sense of the Scriptures . . ." (x, 1). In order to understand a prophetic text, Poe argues, the interpreter must focus on the literal meaning of the words. But interpretation is a to-and-fro process. Consequently the hermeneutist must not only move very close to the page, as it were, but far away from it; if the words he studies are prophetic he must view them against the horizon of the future:

"We mean to say that, in *all* instances, the most strictly literal interpretation will apply. There is, no doubt, much unbelief founded upon the *obscurity* of the prophetic expression. . . . That many prophecies are absolutely unintelligible should not be denied—it is a part of their essence that they should be. The obscurity, like the apparently irrelevant detail, has its object in the providence of God. Were the words of inspiration, affording insight into the events of futurity, *at all times* so pointedly clear that he who runs might read, they would in many cases . . . afford a rational ground for unbelief in the inspiration of their authors . . . for it would be supposed that these distinct words, exciting union and emulation among Christians, had thus been merely the means of working out their own accomplishment. It is for this reason that the most of the predictions become intelligible only when viewed from the proper point of observation —the period of fulfilment." (x, 10)

The interpreter—whether he is reading the faces of an opponent in a game or lines in a text—creates a *figure* and a *ground*, the latter being the general field in which an object appears, the former being the object itself. In his interpretation of *Hamlet*, Poe presents the figure of Hamlet—the concrete, individual phenomenon as given in the play—against the ground, or general field of common experience. He asks, in effect: What do most people know about certain kinds of intoxication? Narrowing down to a smaller group (thoughtful persons), he then asks whether a member of such a group would see an analogy between the behavior of an intoxicated person and the behavior of a mad one.

In "The Mystery of Marie Rogêt" Dupin combines these techniques in order to recreate the consciousness, motivation, and probable behavior of the girl's murderer, of a theoretical gang, and of the girl herself. Employing the third-person, Dupin reconstructs the thinking of the hypothetical killer from a moment just after the murder to the moment he decides to flee: " 'The sounds of life encompass his path. A dozen times he hears or fancies the step of an observer. Even the very lights from the city bewilder him. . . . His sole thought is immediate escape. He turns his back *forever* upon those dreadful shrubberies, and flees as from the wrath to come' " (v, 55). Dupin reasons that a gang of men, by their very numbers, would not have felt the terror of the lone criminal, and, having the advantage of manpower, would have cleaned up any telltale evidence. Since such evidence was found, the involvement of a gang becomes an improbable inference, and Dupin concludes that the murder was the act of an individual. In his reconstruction of the victim's behavior, Dupin identifies through use of the first-person:

"We may imagine her thinking thus—'I am to meet a certain person for the purpose of elopement, or for certain other purposes known only to myself. It is necessary that there be no chance of interruption. . . . I will give it to be understood that I shall visit and spend the day with my aunt at the Rue des Drômes—I will tell St. Eustache not to call for me until dark. . . . Now, if it were my design to return *at all* . . . it would not be my policy to bid St. Eustache call; for, calling, he will be *sure* to ascertain that I have played him false—a fact of which I might keep him for ever in ignorance, by leaving home without notifying him of my intention, by returning before dark, and by then stating that I had been to visit my aunt in the Rue des Drômes. But, as it is my design *never* to return . . . the gaining of time is the only point about which I need give myself any concern.' " (v, 44-45)

In this account Dupin connects "intention" with "design" just as Poe did in his reading of Dickens. The association is not casual for the two terms are used in tandem throughout the criticism,[22] designating, on the one hand, the aims of authors, and on the other the aims of the characters they create. For Dupin as for Poe, every language-using being—

[22] See, for example, Poe's discussion of Hawthorne's *Twice-Told Tales*, xi, 108-109; also, viii, 208; x, 117, 118, 127, 131; xi, 45-61.

a man on the street, an author, a character, or God Himself—is endowed with intentionality. Thus Dupin uses the same methods in reconstructing the thoughts of Marie Rogêt as in determining the aims of the newspapermen whose articles, throughout much of the narrative, are his texts:

"The first aim of the writer is to show, from the brevity of the interval between Marie's disappearance and the finding of the floating corpse, that this corpse cannot be that of Marie. The reduction of this interval to its smallest possible dimension, becomes thus, at once, an object with the reasoner. . . . The paragraph beginning 'It is folly to suppose that the murder, etc.,' however it appears as printed in L'Etoile, may be imagined to have existed actually *thus* in the brain of its inditer—'It is folly to suppose that the murder . . . could have been committed soon enough to have enabled her murderers to throw the body into the river before midnight . . . and to suppose at the same time . . . that the body was *not* thrown in until *after* midnight'—a sentence sufficiently inconsequential in itself, but not so utterly preposterous as the one printed." (v, 22-23)

Dupin perceives a discrepany between intention and achievement and, instead of merely labelling it, demonstrates it through an improvised monologue. Such tactics are common in these stories, which are concerned with solutions to practical and more or less urgent problems. In "The Purloined Letter" Dupin draws an implicit parallel between himself and a schoolboy who was skilled at a certain guessing game. Surmising that the boy was able to identify with the playmate who decided whether the marbles would be "odd" or "even," Dupin asks him to explain his technique: " 'When I wish to find out how wise, or how stupid, or how good, or how wicked is any one, or what are his thoughts at the moment, I fashion the expression of my face, as accurately as possible, in accordance with the expression of his, and then wait to see what thoughts or sentiments arise in my mind and heart, as if to match or correspond with the expression' " (vi, 41). The schoolboy, like Rameau's nephew, is a plastic, "physical" mimic who enters into the very gesture and body of the other. The older, more pensive Dupin, being less concerned with tactics than with the interpretation of a complex circumstantial design, is more "detached." When the reflective mood is upon him he is indeed, as we have seen, a man possessed: "His manner at these moments was frigid and abstract; his eyes were vacant in expression; while his voice, usually a rich tenor, rose into a treble which would have sounded petulantly but for the deliberateness and entire distinctness of the enunciation" (IV, 152). That might be a description of Roderick Usher as his consciousness tunes itself to the harmonies of a world beyond the gulf, or of Vankirk, the character in "Mesmeric Revelation" who communicates with that world and reports on it to the man who has placed him in the mesmeric state. This is one way in which the "beyond" gets into the tales of detection. It also enters through the notion of design, which embraces not only everyday reality and literary creation but the divine creation as well. In his literary application of the idea of design, Dupin anticipates the procedures of Martin Heidegger, who views a statement against a horizon of expression that it fails to reach. The interpreter, in such a case, "fills in" what he perceives to be missing when intention is compared with achievement: " 'The sentence in question has but one meaning, as it stands; and this meaning I have fairly stated: but it is material that we go behind the mere words, for an idea which these words have obviously intended, and failed to convey. It was the design of the journalist to say that . . . it was improbable that the assassins would have ventured to bear the corpse to the river before midnight' " (V, 23). The narrator of "The Mystery of Marie Rogêt," more consciously concerned with the beyond, begins his story with a quotation from Novalis, who saw both a "real" and an "ideal" series of events (V, 2), and ends with an examination of coincidence in light of the "Calculus of Probabilities" (V, 65) and the intentions of God. The idea here is that there are two kinds of design, the human and the divine, but that the connections between them are problematic. That such considerations enter such a work at all affirms once again Poe's tendency to see every phenomenon in relation to something greater than itself. That these considerations are carried no further than they are indicates Poe's recognition that the detective tale had boundaries that it could not cross without becoming another kind of work. What sort of work could deal more fully with these problems will be seen after we have finished our reading of the remaining tales.

"MS. Found in a Bottle"

"Of my country and of my family I have little to say. Ill usage and length of years have driven me from the one, and estranged me from the other" (II, 1). The family in Poe is curiously everything and nothing, a point on some lost horizon and a complete fate. But in reality the two extremes are very close. The narrator of "MS. Found in a Bottle," like Tamerlane, is a man of problematic origins. He has no family history, only a kind of racial mark; he is the extreme ahistorical being. His family exists only as a memory, private and discrete, that he cannot give up. This ahistorical being fears discontinuity as it fears death; consequently, nothing could be more foolish than to sacrifice what little hold he has on his past—this past *must* be mentioned.

No sooner has he done so than he faces a dilemma. He does not know this phenomenon to which he refers. His situation resembles that of a man quickly sketching a landscape. In the background lies something that intrigues him and that he cannot make out. His only solution is to render it quickly, vaguely—better some stroke than none at all. The difference between Poe's narrator and the artist is that the narrator sees it habitually, must render it in his art, can never quite succeed. His second task, in order to minimize his discontinuity, is to give this murky space of time, this mysterious smudge in the background, a quality that will keep it from submerging in the flow of time. The origins must be placed outside of mere history, with all its economic, psychological, social, political variables.

What concept broadens the family's existence in time while saving it from the vagaries of historical succession? The concept of race. There, then, is the rationale underlying the tendency, in so many of the tales, to introduce the family and to enlarge on it while at the same time preserving the narrator's sense of isolation. Here, for example, is the beginning of "William Wilson": "Let me call myself, for the present, William Wilson. The fair page now lying before me need not be sullied with my real appellation. This has been already too much an object for the scorn—for the horror—for the detestation of my race" (III, 299). The first sentence of "Eleonora" reads: "I am come of a race noted for vigor of fancy and ardor of passion" (IV, 236). Similarly, the consort of "Berenice" declares: "My baptismal name is Egaeus; that of my family I will not mention. Yet there are no towers in the land more time-honored than my gloomy, gray, hereditary halls. Our line has been called a race of visionaries . . ." (II, 16). Even when the family is presented at length, as in "The Fall of the House of Usher," the unit is isolated, dehistoricized, "racial": "I had learned, too, the very remarkable fact, that the stem of the Usher race, all time-honored as it was, had put forth, at no period, any enduring branch; in other words, that the entire family lay in the direct line of descent . . ." (III, 275).

Isolated, the narrator of "MS. Found in a Bottle" is full of himself, or rather of his own mind: "Hereditary wealth afforded me an education of no common order, and a contemplative turn of mind enabled me to methodize the stores which early study diligently garnered up" (II, 1). He reads the German moralists and accuses himself of rigid thought patterns and want of imagination, the accusation serving as a strategy for making his fantastic adventures seem credible. But the principal result of this self-portraiture is to reveal a man of high consciousness, a kind of epistemic being who moves through the terrors toward a deeper knowledge.

Poe dealt often with the theme of fatal descent, of a fall into seeming annihilation: "MS. Found in a Bottle," "A Descent into the Maelstrom," "The Pit and the Pendulum," and so on. The interesting thing is that the relationship of victim and victimizer, of man and nature, is rarely direct. Some object—some physical thing made by human beings—insinuates itself between them. Poe's characters do not fall directly into watery abysses; they descend into them on ships. In "MS." there is in fact a double descent, doubly mediated. As the ship on which the victim is a paying passenger is about to break up within the vortex, he falls from it *onto another ship*.

We are rarely conscious, in Poe, of the human origins of a made thing; he makes us aware precisely of its "madeness," its artificiality. Poe confronts and represents, as few authors before him, the alienated and alienating quality of the technological environment. Marx, born within a decade of Poe, discusses the same phenomenon under the heading of reification (*Vergegenständlichung*), the process through which man turns his labor, and in a sense himself, into a thing. Like Marx, Poe was disturbed by the process, but in a less "intellectual" way. The fear his characters experience is a primitive, animistic anxiety, closer to the *Angst* experienced in the German tradition of the grotesque. The source of this fear, as it is presented in the post-Romantic phase of that literature, is a *Tücke des Objekts*, or "malice of the inanimate object."[23] What this produces, to put it simply, is the fear that "things" are "out to get you." One might expect to find these qualities exclusively (given Poe's feelings on the subject) in the technological object: "The air now became intolerably hot, and was loaded with spiral exhalations similar to those arising from heated iron" (II, 3). And later: "As I placed

[23] Wolfgang Kayser, *The Grotesque in Art and Literature*, trans. Ulrich Weisstein (Bloomington, 1963), p. 110.

my foot upon the upper step of the companion-ladder, I was startled by a loud, humming noise, like that occasioned by the rapid revolution of a mill-wheel . . ." (II, 3). As a complement to the literal technological object we are given, then, a technological aura through metaphor. This second degree of mediation occurs, for example, at the end of the following paragraph. Although there is no mediating object here (such as a refracting lens), the light behaves as if there were: "It [the sun] gave out no light, properly so called, but a dull and sullen glow without reflection, as if all its rays were polarized" (II, 5). The water itself is forced from its natural mode of being, and it is at least in part this distortion that precipitates terror: "All around were horror, and thick gloom, and a black sweltering desert of ebony.—Superstitious terror crept by degrees into the spirit of the old Swede, and my own soul was wrapped up in silent wonder" (II, 6).

A second distinguishing characteristic is the peculiar, to-and-fro quality, as of a pendulum swinging, that permeates the description. For the general progress of the ship is not, as one might have thought, downward; it is both downward and upward: "At times we gasped for breath at an elevation beyond the albatross—at times became dizzy with the velocity of our descent into some watery hell . . ." (II, 6-7). The pendulum is a nonce analogy, and in a sense misleading. The narrator achieves a mixed effect of doubleness and inversion, an effect by which one phenomenon is both itself and another, or remains itself even in becoming another. There is, as we have already seen, a zigzag of up and down; we see it again in the second ship (the ship that saves the narrator only to carry him down with it—saves him, in other words, for destruction): "When we first discovered her, her bows were alone to be seen, as she rose slowly from the dim and horrible gulf beyond her. For a moment of intense terror she paused upon the giddy pinnacle, as if in contemplation of her own sublimity, then trembled and tottered, and—came down" (II, 7). She paused as if in contemplation: these few words suggest the elusive oxymoronic motion—of motion shot through with stasis—which pervades the narrative. The phenomenon is familiar in ekphrastic poetry, where the spatial object seems about to free itself into the flow of time. Despite the velocity of the phantom ship, it remains somehow an extratemporal form which at times seems not to be moving at all. The timelessness derives from the velocity itself, which is so extreme that one cannot "keep up" with it. After a while the victim simply gets used to it, much as a driver, in what traffic experts speak of as the "velocitation" phenomenon, gets used to high speed (although periodically, with Poe's victims, there is a return of feeling, one's consciousness reviving once more with the sensation of movement).

This mixed effect of both this and that—of motion that tends toward stasis, of ascents that become descents—casts its shadow on the occupants of the ship as well. Of an old man who passes, the narrator observes: "His manner was a wild mixture of the peevishness of second childhood, and the solemn dignity of a God" (II, 9). With his fall onto the rigging of the second ship, the narrator has entered a new and higher kind of mediation. The space within the annihilating vortex is a space-between. Here one moves in a continuum beyond the realm of habit and custom without, however, attaining the gulf beyond. The space of the voyager is normally horizontal. A ship moves on a surface that is more or less a plane as do animals or vehicles or man himself. Man can also voyage up, as in a balloon ascension, or down, as in a bathysphere. Although he may meander, or get lost, the intentional direction of his movement is generally "straight toward." Now a vortex is as much a space-*toward* as a space-between: in a vortex one is "on the way." But there are differences. The first difference is that one's descent in the vortex is gradual, notwithstanding the velocity of motion. One cannot go down very fast when one is also going round and round. In this connection we are reminded of Poe's concern with gradation, the shades of development by which one condition accedes to another. All that must be said of that subject here is that one cannot breach the gulf beyond all at once: *Novelty* is preceded by stages of the merely novel. The second point I want to make is that the vortex—the pure spiral movement—is the most equivocal of motions. It is a descent that resists descent, a movement that twists away from itself only to be twisted back to itself *by* itself. It is as near to non-movement as any movement can be. At the same time it combines two other kinetic "figures," the circle, traditionally symbolic of harmony and perfection, and the pure descent, symbolic of annihilation and death. The vortex is a function of time, however, as well as of space, an integration of the present and that "spirit of Eld" (II, 13) of which the crew is the corporate embodiment. One of the victim's fears is that the ship, even in that headlong southward rush that separates the two descents into the vortex, will never move enough. What if something stays its motion forever, freezing it in motionless time? "We are surely doomed to hover continually upon the brink of Eternity, without taking a final plunge into the abyss" (II, 12). Cut off from his own past, unable to achieve his future, the victim exists in a kind of indefinite present, an eternal moment of terror.

Toward what fate is the mysterious ship moving? The answer cannot be known, and yet the goal lies, for lack of a better term, within the realm of knowledge. In truth such knowledge is a new mode of being that no human art can render. Consciousness can experience it only by anticipation. Now we can see the function of novelty: it is the human expression of the inexpressible: "A feeling, for which I have no name, has taken possession of my soul—a sensation which will admit of no analysis, to which the lessons of by-gone time are inadequate, and for which I fear futurity itself will offer me no key. To a mind constituted like my own, the latter consideration is an evil. I shall never—I know that I shall never—be satisfied with regard to the nature of my conceptions. Yet it is not wonderful that these conceptions are indefinite, since they have their origin in sources so utterly novel. A new sense—a new entity is added to my soul" (II, 9). One acquires this new sense, despite the physical presence of others, in isolation. The others may also be preoccupied with the challenge to know (for them, too, existence seems a reverie). Yet for the victim nothing remains more opaque than the other: "Incomprehensible men! Wrapped up in meditations of a kind which I cannot divine, they pass me by unnoticed" (II, 9). In the following section the victim himself finds "new room for meditation" (II, 10). What we shall never know is whether the contents of those separate meditations have anything in common. For the others on the ship are not human beings, they are phantasmagoria of time, shapes that move in a realm beyond language, ineffable forms dwelling barely within the sphere that embraces the narrator. It is this that explains their fantastic old age: they are about to pass to the gulf beyond.

Until it "surfaces," the content of one's meditation is also unknown: "While musing upon the singularity of my fate, I unwittingly daubed with a tar-brush the edges of a neatly-folded studding-sail which lay near me on a barrel. The studding-sail is now bent upon the ship, and the thoughtless touches of the brush are spread out into the word DISCOVERY" (II, 10). Again the human impulse is mediated by the technological object: the ground of expression is a thing, a functioning part of a functioning ship. Yet this thing is not here *as* technological; its function in the management of the voyage entirely subserves its epistemological and ontological value. When the sail unfurls, the action does not facilitate motion on the sea so much as it reveals the word. In this act the victim declares himself as one who does not know what he thinks until he hears what he has to say, or until he sees.

The difference between hearing and seeing, between oral and visual expression, may count, in this case, for more than immediately appears. Many efforts have been made to establish Poe's psychosexual stages; curiously, no one seems to have noticed Poe's stages in the sequence, from oral to chirographic to typographic, of verbal expression. This is not the place to examine such a complex problem in detail. Yet we cannot help observing that here, as in "Hans Pfaall," *The*

Journal of Julius Rodman, and *Pym*, the narrative is in the form of a manuscript, and that a central act in the story—the drawing of the word DISCOVERY—is closely related to the act of composing in script. What this form of expression confirms is precisely the narrator's isolation. How few are the narrators in Poe who function orally in a community of men! Speech between characters is scandalously opaque. Consider, for example, the oral "exchange" in "The Cask of Amontillado." The function of Montresor's words is solely to *disguise* (a verbal complement to the mask motif of the carnival). Neither Montresor's nor Fortunato's spoken words penetrate the other. And where are the meaningful oral exchanges between Poe's narrators and their female friends? The narrator does not speak to his lover; he speaks *of* her. I am suggesting, then, that writing substitutes for speech, allowing men who cannot talk directly to other human beings to record their experiences: "Ye who read are still among the living: but I who write shall have long since gone on my way into the region of shadows. For indeed strange things shall happen, and secret things be known, and many centuries shall pass away, ere these memorials be seen of men. And, when seen, there will be some to disbelieve, and some to doubt, and yet a few who will find much to ponder upon in the characters here graven with a stylus of iron" (II, 147). Looking now at the many tales in which the narrator addresses the reader without the mediation of a discovered document, we see another type of substitute for oral, interpersonal communication. For these first-person narratives are monologues, and the reason Poe turned to them may have been similar to the reason he turned to the "manuscript"—the monologue perfectly expresses isolation, expresses it *in* isolation. If we imagine the expanse of a narrative as a communications space, a circumscribed spatial and temporal zone in which the author addresses the reader, then we see that the monologue, like the manuscript, takes up all the space there is. It is a total speech and a speech in isolation.

The crew's reaction to the narrator in "MS. Found in a Bottle" underlines the close relation between language and being: their failure to perceive the word he paints is the corollary of their failure to perceive the fact that he exists. He turns therefore to an audience of readers—becomes in effect an author. To write words that others can read is to prove the reality of his experience and of his very being; it is to put one's faith—as any writer must do, including the man with the stylus—in the guardianship of language. What the reader gets in the bargain is not merely writing but handwriting. A manuscript that shows the author's own hand bears something of his presence both materially and spiritually. It bears it materially insofar as the value of a manuscript resembles the value of a book, which, as Poe explains in the essay on anastatic printing that we considered in discussing the poems, is "a compound of its literary value and its physical or mechanical value as the product of physical labor applied to the physical material" (XIV, 158). It bears his presence spiritually inasmuch as the book is not only "*physique*" but "*morale*" (XIV, 159)—not only body, as it were, but also spirit. In contrast with works printed in type, which we tend (says Poe) to value for physique, the handwritten work, by bringing the reader closer to the writer and the "literary value" (XIV, 158) of his statement, inevitably "elevate[s] the value of its *morale*" (XIV, 159).

The adventure experienced by the narrator tests his ability to interpret and intensifies his will to know. Indeed, the longer the voyage continues, the less the threat to the body and the greater the challenge to consciousness. The vital energies flow upward to the mind; the "passenger" becomes a philosopher-in-motion. In order to determine the nature of the ship, consciousness backs into the problem, as so often happens in the poems, by negation: "What she *is not*, I can easily perceive—what she *is* I fear it is impossible to say" (II, 10).

As consciousness advances in time, recollection grows, for time is circular. In the future one returns to one's origins:

". . . there will occasionally flash across my mind a sensation of familiar things, and there is always mixed up with such indistinct shadows of recollection, an unaccountable memory of old foreign chronicles and ages long ago" (II, 10). There is, then, no pure futurity. There is only a *now* and a *then*, the latter term designating all that was and will be again, the former signifying what is left. Within the *now* are enacted all the tales of victimization, whether by nature, the manmade environment, or by man himself; whereas works set in the afterlife (such as "The Colloquy of Monos and Una," or "The Conversation of Eiros and Charmion") are attempts to render *then*.

The spatial circumstances of the narrator closely approximate, at two points in the tale, his situation in time. I am thinking of the first and second vortices, and the fact that both are, in more than one way, cyclical. The first way relates to the tendency of the vortex to self-repetition: having gone around once, the spiral goes around again, and so on. The second way also involves repetition inasmuch as the first descent into the watery abyss is repeated in the second, providing a return to the point at which one began. As in "The Island of the Fay," which we shall examine at the end of the chapter, the cycle is indissociable from the circle. In the visual sphere, cycle defines itself as circularity, and all the more so in the case of Poe, for whom the circle was a frequent motif. In order to examine this phenomenon we must refer again briefly to the technological milieu. What we have both in "MS." and in "A Descent into the Maelstrom" is a kind of environing chamber. The towering ice that surrounds the ship in the earlier story resembles "ramparts," and "the walls of the universe" (II, 13, 14). In the later story, a similar conception is developed: " 'The boat appeared to be hanging, as if by magic, midway down, upon the interior surface of a funnel vast in circumference, prodigious in depth, and whose perfectly smooth sides might have been mistaken for ebony, but for the bewildering rapidity with which they spun around, and for the gleaming and ghastly radiance they shot forth, as the rays of the full moon . . . streamed in a flood of golden glory along the black walls, and far away down into the inmost recesses of the abyss' " (II, 242). The vortex, in a word, is a kinetic chamber. The narrator's term for this surrounding space, in the final paragraph of "MS." is, appropriately, architectural: "Oh, horror upon horror! the ice opens suddenly to the right, and to the left, and we are whirling dizzily, in immense concentric circles, round and round the borders of a gigantic amphitheatre, the summit of whose walls is lost in the darkness and the distance" (II, 14).

The victim finds himself polarized. On the one hand the prospect of a final descent, which threatens his very being, fills him with horror. On the other hand, that being is epistemic, and will take any risk to know. Therein lies the fatality.

The writer of MS. gives no hint of an external fate directing his life. The nearest thing to it is his heredity, but that, as we have seen, is not very near. His fate is himself, his very being: "To conceive the horror of my sensations is, I presume, utterly impossible; yet a curiosity to penetrate the mysteries of these awful regions, predominates even over my despair, and will reconcile me to the most hideous aspect of death. It is evident that we are hurrying onwards to some exciting knowledge—some never-to-be-imparted secret, whose attainment is destruction. Perhaps this current leads us to the southern pole itself" (II, 14). Poe regularly associates the return to origins with descent. As the primal state is that from which man rises, as from a sleep, so it is that to which he must descend when his vital period is over. The descent is not confined to a watery medium. The place of "demise" may also be in the earth, as in a vault to which one is carried, or a grave into which one is lowered. The chamber may be located anywhere. It can even be above the ground, in an apartment or a house, in which case descent is accomplished by the simple act of lying down.

In geographical terms Poe conceived the ultimate journey as a journey south. There may be a biographical influence here, as Leslie Fiedler argues, for Poe was a Southerner who went north, and who regarded the South as in certain respects his truest home. Or it may be, as Edwin Fussell suggests, that the southern region represented a version of the western frontier, always for Poe a realm of exciting novelty and adventurous possibilities.[24] But whatever else it was, the southern Pole was above all the unknown, a secret space as yet unexplored, a wonderful and terrible gulf beyond. The southern Pole stands as the ultimate space within the realm of human time, ultimate but not final, for the episode of descent is open-ended. It does not end time; it mediates between the old time and the new, "timeless" time that can be known only in the condition of pure novelty. It is an episode because it appears, in a mediate position, between the *now* and the *then*; it is a process broken off, an arrested interval: "But little time will be left me to ponder upon my destiny!—the circles rapidly grow small—we are plunging madly within the grasp of the whirlpool—and amid a roaring, and bellowing, and thundering of ocean and of tempest, the ship is quivering, oh God! and—going down" (II, 14-15).

The ontological economy of the narrative is finally an economy of the present. Between the obscurity of the past and the obscurity of the future lies the space of the episode, which never really ends. The first time the phantom ship is seen descending, the event is recorded in the past: "For a moment of intense terror she paused upon the giddy pinnacle, as if in contemplation of her own sublimity, then trembled and tottered, and—came down." In the final paragraph the emphasis falls on a kind of indefinitely extended now, the dominant grammatical form being the present participle, which renders the event as something still going on: "The circles rapidly grow small—we are plunging madly within the grasp of the whirlpool—and amid a roaring, and bellowing, and thundering of ocean and tempest, the ship is quivering, oh God! and—going down."

[24] Fiedler touches on the problem in *Love and Death in the American Novel* (Cleveland and New York, 1962); for Fussell's more extended analysis see the chapter on Poe in his *Frontier: American Literature and the American West*, pp. 132-174.

"The Narrative of Arthur Gordon Pym of Nantucket"

The ship in the conventional tale of nautical adventure floats within the sphere of praxis; space for the mariner is, traditionally, horizontal, volitional, the space of opportunity and conquest. In *Pym*, on the other hand, space is circumscriptive, non-volitional, a space of impending victimization. The ship is less a vessel than a chamber: in the hold where Augustus secretes him, Pym experiences premature burial.

The boys are nearly drowned on the *Ariel*, while Pym's mode of being aboard *The Grampus* is that of a creature secreted, silent, not known to exist: in a word, the ship is an instrument of victimization. Poe's vessels do not sail to ports: "to ship," in Poe, is to be shipwrecked, or, at the least, to sail off out of control into the unknown. In order to free himself for his victimization, Pym must break certain ordinary human bonds. This he does easily, although it appears for a moment at the beginning of the book that we shall have to do with a normal family: "My name is Arthur Gordon Pym. My father was a respectable trader in sea-stores at Nantucket, where I was born. My maternal grandfather was an attorney in good practice" (III, 5). It is surprising that many readers miss the implications that this opening paragraph lays bare. We notice, first of all, a lack of transition between the first and third sentences. It is not the bare seriality that surprises. What we are not prepared for—that for which we have no grammatical or syntactic foundation—is the way in which the grandfather, and after him Augustus's father Mr. Barnard, completely supplant the mysterious father of sentence two. Anyone else would have gone on to write: "My father having died while I was still quite young, I came under the care of my maternal grandfather," or something of the kind. But Pym, instead of erasing the father, leaps over him to a more remote, more "ancestral" figure, the grandfather, who is easier to reject. In truth, Pym has no family, he belongs rather, as he states early in Chapter II, to a "race." Like other adventurous spirits in Poe he is, from the start, a kind of existentially displaced-person. He also shares with other protagonists a conscious tendency to perverseness. Thus he decides to ship out precisely because of the dangers involved: "For the bright side of the painting I had a limited sympathy. My visions were of shipwreck and famine; of death or captivity among barbarian hordes; of a lifetime dragged out in sorrow and tears, upon some gray and desolate rock, in an ocean unapproachable and unknown. Such visions or desires —for they amounted to desires—are common, I have since been assured, to the whole numerous race of the melancholy among men . . ." (III, 17-18). For another brief moment Pym nearly attains his family. His father, the nullity, does not object to his plans; his mother weeps, and his grandfather vows to disinherit him. But Pym *will* go anyway: the family flares up in order to be quenched. To accomplish his voyage Pym must first perfect his isolation.

It is to this end that he is imprisoned in the darkness of the *Grampus*'s hold, which displays the properties of the ultimate chamber, the coffin: "He brought me, at length, after creeping and winding through innumerable narrow passages, to an iron-bound box, such as is used sometimes for packing fine earthernware. It was nearly four feet high, and full six long, but very narrow" (III, 23). Lapsing into what he only later recognizes as a three-day sleep, Pym discovers that his meat has putrefied, a fact he tries to explain by making the first of several references to the closeness of the atmosphere. These theoretical moments are the first sign of that epistemological urge which will deliver him, like the victim of "The Pit and the Pendulum," to the terrors of consciousness: he cannot "imagine a reason" why Augustus has not returned; he resists the "idea" that Augustus has disappeared forever; he abandons the "notion" that the ship still lingers near Nantucket; and he goes on "Pondering in this manner upon the difficulties of my solitary and cheerless condition. . . ." The first extended encounter with terror comes in the form of a dream:

"While occupied with this thought, however, I fell, in spite of every exertion to the contrary, into a state of profound sleep, or rather stupor. My dreams were of the most terrific description. Every species of calamity and horror befell me. Among other miseries, I was smothered to death between huge pillows, by demons of the most ghastly and ferocious aspect. Immense serpents held me in their embrace, and looked earnestly in my face with their fearfully shining eyes. Then deserts, limitless, and of the most forlorn and awe-inspiring characters, spread themselves out before me. Immensely tall trunks of trees, gray and leafless, rose up in endless succession as far as the eye could reach. Their roots were concealed in wide-spreading morasses, whose dreary water lay intensely black, still, and altogether terrible, beneath. And the strange trees seemed endowed with a human vitality, and, waving to and fro their skeleton arms, were crying to the silent waters for mercy, in the shrill and piercing accents of the most acute agony and despair. The scene changed; and I stood, naked and alone, amid the burning sand-plains of Zahara. At my feet lay crouched a fierce lion of the tropics. Suddenly his wild eyes opened and fell upon me. With a convulsive bound he sprang to his feet, and laid bare his horrible teeth. In another instant there burst from his red throat a roar like the thunder of the firmament, and I fell impetuously to the earth. Stifling in a paroxysm of terror, I at last found myself partially awake. My dream, then, was not all a dream. Now, at least, I was in possession of my senses. The paws of some huge and real monster were pressing heavily upon my bosom—his hot breath was in my ear—and his white and ghastly fangs were gleaming upon me through the gloom." (III, 27-28)

The victim recognizes at the very outset that the experience constitutes a "state" (a word that picks up the sense of "condition" earlier in the paragraph). This state is one of isolation and victimization, and is characterized by an animistic displacement of energy from the mind to external nature. As in "The Masque of the Red Death" some of this energy withholds itself (the roots of the trees "were concealed," the water "lay"). A good deal of it, on the other hand, is released: the trees do wave and the lion does leap. Only the "I" is entirely passive and acted-upon: I was smothered, serpents held me, I fell impetuously to the earth. The springing beast who causes this fall is a more familiar creation than may at first appear. This creature of heated breath and weight and gleaming teeth is a composite of the properties of oppression (these properties being distributed as imagination wills, now in a lover, now in an animal, now in the environment). Although themselves determined (by psychic experiences we lack the data to reconstruct) they are free-floating in respect to their manifestation, like a platonic idea trying on a variety of forms. But if the dream reveals a deep urge to be victimized, it also shows a remarkable congruence between the sleeping and waking worlds. Much of the dream must be interpreted as what Pym calls "anticipative horror" (III, 92), an experience of consciousness that may or may not accord with subsequent experience. The later part of the dream, by contrast, exceeds the consciousness and thus transcends the possibility of illusion. Anticipation becomes prediction (I fear the oppression of a beast and point toward his actual approach) that represents, in turn, a subliminal recognition (I perceive a phenomenon resembling a beast). In the world of Arthur Gordon Pym, the darker reaches of consciousness are directly connected, as by secret passages, to the realm of daylight. The relation parallels the mixture in the narrative of straight adventure and metaphysical quest, the daylight world standing more or less for the first literary type, the concealed world for the second. Wherever the victim turns in these dark, technological spaces he finds himself blocked by metallic barriers. Driven by terror he crawls through the darkness in the hope of deliverance: "At length, upon making a push forward with all the energy I could command, I struck my forehead violently against the sharp corner of an iron-bound crate. The accident only stunned me for a few moments; but I found, to my inexpressible grief, that the quick and violent roll of the vessel had thrown the crate entirely across my path, so as effectually to block up the passage" (III, 31). From the beginning Pym's coffin is a chamber within a chamber (the box that contains him being in turn contained by the hold). All about him is a virtual infinity of walls: "On each side of the narrow passage arose a complete wall of various heavy lumber . . ." (III, 32). Ascending, Pym discovers, in the trap-door over his head, still another confining wall: "It was evident, from the unyielding nature of the resistance, that the hole had either been discovered and effectually nailed up, or that some immense weight had been placed upon it, which it was useless to think of removing" (III, 33). What possesses the capacity to weigh down and at the same time to confine—what but a mass of metal? To his "grief and horror" Augustus discovers that "several fathoms of old chain-cable . . . had been dragged thence to make room for a chest, and were now lying immediately upon the trap!" (III, 55).

We must now consider some further implications of this chamber's non-volitional space. In confining himself to the iron-bound box, Pym surrenders his power to act in the kind of space with which the conventional adventure novel—no less than the realistic or naturalistic novel—is concerned. In his essay "The Upright Posture," the psychiatrist Erwin W. Straus describes this type of space in the following way:

"Within the totality of the new spatial dimensions acquired with upright posture, lateral space is perhaps the most important one. Through the mobility and action of arm and hand, lateral space becomes accessible and relevant for man. In this sector, most of the human crafts originated. Hammer and axe, scythe and sickle, the carpenter's saw, the weaver's shuttle, the potter's wheel, the mason's trowel, the painter's brush—they all relate to lateral space. The list could be extended *ad libitum* but would probably never come to an end, for lateral space is the matrix of primitive and sophisticated skills: of spinning and sewing, stirring and ironing, sowing and husking, soldering and welding, fiddling and golfing, batting and discus-throwing."[25]

[25] *Essays in Phenomenology*, ed. Maurice Natanson (The Hague, 1966), p. 184.

The handling of such space may not have come naturally to Poe, who was committed from early in his career to the pursuit of the pure lyric. But he knew what the magazine reader was paying to get, and adapted himself accordingly. *Pym* is one result; "The Gold-Bug" and the Dupin stories are another. In all of these works there is something like conventional adventurous action. *Pym* offers voyages, fights, hill-climbing, exploration, and the like. In "The Gold-Bug" the narrator and his assistant hunt up a site and dig for buried treasure, while in the detective tales Dupin and his friend stroll about, investigate crimes, and (in "The Murders in the Rue Morgue") set a trap. There is at the same time, in these works, a tendency to pull in the opposite direction, a desire to handle the type of situation with which the author felt more at home. We note, for example, that the walking in the detective tales is essentially heuristic; the animus is a desire to know—to unravel a mystery through the power of consciousness and will. In works with an element of adventure, such as "William Wilson" or "The Pit and the Pendulum," the characters struggle in a manner more typical of classic Poe situations than of the melodramatic pieces on which the works are ostensibly modelled. The duel in "William Wilson" is a struggle of polar forces, each representing different existential possibilities, while the struggle in "The Pit and the Pendulum," characteristically, is between a faceless, arbitrary power and a defenseless being who is fully conscious that he is being manipulated at will. The essential similarity of the adventure tales and the more patently metaphysical works is illustrated by the physical situations of the protagonists in "The Fall of the House of Usher" and "MS. Found in a Bottle." The narrator of the latter is resigned to a physical passivity that is the reflection of his defenseless condition, while at the conclusion of the former work we find Usher merely sitting and rocking as he awaits his end. The function of Poe's countless chambers (and of their variants, such as the coffin, the hold of the ship, and the tomb) is precisely to deny man lateral space. Although the victim can move, he cannot act, in the sense that he can do any of the things that would save him from whatever it is that threatens. Even the normal human operations, such as those enumerated by Straus, are not directed so much toward the material world as toward the achievement of an ontological state. If the walls erected by Poe's masons ("The Black Cat," "The Cask of Amontillado,") are material, they are also existential: to take up mortar and trowel is to victimize the other, and through this process to bring about the victimization of oneself.

It is not surprising, therefore, that Pym finds himself, in the hold of the ship, horizontal and helpless. Whether approaching the iron-bound box for the first time, whether attempting to escape from it or advancing toward the blocked exit—whatever the goal, Pym seems fated to crawl. Although he is sometimes upright, the chief alternative to crawling is lying down. After the storm on the *Grampus*, he is reduced again to the horizontal, while at the end of the novel Pym and his friend are seated, passive and listless, in a drifting canoe. The horizontal makes sophisticated action difficult. On all fours one regresses to what Straus calls "the digestive axis," in which the body moves on a plane, in contrast to the axis of the upright posture, which allows one to move according to the line of vision. The hold in which he is imprisoned being black, Pym has no vision; his regression to the digestive axis corresponds, furthermore, with the total absence of food! To add to his desperation Pym, like Kafka's Gregor Samsa, remains a man even after losing human qualities. On all fours like an animal, Pym finds himself threatened by an actual animal (the dog Tiger), but reacts as a man. In a chamber such as Pym's, the horizontal axis is an axis of terror.

With his return to the "elbow room" of normal lateral space Pym regains his freedom of action, and contributes to the victory of his group over the enemy faction. That is the advantage of the upright posture: it enables you to cope with, and, when necessary, to victimize the other. It is not surprising, then, that so much of Pym's behavior, while in this condition, involves deception, for through deception one can baffle and finally defeat the threatening other: first Pym deceives his grandfather by pretending to be a sailor, then, in Chapters VII and VIII, he masquerades as the corpse of Rogers, an act that leads to the death of the entire enemy party.

But the worst "upright" deception is the one visited upon the survivors of the *Grampus* by the Death Ship. After glancing at two sailors who are lying down, Pym concentrates on a third, who stands, nodding and smiling: "Of a sudden, and all at once, there came wafted over the ocean from the strange vessel . . . a smell, a stench, such as the whole world has no name for—no conception of—hellish—utterly suffocating—insufferable, inconceivable. I gasped for breath . . ." (III, 111). The pattern is a familiar one in the tales: suddenness of sensation, helplessness of the percipient, direct address to the sense that "takes in" the very stuff of the confronted object, threatened loss of vital force symbolized by breath, inexpressible horror. Soon smell gives way to sound, which heightens terror echoically. "As our first loud yell of terror broke forth, it was replied to by something . . . so closely resembling the scream of a human voice that the nicest ear might have been startled and deceived" (III, 112). Pym's advance to knowledge cannot be dissociated from movement in space, for he perceives the hidden horror when a yaw of the vessel—sudden, like the advent of the stench—brings the truth bodily into view: "On his back, from which a portion of the shirt had been torn, leaving it bare, there sat a huge seagull, busily gorging itself with the horrible flesh, its bill and talons deep buried, and its white plumage spattered all over with blood" (III, 112). With the bird we arrive at a second stage of mediation that complements the mediation of technology. We have already seen an animal assimilate the free-floating properties elsewhere attributed to non-organic nature; and later there will be a mysterious white animal with red teeth and claws, regarded by the natives as a noumen and by Pym as a challenge to curiosity. The intention of the devouring bird, on the other hand, is to mediate the impulse to cannibalism: "As the brig moves further round so as to bring us close in view, the bird, with much apparent difficulty, drew out its crimsoned head, and, after eying us for a moment as if stupefied, arose lazily from the body upon which it had been feasting, and, flying directly above our deck, hovered there a while with a portion of clotted and liver-like substance in its beak. The horrid morsel dropped at length with a sullen splash immediately at the feet of Parker. May God forgive me, but now, for the first time, there flashed through my mind a thought, a thought which I will not mention, and I felt myself making a step toward the ensanguined spot" (III, 112-113). Thus, in addition to bringing the possibility of cannibalism to consciousness, the bird also identifies the victim. If the aim of the bird is the mediation of cannibalism, the aim of Pym's speculations about the cause of death—in other words, where the speculations "go"—is to exceed speculation. The function of the mystery is to remain a mystery, and, by so remaining, to prepare for that greater mystery to be encountered at story's end: ". . . but it is utterly useless to form conjectures where all is involved, and will, no doubt, remain for ever involved, in the most appalling and unfathomable mystery" (III, 114).

The truth of cannibalism, for Pym, lies temporarily obscured in his expressed disgust at the idea of eating human flesh: "idea" because the problem centers in his mind, representing civilization's last stand against the rising barbarism of the body; "expressed disgust" because Pym's reluctance arises from the inhibiting presence of the other. As Pym moves toward the ensanguined spot, "I looked upward, and the eyes of Augustus met my own with a degree of intense and eager meaning which immediately brought me to my senses" (III, 113). Although Pym advertises himself as the healthiest of the survivors, the most rational and least prone to regression, he has been gravely tempted. What he fears most is not the prospect of eating another human being, but the prospect of being eaten: "But now that the silent, definite, and stern nature of the business in which I was engaged . . . allowed me to reflect on the few chances I had of escaping the most appalling of deaths—a death for the most appalling of purposes—every particle of that energy which had so long buoyed me up departed like feathers before the wind, leaving me a helpless prey to the most abject and pitiable terror" (III, 127). If being cannibalized exceeds even premature burial as a source of terror, the reason may be found in the nature of matter itself. Annihilation is never final so long as the victim exists in some independent material form; even in premature burial the individual retains identity. Indeed one cannot be a victim without being the victim one is. If I gasp for breath, I gasp as myself. If you victimize me, I am me-being-victimized. But if you consume me, that me is lost; my materiality can no longer be distinguished from yours: I have become you.

Isolation is the condition in which everything transpires: birth, terror, deliverance, burial. Nothing can happen anywhere else, for there is nowhere else. Isolation is that which victim and victimizer possess in common, for each is uniquely himself. When I victimize you I express myself as victimizer to you who express yourself as victim. It is an interesting commentary on Poe's concern with isolation that the only enduring social economy in his fiction is achieved by making one character, in a manner of speaking, the shadow of another. Pym, the son of "a respectable trader in sea-stores" (III, 5) and the grandson of an affluent attorney, has all the marks of good breeding one expects in a young man educated at two private schools. He stands to inherit a valuable estate and is already something of a property owner, possessing as he does a boat large enough for ten passengers, and costing the not inconsiderable sum of seventy-five dollars. By contrast, the "hybrid" Peters (II, 62, 73, 80, 101) is the son of an Indian woman and a fur trader, and seems to own nothing but what he can carry, including the bear-skin with which he hides his baldness. There is something primitive, almost chthonic about Peters, and perhaps—in view of his animal-like qualities and his physical assertiveness, to say nothing of his name—something phallic as well. Each character thus embodies in his own way a different type of civilization: the one an eastern, merchant civilization at an advanced level of marine technology and with a flourishing middle class; the other a western civilization, based also on trading, but less dependent on sophisticated technology and institutions than on personal adaptability and physical prowess. The two represent different mental tendencies as well. Pym stresses the intellect: he analyzes, takes notes, reflects, and finally—at the instigation of a certain Mr. Poe (III, 2)—turns author. Peters, not surprisingly, has a practical intelligence, but one that is intuitive as well. It is he who senses the hieroglyphic intention of the "most northwardly" of the excavations on the island of Tsalal. Pym, showing his kinship to the "business man" and the methodizing narrator of "MS. Found in a Bottle," finds the inference improbable and, in good rationalistic fashion, explains it away.

The second of Pym's three inhumations, like the advent of the stench and the yawing of the Death Ship, takes place suddenly, reducing Pym and his friend from upright efficiency to horizontal helplessness. The critical moment displays all the familiar qualities of breathlessness, weightedness, and the heightening of terror by thought: "As soon as I could collect my scattered senses, I found myself nearly suffocated, and grovelling in utter darkness among a quantity of loose earth, which was also falling upon me heavily in every direction, threatening to bury me entirely. Horribly alarmed at this idea, I struggled to gain my feet, and at length succeeded" (III, 204). Thought does not content itself with intensifying the terrible event; thought deliberates, lingers, cherishes, thought virtually caresses the event: "I firmly believed that no incident ever occurring in the course of human events is more adapted to inspire the supremeness of mental and bodily distress than a case like our own, of living inhumation. The blackness of darkness which envelops the victim, the terrific oppression of lungs, the stifling fumes from the damp earth, unite with the ghastly considerations that we are beyond the remotest confines of hope, and that such is the allotted portion of *the dead*, to carry into the human heart a degree of appalling awe and horror not be tolerated—never to be conceived" (III, 204-205).

Equally difficult to conceive is the nature of the material world that the two investigate by a series of descents. As epistemic being, Pym finds himself in a world of mysteries, of stuffs and weights and textures for which he cannot immediately account. The collective term for these objects of contingent mystery (as distinguished from the absolute mystery of the gulf beyond) is "substance." As concerns the substance Pym encounters and brings to the surface after his dive into the flooded hold of the *Grampus*, the mystery ends quickly: it is merely glass. The same word, a little earlier, functioned less as mystery than as euphemism, the value of the term deriving from the force of covert reference. Applied to the *bêche de mer*, "substance" is a kind of service word, substituting for a term that anyone familiar with the phenomenon would immediately call to mind. The same applies to the mysterious white beast with claws "resembling coral in substance" (III, 180), although here the term perhaps already anticipates the numinous quality that the natives will later attribute to the animal. We see the term applied again, finally, to non-organic nature when Pym and Peters, exploring the alphabetic excavations, discover that the sides of the chasm they have entered "were now entirely uniform in substance, in colour, and in lateral direction, the material being a very black and shining granite" (III, 222-223), whereas above, the surface on one side had been "of marl, granulated with some metallic matter" (III, 222), the same combination discovered after the pair return to the area of the ravine in which their friends were killed. Although Pym never attempts to analyze this strange environment, it appears to foreshadow the more general properties of novelty that the duo discover on their journey south.

The journey has become more than an attempt to know, even in that very broad sense which we have employed throughout these pages. Nor should we see the descent at the beginning of Chapter XXIV as merely an attempt to come down from a hill in order to secure provisions. The movement throughout the last part of the book is a movement into deeper, more primal areas of experience—toward what Merleau-Ponty calls the "ante-predicative," or preverbal, consciousness.[26] The space of the gulf beyond is a space beyond the word: thus the growing concern with the inexpressible. We are not dealing here, however, with the sorts of fears one finds elsewhere in Poe. I am thinking, for example, of that extreme panic that psychoanalytic critics are probably right in attributing, at least in part, to the loss of sexual powers. In fact, the further we move with Pym the less we have to do with fear at all. As the book advances we are increasingly attuned to a further rhythm, that of peril and deliverance. Gradually we see that the function of the great risk is nothing less than the great salvation.

No major fall in Poe—and there are many—is ever merely or even primarily physical. The fall in Poe is ontological.[27] In the chapter we are considering, Peters descends into the gulf (Pym's word) without mishap, as befits a man of praxis. But Pym, the man of dark places, cannot. Upright posture does not help, for he is not really upright. Efficiency in the upright posture presupposes a rootedness that frees the body's most versatile members, the arms, for whatever job needs to be done. The descent of a cliff, on the other hand, is a species of crawling, and hazardous. Under normal circumstances movement on all fours involves little chance of falling, for one is very close to one's base of support; gravity operates, but may not be consciously perceived, and in any case poses no threat. Gravity is the force that animates Poe's fascination with weightedness and descent; and we have already seen

[26] *Phénomenologie de la perception* (Paris, 1945), p. x.

[27] Gaston Bachelard, *L'Air et les songes: essai sur l'imagination du mouvement* (Paris, 1943), pp. 113ff.

the frightening effects of suddenness. A fall into a gulf thus combines two essential terror-producing features. When the gulf happens to be deep, as in the present case, the danger is only intensified.

If Peters descends with his body, Pym descends with his imagination. To disguise his fear, he starts off quickly; but

". . . presently I found my imagination growing terribly excited by thoughts of the vast depth yet to be descended. . . . It was in vain I endeavoured to banish these reflections, and to keep my eyes steadily bent upon the flat surface of the cliff before me. The more earnestly I struggled *not to think*, the more intensely vivid became my conceptions, and the more horribly distinct. At length arrived that crisis of fancy, so fearful in all similar cases, the crisis in which we begin to anticipate the feelings with which we *shall* fall—to picture ourselves the sickness, and dizziness, and the last struggle, and the half swoon, and the final bitterness of the rushing and headlong descent. And now I found these fancies creating their own realities, and all imagined horrors crowding upon me in fact. . . . There was a ringing in my ears, and I said, 'This is my knell of death!' And now I was consumed with the irrepressible desire of looking below. I could not, I would not, confine my glances to the cliff; and, with a wild, indefinable emotion, half of horror, half of a relieved oppression, I threw my vision far down into the abyss. For one moment my fingers clutched convulsively upon their hold, while with the movement, the faintest possible idea of ultimate escape wandered, like a shadow, through my mind—in the next my whole soul was pervaded with *a longing to fall*; a desire, a yearning, a passion utterly uncontrollable. I let go at once my grasp upon the peg, and, turning half round from the precipice, remained tottering for an instant against its naked face. But now there came a spinning of the brain; a shrill-sounding and phantom voice screamed within my ears; a dusky, fiendish, and filmy figure stood immediately beneath me; and, sighing, I sunk down with a bursting heart, and plunged within its arms." (III, 229-230)

No sooner does the descent begin than he forgets about the cliff, so absorbed is he in the challenge to his own being. The nature of this challenge may be viewed in several interesting, recurring, and representative aspects. After the first response of imagination that we have already noted, Pym confronts himself with his own perverseness: I must fall because I am afraid to. The perverseness of the reasoning unveils the hidden intentionality, what Sartre calls the totalizing movement of the act. In order to grasp this act we must divine its futurity—to see, in other words, where it goes. Here Pym assists us with his grammar, defining the crisis of fancy as that in which we anticipate the feelings with which we *shall* fall. We cannot doubt where he wants to go. At the same time, by employing the first-person plural he universalizes the situation, making it common to all men, and thus normalizing the intention: What all men do, I must do. Surrendering responsibility, Pym allows imagination to function autonomously. Suddenly the fancies created by mind create in turn their own realities, all the imagined horrors becoming facts. Now for the first time Pym shows his dialectical bent. In a situation of despair he experiences hope. A moment later, however, the pendulum swings back, abolishing all hope and revealing the hidden intentionality: the urge to risk everything. As Pym is on the verge of letting go, two familiar terror-producing phenomena appear—the vortex and the fearful sound. In situations of peril these are usually encountered early; that they come late in this situation indicates the displacement of peril from the external to the internal world. It is not the cliff as such that threatens; it is Pym's peculiar way of being on the cliff. By falling, Pym openly "expresses" his heretofore concealed design, which is to become the absolute victim. In such a state he cannot see Peters for what he is. Demonstrating its autonomy, the imagination flashes back to Pym the image of the victimizer: "a dusky, fiendish, and filmy figure stood immediately beneath me; and, sighing, I sunk down with a bursting heart, and plunged within its arms." Pym, bound for the gulf beyond, cannot die;

he can only enter a new state: "On recovery, my trepidation had entirely vanished; I felt a new being, and with some little further aid from my companion, reached the bottom also in safety" (III, 230). *I felt a new being*: the statement recalls the ontological nature of the fall even as it identifies Pym's first profound experience of novelty. It also reveals that, beneath his rather boyish and ingenuous exterior, Pym is troubled by the same gratuitous impulses that afflict the victimizer of "The Black Cat" and the victim of "The Imp of the Perverse." The latter has his deepest—and his most conscious—experience of perverseness when, like Pym, he contemplates a fall:

"We stand upon the brink of a precipice. We peer into the abyss—we grow sick and dizzy. Our first impulse is to shrink from the danger. Unaccountably we remain. . . . There grows into palpability, a shape, far more terrible than any genius, or any demon of a tale, and yet it is but a thought, though a fearful one, and one which chills the very marrow of our bones with the fierceness of the delight of its horror. It is merely the idea of what would be our sensations during the sweeping precipitancy of a fall from such a height. . . . And because our reason violently deters us from the brink, *therefore*, do we the more impetuously approach it. There is no passion in nature so demoniacally impatient, as that of him, who shuddering upon the edge of a precipice, thus meditates a plunge. To indulge for a moment, in any attempt at *thought*, is to be inevitably lost; for reflection but urges us to forbear, and *therefore* it is, I say, that we *cannot*." (VI, 149-150)

The descent that occupies the last part of the book is, on the other hand, much slower, and less threatening. Moreover, it leads to a positive goal—the realm of pure novelty. What unites the two kinds of descent (the sudden fall and the journey to the southern Pole) is their ability to bring about a change in being. The notion of southerly movement as a movement down is a familiar conception (one goes "down south," Australia is "down under," and so on). But for Poe downward or southerly motion also suggests (to elaborate on a point made above) that attraction of the unknown and the ultimate that has inspired so many myths, including those involving a return to the womb. A common feature of such myths, Mircea Eliade reminds us, is an "initiatory passage through a *vagina dentata*, or the dangerous descent into a cave or crevice assimilated to the mouth or the uterus of Mother Earth. All these adventures are in fact initiatory ordeals, after accomplishing which the victorious hero acquires a new mode of being."[28] Pym's adventure, which leads him to the farthest reaches of the earth and to a figure not unlike the one Eliade describes, is also a kind of initiatory ordeal. But before he can undergo his initiation into a new kind of being, Pym must endure a series of gradations that are also in a broad sense reductions.[29] The process fulfills the requirements of a Lawrentian lapsing-out, through which the energies of being are released from the hold of consciousness. Sloughing off inessential ties—those of family, for example—the lapsing individual moves toward membership in a more essential unit, the primal couple. In forming that couple, and in advancing toward the realm of pure novelty, Pym and Peters also go through a kind of technological regression. For as long as it lasts, each ship on which Pym finds himself is a complete world. Within the ship Pym lives an important phase of his essential self, a phase of darkness and confinement and depth. In this connection we note that there are no depths beneath the ship, such as you find in Melville. The vessel is its own depth, Pym's watery immersion after the multiple murders on the *Grampus* occurring within the ship. No artifact as civilized as this can endure. Thus all three ships that Pym helps to man (the *Ariel*, the *Grampus*, and the *Jane Guy*) meet destruction. After these relics of an advanced technology are dispensed with, the primal couple revert to the only object that can carry them through to the end—that primitive, preindustrial, aboriginal artifact, the canoe. Pym's

[28] *Myth and Reality*, trans. Willard Trask (New York and Evanston, 1963), p. 81.

[29] Davidson, *Poe: A Critical Study*, pp. 175-176.

"writing" falls within the same pattern. Pym has a notebook and pencil that he carries with him and that represent, along with his clothing, the last material vestige of nineteenth-century civilization. Similarly, the most critical message in the book is the note Augustus writes to Pym. Here Poe returns to the idea that handwriting *re*-presents literally, by transferring something of the author's presence from one sphere to another. He carries the idea further than before by involving the body in the most direct and physical way: the "several lines of MS. in a large hand" (III, 40) are written in Augustus' very blood.

The realm of novelty is anticipated in the strange water the voyagers discover on their island. Although Madame Bonaparte interprets this water as disguised blood,[30] there is no certain proof of this in the text. What is given is a phenomenon that introduces something entirely new to Pym's life: "The very rocks were novel in their mass, their colour, and their stratification; and the streams themselves, utterly incredible as it may appear, had so little in common with those of other climates, that we were scrupulous of tasting them, and, indeed, had difficulty in bringing ourselves to believe that their qualities were purely those of nature" (III, 186). This is not a blood disguising itself as water; it is water which transcends its own nature. That it cannot find what it seeks confirms the transcendental nature of its object: "I am at a loss to give a distinct idea of the nature of this liquid . . ." (III, 186). According to the blood theory, interpretation should make much of the travellers' early scrupulousness about tasting the water, and about its apparent lack of "limpidity." This approach overlooks the fact that once the travellers become acquainted with the true properties of the water, their hesitation passes. To say that the water lacks limpidity is to end where Pym begins. What Pym ultimately discovers is that the water is purer than it looks: "It was, nevertheless, in point of fact, as perfectly limpid as any limestone water in exist-

[30] *The Life and Works of Edgar Allan Poe* has a long and suggestive discussion of the symbolism in *Pym.*

ence, the difference being only in appearance" (III, 186). This water is an extended oxymoron that Pym, unable to grasp its essence, attempts to define by negatives: "It was *not* colourless, nor was it of any one uniform colour—presenting to the eye, as it flowed, every possible shade of purple, like the hues of a changeable silk" (III, 186). The more he comes to know about this water, the more it reveals its hidden futurity. For whatever it may have represented in Poe's psyche, the water is connected in the story with the attractive experiences that lie in Pym's future. In articulating this connection, Pym moreover underlines the positive and transcendental nature of the mysterious flowing substance: "The phenomena of this water formed the first definite link in that vast chain of apparent miracles with which I was destined to be at length encircled" (III, 187).

In his first log entry Pym defines the nature of the realm which he and his companions are entering: "*March 1.** Many unusual phenomena now indicated that we were entering upon a region of novelty and wonder" (III, 238). The transcendental character of this super-nature can be seen in several phenomena. Heat, combined with exhalation, is ordinarily an oppressive force, as in the case of the "beast" that afflicts Pym with its hot breath, or of the prisoner hemmed in by heated walls of iron ("The Pit and the Pendulum"). In both cases heat confronts and dominates (it tends to be both "out there" and "above"). The region of novelty and wonder reverses this relationship, placing the victim atop the source, the heat becoming supportive, like an enormous fluid cradle. Velocity, another common source of terror, is similarly placated and subdued. Pym's remark that "we were still hurrying on to the southward, under the influence of a powerful current" (III, 240) carries no overtone of terror. Even at the end Pym regards his slow southward fall with Augustan calm: "The summit of the cataract was utterly lost in the dimness and distance. Yet we were evidently approaching it with a hideous velocity" (III, 241). There is an element of suddenness in his torpor: "there came over me a sudden listlessness . . ." (III, 241); but the calming nature of the realm smooths away the abruptness of the transition, producing a sense of gradation. We also note the absence of any notion of being enclosed. Despite its technological nature, the canoe is no chamber. Its containment protects rather than oppresses. Nor is it kinetic, the source of motion lying outside its confines.

With the ashy material that continually falls upon the travellers Pym experiences the third and last of his inhumations: "The whole ashy material fell now continually around us, and in vast quantities. . . . We were nearly overwhelmed by the white ashy shower which settled upon us and upon the canoe, but melted into the water as it fell" (III, 241). Despite the fact that it has weight enough to fall, no one touched by this substance perceives any heaviness. So unstable is its nature that the material cannot remain itself—on contacting the water it *becomes* the water. Pym is not describing ashes but the transcendence of ashes.

In examining the phenomenon of darkness we may find it helpful to distinguish between the relative properties of blackness and whiteness that pervade the island section of the book. The natives of the island live in a world of blackness: most of their animals are black, and so are their own teeth (always, in Poe, a sign of essence). Whiteness, perhaps because it rarely occurs, meanwhile takes on the aspect of a noumen, and appears to be surrounded by taboos. After the *Jane Guy* explodes, killing many of the natives, the survivors surround the carcass of the white animal, which Pym had earlier described, with a circle of stakes; in the canoe the whiteness of his companions' shirts and of a handkerchief terrify Nu-Nu, who is so affected by cumulative whiteness that he finally dies. In some ways black and white in Poe work dialectically, each opposing the other and at the same time drawing the other out. One finds, for example, that black, white, and gray dominate both in the tales of terror and in the works that are seemingly most unlike them, the tales of humor and burlesque. But they are also poles of value.

This is not the place to debate the merits of Leslie Fiedler's suggestion that black really means Negro, but at least in one sense it is evidently valid. At the very least, black *includes* Negro, and the proof is that the transcendence at the end of the story is a transcendence for whites alone. Let me elaborate. In the animal world of *Pym* white shows a changing face. It can be repulsive or bad (as in the case of the carnivorous seagull), or numinous (as in the case of the white-haired animal). In the realm of non-organic nature and of man, however, the qualities of whiteness are positive. The water that buoys up the canoe is of a milky hue, while the mysterious figure at the end of the voyage has a skin as white as snow. Moreover—and the significance of the point can hardly be exaggerated—the white human beings on the voyage survive, whereas the black man dies. Nu-Nu's death is an inevitable liquidation. Black in *Pym*, personified by the treacherous natives, is deceit, depravity, evil. When Pym discovers the blackness of the natives' teeth he discovers a proof that they are as morally "dark" as they appear, and as their actions later show them to be. Such beings are not made for transcendence, but only for elimination; thus, on the last recorded day of the voyage, just before Pym and his white companion glimpse the supernal white figure in the distance, the black man suddenly dies.

"And now we rushed into the embraces of the cataract, where a chasm threw itself open to receive us. But there arose in our pathway a shrouded human figure, very far larger in its proportions than any dweller among men. And the hue of the skin of the figure was of the perfect whiteness of the snow" (III, 242). The succession of verbs in these three sentences represents the movement toward that still point that moves even in its stillness, that *concordia discors* that stands at the center of so much mystical writing and the poetry of ekphrasis. *Rushed*; *arose*; *was*: a process involving speed (which is not experienced as speed) gives way to a rising-into-view, and thence to a simple being-there of that which has risen. One could scarcely write a sentence with less action.

After the verb of being, there is only the series of prepositional phrases, creating the effect of successive stasis: of the skin, of the figure, of the perfect whiteness, of the snow. This is not a figure that *does* but a figure that *is*, not a creature of flesh but a being of essence. The prepositions of the sentence strive to render this essence by rendering the attributes of its substance, here viewed as skin. But again we verge upon the inexpressible, for it is not the skin that is at issue; it is the hue. This skin exists as the ashy material exists, on the verge of immateriality; it is matter in its most intangible expression. Nothing better demonstrates the intentionality of these pages than this tendency of the phenomenon to turn into something higher. So, too, with the darkness. As the seemingly opaque water was actually purer than it first appeared, so the darkness is less dark. Darkness is the secrecy of light: "A sullen darkness now hovered above us—but from out of the milky depths of the ocean a luminous glare arose, and stole up along the bulwarks of the boat" (III, 241). Darkness arises again in the final log entry, but not as palpably as whiteness. For as darkness escalates, so does whiteness—first in the birds which fly continuously about, and then in the figure of whiteness. There is perhaps no more interesting attempt, in American literature, to render pure transcendence.

"The Fall of the House of Usher"

"During the whole of a dull, dark, and soundless day in the autumn of the year, when the clouds hung oppressively low in the heavens, I had been passing alone, on horseback, through a singularly dreary tract of country; and at length found myself, as the shades of the evening drew on, within view of the melancholy House of Usher" (III, 273). The hypotaxis of the opening sentence is a paradigm of the relations, in the story, between time, space, and the narrator's self. Everything depends, so to say, on everything else: the temporal priority on the spatial, the continuity of action on both of these, and the terminus of the structure on everything that precedes. "During," a preposition of time, establishes a continuity and a duration that gradually expands until it embraces the whole of a day; while the dependent clause that follows develops visual and spatial details through the mediation of a conjunction of time. At the structural center, "I had been passing alone" confirms the continuity without accounting either for the origin of action or for its goal: continuity precedes origin and intention. The narrator is the one who is already moving, doubly surrounded—on the one hand, by clauses or phrases that depend grammatically upon his action but that his action does not illuminate; on the other, by the space-time that gradually unfurls with and as the flow of the grammar. The increasing specificity of this space-time, instead of clarifying the aim of the narrator's continuity, merely throws it into relief. Obscurity reigns: the day is dark with approaching night, the narrator moves in mystery. We wait for some event, some exertion that will define this actor who does not act. Perhaps he will say where he is going. Instead, I "found myself." The place I arrive at is not my goal; it is the site that perfects my having-come: the purpose of my motion is to discover where I am.

The entire first sentence is the process by which the narrator *comes to consciousness.* He rides as other men walk in their sleep. On waking to his surroundings, he discovers what he does not know. At first there is only the sense of himself here and of a separate presence there, and a profound sensation he cannot define: "I know not how it was—but, with the first glimpse of the building, a sense of insufferable gloom pervaded my spirit" (III, 273). The center of action, which was never more than a kind of inertia, has shifted: scene acts upon spectator, challenging his capacity to know. The scene is mystery, oppression; not dream but dream's aftermath: "I looked upon the scene before me—upon the mere house, and the simple landscape features of the domain—upon the bleak walls—upon the vacant eye-like windows . . . with an utter depression of soul which I can compare to no earthly sensation more properly than to the after-dream of the reveller upon opium—the bitter relapse into everyday life—the hideous dropping off of the veil. There was an iciness, a sinking, a sickening of the heart . . ." (III, 273). Even before the House has been fully constituted—whether by observation, experience, memory, or pure ratiocination—the narrator discovers himself in a world of heaviness, oppression, and submergence: clouds hang oppressively low, the veil of dreams drops off, the heart sinks. Below the level on which one rides or contemplates lie the depths. After declaring the effect of the house "a mystery all insoluble" (III, 274), the narrator concludes that "the analysis of this power lies among considerations beyond our depth" (III, 274). So interdependent are the elements of the narrative that "depth," which is itself lacking in spatiality, is connected immediately with an element of the physical scene: the tarn: "It was possible, I reflected, that a mere different arrangement of the particulars of the scene, of the details of the picture, would be sufficient to modify, or perhaps to annihilate its capacity for sorrowful impression; and, acting upon this idea, I reined my horse to the precipitous brink of a black and lurid tarn that lay in unruffled lustre by the dwelling, and gazed down—but with a shudder even more thrilling than before—upon the remodelled and inverted images of the gray sedge, and the ghastly tree-stems, and the vacant and eye-like windows" (III, 274).

Before examining this "twoness" we should perhaps look back at the first example of it in the story. The parallelistic or complementary structure of the first sentence is so obvious that critics, so far as I am aware, have overlooked it, much as everyone, except Dupin, overlooked the purloined letter which lay in plain view. There are many ways to dissect such a structure. Perhaps the simplest is this:

During / passing / country
at length / found / house

The sentence answers several questions: When did it happen; what was it that happened; where did it happen? More important, it is a grammatical paradigm not only of the narrative as a whole but of the ontological structure it embodies.

Henceforth every significant being, every reflection, act, or state will have its analogy or complement. Thus, to use the leading instance, the destruction of Lady Madeline necessitates the destruction of her brother, and, in turn, the submergence of the House. The relationship is not symbiotic, as might appear from the fact that the two, in a manner of speaking, nourish each other. There is too much healthy reciprocity and sunlight in the model of symbiosis. The relationship of Usher to his sister is dark and airless, a nourishing of the other in order to sustain oneself, a destruction of the other in order to be oneself destroyed. This adversary function of the other in relation to his complement prevails also in the confrontation between the narrator and the scene before him. The scene bears in upon the consciousness with the brute force of fact. It is powerfully, oppressively there. But what is one to do about it? It is useless to speak of resisting its force, let alone of destroying it (as one might destroy or will away another human being). The only way to free oneself from the source of oppression is to change one's relation with it.

It is for this reason that the narrator, after pausing, decides once more to move. But the decision is simplistic. The narrator reminds us of the narrator of "MS. Found in a Bottle" or of "The Business Man," those devotees of method whose existence is a quest for simple answers. He fails in his effort just as Usher fails when he tries to explain the mysterious sentience of inorganic things by reference to "the method of collocation of these stones" with which the House was built (III, 286). They fail because each envisages the problem as one of practical relation, of the way things fit together in the material world. But the problem is irrelation, that quality which, in *Eureka*, becomes the chief means of defining the absolute. Conceptual models such as "the whole and its parts" are of little help. It would be more accurate to say that the complementary, interpenetrating phenomena that the narrator confronts compose a whole with aspects that present themselves to consciousness successively. That is why, when the narrator reins up to the brink of the tarn, he discovers nothing new. He merely witnesses the scene from a different perspective: nothing changes but his own relation to what is beyond relation.

The water of the tarn—the medium between the *now* of present consciousness and the *then* of the gulf beyond—is opacity, prevention, an expanse of matter that, merging the properties of the wall and the mirror, keeps the world in its place by throwing its own image back upon it. The mirror-water-wall circumscribes and by circumscribing perfects, making the scene a kind of infinity to itself, which threatens to absorb the being of any human actor who comes within its sphere: peering into the tarn, the "reflecting" narrator can find no image of himself!

He is nonetheless highly self-conscious. Indeed, there is nothing of which he is more conscious than his own consciousness, the field of concern to which everything in the first part of the story—even the management of the horse—is subordinated. After recalling that his glimpse into the tarn had only deepened his original impression, he declares, "There can be no doubt that the consciousness of the rapid increase of my superstition—for why should I not so term it?—served mainly to accelerate the increase itself. Such, I have long known, is the paradoxical law of all sentiments having terror as a basis" (III, 276). The passage attempts to account for the disquiet the narrator feels on perceiving that the house and its environs are surrounded by "an atmosphere peculiar to themselves and their immediate vicinity—an atmosphere which had no affinity with the air of heaven, but which had reeked up from the decayed trees, and the gray wall, and the silent tarn—a pestilent and mystic vapour, dull, sluggish, faintly discernible, and leaden-hued" (III, 276).[31]

[31] The role of atmosphere, from the standpoint of the history of ideas and of nineteenth-century science, is discussed in Leo Spitzer, "A Reinterpretation of 'The Fall of the House of Usher,'" pp. 51-66; in I. M. Walker, "The 'Legitimate Sources' of Terror in 'The Fall of the House of Usher,'" pp. 585-592; and Herbert F. Smith, "Usher's Madness and Poe's Organicism: A Source," *American Literature*, 39 (1967), pp. 379-389.

Besides the opposition put forward by the world, there is an opposition within the self, a contradiction that resists the impulse to take in fully what one's senses record. It is this that makes the narrator a skeptic and a rationalist, warning him that what he sees may be an illusion. The advantage of this approach, as a literary strategy, is obvious. We find it easier to accept the fantastic when we are accompanied on our trip by a cool-headed doubter. But the story claims that the fantastic events involving the Ushers are true, a part of everyday reality. The narrator's role is to observe, to become involved, and finally to validate the happenings in the House. Above all, the "fancy" he entertains comes true in the narrative itself, so that we find produced, in the end, the actual results of what was first attributed to excessive mental excitement. In living the truth of the House of Usher the narrator lives the illusion of illusion.

The edifice itself embodies an even more difficult paradox. One might call the building a *concordia discors* except that the discordant elements are not fully reconciled. It might better be described as a kind of unstable compound. The narrator defines its principal feature as "an excessive antiquity," following this thematic statement with two sentences of amplification (dealing with discoloration and fungi). Now comes a turn: "Yet all this was apart from any extraordinary dilapidation" (III, 276). The sentence that follows appears to extend the qualification: "No portion of the masonry had fallen; and there appeared to be a wild inconsistency between its still perfect adaptation of parts, and the crumbling condition of the individual stones. In this there was much that reminded me of the specious totality of old woodwork which has rotted for long years in some neglected vault, with no disturbance from the breath of the external air" (III, 276-277). The first clause presents no problem; the difficulty begins with the conjunction. Logic would dictate a development on the following lines: no portion of the masonry had fallen; and there appeared, moreover, to be no inconsistency between its parts; and so on. This changes the sense quite radically, of course. In order to preserve the sense and escape contradiction, one would have to replace the "and" with a "yet" or a "but": no portion of the masonry had fallen; yet there appeared to be a wild inconsistency, etc. (An inconsistency, in other words, which suggests that it might fall before long.) The narrator has trapped himself between an inclination, on the one hand, to perceive that the House, though old, shows no likelihood of falling; and on the other, to perceive exactly the opposite. The more he argues, the likelier does this "opposite" become. After stating in sentence five of the paragraph that the edifice reveals no extraordinary dilapidation, he likens it two sentences later to rotting woodwork. Its unity has become specious. As though sensing that he has gone too far, he cuts off the speculation: "Beyond this indication of extensive decay, however, the fabric gave little token of instability" (III, 277). But that will not do either, for despite the ostensible premises of the "argument," the drift of the paragraph is toward decay and imminent fall. Nothing would foreshadow this better than a fissure running all the way from the top of the building down into the tarn. In establishing this, however, the narrator would get caught with his contradictions showing. The solution is to displace the observation to a hypothetical other, an observer: "Perhaps the eye of a scrutinizing observer might have discovered a barely perceptible fissure, which, extending from the roof of the building in front, made its way down the wall in a zigzag direction, until it became lost in the sullen waters of the tarn" (III, 277).

Before going any further with our inspection of the edifice, we may find it helpful to look for a moment at its principal occupant. Our first hint that Usher is the true center of interest is his authorship of an "M.S." (III, 274), that chirographic product of extreme experience. Through Usher's writing the narrator understands and accepts his mission: he will be the one who is near. Being near, in this case, means being with Usher *in* Usher's mansion; the distinction is important. For Usher cannot leave. The narrator can only help him where Usher is and Usher *is* only in the House of Usher. His claustration, like that of Egaeus, is habitual, and, in light of the family past, even hereditary. Behind the present, which is loneliness and a sense of fatedness, looms descent—as far back as one can see, the family seems headed for this one point in time. Descent is not a multiplication in many directions, as in the concept of the family tree; descent is intensification with circumscription: "I had learned, too, the very remarkable fact, that the stem of the Usher race, all time-honoured as it was, had put forth, at no period, any enduring branch; in other words, that the entire family lay in the direct line of descent . . ." (III, 275). At the end of the line is that present moment in which one lives the impossibility of a future. Roderick knows that Madeline will perish and that he will perish in the terrors of that knowledge. To be of the Usher race is to exist at the limits of the bodily, at that point where flesh turns into nothingness. Race is not the will to live but the will to live out.

Allen Tate complains that Usher's extreme sensitivity "is not 'regulated' to the forms of the human situation; it is a mechanism operating apart from the moral consciousness. We have here something like a capacity for mere sensation, as distinguished from sensibility, which in Usher is atrophied. In terms of the small distinction that I am offering here, sensibility keeps us in the world, sensation locks us into the self, feeding upon the disintegration of its objects and absorbing them into the void of the ego."[32] It would perhaps be nearer the mark to say, at least where Usher is concerned, that sensation is the individual's way of keeping in touch with the world, in the material sense, while sensibility is his way of holding his interests and those of the world in some sort of balance. It may not be a "normal" balance, when measured by the standards of some other being, but within the life-world of the individual, with its special demands, it has its own kind of sense. The problem for Usher is how to live

[32] "Our Cousin, Mr. Poe," in his *The Man of Letters in the Modern World* (see "Foreword," n. 17), p. 138.

"on the brink" without losing all sense of equilibrium, or what Rollo May would call "centeredness." From a phenomenological point of view, says May, neurosis "is seen not as a deviation from my particular theories of what a person ought to be, but precisely as the method the individual uses to preserve his own centeredness, his own existence. His symptoms are his way of shrinking the range of his world in order that his centeredness may be protected from threat; a way of blocking off aspects of his environment that he may be adequate to the remainder. We now see why the definition of neurosis as a 'failure of adjustment' is inadequate. An adjustment is exactly what a neurosis is; and that is just its trouble. It is a necessary adjustment by which centeredness can be preserved; a way of accepting nonbeing in order that some little being may be preserved."[33]

Usher's problem is that his existential center of gravity (what Tate would call his self) tends to shift away from him—to be "out there" in the miasmal atmosphere, in the "*physique*" (III, 281) of the House, and above all in his consubstantial twin. As Tate himself points out in the same essay, speaking of the two surviving Ushers: "Their very birth had violated the unity of their being" (p. 140). This is a corporeal separation, a splitting of the living substance, but it is an experience of consciousness too: Usher's "MS.," the narrator recalls, "gave evidence of nervous agitation arising both from an 'acute bodily illness' and 'a mental disorder' " (III, 274). Usher's plight foreshadows that of Agathos, the angel in "The Power of Words" whose consciousness is gripped by the knowledge that an essential part of his being exists in a state of separation. There the separated part is a star that the power of Agathos' words has spoken into life—a relatively small thing in space that he can sit (if that is the appropriate posture for an angel) and contemplate. In Usher's case the separation is diffused rather than localized: it is all

[33] "On the Phenomenological Bases of Psychotherapy," in *Readings in Existential Phenomenology*, eds. Nathaniel Lawrence and Daniel O'Connor (Englewood Cliffs, N.J., 1967), p. 370.

around him, in the air, in the body and soul of his sister, in the body and soul of his House.

The limits of this diffusion are set by the House, or rather by what might be called the Usher place of residence, since the tarn and the surrounding vegetation belong to it as well. Ernst Cassirer, Mircea Eliade, and O. F. Bollnow have shown how the founding of a residence consecrates a certain space, taking it out of the ordinary world and making it, in effect, sacred.[34] The dwelling place becomes a little infinity unto itself, separated from the "profane" space that surrounds it. The House of Usher is such a place: inner-directed, inviolable, self-contained. There is something baffled, however—something almost demonic—about its interiority. It is dark and comfortless and, what is worse, impossible to "know": "The windows were long, narrow, and pointed, and at so vast a distance from the black oaken floor as to be altogether inaccessible from within. . . . the eye . . . struggled in vain to reach the remoter angles of the chamber, or the recesses of the vaulted and fretted ceiling" (III, 277-278). If the chamber in "The Philosophy of Furniture" is a vision, Usher's is a nightmare.

The House is presented, like the doomed-city of the poems, in a "late" phase—a period of time that must soon end because the House is nearing its predestined term. Its troubles—its "disease," if you will—can be traced in a measure to "the biological phenomenon which might be described as 'colonial organicism,' symbiosis, or mutualism. It begins with vegetable sentience, but goes much farther than that. The algae of the house of Usher have organized themselves—the stones of the house, the air around them, and even the mind of Usher himself—into what can only be described as a single, unified organism. What has happened with Roderick and his house is an example of aberrant *micro*cosmic organicism. Where the universe of Poe's *Eureka* is apparently equiposed between the forces of attraction and repulsion . . . the House of Usher

[34] Bollnow, "Lived-Space," trans. Dominic Gerlach, *Philosophy Today*, 5 (1961), pp. 31-39.

—which includes the family, Roderick himself, and of course the building—has *refined* itself to a special condition within the larger cosmos of general organization."[35]

The kinetic element in the House is embodied for a time in its chief occupant, who is undergoing a continuous and rapid transformation: "Surely, man had never before so terribly altered, in so brief a period, as had Roderick Usher!" (III, 278). That the change is rapid and still in process suggests, even before the narrator has established his presence, that he has come too late and that Usher's passage to the gulf beyond has already begun. The Usher heir is surrounded by a kind of nimbus that sets him off from normal human beings as the exterior miasma sets off the house: "The silken hair, too, had been suffered to grow all unheeded, and as, in its wild gossamer texture, it floated rather than fell about the face, I could not, even with effort, connect its Arabesque expression with any idea of simple humanity" (III, 279). Usher's hair corresponds, as Maurice Beebe has shown, to the minute fungi hanging from the eaves of the house, much as the inconsistency in the stones corresponds to an inconsistency in Usher's manner.[36] Similarly, the leaden-hued vapor of the tarn finds its complement in the leaden quality of Usher's voice (III, 279). More significant, perhaps, is Usher's ability to radiate his influence into the very atmosphere: his is "a mind from which darkness, as if an inherent positive quality, poured forth upon all objects of the moral and physical universe, in one unceasing radiation of gloom" (III, 282). "The Fall of the House of Usher," as Beebe points out, states in narrative terms what Poe was later to formulate conceptually in *Eureka*.[37] Roderick Usher represents a late stage of the diffusion that, working against the counterforce

[35] Smith, "Usher's Madness and Poe's Organicism," p. 387.

[36] "The Universe of Roderick Usher," *Personalist*, 37 (1956), pp. 147-160.

[37] E. Arthur Robinson, "Order and Sentience in 'The Fall of the House of Usher,'" *PMLA*, 76 (1961), pp. 68-81, also reads the tale in the light of *Eureka*, as well as "The Colloquy of Monos and Una."

of attraction, constitutes the universe as presently known. All life, according to this theory, is a radiation or diffusion from a simple essence. The particles that radiate tend by their very nature to return to their primal oneness; Poe calls this process attraction and sees it exemplified in gravity. So long as the particles exert their diffusive energy, the power of attraction will be resisted. But eventually the energy will slacken, allowing the universe to contract to the point of its origin. Usher, when we see him, is at a point in existence where the diffusion, nearing its end, prepares the way for a dissolution that is actually a return to oneness.

In this weakening diffusion Usher inhabits the last reach of existence, where flesh is about to dissolve into spirit. A man who can paint ideas has already begun to transcend mortal existence. Normal stimuli affect him, accordingly, as they might affect an angel. Everything that is not rarefied oppresses—food, clothing, smells, lights, sounds—as if to suggest that only those about to quit ordinary life can fully perceive its basic materiality. But there is pain in the quitting. The longer he stares at his contracting future, the more terrible it becomes: " 'I have, indeed, no abhorrence of danger, except in its absolute effect—in terror. In this unnerved—in this pitiable condition—I feel that the period will sooner or later arrive when I must abandon life and reason together, in some struggle with the grim phantasm, FEAR' " (III, 280). Usher's speech is more cry than communication: When I speak I solicit nothing from you, neither action nor response. I speak in order to perfect my condition—to allow the predictions of my heritage to come true. The narrator never fully participates in the existential ballet of brother and sister. It is Roderick and Lady Madeline who form the primal couple. As an outsider temporarily on the inside, the narrator provides the focal consciousness through which the strange fate of the House of Usher becomes credible. But the ontological economy remains, as in the tales about women, an economy of two. So complete is this economy, so fully does it take up all its living space, that the advent of a third radically affects the balance of the original two. When Usher and the narrator are together, the Lady Madeline is apart. After his arrival the narrator catches only a glimpse of her before she withdraws: "Hitherto she had steadily borne up against the pressure of her malady, and had not betaken herself finally to bed; but, on the closing in of the evening of my arrival at the house, she succumbed . . . to the prostrating power of the destroyer" (III, 282). The narrator approaches the lady's person only in the act of removing her, after she has been placed in her coffin, from her quarters. When the lady returns to the inner house from the vault, the narrator, in turn, is himself displaced, the reunion of the two forcing the third out of their living space and back into the obscurity from which he emerged.

Usher's behavior toward his sister can be seen from two perspectives. The reader will recall that a double perspective was available in "Al Aaraaf" as well, one directed toward the poetic order of events, the other directed toward the chronological order which the poetic version deliberately scrambled. In "The Fall of the House of Usher," however, there is no need to untangle the sequence of events, which is relatively straightforward. The narrator arrives, meets with Usher, helps inter the Lady Madeline, and so on. The "doubleness" in the tale results from the gap between the pattern experienced by the narrator and revealed by him as the story moves along, and the pattern experienced by Usher but revealed only in retrospect. In the first instance we see, hear, and feel simultaneously with the narrator. In the second we experience the pattern of events through Usher—but later, and all at once. That his sister has been buried alive does not become clear, for example, until Usher reveals it; but once acquired, this new knowledge casts light on everything that has gone before: suddenly, in retrospect, Usher's demeanor and attitude assume a significance they had previously lacked. The difference between the one and the other pattern—really the difference between the one and the other consciousness—is illustrated by the way the two men react to the sounds that coincide with elements in the tale being read aloud by the narrator. The narrator hears mysterious, coincidental noises; Usher hears his sister struggling in the tomb. Each perception goes its own way until, near the end, Usher reveals the truth: " '*We have put her living in the tomb*! Said I not that my senses were acute? I *now* tell you that I heard her first feeble movements in the hollow coffin. I heard them—many, many days ago—yet I dared not—*I dared not speak*!" (III, 296). Usher's friend now knows what Usher knows, the two patterns converging in a moment of utterance that is also, characteristically, a moment of confession.

The crime that this confession exposes is arrived at by a somewhat circuitous route. Usher first of all announces that his sister is dead, and enlists the aid of the narrator in laying her to rest; to the latter's eyes, moreover, she is obviously a corpse. Yet Usher is unwilling to bury her in the customary way. Usher "stated his intention of preserving her corpse for a fortnight, (previously to its final interment,) in one of the numerous vaults within the main walls of the building. The worldly reason, however, assigned for this singular proceeding, was one which I did not feel at liberty to dispute. The brother had been led to his resolution (so he told me) by consideration of the unusual character of the malady of the deceased, of certain obtrusive and eager inquiries on the part of her medical men, and of the remote and exposed situation of the burial-ground of the family" (III, 287-288). It is not impossible, of course, that Usher believes, or suspects, that Madeline is actually in a comatose state. Unfortunately the narrator has no way of knowing, and it is a point to which Usher never explicitly addresses himself. The brother's stated aim, in any case, is a reasonable one: he wants to protect the sister from the prying eyes and prying tools of the physicians. The explanation is supported, furthermore, by the look of the family doctor, who "wore a mingled expression of low cunning and perplexity" (III, 277) on his "sinister" countenance (III, 288). Since this still leaves some latitude for interpretation, the most we can conclude with certainty is that Usher knows the true state of his sister, at least from the time he hears her struggles in the vault, and that his victimization of her, even if it is essentially an act of omission, is henceforth conscious.

To rescue the sleeper, the guardian has only to exercise the power of words. This he fails to do, with the result that Madeline, like the protagonist of "The Premature Burial," is threatened with annihilation through the loss of breath: the guardian tries, in effect, to suffocate the sleeper. The story being built of analogies and complements, it is not surprising that the sleeper's return should be accompanied by a wind that possesses a "fierce breath" (III, 297), or that her body should press down upon the guardian much as the clouds press down upon the House. Usher by his silence has forced his sister to endure a *separation* of which the inevitable aftermath—given the indissoluble bond between the twins—is *reunification.* What Madeline overcomes is not mortality, as in the case of the other returning ladies, who expire and come back to life. What Madeline overcomes are things that keep her from her brother: the door of her vault, the door of the chamber where Usher awaits, and the physical space between them. Here is a triumph not only of will but of body, for this woman simply overpowers all matter that gets in her way. Corporeality is equally central to her final moment with her brother, the reunification of the two being figured by their physical convergence: body to body, the pair fall from life as we know it to life as we know it not.

The House maintains, as noted above, a close relationship with the world of external nature. So dominant is the House in this relationship, however, that nature seems to belong to the House more than the House to nature. The storm that arises near the end is, as Hegel might say, a storm *for* the House. The term nature, as a description of the phenomena outside the walls, is obviously inadequate, for the occupants of the House are ultimately creatures of the same nature—ultimately but not immediately. Whereas the nature exemplified by the storm still exists in the *now*, Roderick and Madeline are in passage toward *then*. Nature remains vital, active, mobile, while the Ushers become increasingly lifeless and effete, a distinction dramatized by the contrast between the whirlwind and the increasing powerlessness of Roderick Usher, who finally sits facing the door, rocking mechanically, while awaiting the return of his sister from the vault. It appears for a time that it is this external nature which both Usher and the narrator fear. Motion appears in the House only through the operation of external natural forces: "I endeavoured to believe that much, if not all of what I felt, was due to the bewildering influence of the gloomy furniture of the room—of the dark and tattered draperies, which, tortured into motion by the breath of a rising tempest, swayed fitfully to and fro upon the walls, and rustled uneasily about the decorations of the bed" (III, 290). What nature has, man has not. Thus the narrator now finds himself in the same helpless position, relative to forces outside himself, as at the beginning of the story. Something has usurped his power to act, transforming him into a victim. The oppressor frightens, weighs down, imprisons, steals breath: "An irrepressible tremour gradually pervaded my frame; and, at length, there sat upon my very heart an incubus of utterly causeless alarm. Shaking this off with a gasp and a struggle, I uplifted myself upon the pillows . . ." (III, 290). The qualities of oppressiveness and weight attributed to animals in *Pym*, "The Black Cat," and "Metzengerstein," are here transferred to something more abstract, but they are the same qualities. The storm has equally familiar properties, such as velocity, which are evidenced in the tales of individual peril in a hostile nature. But this tempest is not, as in the tales of descent, a storm-in-itself; it is entirely complementary, and in two ways: first, in relation to the turbulence in Usher himself, and second, as an anticipation of the revivified Lady Madeline. At first "change" seems limited to Usher: "And now . . . an observable change came over the features of the mental disorder of my friend" (III, 289). In the storm change is made external, circumambient, all-encompassing. Usher is no longer a man changing in a world; he is a man in a world changing. His end now looms before him like a terrible wall erected by the very atmosphere that has conditioned the existence of his race, an atmosphere rendered kinetic by the rapid changes it enspheres: "The exceeding density of the clouds (which hung so low as to press upon the turrets of the house) did not prevent our perceiving the life-like velocity with which they flew careering from all points against each other, without passing away into the distance. . . . But the under surfaces of the huge masses of agitated vapour, as well as all terrestrial objects immediately around us, were glowing in the unnatural light of a faintly luminous and distinctly visible gaseous exhalation which hung about and enshrouded the mansion" (III, 291).[38]

The purest expression of this life-like velocity is the whirlwind that agitates the clouds against themselves. Man naturally regards a great wind as a threat, as Conrad explained in "Typhoon": "This is the disintegrating power of a great wind: it isolates one from one's own kind. An earthquake, a landslip, an avalanche, overtake a man incidentally, as it were—without passion. A furious gale attacks him like a personal enemy, tries to grasp his limbs, fastens upon his mind, seeks to rout his very spirit out of him."[39] Usher's storm does the same; the difference is in Usher's complicity. The repeated correspondences between the "Mad Trist" and the sounds from within the house signal the approach of the Ushers' dissolution. Recognizing this, Roderick seats himself facing the door so as to receive directly the impact of his fate. A horizontal posture, under the circumstances, would be too passive; Usher is expectant, ready, willing to cooperate. But the upright will not answer either, because there is nothing he can do. He assumes instead an in-between position in

[38] These and other lighting effects are discussed in Oliver Evans, "Infernal Illuminations in Poe," pp. 295-297.

[39] *The Concord Edition of the Works of Joseph Conrad* (New York, 1928), XXII, 40.

which he rocks mechanically back and forth, like a pendulum, his body possessed by a force more powerful than himself.

The life-like character of the wind foreshadows the return of the living Lady Madeline, whose presence Usher announces in a speech that completes his victimization: "I *now* tell you that I heard her first feeble movements in the hollow coffin. I heard them—many, many days ago—yet I dared not—*I dared not speak*! And now—to-night—Ethelred—ha! ha!—the breaking of the hermit's door, and the death-cry of the dragon, and the clangour of the shield!—say rather, the rending of her coffin, and the grating of the iron hinges of her prison, and her struggles within the coppered archway of the vault!' " (III, 296). In the end there is not a single rhythm but a whole series of coordinated and interdependent repetitions and rhythms: the sounds that link the "Mad Trist" to the sounds from the vault, Usher's back-and-forth motion in the chair, his sentence constructions, the footsteps of Madeline and the very beating of her heart: " 'Have I not heard her footstep on the stair? Do I not distinguish that heavy and horrible beating of her heart?' " (III, 296). Such hearing differs radically from the hearing of the murderer in "The Tell-Tale Heart," who probably hallucinates the sound of the heartbeat, and from that of the present narrator, who heard nothing that might not have been perceived by any other normal human being. Usher's hearing, on the other hand, surpasses nature, and the proof is his ability to perceive the presence of the Lady Madeline outside the door: "As if in the superhuman energy of his utterance there had been found the potency of a spell—the huge antique panels to which the speaker pointed, threw slowly back, upon the instant, their ponderous and ebony jaws. It was the work of the rushing gust—but then without those doors there DID stand the lofty and enshrouded figure of the Lady Madeline of Usher" (III, 296). On that "but" rests the whole balance in the narrative between the supernatural and the everyday. Up to the conjunction, the skeptical side of the narrator prevails; when the Lady Madeline actually appears, skeptic becomes believer.

The climactic fall that ends the story occurs in two parts, or rather in a single process with two aspects. The first is the mutual descent of brother and sister, who expire simultaneously in one another's arms. A sense of process—of a continuous movement in time—is achieved by a hypotactic sentence structure that stretches the moment out while knitting the two dissolutions so seamlessly together that no analysis will ever prove whether one transpired before the other: "For a moment she remained trembling and reeling to and fro upon the threshold, then, with a low moaning cry, fell heavily inward upon the person of her brother, and in her violent and now final death-agonies, bore him to the floor a corpse, and a victim to the terrors he had anticipated" (III, 296).

By his immediate flight the narrator confirms his belief—if any confirmation were needed—in the reality of what he has seen. Now he must withdraw, for the Ushers alone are privileged to endure the fate of their House. It is not that he escapes. The fact is he cannot stay; the ontological economy will not support him. Brother and sister fall for and with one another, inwardly, into a House that is at once the property and the being of the race:

"Without affinity to the air of heaven, reflected in the waters of its own tarn, the House of Usher exists only in the dense vapor issued from its ground. It has, so to speak, created its own space. It has also created its own particular duration. Not only does it exist in the spherical continuity of its own surroundings, but also in the linear continuity of the family it shelters. This 'has perpetuated itself in direct lineage.' So in the absence of connection with the air of heaven there must be added the 'absence of the collateral branch.' In the same way in which the house is enclosed in its own singular atmosphere, so too, its inhabitants are the prisoners of their own time, which cannot be mingled with that of the outside world."[40]

[40] Georges Poulet, *Metaphorphoses of the Circle*, trans. Carley

The second and final phase of the process is the fall of the edifice itself. As the narrator watches, the fissure he had earlier detected "rapidly widened—there came a fierce breath of the whirlwind—the entire orb of the satellite burst at once upon my sight—my brain reeled as I saw the mighty walls rushing asunder—there was a long tumultuous shouting sound like the voice of a thousand waters—and the deep and dark tarn at my feet closed sullenly and silently over the fragments of the 'House of Usher' " (iii, 297). In this submergence the inward-tending, self-completing quality of the Ushers' falling embrace is brought to its own peculiar perfection, the whole structure expiring downward with the pair as the Lady Madeline expired downward on her consubstantial twin. The sense of fateful climax is enhanced by the convergence of terror-producing effects: velocity, suddenness, oppressive breath and ominous sound; there is a suggestive parallel, moreover, between the Lady Madeline and the narrator, whose brain "reeled" (iii, 297) just as the lady's body had reeled a moment before.

For the narrator of "MS. Found in a Bottle," for Pym and for the Ushers, earthly existence is climaxed by an experience of transition figured as a descent or a "going-down."[41] Such an experience must be distinguished from those moments of "leave-taking" which rank, according to Georg Lukács, among the crucial events of literature as well as of life.[42] To take one's leave is to hesitate for a time between presence and absence. Volition and chance play a role: there is the

---

Dawson and Elliott Coleman in collaboration with the author (Baltimore, 1966), pp. 201-202.

[41] Joseph Moldenhauer, "Murder as a Fine Art," pp. 295-296, observes that "the 'going down' of Poe's protagonists symbolizes a return to the mother, to soporific warmth and darkness, to the womb." Later he states that " 'going down' into the aesthetic death state is surely fraught with terrific anxieties and physical torments. But madness and pain are the necessary stage of the protagonist's progress toward Unity, just as the poet must suffer frustration and anguish in striving to perfect his power."

[42] *The Historical Novel*, trans. Hannah and Stanley Mitchell (Boston, 1963), p. 100.

possibility of being talked into staying, or of a simple change of heart, and these provide the tension that renders the situation "full of moment." But we find no such tension in these tales of Poe. There is not the slightest doubt that the characters will go—they have no choice. If there is a pause near the end of "MS. Found in a Bottle," it is because the ship is on the brink and not because the protagonist is having second thoughts. All of the principals in these tales are subject, like their counterparts in the poems, to some overpowering external influence. In the poems this tended to express itself in a vaporous medium descending onto the victim. In the world of the tales, which is more "physical" and more expansive, the medium gets bigger and wetter, becoming now a tarn, now a giant vortex, now the Antarctic Sea; instead of being dampened or vaguely threatened, the victim is now totally immersed. Each climax is an experience, as Poe says in *Eureka*, of "absolute Irrelation," in which a power greater than my own—a power numinous, vast, unknown—draws me not so much *to* itself as *back within* itself. To go down is to be drawn as an irresistible gravitational pull to one's original state: it is, in a word, to go home.

Any account of the experience is limited, for the story must necessarily end before the journey is complete. Poe concludes the two earlier works through the device of a manuscript that has been broken off, so that the reader is left hanging (though less so in *Pym*, where there is an attempt to round the story off with a "Note"). The ending of "The Fall of the House of Usher" is also abrupt, but in a different way. Here there is no break in the continuity of the account. The first-person stays to the end, watching the House as it sinks, like the city in the sea, into the watery depths. But this is only the end as *he* sees it. Unlike the narrator of "MS. Found in a Bottle" and *Pym*, this witness is not an immediate participant in the process of descent, and must therefore confine himself to a distant and "outside" view; thus the climactic moment, which for the Ushers is a return and a reunification, assumes the form in the narrator's perception of a disappearance and a termination. The narrator is technically speaking

—to use Wayne C. Booth's useful term—a reliable narrator. But the source of exclusion is ontological as well: "The narrator is, of course, a visitor from another world, the macrocosmic world of balanced attraction and repulsion. His response to the collocation of Usher's house is a subconscious cognition of the dangerous unification and organization of the Usher total ambience."[43] The narrator belongs, in short, to a different order of being from the Ushers, just as their ancestral dwelling belongs to a different order of being from the landscape to which he retreats.

For Usher's friend, as for Ligeia's lover, there is nothing to do, in the end but name: the final words in this story about the House of Usher are precisely the words, the *House of Usher* (III, 297). This vocal gesture designates nothing new, but confirms an already existing identity. The final naming becomes a parodic Word within the Word, a presence of the absolute turned inward on itself, a force transforming its presence into its own absence. The fall of the House of Usher is the fall of being—through matter—into the gulf beyond.

"WILLIAM WILSON"

A man ridden with guilt offers his confession as he nears the end of his life. Wilson in this respect resembles Tamerlane. Wilson is also, like Tamerlane, dependent on a power outside himself. This power works on him, however, through heredity, whereas Tamerlane is manipulated by an agency that bypasses the mediation of the family in order to work directly on his spirit. The willfulness that makes Wilson "a prey to the most ungovernable passions" (III, 300), derives, in his own words, from the "race" (III, 299) that has endowed him genetically with "the family character" (III, 300). Yet as in *Pym*, "MS. Found in a Bottle," or "Berenice," the family is given only to be taken away: no sooner have the parents started to materialize than they evaporate; by the end of the single paragraph devoted to the subject, Wilson has

[43] Smith, "Usher's Madness and Poe's Organicism," p. 388.

isolated himself: ". . . I was left to the guidance of my own will, and became, in all but name, the master of my own actions" (III, 300). But in exercising this power he is actually—like his counterparts in these other works—*in* the power of a force beyond himself: namely, that heredity which determines, physically and spiritually, the very substance of his being. Another man might keep such information to himself, but not William Wilson, who wants to be "recognized" as even more powerless than he is: "I would fain have them believe that I have been, in some measure, the slave of circumstances beyond human control. I would wish them to seek out for me, in the details I am about to give, some little oasis of *fatality* amid a wilderness of error" (III, 300). If other men will only grant this, Wilson will be morally absolved. We also see, in Tamerlane, a concern with absolution. Tamerlane, however, is relatively indifferent to the opinions of others and openly scorns his sole auditor, the priest. Tamerlane lives solely in the gaze of God. It was a supernal force that made him what he is; it is a supernal force alone that can shrive him of his sins. But William Wilson cares much for the opinions of fellow men. He lives, in Sartre's terms, in the gaze of the other (*l'autre*) and the others (*l'autrui*). That is why the second Wilson's implicit rejection of his values threatens him; it is the incriminating gaze of the other. That is why so much depends on the attitudes of one's peers, whose collective gaze can either endorse rejection, which would condemn the first Wilson, or repudiate it, which would save him.

William Wilson also relates, like Tamerlane, to a "beyond," but more indirectly. The first hint that his fate is superintended by some higher power is pressed, as we have already seen, through the mediation of the family. The second mediator is the house:

"But the house!—how quaint an old building was this!—to me how veritably a palace of enchantment! There was really no end to its windings—to its incomprehensible subdivisions. It was difficult, at any given time, to say with certainty upon which of its two stories one happened to be. From each room to every other there were sure to be found three or four steps either in ascent or descent. Then the lateral branches were innumerable—inconceivable—and so returning in upon themselves, that our most exact ideas in regard to the whole mansion were not very far different from those with which we pondered upon infinity." (III, 303)

Generically speaking, the section of the tale dealing with the school, of which this house is a part, is an idyll; while the house itself is a kind of *locus amoenus* or ideal place—a *topos* with, as E. R. Curtius has shown, countless variations.[44] But neither the generic perspective nor the perspective of *topoi* explains the exhilaration in the passage, which is one of the most buoyant in all of Poe's writings. This quality, in addition to the fact that the description concerns a memory from childhood, identifies the edifice as, in Gaston Bachelard's terms, a *maison onirique*: there is for each of us "une maison onirique, une maison du souvenir-songe, perdue dans l'ombre d'un au-delà du passé vrai." Such a house is literally a world in itself: "Car la maison est notre coin du monde. Elle est—on l'a souvent dit—notre premier univers. Elle est vraiment un cosmos."[45] Within this general pattern the house takes on whatever local characteristics the individual imagination wants to give it. The special characteristic of William Wilson's house is that it challenges the mind's desire to know, only to baffle that desire by proving inexhaustible. "Then the lateral branches were so *innumerable —inconceivable*—and so returning in upon themselves, that our most exact ideas in regard to the whole mansion were not very far different from those with which we pondered upon *infinity*" (III, 303; italics mine). The nature of the house thus accords with Poe's ideas about the limits of the human ability to know, and about the role of matter in relation to those limits. In "The Power of Words" Agathos

[44] *European Literature and the Latin Middle Ages*, trans. Willard R. Trask (New York, 1953), pp. 192-200.

[45] *La Poétique de l'espace* (Paris, 1957), pp. 33, 24.

explains that "of this infinity of matter, the *sole* purpose is to afford infinite springs, at which the soul may allay the thirst *to know* which is for ever unquenchable within it—since to quench it would be to extinguish the soul's self" (VI, 140). The third mediator of the beyond, more problematic than the other two, is the second William Wilson, in whom the first "discovered, or fancied I discovered, in his accent, his air, and general appearance, a something which first startled, and then deeply interested me, by bringing to mind dim visions of my earliest infancy—wild, confused and thronging memories of a time when memory herself was yet unborn. I cannot better describe the sensation which oppressed me than by saying that I could with difficulty shake off the belief of my having been acquainted with the being who stood before me, at some epoch very long ago—some point of the past even infinitely remote" (III, 311).

The second William Wilson relates to the first as the cat will relate to the narrator of "The Black Cat." Even in the act of frustrating the first Wilson, the second reveals "a certain most inappropriate, and assuredly most unwelcome *affecionateness* of manner" (III, 306). Wilson responds to all displays of goodness (again in a way that anticipates "The Black Cat") with gratuitous acts of evil. His perverseness is nowhere more evident than when he cheats at cards and keeps the winnings despite an already enormous fortune. The second Wilson, by contrast, is good, and tries to bring out what goodness there is in the first. Yet we are less aware of the good in the second than of the evil in the first. This is because the Good tends to exist, for Poe, "elsewhere." It can be in a woman, or in a God, or, as in this case, in another man. But it is always a thing apart—something from which I am alienated; something that *I* do not have. Consequently, no matter how hard he tries, the second Wilson can never reach the first, who sees the other but does not recognize him. By refusing to face the incriminating gaze of the other, I reject the potential not only for the good in me but for the godly.

As a mediator the other comes to me as an alerting—and if I heed him, a saving—presence. What the other alerts me to is the sin of putting myself before all others—the sin of Tamerlane, of Angelo and Ianthe, and later, as we will see in the first of the dialogues, of mankind as a whole.

That the other schoolboys do not perceive the similarity between the two classmates puzzles the first Wilson for a time. Being theoretically inclined, like most of Poe's characters, he concludes: "Perhaps the *gradation* of his copy rendered it not so readily perceptible; or, more possibly, I owed my security to the masterly air of the copyist, who, disdaining the letter, (which in a painting is all the obtuse can see,) gave but the full spirit of his original for my individual contemplation and chagrin" (III, 309-310). This explanation overlooks the extent to which the first Wilson magnifies the imitation in his own mind; but it recognizes the significant fact that the first Wilson is *himself* the link between the *other* and the *others.* I magnify out of a sense of inferiority, which is privately felt, and which merges eventually with a sense of guilt. Guilt, too, is privately felt, although it is an emotion brought on by my relations to others. Guilt is a failure to meet their standards or expectations; I burn with shame beneath the incrimination of their gaze. As it happens, they do not see my inadequacy or guilt any more than they see the likeness between myself and the other. No matter. They have a pair of mediators who act in their behalf. One of these is my counterpart, the second Wilson, who acts as their surrogate, never allowing me to forget my failings. The other is myself. When I experience guilt I feel the gaze of the others as it is refracted not only in the gaze of the second Wilson, but in my own. I see the others, I read the judgment in their eyes, then draw it into myself. My guilt is internalized social rejection. If I spare one of my gambling victims it is "rather with a view to the preservation of my own character in the eyes of my associates, than from any less interested motive . . ." (III, 318). When my companions, disturbed by my behavior, encircle me, staring, "I could not help feeling my cheeks tingle with the many burning glances of scorn or reproach cast upon me by the less abandoned of the party" (III, 318).

The second Wilson brings on this and other exposures through a series of confrontations, of which four are described in detail. In the first confrontation, which occurs at the original school, the corrupt Wilson steals into the chamber of the other. The second confrontation takes place in a vestibule in Eton, the third during the card game in which Wilson ruins Glendinning. The two Wilsons confront one another for the last time in Rome, as the first Wilson heads for a meeting with a married woman. The first confrontation recalls the sleeper poems and anticipates "The Tell-Tale Heart," in which the victimizer contemplates his victim before murdering him. Wilson never carries out the misdeed he plans (a practical joke) because of something he sees, or partly sees, in the appearance of the other: "Gasping for breath, I lowered the lamp in still nearer proximity to the face. Were these —*these* the lineaments of William Wilson? I saw, indeed, that they were his, but I shook as if with a fit of the ague in fancying they were not. What *was* there about them to confound me in this manner? I gazed;—while my brain reeled with a multitude of incoherent thoughts" (III, 312). His situation resembles that of the guardians who, in the sleeper poems, fail to remember. Wilson's shortcoming, however, is twofold. It is, first, a failure to recognize. All the facts indicate that he and the other share in the same identity, but it is the one fact he cannot perceive. His shortcoming is also a failure to remember. A few months away from the school are enough "to enfeeble my remembrance of the events at Dr. Bransby's, or at least to effect a material change in the nature of the feelings with which I remembered them. The truth—the tragedy—of the drama was no more. I could now find room to doubt the evidence of my senses . . ." (III, 313). The two failures are complementary. Failure to recognize protects me now, at the moment of confrontation; failure to remember protects me later from the cumulative effect such moments would have if

I were ever to put them all together. But inevitably, by the same process, forgetting condemns me, by preventing me from recognizing the other through whose agency alone I can be saved.

In neither of the next two confrontations is the second Wilson seen by the others. There is no one else in the vestibule, which in any event is dimly lit; and the entry of the second Wilson into the card room extinguishes the candlelight. The other is essentially, in both cases, an oral presence —an elaboration on the notion of the "voice of conscience." His partial viability is a corollary, at the same time, of the incomplete way in which the first Wilson perceives him. For not until the final confrontation does he comprehend the relevance of the other for himself. In this confrontation, as in the first, the two meet face to face. They are not alone together, however, until the first Wilson drags the second, masked, into a secluded space that is the complement of the chamber in which the first confrontation took place. As we have seen, there is often some circumstantial element that obscures the confrontation: the dimness of the vestibule, for example, or the darkness in the card room. The mask, which stays on during the sword fight, is another of these elements, a kind of barrier at which the first Wilson's mind is only too glad to stop. The entire story is a mixture of just such commonplace elements with the mysterious or the improbable (the coincidences of name, age, and appearance that link the two Wilsons, the desire of the second to imitate and pursue the first). To reduce the second Wilson to the status of a hallucination, as a recent critic has attempted to do, is merely to make the story palatable to a psychologically oriented twentieth-century taste.[46] Such modernization unfortunately leaves no place

[46] Patrick F. Quinn, *The French Face of Edgar Poe*, sees the second Wilson as "a mental projection and only that" (p. 221). Quinn is nearer my own view, and the view of such French commentators as Maurice Blanchot and Gaston Bachelard, when he states that "to read Poe properly we should realize that the experience which his stories uniquely offer us is that of participating in the life of a great ontological imagination" (p. 274).

in the tale for the element of sheer mystery that Poe, in keeping with his own inclinations and the taste of his times, built into it. The second objection that can be raised against such a reading is that it causes us to miss one of the main points of the narrative: that William Wilson is not crazy but *bad*. If Poe is only fitfully concerned with right and wrong, as we are often told, the greater the reason to test the quality of his Moral Sense (as he was calling that faculty when Henry James was still a child)[47] when it unmistakably appears. The third objection is that, by concentrating on a single element in the tale, we lose sight of other, equally important, elements both in themselves and in their interrelations. When William Wilson's moment of recognition finally comes, it comes through a *combination* of the improbable, the circumstantial, and the psychological. The improbable: the other Wilson carries on to the end of his life the mission of representing to the first Wilson the latter's potential for good. The circumstantial: the recognition comes about only after the mask is dropped—which lets the first Wilson see the other's face for the first time in years. The psychological: when Wilson looks back at his counterpart (after being distracted for a moment by a noise at the door) he sees "a material change in the arrangements at the upper or farther end of the room. A large mirror,—so at first it seemed to me in my confusion—now stood where none had been perceptible before; and, as I stepped up to it in extremity of terror, mine own image, but with features all pale and dabbled in blood, advanced to meet me with a feeble and tottering gait" (III, 324-325).

[47] In "The Poetic Principle" Poe divides "the world of the mind" into "the Pure Intellect, Taste, and the Moral Sense. I place Taste in the middle, because it is just this position which, in the mind, it occupies. It holds intimate relations with either extreme; but from the Moral Sense is separated by so faint a difference that Aristotle has not hesitated to place some of its operations among the virtues themselves. Nevertheless, we find the *offices* of the trio marked with a sufficient distinction. Just as the Intellect concerns itself with Truth, so Taste informs us of the Beautiful while the Moral Sense is regardful of Duty" (XIV, 272-273).

The first Wilson may be corrupt, but he is not mad. He recognizes that the vision is an illusion, just as he recognizes a moment later an even more startling truth: "Not a thread in all his raiment—not a line in all the marked and singular lineaments of his face which was not, even in the most absolute identity, *mine own*!" (III, 325). "Ligeia" and the other tales about women conclude with the same kind of recognition and the same kind of sentence—a sentence with a sting in the tail, as Louis Untermeyer might have said. But the endings of "Ligeia" and "William Wilson" differ in at least two important respects. One difference involves the role of the other. In "Ligeia" the other is spatially near but ontologically far. The narrator can recognize Ligeia, he can see that she is there, but he can never identify with her, for her mode of being is alien to his own. In "William Wilson," by contrast, the confronting individuals are ontologically near: when the first Wilson sees the face of the second he contemplates his own, the mediation of the other representing the sole means by which he is able to confront himself. This does not mean, as a "psychological" reading would imply, that I who am real see myself in the other, who is not. It means, rather, that the other who is real is seen by myself as though he *were* myself. Indeed, it is precisely because the other is a reality that I can see the reality of myself. This desire to see the truth, and to say it, is embodied in a style characterized, as Donald Barlow Stauffer has shown, by such properties as orderliness, abstraction, parallelism, and that eighteenth-century *ordonnance* which found favor with Tate.[48] The style is marked as well by asides or parenthetic expressions that demonstrate, as Stauffer points out, Wilson's desire to analyze and moralize. Wilson's self-interruptions, one might add, tend to be self-contradictions: "I discovered, or fancied I discovered . . ." (III, 311); ". . . he avoided, or made a show of avoiding me" (III, 310). He is also inclined to negations and negative conjunctions: but, although, cannot, however. This

[48] "Style and Meaning in 'Ligeia' and 'William Wilson,'" *Studies in Short Fiction*, 2 (1965), pp. 316-318, 321-330.

means that Wilson does to himself in his language what the other has done to him in his life: through his speech he reenacts, in effect, the other's attempts to challenge him and check him, in the hope of bringing him nearer the truth.

It is idle to say that the first Wilson might have been saved by the second Wilson if only he had recognized the truth in time, because in Poe's world you never do. Witness Tamerlane, who does not know what he desires until he has lost any chance of having it. William Wilson, in the same way, never really lives until the moment when—in seeing the truth of his being embodied in another—he ceases to exist.

"The Masque of the Red Death"

The central event in this tale is a victimization of the third-person: a singular form, *he* (Prince Prospero) and a plural, *they* (the Prince's guests). Fearing the plague that is devastating the countryside, and desiring an environment in which they can indulge their fancies, the Prince and his party lock themselves behind the abbey walls, creating thereby the conditions of their own premature burial: "A strong and lofty wall girdled [the castle] in. This wall had gates of iron. The courtiers, having entered, brought furnaces and massy hammers and welded the bolts" (IV, 250). If the depopulated countryside resembles the vacant landscape in "The Valley of Unrest," the castle resembles "The Haunted Palace." Lacking an experiencing consciousness with which to identify, we watch the masque as outsiders, in much the same way that the travellers watch the occupants of the haunted palace. There is, secondly, as in the poem, a sudden, gratuitous change: at one moment death is apparently absent; a moment later, he is present, and everyone starts to die. And, finally, there is the same kind of intense, obsessive activity, ending, as in the poem, with a rush. In this case the hurrying is dual. There is, first, the "slight rushing movement" of the group toward the intruder, and moments later the more impulsive movement of Prospero, who "rushed hurriedly" toward the intruder through each of the six chambers. As in the other tales, velocity expresses anxiety, and heightens it. But the anxiety in the castle is not something that, at a certain point, enters the scene; it is something that is already there. In securing the walls and doors, the courtiers are locking *in* more than they are locking *out*: "They resolved to leave means neither of ingress or egress to the sudden impulses of despair or of frenzy from within" (IV, 251). By what logic could someone seized by a frenzy *within* the castle ever seek *ingress*? Obviously, such a person would want to go out. The statement is contradictory because in the space of it there is a shift of interest from, as it were, outside to inside—from a condition that is overt to one that is immanent. Up to the word "ingress," the sentence seems to be oriented toward the external world. If it were broken off at this point, we would presumably expect the missing portion to say something about keeping the disease out and the people in. That of course is not what occurs. Ingress and egress are paired a little too automatically here, like those "gummed strips of words" that Orwell refers to in his analysis of linguistic abuses. They are a set, like "in or out," "come or go." The danger in using such a set is that you may conceal from your reader that you are leaning more heavily here on "egress," for, as we move on in the sentence, we see that the concern is with the behavior of people who will want, like the occupants of the haunted palace, to rush *out*. For this, too, is a haunted palace—a circumscribed space that, from the time it is closed in on itself, is already tenanted by the power that its walls supposedly exclude.

That power is the phantom mummer, death. But the appeal of death, as we have seen, lies in its capacity to free man into the gulf beyond the gulf beyond. Death mediates in the direction of new life, or rather, since Poe's time is cyclical, toward an absolute anterior existence. We have now come back to the point at which we arrived earlier. If death is not ultimately possible, it is possible relatively. Ordinary human death, like ordinary human life, transpires within the field of relation. Whereas the godhead of *Eureka* is an absolute Irrelation, the human power is precisely one of relations, ratios, and proportions (whence Poe's great fondness for such phrases as "in ratio to," "in proportion to," and so on). In other words, although Poe conceives of death as ultimately a mode of transcendence, his characters may not do so; and the "ratio," as he would say, applies in the same way to "I" and "he." The flow of destructive power between these two grammatical and ontological persons is rarely from third to first. "I" can kill "him" or "her" but neither can kill "me." Only nature has ultimate power over the first-person, but nature, even when it most victimizes, gathers the victim into its infinite self, as a mother takes in a child; it does not shuck him of his life and discard the shell ("MS. Found in a Bottle," "A Descent into the Maelstrom," *Pym*, "Hans Pfaall," and all the stories of the after-life).

To this extent the "he" and "they" of "The Masque of the Red Death" are subject to the worst that time can offer. We may now examine these creatures in the hopes of defining their fate and the fate of their world. Poe shows, in this creation, more social consciousness than one expects of him, the tone of the second paragraph suggesting a degree of moral distaste for the court's desire to sequester itself. But this consciousness vanishes almost as soon as it appears. There are, for example, no "people" who might visit death upon their defaulting masters (who, as an incidental result of excluding the lower classes, must do their own manual labor). The real interest in the story is man's relation to his own mortality. What has the Prince done to warrant his punishment? For one thing, he has indulged the universal human tendency to *perverseness*, first, by turning from his subjects, and, second, by walling himself and his court into a space from which there can be no escape. But more importantly he has attempted to supplant God's creation with a creation—a model, as it would be called in "Al Aaraaf"—of his own. In the words of Leibniz, the philosopher most quoted by Poe, man replaces God's "equivocal" relationship with the created world (by which the creating agent works in a medium different from himself) with a "univocal" relationship (in which the agent and his creation are of the same kind).[49]

What better recourse, in such a situation, than to revel in one's own reality-denying fantasies? Accordingly, Prospero turns the abbey into a *maison onirique*. Most authors conceive of houses, Bachelard suggests, as verticalities linking an up with a down. But Prospero's dwelling stretches out horizontally. Instead of a space for descent, the author provides a space for walking, for dancing, for listening to music. He presents it, furthermore, in a series of gradations, from blue through purple to green to orange to white to violet to black.[50] That we have to do with gradations rather than with an uncoordinated sequence can be seen from the climactic nature of the seventh and black apartment that quickly takes dominion. Nothing ever really happens in the other rooms, which seem to exist in order to bring the black apartment into perspective; in addition, the black apartment gets by far the fullest treatment, and it is within its precincts that the critical scene transpires. The arrangement of the series is so managed, finally, that the visitor also enjoys the highly favored property of the "novel effect" (IV, 251). All of this conspires to make the last apartment, with its black draperies and its blood-colored windows, the ultimate existential space. The chamber has become, in effect, a *Burgverliess*, the foolproof Gothic dungeon from which no prisoner ever escapes.[51] In his blindness the Prince does not perceive this; nor does he perceive that in and through the apartment (which stands at the sym-

[49] *The Monadology and Other Philosophical Writings*, trans. and ed. Robert Latta (Oxford, 1898), p. 238, n. 61.

[50] Walter Blair, "Poe's Conception of Incident and Tone in the Tale," *Modern Philology*, 41 (1944), pp. 228-240, identifies the rooms with the seven ages of man. For Nina Baym, "The Function of Poe's Pictorialism," *South Atlantic Quarterly*, 65 (1966), pp. 46-54, the rooms show that excessive indulgence in imagination can lead to insanity.

[51] Einor Railo, *The Haunted Castle: A Study of the Elements of English Romanticism* (London, 1927), p. 139. Kane, "Edgar Allan Poe and Architecture," pp. 149-160, shows Poe's indebtedness to the haunted castle of the Gothic novel and enumerates the characteristics of his fictional architecture.

bolic western extreme of the series) death is "already here": the black apartment is his scenic presence.

The rooms are meant to accomplish several overlapping aims. One aim is to vanquish mutability by transforming time into space—by embodying variety, change, and sequence in a purely architectural form. Thereby Prospero realizes a second aim, which is to allow his ego to expand to the fullest possible degree, so that everyone is living almost literally inside him: within his walls, within his will, within his taste. It is in fact this desire for all the fullness one can get, this insatiable desire to *be* everywhere, which gives impetus to Poe's entire cosmology. The "hero" of "The Masque of the Red Death" is like a grotesque version of the expansive consciousness in *Eureka*, which transforms itself not only into the universe but into God Himself.

As we have often noticed, and as W. H. Auden reminds us, Poe was fascinated by conditions or states of being. Auden, indeed, divides Poe's tales according to the type of state they express. There are narratives concerned with "states of willful being," such as "Ligeia"; with self-destructive states in which the "ego and the self are passionately hostile," such as "The Imp of the Perverse"; and with "the state of chimerical passion, that is, the passionate unrest of a self that lacks all passion," such as "The Man of the Crowd." Finally, Auden puts the horror tales and the tales of ratiocination together "for the heroes of both exist as unitary states."[52] "The Masque of the Red Death," too, is about states. We do not read about things that happened; we read about things which were: "There were buffoons, there were improvisatori, there were ballet-dancers, there were musicians, there was Beauty, there was wine. All these and security were within. Without was the 'Red Death' " (IV, 251). The masque is an accompaniment to the Prince's imagination: "There were much glare and glitter and piquancy and phantasm—much of what has been since seen in 'Hernani.' There were arabesque figures with unsuited limbs and appointments. There were de-

[52] *The Recognition of Edgar Allan Poe*, p. 221.

lirious fancies such as the madman fashions. There were much of the beautiful, much of the wanton, much of the *bizarre*, something of the terrible, and not a little of that which might have excited disgust" (IV, 254). We should appreciate that these predicates are not mere copula. A verb of being is a verb of *being*. All words—nouns, adverbs, adjectives, pronouns—have being. If they did not, we could not talk about them. There is no such thing as a grammar without ontological implications; there is no syntax that cannot be approached not only from a philological but from an ontological point of view. Although Poulet has suggested (to return to our text) that death "enters" this scene, it is in fact already there. Death, to borrow a term from Lawrence, is "realized"; it has no need to enter the abbey in order to be there, it has only to be recognized. We hear nothing therefore about entry. We are told, rather, that "there were many individuals in the crowd who had found leisure to become aware of the presence of a masked figure which had arrested the attention of no single individual before" (IV, 255). In order to die, Prospero has but to perceive. The Prince expires, accordingly, not from the disease, but from a recognition so intense that he falls swooning onto his own upturned dagger (suggestively, a technological instrument).

That the principal action of the Prince's should be a kind of non-action (a loss of consciousness and a fall) indicates the temporal quality of the narrative, which is a rhythm of motion and stasis, motion coming into being, as it were, dialectically, by a consciousness of its absence. The dancers pause more than they dance, the musicians interrupt a music they have not made. With the chiming of the hour "the musicians of the orchestra were constrainted to pause, momentarily, in their performance, to hearken to the sound; and thus the waltzers perforce ceased their evolutions; and there was a brief disconcert of the whole gay company . . ." (IV, 253). Even after the moment of terror passes, the musicians do not play. They look at one another, they smile at their own edginess, they vow that they will not cease again; and then, an hour later, without any mention of their having played, "there came yet another chiming of the clock, and then were the same disconcert and tremulousness and meditation as before" (IV, 253).

Even the "action" words are strangely static. We have, for example, a "slide" in the third paragraph. But its function here is to represent a state, a *possibility* of sliding, not to render a determinate event within the narrative. The sentence is a generalization about an architecture *not present* in the scene: "In many palaces, however, such suites form a long and straight vista, while the sliding doors slide back nearly to the walls on either hand . . ." (IV, 251). Closely examined, many verbs are even less active than they appear. The "looked" that occurs in the same paragraph depicts a position, a configuration in space, entirely static and removed from the realm of human behavior: "To the right and left, in the middle of each wall, a tall and narrow Gothic window looked out upon a closed corridor which pursued the windings of the suite" (IV, 251). The pseudo-motion continues in the use of "pursued," anticipating a similar use of the past tense of "follow" a few sentences later: "But in the corridors that followed the suite. . . ." One might also point out the number of verbs that convey a sense of inertia, weight, or lassitude: *hung, shrouded, failed, lay*, and so on.[53] The most "active" element in the apartments is the firelight that streams in through the windows: "And thus were produced a multitude of gaudy and fantastic appearances. But in the western or black chamber the effect of the fire-light that streamed upon the dark hangings through the blood-tinted panes, was ghastly in the extreme and produced so wild a look upon the countenances of those who entered, that there were few of the company bold enough to set foot within its precincts at all" (IV, 252). To this extent the rooms are kinetic, although

[53] Poe's fascination with weightedness and related phenomena is discussed in Gaston Bachelard, *L'Eau et les rêves: essai sur l'imagination de la matière* (Paris, 1942), pp. 63-96.

"was" continues to predominate along with a tendency to render a given effect (in this case the condition of fear) more vivid than its cause. The clock comes closer to an active state: "Its pendulum swung to and fro with a dull, heavy, monotonous clang; and when the minute-hand made the circuit of the face, and the hour was to be stricken, there came from the brazen lungs of the clock a sound which was clear and loud and deep and exceedingly musical, but of so peculiar a note and emphasis that, at each lapse of an hour, the musicians of the orchestra were constrained to pause . . ." (IV, 252-253). An action that produces a stasis: the fire and the clock contribute both, for the two are equally alive and equally destructive.

Within the Prince's *Burgverliess* we find, among the human beings, an absence of force; or, to put it another way, a negative capacity, the power of ceasing to move and, extending from that, of ceasing to be. In such a world human beings do not act; they are acted upon. In order to act upon human beings, the clock, a technological instrument, must be able to operate within their sphere. It must, as it were, cross over, manifesting itself as a vital being: thus, as heated metal has "breath," so the clock has a "voice," its rhythm inevitably suggesting the rhythm of the heartbeat. Finally, when the human lives have passed so must those of the clock and the fire: "And the life of the ebony clock went out with that of the last of the gay. And the flames of the tripods expired" (IV, 258).

"The Masque of the Red Death" is anticipated, in certain ways, by "Shadow. A Parable." Threatened by a plague, oppressed by "feelings more intense than terror for which there is no name upon the earth" (II, 147), Oinos retires with a small company of friends who, as Poulet has noted, enclose themselves in much the same way as Prospero's revellers: "And to our chamber there was no entrance save by a lofty door of brass: and the door was fashioned by the artizan Corinnos, and, being of rare workmanship, was fastened from within. Black draperies, likewise, in the gloomy room, shut out from our view the moon, the lurid stars, and the peopleless streets . . ." (II, 148). Here the sense of inertia and lassitude is even more pronounced: "A dead weight hung upon us. It hung upon our limbs—upon the household furniture—upon the goblets from which we drank; and all things were depressed, and borne down thereby . . ." (II, 148). How does mortality manifest itself among the company? By already being there: first, in the sensation of weight and incipient descent in the passage just quoted; second, in the person of a corpse that lies upon the floor, "the genius and the demon of the scene" (II, 149); and, third, in the person of death himself. As in "The Masque of the Red Death" death announces his presence by a cessation. Suddenly Oinos stops singing, the echoes of his voice "rolling afar off among the sable draperies of the chamber. . . . And lo! from among those sable draperies where the sounds of the song departed, there came forth a dark and undefined shadow . . ." (II, 149). This is not an entry from without but an emergence from within. The chamber is one of those "sacred" places discussed above, an area carved out of the external and "profane" space around it. It is at once internal and centrifugal, its draperies serving as a kind of inner-directed wall, from which the shadow issues forth like a visual echo of Oinos' fading voice. Self-contained, the chamber possesses a door by which one cannot escape. This door, which death covers with its shadow in the final paragraph, is only a denied possibility, a barrier that, in cutting off escape, converts the chamber into a space of terror.

For Prince Prospero alone does the abbey in "The Masque of the Red Death" become the ultimate space of terror. Although the guests suffer greatly from fear, they die from the disease. But Prospero dies from the terror itself—his fright causing him to fall upon the blade he has dropped. Before a greater power, the Prince's autonomous creations—his attempt to extend time through space—are as nothing. The masque becomes what it already was, the masque not of Prince Prospero but of the Red Death.

"The Pit and the Pendulum"

"The Pit and the Pendulum" begins in repetition: "I was sick—sick unto death with that long agony. . . . The sentence —the dread sentence of death—was the last of distinct accentuation which reached my ears" (v, 67). Again we are confronted with a to-and-fro, back-and-forth quality; the difference is that here the quality is rendered as cycle: "After that, the sound of the inquisitorial voices seemed merged in one dreamy indeterminate hum. It conveyed to my soul the idea of *revolution*—perhaps from its association in fancy with the burr of a mill-wheel" (v, 67). "Revolution" suggests two things: a transition from one kind of sensation to another, and the drawing of these sensations together in a merger—as if a wheel, in rapidly touching two opposed points one after the other, were thought of as bringing them momentarily together. First the victim records sound; then silence, "for presently I heard no more" (v, 67). There is a brief swing to sight, to a kind of visualization of sound, as he watches the lips of judges, white, "thin even to grotesqueness." Another swing carries vision to the seven candles that are followed in turn by the tactile sensation of the galvanic battery. After a moment music supersedes, in fancy, only to be superseded by a return to silence. The total effect is of an imperfect synesthesia, a merger of the senses that does not deprive the senses of their discreteness.

The "idea of revolution" states abstractly what is rendered concretely in the interrelated rhythms of the story: the repetition of words in the initial and later paragraphs, the clocklike swinging of the pendulum, and the cyclical nature of the torture itself, whereby the narrator experiences suffering, respite, then renewed suffering. Rhythm, like so many other things in Poe, is metastable. In "The Poetic Principle" it represents the foundation of poetry, which the essay defines quite simply as "*The Rhythmical Creation of Beauty*" (xiv, 275). The cosmogony goes further, carrying rhythm into the very center of being, so that the universe itself becomes a great body breathing awesomely out and awesomely in.

Rhythm, cycle, and revolution are closely connected with the idea of circularity, the circle being the constant expression of that principle of continuity which those other phenomena embody in flux. In the landscape tales and in *Eureka,* rhythm and circularity are essentially affirmative; here they are negative. "The Pit and the Pendulum" might be subtitled: "The Rhythmical Creation of Terror," as might "Ligeia," for each narrative depends not so much on the mere association of terror as on the compounding of it through a pattern of repetition. The same inversion affects the phenomenon of the "center," which signifies in the landscape and cosmological writings a kind of ideal point (a term we will meet again below) in reference to a surrounding circumference, sphere, circle—or universe. In the present tale, by contrast, the center is a place of intense victimization. Forced back by the impinging walls, the narrator shrinks "to the centre of the cell" (v, 85) only to discover that this point of space holds even greater terrors: the advancing walls assume the shape of a lozenge "with a rapidity that left me no time for contemplation. Its centre, and of course, its greatest width, came just over the yawning gulf. I shrank back—but the closing walls pressed me resistlessly onward. At length for my seared and writhing body there was no longer an inch of foothold on the firm floor of the prison. I struggled no more, but the agony of my soul found vent in one loud, long, and final scream of despair. I felt that I tottered upon the brink—I averted my eyes—" (v, 86). The circumscription of space, the anticipation of the fall, the interpretation of design: all of these phenomena that are potentially or actually "good" in other contexts, here assume a victimizing aspect. The same applies, though in a different way, to the pendulum. This instrument has a special relation to circularity by virtue of its movement, which is that of an arc or incomplete circle, and by virtue of the "crescent" (v, 78) it swings across the prisoner's horizontal body. But the meaning of this form depends, as in the case of these other phenomena, on the totality within which it appears. As an element of the landscape in "The Island of the Fay," the crescent form is natural, picturesquely irregular, and restorative; as an element of that claustrophobic landscape that is the prison, it is unnatural, mechanically regular, and destructive.

Like Pym, Hans Pfaall, and the man in the vortex, the narrator communicates his sensations by writing: "I saw the lips of the black-robed judges. They appeared to me white—whiter than the sheet upon which I trace these words . . ." (v, 67). What we experience, in this consciousness with which the writing enables us to identify, is not so much an action as a state. The victim attempts

". . . to regather some token of the state of seeming nothingness into which my soul had lapsed . . ." (v, 69)

"Then the mere consciousness of existence, without thought—a condition which lasted long. Then, very suddenly, *thought*, and shuddering terror, and earnest endeavor to comprehend my true state." (v, 70)

"Yet not for a moment did I suppose myself actually dead. Such a supposition, notwithstanding what we read in fiction, is altogether inconsistent with real existence;—but where and in what state was I?" (v, 71)

This first-person is a man, like the typical voyager or lover, to whom things happen. He does not act but is acted-upon: "States—in contrast with qualities which exist 'potentially' —give themselves as actually existing. Hate, love, jealousy are states. An illness, in so far as it is apprehended by the patient as a psycho-physiological reality, is a state. In the same way a number of characteristics which are externally attached to my person can, in so far as I live them, become *states*. Absence (in relation to a definite person), exile, dishonor, triumph are states. . . . A quality furthermore is an innate or acquired disposition which contributes to *qualify* my personality. The state, on the contrary, is much more accidental and contingent; it is *something which happens to me*."[54]

[54] Jean-Paul Sartre, *Being and Nothingness: An Essay on Phenomenological Ontology*, trans. Hazel Barnes (New York, 1956), p. 162.

Viewing the figure of Poe's first-person against the ground of Sartre's definition, we see the need for two qualifications. First, the victim's trouble is not a malady as such, but a state of affliction brought on by the conditions of his imprisonment. (That the state is both psychical and physical, as in Sartre's definition, is self-evident, since every page describes some agony of the body that is also an agony of the mind.) The second qualification is that the prisoner's state is a mixture of the accidental and contingent of which Sartre speaks, and of the absolute and irrelative of which Poe himself speaks. The narrator's state is accidental and contingent insofar as he happens to have been caught by the Inquisition and placed in confinement. It is absolute and irrelative because it is his nature to be caught and confined. Such a man declares: *what happens to me occurs because of the way I am.*

Returning to the opening paragraph, we discover vincula that are mainly conjunctive and temporal: *And then, At first, but then, all at once, while, long, but just as, at length, And then, Then* (v, 68). The to-and-fro cyclical effect of the paragraph, partly a result of repetition and partly the result of the rather mechanical coordination in the grammar, is based upon the systolic, diastolic rhythm of the body: "Very suddenly there came back to my soul motion and sound—the tumultuous motion of the heart, and, in my ears, the sound of its beating. . . . Then again sound, and motion, and touch —a tingling sensation pervading my frame" (v, 70). With the return of consciousness, the body's possibilities for perceptual anguish are increased: "I struggled for breath. The intensity of the darkness seemed to oppress and stifle me. The atmosphere was intolerably close" (v, 71). The body now has mind enough to ask, "but where and in what state was I?" (v, 71). The problem recalls Leibniz's suggestion that the body is "momentary mind, i.e. mind without memory" (*mens momentanea, seu carens recordatione*).[55] The

[55] *The Monadology*, p. 230, n. 34. In Leibniz, memory plays an even more central role, the name of "souls" being conferred only upon those Monads or Entelechies which possess, in addition to superior perception, the faculty of memory (para. 19).

narrator approaches the problem through two complementary terms, consciousness and memory, of which the first is the more encompassing. The narrator does not merely argue, however, for the importance of consciousness (in itself or as a corollary of terror); he argues for infinite consciousness and for finite unconsciousness.

Consciousness can never be wholly lost. One loses consciousness in order to recover it. Consciousness alone has true duration; unconsciousness—and the annihilation of which it is the sign—resembles a temporary loss of focus, an absence that prepares one for the return of a continuous, immortal presence. Although the narrative is a descent in darkness and seeming death (sickness-unto-death was the victim's condition at the outset), in truth death cannot be:

"I had swooned; but still will not say that all of consciousness was lost. What of it there remained I will not attempt to define, or even to describe; yet all was not lost. In the deepest slumber—no! In delirium—no! In a swoon—no! In death—no! even in the grave all *is not* lost. Else there is no immortality for man. Arousing from the most profound of slumbers, we break the gossamer web of *some* dream. Yet in a second afterward, (so frail may that web have been) we remember not that we have dreamed. In the return to life from the swoon there are two stages; first, that of the sense of mental or spiritual; secondly, that of the sense of physical, existence. It seems probable that if, upon reaching the second stage, we could recall the impressions of the first, we should find these impressions eloquent in memories of the gulf beyond. And that gulf is—what? How at least shall we distinguish its shadows from those of the tomb? But if the impressions of what I have termed the first stage, are not, at will, recalled, yet, after long interval, do they not come unbidden, while we marvel whence they come? He who has never swooned, is not he who finds strange palaces and wildly familiar faces in coals that glow; is not he who beholds floating in mid-air the sad visions that the many may not view; is not he who ponders over the perfume of some novel flower —is not he whose brain grows bewildered with the meaning of some musical cadence which has never before arrested his attention." (v, 68-69)

Leibniz' attempt to prove that the soul is more than an ordinary monad is very close to the narrator's attempt to prove that consciousness can return from the gulf beyond. I quote paragraph 20 of the *Monadology*: "For we experience in ourselves a condition in which we remember nothing and have no distinguishable perception; as when we fall into a swoon or when we are overcome with a profound dreamless sleep. In this state the soul does not perceptibly differ from a bare Monad; but as this state is not lasting, and the soul comes out of it, the soul *is* something more than a bare Monad." Recovering from its swoon, the soul discovers that it is conscious of perceptions, which can only mean that it must have been perceiving before waking.

"Man and other beings . . . are portions of this unparticled matter [of which the universe is composed], individualized by being incorporated in the ordinary or particled matter. Thus they exist rudimentally. Death is the painful metamorphosis. . . . But for the necessity of the rudimental life, there would have been no stars—no worlds—nothing which we term material. These spots are the residences of the rudimental things. At death, these, taking a n[e]w form, of a n[o]vel matter, pass everywhere, and act all things, by mere volition, and are cognizant of all secrets but *the one*—the nature of the volition of God—of the agitation of the unparticled matter."[56]

But this consciousness which saves one from the abyss of nonentity is also a trap. For the continuity it represents exists by virtue of a possible discontinuity: to be continuous is *not* to be *dis*continuous, and only consciousness can make the distinction. The issue may be refined further by pointing out that this possibility is an illusion. There can be, ultimately, no end of consciousness but only an illusion of an end. The

[56] *The Letters of Edgar Allan Poe*, ed. John Ward Ostrom (Cambridge, Mass., 1948), I, 260. The passage closely resembles a passage in "Mesmeric Revelation," v, 252.

victim, that is to say, cannot die; he can only think he can die. Inasmuch as this system excludes the ultimate possibility of extinction, the most that can be allowed is a false or momentary possibility of extinction. *The story is about the victim's illusion that he will die.* The narrative will finally go, by a circular process where it was willed to go, ending where it began—with a man alive.

Terror arises from consciousness because, for the interval that the main narrative occupies, it does not yet know the truth. The rationale of the long passage quoted above is a rationale of memory; the terrors of pit and pendulum are those of an earlier pre-recollective state. The tension we feel in the paragraph that follows our long quotation arises from the conflict between a rational position that is not yet "earned" and the pressure of pure sensation. The rational side whispers, None of this can really be: you are experiencing merely a "state of seeming nothingness" or a "condition of seeming unconsciousness" (v, 69-70). To which the sensational side replies, You are really going to die—or at least it *seems* so: "These shadows of memory tell, indistinctly, of tall figures that lifted and bore me in silence down—down—still down—till a hideous dizziness oppressed me at the mere idea of the interminableness of the descent. They tell also of a vague horror at my heart, on account of that heart's unnatural stillness. Then comes a sense of sudden motionlessness throughout all things; as if those who bore me (a ghastly train!) had outrun, in their descent, the limits of the limitless, and paused from the wearisomeness of their toil. After this I call to mind flatness and dampness; and then all in *madness*—the madness of a memory which busies itself among forbidden things" (v, 70).

Consciousness returns by gradations: first, consciousness of existence without thought, then, suddenly, consciousness *with* thought. In this latter moment terror peaks. The subject of the "swoon" has lapsed back into his normal, conscious state. He has become again the man who must know; he is once again intermediate, a being between. The gulf beyond lies doubly beyond—beyond him in the past, half-remembered because barely experienced, and beyond him in the future. The space that separates him from the full experience is a space of terror. It is also the space of the tomb, for, as the victim explains, the gulf lies always beyond the tomb. We are hardly surprised, then, that he wakes to the fear that he has been entombed: "A fearful idea now suddenly drove the blood in torrents upon my heart, and for a brief period, I once more relapsed into insensibility. Upon recovering, I at once started to my feet, trembling convulsively in every fibre. I thrust my arms wildly above and around me in all directions. I felt nothing; yet dreaded to move a step, lest I should be impeded by the walls of a *tomb*" (v, 71-72).

There are plain traces, here, of hysteria. All the *no*'s, for example, are exclamations. We are everywhere conscious of the victim's will, of something bordering on sheer stubbornness. He does not declare that consciousness was retained: rather, "I . . . will not say that all of consciousness was lost." There is something of the same insistence in "Morella" when the narrator speaks of "the notion of that identity *which at death is or is not lost forever* . . ." (II, 29), the italicized remark recalling the prisoner's words about consciousness. We shall find a like show of will at those points in *Eureka* where the author, in order to convey an important idea, bears down with unusual vocal or rhetorical pressure.

Despite his physical suffering, perhaps because of it, the mind of the narrator strives for the "heart of the matter," for the essence of its own condition. The goal is a kind of pure, primal state of feeling, not unlike the one Peirce describes in his analysis of monads: "Imagine me to make and in a slumberous condition to have a vague, unobjectified, still less unsubjectified, sense of redness, or of salt taste, or of an ache, or of grief or joy, or of a prolonged musical note. That would be, as nearly as possible, a purely monadic state of feeling."[57] The quest in "The Pit and the Pendulum" is even more radi-

[57] *The Collected Papers of Charles Sanders Peirce*, I, para. 303.

cal and more abstract. The narrator does not speak, for example, of being carried forever, but of "the interminableness of the descent." Similarly, the heart is not stilled—it *has* a stillness. The function of these "-ness" words is precisely to focus, as much as unassisted consciousness can, on essence. In two paragraphs one finds the following substantives: *nothingness, unconsciousness, dizziness, interminableness, stillness, motionlessness, wearisomeness, madness* (twice), *consciousness, forgetfulness, earnestness*, and *the limitless.*

Having investigated his state, the victim must discover the nature of the space in which, through terror, he has returned to the sense of his own being. In most of the tales, space represents a field of behavior more or less coextensive with the "set" of one's existence. It is the area in which one acts, as in the case of the victimizers, or in which one is acted upon, as in the case of the victims. In the second case, of which the present narrative furnishes an example, space is generally non-volitional, rectilinear, constrictive and deep, or buried, its extreme forms being the coffin or the vault, which are merely diminished chambers. It is in this space that the possibilities of terror are most fully explored.

Stretching his hands, the victim discovers himself surrounded by "a wall, seemingly of stone masonry—very smooth, slimy, and cold." Slime, as any reader of post-*Otranto* fiction knows, is an important feature of the Gothic terror complex. Although slime is technically a natural, organic phenomenon, it exists in the tale of terror as a mutation of architecture, a deliquescence of physical structures:

"Slime is the agony of water. It presents itself as a phenomenon in process of becoming; it does not have the permanence within change that water has but on the contrary represents an accomplished break in a change of state. . . . Nothing testifies more clearly to its ambiguous character as a 'substance in between two states' than the slowness with which the slime melts into itself. . . . The symbol of the body of water seems to play a very important role in the construction of pantheistic systems; it reveals a particular type of relation of being to being. But if we consider the slimy, we note that it presents a constant hysteresis in the phenomenon of being transmuted into itself. . . . To touch the slimy is to risk being dissolved in sliminess."[58]

The olfactory complement of slime—which this analysis of Sartre's does not consider—is odorous vapor, or miasma. Falling for the second time, the narrator finds his head suspended over nothingness: "At the same time my forehead seemed bathed in a clammy vapor, and the peculiar smell of decayed fungus arose to my nostrils" (v, 74). The pattern of this sequence, then, is one of increasing rarefaction: from slime we move to vapor and then to sheer emptiness, directly accessible to no sense, of the pit. The pit never becomes a chamber because it is never occupied. Beneath the victim the pit looms as the possibility of the ultimate fall, of emptiness, loss of being, void. In this connection the design of the pit may mock the notion of the circle as the perfect form, or it may do quite the reverse. As the way to seeming annihilation, as the way back to primal origins, the pit may truly offer, through the possibility of descent, the ideal "way out." To escape such a means would be to transcend what the narrator calls the "moral horrors," whereas the concern of the story is to survive them. The problem is not how to descend to the gulf beyond; the problem is how to stay away from the pit.

Between the victim and survival stands the wall: "What I had taken for masonry seemed now to be iron, or some other metal, in huge plates, whose sutures or joints occasioned the depression. The entire surface of this metallic enclosure was rudely daubed in all the hideous and repulsive devices to which the charnel superstition of the monks has given rise. The figures of fiends in aspects of menace, with skeleton forms, and other more really fearful images, overspread and disfigured the walls" (v, 76-77). The immediate urge to know has been satisfied. The victim can now make out the details of the chamber. In a continuation of the to-and-fro

[58] *Being and Nothingness,* pp. 607-608.

movement discussed at the outset, his attention now shifts back to himself. The supine and bound condition he discovers borders on the extreme of non-volitional space (the extreme being, of course, premature burial in a coffin). With the descent of the pendulum, which the victim now perceives, the chamber reveals itself as a destructive machine. There is a certain similarity between this victimization and that in Kafka's "In der Strafkolonie." Poe's victim and Kafka's condemned man are equally helpless and immobile. Moreover, their situation exploits to the limit the possibilities of conscious terror and duration, to which is added a wholly synesthetic heightening of agony (the blade is simultaneously sight, sound, odor, and touch). Besides the obvious stimuli of sight and sound, there are the subtler oppressions of smell and taste (both machines being supplied with food) and touch (Poe's narrator has tactile contact with rats, among other things, while the condemned man is literally embraced by his machine). I omit the sergeant, who elects to submit to the machine, as too different from Poe's victim to warrant comparison.

The greatest difference between the situations created by the two authors is in perspective. Whereas Kafka offers several points from which the reader may take a sighting on the story's symbolic value (the explorer's, the sergeant's, and so on), Poe offers only one. The single perspective offered has, however, a dual aspect, or, if you prefer, a serial one. The victim first interprets the descending pendulum as the source of imminent death; then later reinterprets it, more accurately, as the means of immediate release. In "MS. Found in a Bottle," as here, the space of terror was also the space of illusion: the source of terror lay in a durative consciousness that believed it foresaw its own end. The illusion in "The Pit and the Pendulum," on the other hand, is virtually self-revealing. After the blade severs his bonds the narrator realizes what his victimizers always knew: that the goal of the pendulum was not his death but his liberation.

Although Jean-Paul Weber has identified the pendulum as an important example of Poe's fascination with clocks,[59] he does not notice that the chamber is itself a clock. In his relation to the descending blade, the narrator resembles Signora Psyche Zenobia, heroine of the burlesque "A Predicament. The Scythe of Time," who enters a clock tower and is decapitated: "Turning my head gently to one side, I perceived, to my extreme horror, that the huge, glittering, scimetar-like [sic] minute-hand of the clock, had, in the course of its hourly revolution, *descended upon my neck*" (II, 290).[60] In both cases, time fails to destroy, the narrator of "The Pit and the Pendulum" being rescued, whereas Psyche Zenobia lives on to describe her pseudo-death and dismemberment. This pendulum is not a true clock, but a device for heightening consciousness and thus terror: "What boots it to tell of the long, long hours of horror more than mortal, during which I counted the rushing vibrations of the steel! . . . Days passed—it might have been that many days passed—ere it swept so closely over me as to fan me with its acrid breath" (V, 79). To the rhythm of the blade, body and mind reply with a rhythm of their own, passing now into an "interval of utter insensibility," now "lapsing into life" (V, 79), now oscillating between extremes: "To the right—to the left—far and wide—with the shriek of a damned spirit; to my heart with the stealthy pace of the tiger! I alternately laughed and howled, as the one or the other idea grew predominant" (V, 80-81). But the chamber is a clock only temporarily, the design of the room-machine being adaptable to the requirements of the victimization. From an instrument exerting a pressure primarily mental, the machine evolves, by gradation, into an instrument of physical pressure, and starts literally to push the victim toward what seems his ultimate fate. From moving blade to moving walls: whereas the

[59] "Edgar Poe ou le thème de l'horloge," *Nouvelle Revue Française*, 68 and 69 (1958), pp. 301-311, 498-508.

[60] The connection is made by Auden, *The Recognition of Edgar Allan Poe*, p. 223.

vortex was a motion with architectural features, the chamber is architecture in motion.

I suggested above that Poe represents more than most writers the threatening qualities of human artifacts. His characters find themselves impinged upon, pressured, constricted, as though the world of things were not merely "other" but "anti." In this Poe merely throws into relief the property of violence that characterizes the world of *homo faber*. "Fabrication, the work of *homo faber*, consists in reification. Solidity . . . comes from the material worked upon, but this material itself is not simply given and there. . . . Material is already a product of human hands which have removed it from its natural location, either killing a life process, as in the case of the tree . . . or interrupting one of nature's slower processes, as in the case of iron, stone, or marble. . . . This element of violation and violence is present in all fabrication, and *homo faber*, the creature of the human artifice, has always been a destroyer of nature."[61]

What happens when an "artifice" possesses a will of its own and even the power of autonomous action? In a pure form the result is that *Tücke* in which the inanimate world acts upon man as if it were alive. Rebelling against human control, objects harass and sometimes even destroy their human masters. Does Poe subscribe, in the present story, to the possibility of such animistic behavior? Not entirely, for the pendulum and the walls are still being manipulated by human will. Working against this view, on the other hand, are three considerations: first, the victimizers, like all victimizers in Poe, have already largely reified themselves, which is to say that by making another into an object they have made mere objects of themselves (an idea to which we shall return); second, their will is so gratuitous, so "off-stage" and invisible, as to approximate the invisible and perverse control that we see in the pure *Tücke*; and, thirdly, the invisible victimizers are in any case less real for the victim than the things which immediately oppress him.

[61] Hannah Arendt, *The Human Condition* (Chicago, 1958), p. 139.

The second of those things, the walls, represent the technological environment in its most aggressive form. The space of terror, always opposed to man, now attacks him through physical constriction and oppression. Considering how frequently these qualities are associated in Poe, it is remarkable that they have not been more closely examined. The association may attach itself to a signal (as in "MS. Found in a Bottle," where the air is likened to heated iron) or as a phenomenon that threatens destruction by enclosure (the copper-plated vault of "The Fall of the House of Usher").[62] The walls in the present narrative are doubly endowed, for in addition to enclosing their victim they deprive him of his very breath: "Even while I breathed there came to my nostrils the breath of the vapor of heated iron! A suffocating odor pervaded the prison! A deeper glow settled each moment in the eyes that glared at my agonies! A richer tint of crimson diffused itself over the pictured horrors of blood. I panted! I gasped for breath! There could be no doubt of the design of my tormentors—oh! most unrelenting! oh! most demoniac of men! I shrank from the glowing metal to the centre of the cell. Amid the thought of the fiery destruction that impended, the idea of the coolness of the well came over my soul like balm" (v, 85). In terms of the four elements that Bachelard has analyzed, metal is a merger of fire and earth. Further, it represents the merger of human effort with natural existence; it is nature mediated. Nothing appalls the imagination of Poe more than this quality of being two things at once. Whereas *im*-mediate nature offers submergence, oblivion, release, and return to origin, mediated nature—the world of technology, or reified human time—is a world of consciousness, terror, impingement, and destruction without

[62] Metallic qualities appear throughout Poe's work. One finds them, to cite only a few examples, in the storm cloud of "MS. Found in a Bottle," in the substance from which Hans creates his launching gas in "The Unparalleled Adventure of One Hans Pfaall," and, of course, in the hold of the ship in *Pym*. Poe was intrigued by related qualities in the technology of his age; see his essay on "Street Paving," XIV, 164-169.

transcendence. In facing the metallic threat consciousness faces, not a mere neutral object, but the object in the fullness of its heritage of will and violence. In order for metal to be, man must make a thing—lifeless and inert—where before there was a process. But the imagination in a state of terror is too animistic for such distinctions. It is a fusing and fusion-minded imagination that sees the destructive capacity that went into the object as still inhering in that object. The imagination shrinks at the thought of being possessed by this thingish being which, for all its mere materiality, threatens to become more "living" than its victim. In the passage above, the metal walls *have* breath whereas the human victim is *deprived* of breath! The wall, in short, threatens to possess his being.

Fire is change, conversion, transformation. Being itself a metamorphosis, it would revenge itself (so the animistic imagination believes) by completing the ontological cycle—by changing the human being into itself. Herein lies the reason for Poe's emphasis upon olfactory terror, for the sense of smell is the sense that takes the stimuli into itself, odor being, scientifically, the transmission of particles of a substance into the perceiver. The function of the monstrous decorations on the wall is to reinforce this immediate peril on a more imaginative and ideational level.

Peering down into the abyss from its deadly brink, the victim discerns in the awful lustre thrown off by the glowing metal—the inexpressible. As the vague and the indefinite were for Poe qualities of Beauty so were they qualities of Terror. For the property of vagueness is to have no property, but rather, like Melville's whiteness, to enhance whatever property is brought within its range. One need not define what the narrator sees in the abyss. Like vagueness, the abyss is a nothingness, a space of terror waiting to be peopled with one's private phantoms.

From his terrors the victim is rescued by the whole teleology of the narrative, the goal of the adventure being, not to die, but to be rescued. What happens to this helpless, imperilled man as he totters "over the yawning gulf" (v, 86)? *Deus ex machina* and salvation. The abruptness of the *dénouement*, in which the rescuer is literally whisked onto the scene, is figured by the lack of transition at the end of the next-to-last paragraph: "I struggled no more, but the agony of my soul found vent in one loud, long, and final scream of despair. I felt that I tottered upon the brink—I averted my eyes—" (v, 86).

There is no transition because there is no transitiveness. The conclusion of the story is less an action in its own right than the perfecting of a condition. The man who rescues the prisoner is one of those vague figures who keep turning up at the height of an experience—as in *Pym*, "The Masque of the Red Death," or "Shadow. A Parable"—as though to announce that the story is approaching a boundary it may not pass. Such a figure cannot be bothered with the mechanics of "arriving": he is by definition the one-who-is-simply-there: "There was a discordant hum as of human voices! There was a loud blast of many trumpets! There was a harsh grating as of a thousand thunders! The fiery walls rushed back! An out-stretched arm caught my own as I fell, fainting, into the abyss. It was that of General Lasalle. The French army had entered Toledo. The Inquisition was in the hands of its enemies" (v, 86-87). The dominant verbal form in this passage of ostensible action is a conjugation of the infinitive *to be*: *was, was, was, was, was.* Some action under the circumstances could hardly fail to occur. But it is the least action that Poe can get away with, the least the reader will tolerate. Toledo, the General, the Inquisition, the army—all are, for practical purposes, afterthoughts. In the last analysis it is neither its exotic setting or its melodramatic trappings that has made the tale endure, but the fact that it portrays a man who is imprisoned under threat of torture and death. Such a being experiences suffering and relief, tension and calm, despair and hope. Such a being is, in short, a man. The "condition of the prisoner," says Gabriel Marcel, "can be taken as the symbolic expression of the human condition in general. Our existence is so structured that it can seem an imprisonment in a time cut off by the one certainty which cannot be doubted, the death-sentence which hangs over every one of us . . . my situation differs in no way from that of the torture victim imprisoned in a space whose walls come imperceptibly closer from minute to minute."[63] It is that universal and inescapable situation which Poe, in the present work, has sought to embody.

"The Tell-Tale Heart"

The moon in "Irenë" watches the sleeper and worries about the harmful effects of an influence it does not recognize as its own. The first William Wilson watches *his* sleeper, the other Wilson, with full knowledge of the harm he intends, then fails to inflict it. The relation of the sleeper and the watcher in "The Tell-Tale Heart" is similar but more extreme. Here the watcher has no guardian role, as in the sleeper poems; unlike the first Wilson, he is not intimately involved with the sleeper, who means nothing to him. The defiant attitude of the second Wilson provides some slight justification for the behavior of the first; but even this is lacking in "The Tell-Tale Heart." The murderer's choice of victim is completely gratuitous. It is also completely conscious, for this first-person, to an even greater extent than Poe's other criminals, is a man who loves to wallow in his own mind. His theory about the old man's eye making his blood run cold satisfies that love. At the same time it provides a protection not unlike the one Egaeus provides for himself when he turns a big threatening object into a small manageable one. Drunk with his own shrewdness, the murderer expands verbally in all directions, as though by taking up all the space there is he could become the absolute of his own fiction, its center of motive and power. The murderer exists in a world of signs that he invents and that he wills himself to believe. This is not to say that he invents, for example, the

[63] "Desire and Hope," in *Readings in Existential Phenomenology*, p. 283.

old man's eye, which obviously exists independently of his perception of it. But it is the speaker who makes the eye exist as a sign. In contrast to other men who signify in order to connect and illuminate, this man signifies in order to separate and conceal. In explaining his behavior, he chooses points and details that protect him from dangerous confrontations with his inner self by making him appear not only sane but highly rational. His wall of rationality is, of course, transparent, for his arguments, proofs, and analyses are simply too "technical" to be believed: "Oh, you would have laughed to see how cunningly I thrust [my head] in! I moved it slowly—very, very slowly, so that I might not disturb the old man's sleep. It took me an hour to place my whole head within the opening so far that I could see him as he lay upon his bed. Ha!—would a madman have been so wise as this?" (v, 89). This is no ordinary mystification but a self-mystification, in which the creator himself believes and of which he is therefore the victim.

Unlike the normal, responsible communicator, this speaker underlines his argument at its weakest point. One thing that will never persuade anyone of his rationality is the mere deliberateness of his bodily movements; yet this is precisely what he chooses to emphasize: "And then, when my head was well in the room, I undid the lantern cautiously—oh, so cautiously—cautiously (for the hinges creaked)—I undid it just so much that a single thin ray fell upon the vulture eye" (v, 89). Unlike the responsible communicator, he dwells upon the obvious: "The old man was dead. I removed the bed and examined the corpse. Yes, he was stone, stone dead. I placed my hand upon the heart and held it there many minutes. There was no pulsation. He was stone dead" (v, 92). The rhythms of the narrator's speech express a peculiar will. It is not the will to certainty that we see in William Wilson, who is concerned to get things right, down to the last shade of meaning. The narrator in "The Tell-Tale Heart" exhibits a will to convince. If Wilson wants to know and be known, the murderer wants to believe and be believed. To convince his imaginary auditors is, of course, only part of the task; he must also convince himself. His insistence that the old man is dead is for his own benefit as much as for ours, and the same can be said of his insistence that he is sane. The rhythms of this man's speech are, in fact, doubly revealing, for while they show the strength of his will they also show (like the verbal repetitions in "The Pit and the Pendulum") the depths of his terror. There is nothing contradictory about being willful and assertive on the one hand while being fearful and defensive on the other. A man such as Poe describes asserts himself *because* of his fear. If he compels, it is because he is compulsive.

After so many "manuscript" stories, here is a story told by a voice. Despite the lack of a specific auditor, as in "Tamerlane," the narrator's phrasing, diction, and punctuation are those of a man who speaks, or thinks he speaks, in the hearing of another. His opening remark has the quality of a spontaneous vocal reply: "True!—nervous—very, very dreadfully nervous I had been and am; but why *will* you say that I am mad?" (v, 88). The repeated addressing of a second-person in the opening section adds to the effect. The tale becomes a kind of hysterical conversation-poem dominated by a speaker whose voice rises from a middle register of argument to a top register of shouted confession. Such a speaker lives in an intensely acoustic space: life hinges literally on sound, or on silence, which is the temporary absence of sound and its imminent return. By this acoustic space consciousness is surrounded and returned to itself as the echoes of a voice are returned to a speaker by an encompassing wall. In such a space I hear the other even as I hear myself. I share his silence and his sounds, his consciousness and his fears, and can therefore interpret the design of my own:

"Presently I heard a slight groan, and I knew it was the groan of mortal terror. It was not a groan of pain or of grief—oh, no!—it was the low stifled sound that arises from the bottom of the soul when overcharged with awe. I knew the sound well. Many a night, just at midnight, when all the world slept, it has welled up from my own bosom, deepening, with its dreadful echo, the terrors that distracted me. . . . I knew what the old man felt, and pitied him, although I chuckled at heart. I knew that he had been lying awake ever since the first slight noise, when he had turned in the bed. His fears had been ever since growing upon him. He had been trying to fancy them causeless, but could not. He had been saying to himself—"It is nothing but the wind in the chimney—it is only a mouse crossing the floor," or "it is merely a cricket which has made a single chirp." (v, 90-91)

Sound afflicts the victimizer both inwardly and outwardly, in the realm of his consciousness and in the public realm of everyday reality. What causes him to speak out at last, declaring his crime and offering himself as a victim, is the illusion that the one has crossed over into the other. As the narrative progresses, the sound of the rhythm that the speaker hears inwardly advances (so he feels) from inner space to outer. This rhythm is introduced analogically: "A watch's minute hand moves more quickly than did mine" (v, 89). As the victimizer contemplates his victim the rhythm begins to assert its autonomy: ". . . now, I say, there came to my ears a low, dull, quick sound, such as a watch makes when enveloped in cotton. I knew *that* sound well, too. It was the beating of the old man's heart. It increased my fury, as the beating of a drum stimulates the soldier into courage" (v, 91). The process is a kind of one-sided reciprocity in which the victimizer feeds upon the terror he arouses, turning the object of his torture into the object with which he tortures himself: "Meantime the hellish tattoo of the heart increased. It grew quicker and quicker, and louder and louder every instant. The old man's terror *must* have been extreme! It grew louder, I say, louder every moment!—do you mark me well? I have told you that I am nervous: so I am. And now at the dead hour of the night, amid the dreadful silence of that old house, so strange a noise as this excited me to uncontrollable terror" (v, 91-92). The circuit of terror thus ends where it begins, in the victimizer. The victim's terror, which also deserves to be recognized, is a natural response to a danger from the outside. But the victimizer is reacting to a danger in himself, the victim serving as a mediator whose duty it is to heighten the murderer's consciousness of his own sensations. The victimizer acts upon the victim, finally, so as to become himself a victim.

Throughout the process the victimizer enjoys the poise of upright posture while the sleeper is stretched out flat in the classic posture of the one-who-is-acted-upon. When the speaker places the body beneath that horizontal wall that he calls a floor he takes the victimization as far as it will go, the victim being at once recumbent, dead, and buried. By this burial the victimizer attempts to architecturalize his relationship to the victim, to demonstrate with the solidity of matter that victimizer and victim are separate, when in fact they are inseparable.[64] Each occupies a chamber he cannot leave. To the victim this chamber is a space of pure bondage. But the chamber confines the victimizer as much as it confines the victim. For the victim acts in the chamber so as to deprive himself of the power to act: by that same act which creates a chamber for his victim, the victimizer creates a chamber for himself. Victimization is a reciprocal state, and the chamber is its inevitable locale.

Having willed a separation between himself and his victim, the narrator must now, in order to become himself a victim, dissolve it. This is the function of the final emission of sound. Little by little the victimizer perceives that the sound which distresses him emanates from outside himself, unaware that it merely externalizes a desire in himself: "The ringing became more distinct:—it continued and became more dis-

[64] The close relationship of victim and victimizer is demonstrated by E. Arthur Robinson, "Poe's 'The Tell-Tale Heart,'" *Nineteenth-Century Fiction*, pp. 376-378.

tinct: I talked more freely to get rid of the feeling: but it continued and gained definiteness—until, at length, I found that the noise was *not* within my ears" (v, 93-94). The world of the victimizer-speaker has turned itself inside out. In the phase of temporary silence—of an acoustic space charged with withheld sound—he had been master, the proof of his mastery being his ability to extend time through his own slowness. As he loses control, the withheld sound releases itself and quickens: "It was *a low, dull, quick sound—much such a sound as a watch makes when enveloped in cotton*" (v, 94). A rhythm growing steadily louder is the aural complement of velocity, which is complemented further by the staccato of the speaker's language: "I felt that I must scream or die! and now—again!—hark! louder! louder! louder! *louder!*" (v, 94).

Now the victimizer speaks for the first time so as to be heard by those in his presence: " 'Villains!' I shrieked, 'dissemble no more! I admit the deed!—tear up the planks! here, here!—it is the beating of his hideous heart!' " (v, 94). In speaking, the murderer confesses and in confessing realizes his secret aim: to reveal himself as the victim he has always secretly been.

"The Black Cat"

Here as in "Berenice" and "The Tell-Tale Heart" a man confesses to the evil he has done. He distinguishes himself in important ways, however, from his predecessors. Egaeus does not know what he has done, and the murderer does not know that what he has done is wrong. The narrator of "The Black Cat," by contrast, knows what he is doing, and recognizes that he should not be doing it. Far from protesting too much about his sanity, he admits his excitability, and the perverseness of his deeds. He differs from the other narrator, furthermore, in his mode of relating to others and to the world. To understand this mode it will be necessary to distinguish between the relative function in a variety of narratives of the psychological and of the supernatural.

The will to self-victimization causes the narrator of "The Tell-Tale Heart" to imagine that he hears the beating of the old man's heart. The police do not hear it because it is confined to the murderer's consciousness, which is why he must tell them about it. As in "Berenice," the external world depicted here is a recognizable one, while the narrating consciousness through which it is experienced is grossly distorted. At the end of each story Poe offers a perspective on the narrator by bringing in representatives of the normal world: in "Berenice" the servant, in "The Tell-Tale Heart" the detectives. The servant sees the evidence of his senses, thereby underlining the extent of Egaeus' estrangement from reality. By bringing Egaeus to consciousness he also provides the instrumentality through which Egaeus can complete his victimization. He is, in short, a mediator. The policemen mediate too, but in a different direction. Here the problem is reversed. The first-person is conscious of something of which the others, the policemen, are unaware, but which, if his victimization is to be completed, they must finally recognize: thus his confession. Egaeus' *lack* of consciousness and the murderer's *hyper*consciousness are both, therefore, deviations from a norm that is brought to bear on them in the climax of each work. The fact that both narrators are so obviously unbalanced and that neither story involves the supernatural indicates that the interest of both works is predominantly psychological.

In "Ligeia" or "The Fall of the House of Usher" the psychological element works in a different way. In both we see the struggle between life and death, and between dream and reality, in the consciousness of a man who finds himself confronted with a supernatural event: in the one case, the return to life of the deceased Ligeia; in the other, the simultaneous demise of the consubstantial twins and the supernatural submergence of the House. That these events are given as real in no way prejudices the psychological validity of the tales, each of which shows, in its own way, what happens to the consciousness of a man who is faced with an event that he can neither understand nor control. Both tales deal, in other words, with the *psychology of the supernatural*: with the way mysterious things happen in the world, and with the way the human mind reacts to them.

In "The Black Cat," on the other hand, the supernatural element is notably lacking. Superficially, the narrator is faced with a many-faceted *Tücke*: first, the dead cat is memorialized in plaster; second, an image of the gallows materializes on the breast of its successor; finally, the second cat exposes the murderer by howling from the tomb of the dead wife. But a real *Tücke* is mysterious, fantastic, supernatural, and this series of events is not. The first event in the series, the reappearance of the first cat, is explicitly accounted for:

"The walls, with one exception, had fallen in. This exception was found in a compartment wall, not very thick, which stood about the middle of the house, and against which had rested the head of my bed. The plastering had here, in great measure, resisted the action of the fire—a fact which I attributed to its having been recently spread. About this wall a dense crowd were collected, and many persons seemed to be examining a particular portion of it with very minute and eager attention. The words 'strange!' 'singular!' and other similar expressions, excited my curiosity. I approached and saw, as if graven in *bas relief* upon the white surface, the figure of a gigantic *cat*. The impression was given with an accuracy truly marvellous. There was a rope about the animal's neck.

"When I first beheld this apparition—for I could scarcely regard it as less—my wonder and my terror were extreme. But at length reflection came to my aid. The cat, I remembered, had been hung in a garden adjacent to the house. Upon the alarm of fire, this garden had been immediately filled by the crowd—by some one of whom the animal must have been cut from the tree and thrown, through an open window, into my chamber. This had probably been done with the view of arousing me from sleep. The falling of the other walls had compressed the victim of my cruelty into the substance of the freshly spread plaster; the lime of which, with the flames, and the *ammonia* from the carcass, had then accomplished the portraiture as I saw it." (v, 147-148)

That is a rational account but it is not a rationalization. The reality of the phenomenon is validated, like the reality of the cat's cry at the end, by its public nature. By submitting the phenomenon to a combination of deductive and inductive analysis, in the manner of Dupin, the narrator has simply interpreted its design. If his accounts sound like bad science, by twentieth-century standards, it is well to remember that the map of the material universe was less charted in Poe's day than in ours, and that a mind like Poe's did not have to restrain its speculations about the behavior of matter for fear of being corrected by a reader with a Ph.D. in chemical engineering; readers of *Bleak House* will also recall Dickens' receptivity to the notion that human beings could be destroyed by spontaneous combustion. The psychological interest in the passage above is in the narrator's *reaction* to the event: "Although I thus readily accounted to my reason . . . for the startling fact just detailed, it did not the less fail to make a deep impression upon my fancy. For months I could not rid myself of the phantasm of the cat . . ." (v, 148). The second event of the series, the emergence of the gallows on the breast of the second cat, is equally phantasmal. The narrator sees, in this instance, in the same self-induced, hallucinatory way that the narrator of "Tell-Tale Heart" hears. The interesting thing, again, is that he recognizes the phantasm for what it is: "one of the merest chimaeras it would be possible to conceive" (v, 150). The chimerical appearance of the gallows design has such impact on him, he explains with detachment, because of the state of "terror and horror" with which the creature habitually fills him. The last event in the series, the cry of the cat from the tomb, is also circumstantially accounted for: while the narrator was busy constructing the wall, the animal slipped past him into the presence of the corpse, there to remain until he caused it to vocalize by rapping loudly on the wall with his cane (v, 155). The psychology in the story is, then, a psychology of the abnormal, but not of the supernatural. In summary, "Ligeia" and "The Fall of the House of Usher" are tales in which the supernatural is experienced, while "The Tell-Tale Heart" and "The Black Cat" are tales in which it is only imagined.

In *The Rime of the Ancient Mariner*, which Poe knew and admired, Coleridge had also dealt with a man who confessed to taking an innocent life.[65] The crime, moreover, was perverse, in that the Mariner had no adequate motive for making the albatross his victim. The Mariner, as a result, is haunted by the memory of the deed: he can no more forget what he has done than he can forgive himself for having done it, and so he performs, in confession after confession, a lifelong penance. The narrator of "The Black Cat" is also haunted by the memory of what he has done. But unlike the Mariner he is oriented toward the future. What appals him is the certainty that he will repeat the offense, for the impulse to perverseness is irresistible: "And then came, as if to my final and irrevocable overthrow, the spirit of PERVERSENESS. Of this spirit philosophy takes no account. Yet I am not more sure that my soul lives, than I am that perverseness is one of the primitive impulses of the human heart—one of the indivisible primary faculties, or sentiments, which give direction to the character of Man. . . . It was this unfathomable longing of the soul *to vex itself*—to offer violence to its own nature—to do wrong for the wrong's sake only—that urged me to continue and finally to consummate the injury I had inflicted upon the unoffending brute" (v, 146). What was merely implicit in Coleridge's work is here raised to the level of intense consciousness, and erected into a theory. This comes about, at least in part, because Poe has freed his treat-

65 Poe's debt to the *Rime* is shown by Darrel Abel, "Coleridge's 'Life-in-Death' and Poe's 'Death in Life,'" *Notes and Queries*, n.s. 2 (1955), pp. 218-220. On the Coleridgean influence in general see, *inter alia*, Marvin Laser, "The Growth and Structure of Poe's Concept of Beauty," *ELH*, 15 (1948), pp. 69-84; Campbell, *The Poems of Edgar Allan Poe*, pp. xliv ff.; and Mabbott, p. xxvii. Poe's judgment of Coleridge is given in the Drake-Halleck essay (VIII, 284-285).

ment of the problem from the religious framework in which Coleridge had located it. In Coleridge the perverse deed is followed by guilt, punishment, and redemption. Poe's character, by contrast, feels little guilt. After cutting out the eye of the first cat, "I experienced a sentiment half of horror, half of remorse, for the crime of which I had been guilty; but it was, at best, a feeble and equivocal feeling, and the soul remained untouched" (v, 145-146). After he has killed his wife, "The guilt of my dark deed disturbed me but little. . . . I looked upon my future felicity as secured" (v, 154). For those who cannot attain redemption there is only punishment; consequently we see the transgressor, throughout the story, torture himself in his own consciousness, only to be handed over at the end, through the discovery of his deed, to the punishment of society as well. It is as if the wide Coleridgean world had collapsed in on itself: no guilt, no redemption, no desire to save others, as the Ancient Mariner sought to do, from one's own fate. The world of Poe's narrator lacks all claim to cosmic dimension. It is a hermetic world, airless and small, like a parody of a monad. It is no accident that the first-person dwells on the domestic nature of his story: it is a "most homely narrative" which he pens, "a series of mere household events" (v, 143). This is partly rationalization, for the events are extraordinary, and it is uncomfortable to face them. But the statement also has its truth: this is a domestic tragedy—or better, perhaps, a melodrama—about an individual who is in many ways typically bourgeois. A man of means, he owns his own home and can afford a servant; he is also a family man who married early and who, lacking children, maintains a number of pets. Like a good bourgeois he escapes from the problem of the household by retreating to his private bottle or to his pub. But no one in Poe ever really wants to be bourgeois. Everyone wants to be regal—to reign over others with the same absolute power that a king enjoys over his subjects or a wealthy man over the things he owns. Such a being needs breathing room, both figuratively and literally: the "loss of breath" syndrome is merely an extreme version of the chronic fear of being deprived of life. So long as the others, pets or persons, do not transcend the "property" relation, or resist his "territorial imperative," they are safe from the protagonist's wrath. But once they assert themselves they are immediately imperilled. The least the victimizer will do (as in such "love stories" as "Ligeia") is withdraw himself; the worst is that he will deprive the other of its depriving life.

As the vulture eye is to the murderer in "The Tell-Tale Heart," so is the cat to the narrator of the story before us. It is not the depriving other as such, but represents the other, in this case the wife. Unwilling to attack her directly, he assaults a mediator, the cat, which his wife has procured and which she thinks he loves. The second cat intensifies, as it were, the first, accelerating the process by which the husband's resentment against the wife rises to the surface of the affection in which it is submerged:

"When it reached the house it domesticated itself at once, and became immediately a great favorite with my wife.

"For my part, I soon found a dislike to it arising within me. This was just the reverse of what I had anticipated. . . ." (v, 149)

The cat represents the subhuman world, and through this representation brings into the open the speaker's overpowering pride: "And *a brute beast*—whose fellow I had contemptuously destroyed—*a brute beast* to work out for *me*—for me a man, fashioned in the image of the High God—so much of insufferable wo!" (v, 151). The companion of such pride, as in "Tamerlane," is powerlessness, as the first-person goes on in the following sentence to explain: "Alas! neither by day nor by night knew I the blessing of Rest any more! During the former the creature left me no moment alone; and, in the latter, I started, hourly, from dreams of unutterable fear, to find the hot breath of *the thing* upon my face, and its vast weight—an incarnate Night-Mare that I had no power to shake off—incumbent eternally upon my *heart*!" (v, 151).

Even when he takes the initiative of *homo faber*, the result is the same: it is he who is victimized. By walling-up the wife he has murdered he would effect a permanent separation. But matter in Poe is always something more than matter. The wall is not merely an inert thing; it is also an instrumentality. In this regard the difference between the bas-relief wall in the upper chamber and the tomb wall in the lower is more apparent than real. Although each is animated by a different victimizing agency (the cat or "the world" in the first case, the confession-prone speaker who calls attention to the newly plastered wall in the second), both become instruments of victimization. By perversely calling the policemen's attention to the wall, the speaker allows the wall to become a medium of transmission. The cat, the narrator's constant partner in this existential ballet, completes the circuit by responding echoically to the narrator's heavy rapping on the brickwork: "No sooner had the reverberation of my blows sunk into silence, than I was answered by a voice from within the tomb! —by a cry, at first muffled and broken, like the sobbing of a child, and then quickly swelling into one long, loud, and continuous scream, utterly anomalous and inhuman—a howl —a wailing shriek, half of horror and half of triumph, such as might have arisen only out of hell, conjointly from the throats of the damned in their agony and of the demons that exult in the damnation" (v, 155). The terror of the sound consists partly in the suddenness of its onset. That he was equally appalled by the *gradual* appearance of the gallows in the second cat's white patch suggests that velocity does not terrify in itself, any more than gradualism, in itself, necessarily pleases. Velocity is one thing for a Hans Pfaall, who has elected to try a balloon ascent, and quite another for a man who is being swept helpless toward an abyss. The same qualification applies to slowness, which can appeal, as it does to the cosmogonist in Poe, or terrify, as in the case of the present victimizer who suffers, in much the same way as the victim of "The Pit and the Pendulum," in a situation combining heightened consciousness of a terror-producing object with extreme duration.

The practical virtue of sound as a source of terror is its ability to bypass material interference. A wall blocks out most of the senses—sight, taste, touch or smell; through a wall one can only hear. Sound can also appear to bypass the chain of cause and effect, for it is invisible and its origins are often obscure. Poe maximizes the terror-producing capacity of sound by reserving it, in general, for moments of crisis. However intense may be the effect of terror on consciousness, something is always held back for the final outburst (which, whatever the local variations, is always essentially a cry). Thus the initial utterance in the tales occurs, characteristically, just before they end. Only when the desire for victimization has been successfully uttered does victimization call itself complete. Utterance in solitude is not enough; the victim who speaks must be heard, for his victimization is a reciprocity: " 'By the bye, gentlemen, this—this is a very well constructed house. . . . I may say an *excellently* well constructed house. These walls—are you going, gentlemen?—these walls are solidly put together;' and here, through the mere phrenzy of bravado, I rapped heavily . . . upon that very portion of the brick-work behind which stood the corpse of the wife of my bosom" (v, 155).

Where other murderers have secret stores of guilt, the murderer of the cat has stores of pride. As psychologists remind us, the man who takes another's life is sometimes an exhibitionist whose act is not completed until he witnesses its acknowledgment by others; thus his urge to confess. But there is nothing merely supplementary—at least for Poe's victimizers—in this final phase. Poe's victimizers go further. Full of themselves, they liquidate every threat to the sacred isolation of their being, then ask for recognition. But this recognition is not merely confirmatory; it is a mediation that ushers the murderer out of his role of victimizer and into the role of victim.

"The Premature Burial"

"To be buried while alive, is, beyond question, the most terrific of these extremes which has ever fallen to the lot of mere mortality" (v, 256). The chief source of terror in premature burial—as in that earlier account of claustration, "The Pit and the Pendulum"—is consciousness. An artillery officer the narrator reads about in a Leipzig medical journal was conscious for more than an hour after burial; a Londoner who survived a similar experience was constantly aware of everything that happened to him. From these figures the narrator develops a ground (to use once more the terminology introduced in connection with the detective tales) of which the common elements are, among others, suffocation, constriction, silence. But the extreme state of suffering is attained only when these things are combined "with thoughts of the air and grass above, with memory of dear friends who would fly to save us if but informed of our fate, and with consciousness that of this fate they can *never* be informed . . ." (v, 263). Having advanced in a circle from figure to ground, the narrator-victim, still working circularly, develops another figure, whose "condition of hemi-syncope" involves "a dull lethargic consciousness of life and of the presence of those who surrounded my bed . . ." (v, 265). It is himself.

This first-person is another of Poe's sleepers. Indeed he talks explicitly not only about his trances, but about his day-to-day sleeping habits. The peculiar feature of his sleep is the forgetfulness that afflicts him upon returning to consciousness. William Wilson's forgetfulness, as we saw, afforded protection over the short term and victimization over the long. What this narrator's forgetting shows, on the other hand, is an inability to get hold of the real. He is afflicted perpetually by dreams, phantasies, visions, ideas—everything that consciousness can create in order to perfect its own suffering: "My fancy grew charnel. I talked 'of worms, of tombs and epitaphs.' I was lost in reveries of death, and the idea of premature burial held continual possession of my brain" (v,

266). The narrator's troubles have a family kinship with the troubles of Don Quixote, or Calderón's Segismundo, in *La vida es sueño*: the issue for all, in the broadest sense, is the relation of appearance to reality, of illusion to *desengaño*; in a more immediate sense, it is the problem of finding a cure. This sufferer's cure involves an encounter with two visions. The first is a dream vision in which an otherworldly figure reveals the agonies of the dead, while the second vision arises from more ordinary circumstances. The being who appears in the first vision is a mediator whose mission is to make the narrator more conscious of the realm beyond life. To this end the mediator shows him "the graves of all mankind." Peering into them, the narrator observes that "the real sleepers were fewer, by many millions, than those who slumbered not at all; and there was a feeble struggling; and there was a general sad unrest; and from out the depths of the countless pits there came a melancholy rustling from the garments of the buried" (v, 267). Mankind's collective grave is a valley of unrest with a single guardian spirit. This is, of course, the being in the vision, "the unseen figure" through whose agency the narrator is forced, as the first William Wilson was forced by his shadowy counterpart, to confront something he would shun. Like the flowers in the valley of unrest, the unseen figure trembles in sympathy with the forgotten ones and hints that the narrator is guilty for not doing the same: " 'How canst *thou* tranquilly sleep? I cannot rest for the cry of these great agonies' " (v, 267). The narrator does face the spectacle that the figure then presents him, and is affected by it as by the other "phantasies" that haunt him even when he is awake.

The second vision, which is very different, enables him to put such things out of his mind. The narrator is on a river trip when his boat is overtaken by a sudden storm reminiscent of the storm in "MS. Found in a Bottle." The narrator beds down in a narrow and confining berth, but on waking his forgetfulness prevents him from recognizing his situation, and he imagines that he has been prematurely buried: ". . . and the whole of my vision—for it was no dream, and no nightmare —arose naturally from the circumstances of my position—from my ordinary bias of thought—and from the difficulty, to which I have alluded, of collecting my senses, and especially of regaining my memory, for a long time after awaking from slumber" (v, 272). When the narrator resolves, as a result of this experience, to give up his charnel imaginings, his disease disappears, revealing to him the intimate connection between consciousness and the everyday world, a connection the two visions also confirm. Other late works of Poe show interest in the everyday world. "Mellonta Tauta" offers a burlesque perspective on American history, while "The Thousand-and-Second Tale of Scheherezade" explores with similar techniques curiosities of the natural world and technology. "The Domain of Arnheim" and "Landor's Cottage" deal with landscape gardening, "Mesmeric Revelation" and "The Facts in the Case of M. Valdemar" with mesmerism, and "Von Kempelen and his Discovery" with a process for turning base metals into gold. Reflecting this concern—this desire to show wherever possible the influence of the everyday world on consciousness—there is a tendency toward the problem-solving narrative in which someone, as in "The Premature Burial," undergoes an illusion of which he is subsequently cured. In "The Elk" the arrival of an animal tender destroys the dreaminess inspired in the narrator by the "apparition" (v, 161) of the beautiful creature. The oblong box in the story of the same name proves to be a coffin, invalidating the narrator's speculations about it and clearing up the several mysteries it had inspired. The narrator of "The Spectacles" falls in love with a beautiful young woman who proves, once he has his glasses on, to be an ugly old one. In "The Sphinx" a man whose fancy has been made morbid by a plague, and a preoccupation with omens, suffers the illusion that a bug on the window near his eye is a monster approaching from afar. Interwoven with this pattern is a continuing, explicit concern with the beyond. We have seen such a concern already in "The Mystery of Marie Rogêt," with its parallels between real events and ideal ones; in "The Domain of Arnheim," where the handiwork of man is revealed in the full design of nature and God; and we shall see it yet again, in the following chapter, when we consider "Mesmeric Revelation" and "The Power of Words." This dual concern with reconciliation, and with seeing life whole in all its detail and grandeur, is prefigured in the new life that the narrator of "The Premature Burial" is able, following his cure, to pursue:

"The tortures endured, however, were indubitably quite equal, for the time, to those of actual sepulture. They were fearfully—they were inconceivably hideous; but out of Evil proceeded Good; for their very excess wrought in my spirit an inevitable revulsion. My soul acquired tone—acquired temper. I went abroad. I took vigorous exercise. I breathed the free air of Heaven. I thought upon other subjects than Death. I discarded my medical books. 'Buchan' I burned. I read no 'Night Thoughts'—no fustian about church-yards—no bugaboo tales—*such as this*. In short, I became a new man, and lived a man's life." (v, 273)

This reborn being does not exaggerate his accomplishment, and certainly he does not forget his mortality. There is a somber, Augustan quality about this reconciliation, just as there is something in it—if the word is not too strong—of the sublime: "There are moments when, even to the sober eye of Reason, the world of our sad Humanity may assume the semblance of a Hell—but the imagination of man is no Carathis, to explore with impunity its every cavern. Alas! the grim legion of sepulchral terrors cannot be regarded as altogether fanciful—but, like the Demons in whose company Afrasiab made his voyage down the Oxus, they must sleep, or they will devour us—they must be suffered to slumber, or we perish" (v, 273). There are thus, from the beginning of new life, distinct limits on the human ability to know. Even in Aidenn, whose terrain we are shortly to explore, there are things that cannot be known, for like the earth Aidenn exists within something larger than itself. This new, angelic life affirms the infinite plenitude of being, and by that very fact assures that there will always remain some horizon of knowledge that consciousness can never cross.

Landscape Tales

Each work in this group attempts to capture the genius of some scene, or to embody in the physical world certain strongly held ideas about unity, ideality, God, human creativity, and the material Creation itself. In contrast with the other imaginative prose works, there are virtually no characters in these pieces, and virtually no conflict. When there is a character, such as Ellison in "The Domain of Arnheim," he is an idealized type detached from the pressures that normally beset human beings in Poe's world. The only approximation of conflict is in "The Island of the Fay," where the dark and light sides of the island embody, respectively, death and life. The tensions are muted by the ethereality of the atmosphere and by the fact that the Fay is a being purer and higher than any human creature, and therefore implicitly nearer to God.

The idea expressed in the epigraph to "The Island of the Fay," *Nullus enim locus sine genio est*, is elaborated in the narrator's discussion of "the genius of the scene" (IV, 194), in the opening paragraph. This is not as yet a particular scene, but any scene of natural grandeur experienced in solitude:

"To me, at least, the presence—not of human life only—but of life in any other form than that of the green things which grow upon the soil and are voiceless—is a stain upon the landscape—is at war with the genius of the scene. I love, indeed, to regard the dark valleys, and the grey rocks, and the waters that silently smile, and the forests that sigh in uneasy slumbers, and the proud watchful mountains that look down upon all—I love to regard these as themselves but the colossal members of one vast and animate and sentient whole—a whole whose form (that of the sphere) is the most perfect and most inclusive of all; whose path is among associate planets; whose meek handmaiden is the moon; whose mediate sovereign is the sun; whose life is eternity; whose thought is that of a God; whose enjoyment is knowledge; whose destinies are lost in immensity; whose cognizance of ourselves is akin with our own cognizance of the *animalculae* which infest the brain—a being which we, in consequence, regard as purely inanimate and material, much in the same manner as these *animalculae* must thus regard us." (IV, 194)

The passage is at once an expansion and a contraction—an opening out toward infinity, followed by a return movement toward the finite. Within this larger design there are others that duplicate it in miniature. The vision that starts from the vantage point of the first-person reaches out to include valleys, rocks, waters, forests, and mountains. This opening phase of the larger expansive movement is repeated in miniature in the next clause (beginning "I love to regard"), which again starts from the vantage point of the "I" and again expands, so that by the end of it we have come to the spherical whole within which the particular elements of the landscape (valleys, rocks, waters, forests, and mountains) are contained. We now circumnavigate this whole, attribute by attribute, dependent clause by dependent clause, until the observation that its destinies "are lost in immensity." The sentence here begins, without a break in its grammatical unity, a reverse movement back toward the human orientation that was its point of departure. The whole of which we were heretofore taking implicit cognizance now takes explicit "cognizance of ourselves." The focus continues to narrow as we shift down to the scale of those tiny beings which are within our brain much as we are within the sphere whose thought is God. The concluding clause ("a being which we . . . regard as purely inanimate and material") then links itself to the "vast animate and sentient whole" that is its grammatical antecedent. The effect of this long-delayed connection is to hold us—while we experience the attributes referred to above—in suspense: we feel that we do not yet know "where we are going." The fact is we are going back again in a final miniature version of the overarching movement, first toward the great being of which we are all a part, then toward the little beings (the *animalculae*) that are a part of us. We can now see that the movement has been designed so as to come back to its human point of origin, for the sentence that began with "I" has ended with "us." If the thematic center of the sentence is a circular form—the sphere—there is circularity therefore in the form of the sentence itself. There is also, to conclude, a final widening movement, the isolated first-person singular having been expanded into the collective first-person plural.

That the description embraces the Creation in a material as well as a spiritual sense is implied by words like "colossal members" and "form," by the fact that these words immediately follow the enumeration of elements in the physical terrain, and by the attention near the end of the passage to entities in the brain. If the form thus depicted is at least implicitly physical, it is physical in a distinctive way. This form with colossal members follows a path, has a handmaiden and a sovereign, lives and thinks, knows and enjoys knowing, and is destined for a fate that cannot be foreseen. If its form were not spheroid and it were not so near to God, this being could be human, a fact that may serve as a reminder of Poe's willingness to regard the entire hierarchy of beings, from the lowest animal entities through the angels, spirits, and fays, as somehow focussed in man. We shall have more to say on this matter below.

"The Island of the Fay" tells how a being outside the human order fulfills its existence by making a circuit of an island that embodies the brightness of life and the darkness of death. The progress of the Fay is experienced both as a "revolution" (IV, 199), which emphasizes its spatial dimension, and as a "cycle" (IV, 199), which emphasizes its temporal dimension. Although Poe tries as always to do justice to both dimensions, there is a tendency in this work to give space precedence over time, or—what amounts to the same thing—to show time shading into space. The tendency can be seen in his approach to the cyclical: "The cycles in which the stars move are those best adapted for the evolution, without collision, of the greatest possible number of bodies" (IV, 194). The statement, with its Leibnizian sense of confident self-sufficiency, interprets the cyclical design of the universe as the constituting of material plenitude. It is the very fact that there is so *much* matter that provides the basis of this confidence: "Nor is it any argument against bulk being an object with God, that space itself is infinite; for there may be an infinity of matter to fill it" (IV, 195). When we watch the shadow of Fay being absorbed by the water, we are therefore watching an early phase of the process by which that being will be gathered into the infinity of the material creation. As space assimilates time, in other words, so does matter assimilate spirit.

The process is in operation even before the Fay appears. The starting point is the account of the narrator's journey, which follows some three pages of cosmological speculation: "It was during one of my lonely journeyings, amid a far-distant region of mountain locked within mountain, and sad rivers and melancholy tarns writhing or sleeping within all—that I chanced upon a certain rivulet and island. I came upon them suddenly in the leafy June, and threw myself upon the turf, beneath the branches of an unknown odorous shrub, that I might doze as I contemplated the scene. I felt that thus only should I look upon it—such was the character of phantasm which it wore" (IV, 196). The first orientation, as at the opening of "The Fall of the House of Usher," where the word *during* is equally prominent, is temporal. The subsequent orientation is spatial, as we encounter twice in a row that central and centralizing preposition, *within*. In the second sentence the shift is repeated, the time-phrase "suddenly in the leafy June" giving way to the space-oriented phrases, "upon the turf, beneath the branches of an unknown odorous shrub." The spatial emphasis results in part from the action described in the sentences and in part from the sheer preponderance of spatial words (five as against three). Moreover, the phrase "suddenly in *leafy* June" already contains an allusion to the physical landscape within which the narrator, again like his predecessor before the Usher estate, is about to linger.

The Usher analogy may be extended, for the narrator contemplates the distant, silent Fay much as the narrator of the other tale contemplates the distant, silent Lady Madeline. This man, too, is at a remove when the climax comes, and, like the witness to the fall of the Ushers, can testify only to a disappearance from sight. His involvement with the Fay, however, is one of anticipation and parallel. Thus the final rest of the Fay is preceded by the rest of the narrator who sinks down and becomes immobile. At the same time the language of the description anticipates, as we have just seen, the assimilation of time to space that will characterize the Fay's demise. This assimilation is furthered on another level by the narrator's interpretation of the shadows he sees: "The shade of the trees fell heavily upon the water, and seemed to bury itself therein, impregnating the depths of the element with darkness. I fancied that each shadow . . . separated itself sullenly from the trunk that gave it birth, and thus became absorbed by the stream . . ." (IV, 198).

Applying the same analysis to the journey of the Fay around the island, he concludes: " 'The revolution which has just been made by the Fay . . . is the cycle of the brief year of her life. She has floated through her winter and through her summer. She is a year nearer unto Death: for I did not fail to see that as she came into the shade, her shadow fell from her, and was swallowed up in the dark water, making its blackness more black' " (IV, 199). "Cycle," with its temporal connotation, gives way in the concluding paragraph to its spatial complement, "circuit": "And again and again she made the circuit of the island . . . and at each issuing into the light, there was more sorrow about her person . . . and at each passage into the gloom, there fell from her a darker shade, which became whelmed in a shadow more black" (IV, 199). Again the Ushers come to mind, for this Fay is one of the last survivors of an old "family" line: " 'This is the haunt of the few gentle Fays who remain from the wreck of the race' " (IV, 198), the narrator observes, implying that the House and the island are both enclosures in which one waits for earthly existence to reach its appointed term.

The narrator's closing statement, "I beheld her magical figure no more" (IV, 199), suggests that the loss of the female being, if not as intensely painful as the loss of one's beloved, takes a genuine emotional toll. The experience has nevertheless its positive side. The narrator has witnessed the reality of a higher order of being; he has seen that there is an intermediate existence lower than the divine but higher than the human. The sobering realization that the Fays are subject to mutability is offset by two considerations. One is that the Fay suffers less because she has less long, in earthly terms, to live (each higher gradation of being is nearer the phase of universal consolidation when time and space contract in a rush to an ineffable vanishing point, and is therefore nearer the rejuvenating sources of life). The other consideration is that the being of the Fay, as of all creatures, is ultimately contained within the being of God Himself: "As we find cycle within cycle without end—yet all revolving around one far-distant Godhead, may we not analogically suppose, in the same manner, life within life, the less within the greater, and all within the Spirit Divine?" (IV, 195).

Like the Fay, the protagonist of "The Domain of Arnheim" is fated to a "brief existence" (VI, 176), suggesting that he is closer to the ideal than the rest of us. While denying that man in general is capable of improvement, he is himself the embodiment of those ideas about human perfectibility which were advanced by thinkers like Turgot, Price, Priestley, and Condorcet.[66] The eighteenth century stands behind his aes-

[66] All of these thinkers are mentioned in the text. What is not mentioned is Ellison's debt to contemporary landscape theories, especially those of the influential Andrew Jackson Downing, whose *Treatise on Landscape Gardening* appeared in 1841. See Charles L. Sanford, "Edgar Allan Poe: A Blight upon the Landscape," *American Quarterly*, 20 (1968), pp. 54-66, and Brooks, *The World of Washington Irving*, pp. 364-365.

thetic theories as well, for Ellison happily subscribes to philosophical materialism, and the idea that nature should be improved by the application of human genius: "In the widest and noblest sense he was a poet. He comprehended, moreover, the true character, the august aims, the supreme majesty and dignity of the poetic sentiment. The fullest, if not the sole proper satisfaction of this sentiment he instinctively felt to lie in the creation of novel forms of beauty. Some peculiarities, either in his early education, or in the nature of his intellect, had tinged with what is termed materialism all his ethical speculations; and it was this bias, perhaps, which led him to believe that the most advantageous at least, if not the sole legitimate field for the poetic exercise, lies in the creation of novel moods of purely *physical* loveliness" (VI, 180-181). Ellison rejects sculpture, as he rejects the other plastic arts, for being "too limited in its extent and consequences" (VI, 181), which amounts to saying that he needs a more expanded medium. In the plastic arts, furthermore, there is a separation between subject and medium. In order to capture the skin tone of a model, the portraitist must work in the foreign medium of paint; to catch the movement of living flesh, the sculptor must work in the equally foreign medium of stone. Since the skin is always a more wonderful thing than pigment or granite, there is no question of the painter or the sculptor being able to exalt or idealize nature; the best either can do is imitate. In the case of landscape design, on the other hand, such separation does not exist. Here there is nothing *but* the medium: the artist is not obliged to approach nature because he is already *in* it. He is therefore free to idealize and exalt rather than imitate. He enjoys this freedom, however, only because of the fallen state of the Creation:

"I repeat that in landscape arrangements alone is the physical nature susceptible of exaltation, and that, therefore, her susceptibility of improvement at this one point, was a mystery I had been unable to solve. My own thoughts on the subject had rested in the idea that the primitive intention of nature would have so arranged the earth's surface as to have fulfilled at all points man's sense of perfection in the beautiful, the sublime, or the picturesque; but that this primitive intention had been frustrated by the known geological disturbances—disturbances of form and color-grouping, in the correction or allaying of which lies the soul of art. The force of this idea was much weakened, however, by the necessity which it involved of considering the disturbances abnormal and unadapted to any purpose. It was Ellison who suggested that they were prognostic of *death*. He thus explained:—Admit the earthly immortality of man to have been the first intention. We have then the primitive arrangement of the earth's surface adapted to his blissful estate, as not existent but designed. The disturbances were the preparations for his subsequently conceived deathful condition." (VI, 183-184)

In the sphere of human creativity the landscape artist plays God by realizing his own designs in the very substance of the material world. Ellison surmises that a poet with enough money could " 'so imbue his designs at once with extent and novelty of beauty, as to convey the sentiment of spiritual interference' " (VI, 187). The effect would lift the landscape, as it were, to a higher level, producing the kind of terrain that would exist if we could imagine " 'the Almighty design to be *one step* depressed—to be brought into something like harmony or consistency with the sense of human art . . .' " (VI, 187). One would gather, on seeing a landscape so designed, that it was in the care " 'of beings superior, yet akin to humanity' " (VI, 188), like the Fays, perhaps, or like " 'the angels that hover between man and God' " (VI, 188).

The human or "artificial" element in the landscape is not only acknowledged by Ellison, but consciously defended, on the theory that you make a thing more than human by putting in it more of the human. Nature is accordingly architecturalized. Even on the river that approaches the house one is surrounded by walls (VI, 191, 194, 195). Ellison avoids, however, the rectilinear shapes that are associated in Poe with death and burial, preferring the form, at once more natural and more ideal, of the circle, and its variants, the curve and the crescent. "At every instant the vessel seemed imprisoned within an enchanted circle, having insuperable and impenetrable walls of foliage, a roof of ultra-marine satin, and *no* floor . . . " (VI, 191). Descending, the vessel, which is itself an irregular crescent (VI, 193), enters "a circular basin" (VI, 192), follows along the wall "in an infinity of curves" (VI, 194), later to leave the "gentle and extensive curve" of this body of water for "a rapid descent into a vast amphitheatre entirely begirt with purple mountains, whose bases are laved by a gleaming river throughout the full extent of their circuit" (VI, 195). In the word "point" the narrator finds a term that is between the material and the spiritual realms, providing a way of connecting a variety of phenomena. The "points" formed by the prow of the visitor's boat (VI, 193) are the culmination of its curvilinear shape: "The poop and beak of this boat arise high above the water, with sharp points, so that the general form is that of an irregular crescent" (VI, 193). Later in the paragraph the noun becomes a verb in order to suggest the progress of the vessel: "It slowly swings itself around until its prow points toward the sun" (VI, 193). At the other extreme the point is a phenomenon in consciousness, something about which Ellison thinks or on which he makes up his mind (VI, 188, 180). "Point" also designates elements of beauty: "No pictorial or sculptural combinations of points of human loveliness do more than approach the living and breathing beauty" (VI, 183), and, as shown by the opening sentence in the long quotation above, it specifies the single crucial aspect of nature that is susceptible of improvement. Finally, it is our orientation toward a point, in the spatial sense, that makes it possible to assume a vantage point, in the sense of a mental perspective: " 'Now,' said my friend, 'what we regard as exaltation of the landscape may be really such, as respects only the moral or human *point of view*. Each alternation of the natural scenery may possibly effect a blemish in the picture, if we can suppose this picture viewed at large—in mass—from some point distant from the earth's surface, although not beyond the limits of the atmosphere" (VI, 184).

The improvements effected by Ellison illustrate the redemptive capacity of human art.[67] In the landscape he designs there is nothing of the uneasiness found in other imaginary places, such as "The Valley of Unrest," nor any power of victimization. His domain is the embodiment of beauty, order, and serenity. Within it one undergoes, not merely in safety but with actual pleasure, sensations that elsewhere have produced the most intense horror: thus the entire journey is an experience of claustration (one is imprisoned in an enchanted circle); of motion within the confines of an artifact over which one has no control; of descent, and of "gradually accelerated velocity" (VI, 193). Poe's aim is not to repeat the familiar, but to reveal familiar states and processes in their affirmative aspect. Thus the basin of water into which the narrator gazes is like the tarn of Usher absolved of its sinister darkness: it is an "inverted Heaven" in which one watches "the duplicate blooming of the hills" (VI, 192). Ellison is even, like other protagonists, threatened with a vortex—"the common vortex of unhappiness which yawns for those of preeminent endowments" (VI, 177)—but is spared by the "instinctive philosophy" (VI, 177) within him. Finally, like Tamerlane, Ellison faces, near the end, a gate with streaming rays (VI, 195). But whereas Tamerlane was confronted by the iron gate of death and by rays of painful truth, the narrator of "The Domain of Arnheim" faces nothing more threatening than a handsome portal of gold and a bright sun. The concluding passage, with its unworldly architecture and its air of breathless climax, reminds us less of the city in the sea than of the towering ethereal structure in Part II of "Al Aaraaf" or the "dome in air" in Coleridge's "Kubla Khan": "Meantime the whole Paradise of Arnheim bursts upon the view. There is a gush of entrancing melody; there is an oppressive sense of strange sweet odor;—there is a dream-like intermingling to

[67] Rans, *Edgar Allan Poe*, p. 84.

the eye of tall slender Eastern trees . . . and, upspringing confusedly from amid all, a mass of semi-Gothic, semi-Saracenic architecture, sustaining itself as if by miracle in mid-air, glittering in the red sunlight with a hundred oriels, minarets, and pinnacles; and seeming the phantom handiwork, conjointly, of the Sylphs, of the Fairies, of the Genii, and of the Gnomes" (VI, 195-196). The vision ends on a note of onomastic heightening, the realm in question ceasing to be the Domain and becoming instead the *Paradise* of Arnheim.

Poe has not yet reached the point, however, of equating the creativity of man with that of God, or in other respects merging the human and the divine. Ellison indeed modestly allows for the possibility that the results of his labors may look very different from a higher perspective. As he observes in the passage on "point of view," there may be a class of "earth-angels" to whose "death-refined appreciation of the beautiful" (VI, 185) our improvements may seem as blemishes, our harmonies as chaos. What such beings do in fact experience will be seen when we turn below to the dialogues.

"Landor's Cottage," which bears the subtitle, "A Pendant to 'The Domain of Arnheim,' " presents a kind of indoor version of the ideal landscape. We are allowed not only to glimpse the exemplary edifice, as in "The Domain of Arnheim," but to cross its threshold and examine its chambers and contents from the inside. The result is a down-to-earth, domesticated recasting of the central ideas put forward by Ellison. The roofs of the two larger "compartments" of the house sweep down "with a long concave curve" (VI, 265), while the rivulet of the vale loses itself in a lakelet of "roughly oval" form (VI, 262) with banks which are "*rounded*, rather than sloped, off into the clear heaven below" (VI, 262). These features confirm the narrator's general impression that "there were few straight, and no long uninterrupted lines. The same effect of curvature or of color, appeared twice, usually, but not oftener, at any one point of view. Everywhere was variety in uniformity. It was a piece of 'composition,' in which the most fastidiously critical taste could scarcely have suggested an emendation" (VI, 257). "Point of view" merges, typically, with the spatial point from which one achieves perspective in the first place: "The point of view from which I first saw the valley, was not *altogether*, although it was nearly, the best point from which to survey the house" (VI, 264-265). The term shows its flexibility by elsewhere denoting a particular spot that is also an area of transition: "Its three trunks separated from the parent . . . were not more than four feet apart at the point where the largest stem shot out into foliage . . ." (VI, 260; cf. VI, 261).

The "enchanted circle" in which the narrator of "The Domain of Arnheim" was happily imprisoned had both a roof and a sky, but, being a transparent body of water, no floor in the ordinary sense. By contrast, the domain of Landor, which the narrator explores by foot rather than by boat, has two. The first provides that specifically earthly foundation which is lacking in Ellison's more ethereal landscape: "The road . . . bore no resemblance to any road I had before seen. The tracks of which I speak were but faintly perceptible—having been impressed upon the firm, yet pleasantly moist surface of —what looked more like green Genoese velvet than anything else. It was grass, clearly—but grass such as we seldom see out of England—so short, so thick, so even, and so vivid in color" (VI, 256). It will be seen that this piece of earth is at once novel and, what is more to the point, artificial. The next logical step is to carry the idea of the floor into an even more architecturalized setting: "The general floor of the amphitheatre was *grass* of the same character as that I had found in the road: if anything, more deliciously soft, thick, velvety, and miraculously green" (VI, 261). This is true *terra firma*, a piece of earth that human design and human labor have rendered not only beautiful but comfortable and secure. In addition to noting the characteristics of Landor's extramural floor, the narrator also praises the qualities of the road, which manages to be wide enough for "a Virginian mountain wagon" (VI, 256) and artful enough to be picturesque, and of the smaller paths with their solid footing: "The piazzas of the main building and western wing had no floors, as is usual; but at the doors and at each window, large, flat, irregular slabs of granite lay imbedded in the delicious turf, affording comfortable footing in all weather" (VI, 266).

The indoor equivalent of the amphitheatre's grassy floor is the carpet: "on the floor was an ingrain carpet, of excellent texture—a white ground, spotted with small circular green figures" (VI, 270). This carpet—the soul of an apartment, as it will be called in "The Philosophy of Furniture"—thus repeats within the walls of the cottage the pattern of circularity without. Above are simple appointments: unostentatious furniture, lithographs, wallpaper of abstract design, an astral lamp, bouquets, all unified because "designed by the same brain which planned 'the grounds' . . . " (VI, 270). In "The Philosophy of Furniture" the same elements, slightly changed, will reappear, as will one other characteristic of Landor's cottage that distinguishes it significantly from the domain of Arnheim. I refer to the fact that this ideal place is inhabited: beyond the door there are actual people, or to be more precise, one actual person, since Landor himself is quickly disposed of in favor of the more characteristic and more Poesque figure of the welcoming female presence:

"Instantly a figure advanced to the threshold—that of a young woman about twenty-eight years of age—slender, or rather slight, and somewhat above the medium height. As she approached, with a certain *modest decision* of step altogether indescribable, I said to myself, 'Surely here I have found the perfection of natural, in contradistinction from artificial *grace.*' The second impression which she made on me, but by far the more vivid of the two, was that of *enthusiasm.* So intense an expression of *romance*, perhaps I should call it, or of unworldliness, as that which gleamed from her deep-set eyes, had never so sunk into my heart of hearts before. I know not how it is, but this peculiar expression of the eye, wreathing itself occasionally into the lips, is the most powerful, if not absolutely the *sole* spell, which rivets my interest in woman. . . . The eyes of Annie (I heard some one from the interior call her 'Annie, darling!') were 'spiritual gray;' her hair, a light chestnut: this is all I had time to observe of her." (VI, 268-269)

Like other descriptions in the present group of works, this one is full of echoes, the gracefulness of the woman's step recalling the female lovers in other tales, the eyes recalling virtually every woman in Poe, but particularly the title character in the poem "For Annie." The brevity of the narrator's contact with her reminds us of his predecessor's contact with the Fay, and perhaps also the brevity of Ellison's existence or of any being representative of the ideal, while Helen comes to mind as the forerunner of this figure who rewards the wanderer with the mere fact of her presence.

The sole inhabitant of the apartment in "The Philosophy of Furniture" is a figure slumbering on a sofa (XIV, 106, 108), in short a sleeper whose state embodies the quality of "*Repose*" (XIV, 108) suggested by the paintings in the room. As these art works are the equivalent of the lithographs in Landor's cottage, so are the encircling entablature and the abstract designs in the carpet (XIV, 107) the equivalent of indoor and outdoor patterns in that domain. The center of interest and the fullest embodiment of circularity is to be found, as in "Landor's Cottage," on the floor:

"The soul of the apartment is the carpet. From it are deduced not only the hues but the forms of all objects incumbent. . . . As regards texture, the Saxony is alone admissible. Brussels is the preterpluperfect tense of fashion, and Turkey is taste in its dying agonies. Touching pattern—a carpet should *not* be bedizzened out like a Riccaree Indian—all red chalk, yellow ochre, and cock's feathers. In brief—distinct grounds, and vivid circular or cycloid figures, *of no meaning*, are here Median laws. . . . As for those antique floor-cloths still occasionally seen in the dwellings of the rabble—cloths of huge, sprawling, and radiating devises [sic], stripe-interspersed, and glorious with all hues, among which no ground is intelligible—these are but the wicked invention of a race of time-servers and money-lovers—children of Baal and worshippers of Mammon—Benthams, who, to spare thought and economize fancy, first cruelly invented the kaleidoscope, and then established joint-stock companies to twirl it by steam." (XIV, 103-104)

As in his critical and theoretical writings, Poe places beauty above meaning, the abstract and general above the particular and the concrete. We also find in those writings the same insistence on firmly held principles, and, as its inevitable complement, the disdain of opposing views. This is my world, he seems to say, and I will design it in my own fashion. The preliminary step is to destroy bad taste while presenting in the abstract the tenets of the good taste that must supplant it; the final step is to embody that taste in an actual architectural space. The "narrative" falls, accordingly, into two parts and two manners: the first, which takes up about two-thirds of the pages, is a mixture of earnest advocacy and stringent satire; the second, devoted to the apartment, is a serious, almost pious description of the embodied ideal.

As to the contents of the chamber, "The Philosophy of Furniture" might be said to take up where "Landor's Cottage" leaves off, except that the appointments of the sleeper's room have a fullness, a plenitude, lacking in the cottage. The astral lamp that is briefly mentioned in "Landor's Cottage" becomes a thoroughly limned "lamp of Argand" (XIV, 104), while the lithographers are replaced by several specific types of paintings, including landscapes by Chapman and Stanfield, which bring in a domesticated "outdoor" element, and portraits of ladies by Sully, which provide the feminine element that was a central feature of the hominess in "Landor's Cottage."

Against glare, glitter, and sheer ostentation the narrator holds up the principles of softness, restraint, and, embracing all, simplicity. The problem with the ordinary American apartment, he says, is not that it has no curves; the problem is, that if it has any at all, it will have too many: "If curved lines occur, they are repeated into unpleasant uniformity" (XIV, 103). Whereas the man with more money than taste will be "insensibly led to confound the two entirely separate ideas of magnificence and beauty" (XIV, 102), an individual of modest means (XIV, 106), distinguishing between the two, will pursue the beautiful within a smaller compass. To choose an apartment that is too grand or showy is to violate order not as conspicuously perhaps as the malefactors sought by Dupin and the police, but just as surely. Such an apartment reveals "a want of keeping. We speak of the keeping of a room as we would of the keeping of a picture—for both the picture and the room are amenable to those undeviating principles which regulate all varieties of art; and very nearly the same laws by which we decide on the higher merits of a painting, suffice for decision on the adjustments of a chamber" (XIV, 102). To say this is to state generally what has already been shown concretely by those "Median laws" which govern the choice of decorate grounds and figures (XIV, 104), and to anticipate the notion of lawful cosmic design which will be a central element in *Eureka.*

Concluding Remarks

In prose fiction Poe found that he could have it both ways. He could continue to deal with the problems that interested him: power and powerlessness, arbitrary victimization, the reciprocity of body and soul, the need for unity and affirmation, and so on. At the same time he could expand into novel areas or explore old areas in ways that were not admissible under the tenets of his severe poetic theory. Thus one continues to find, as in the poems, victimizations that are subtle, problematic, or complex ("Ligeia," "The Fall of the House of Usher") but also out-and-out crimes against the person ("The Tell-Tale Heart," "The Mystery of Marie Rogêt"), performed in a social setting wider and more varied in texture than any to be found in the verse. Similarly, in the detective tales Poe reaches out to examine patterns of human events in all their interrelatedness, and even tries to convey a sense of urban life. Yet few would suggest that these works are less serious than the poems, or that they presented less of a challenge to Poe's creative consciousness. The same applies to *Pym*, in which Poe depicts the vicissitudes of maritime travel and exploration without prejudice to the story's metaphysical claims. "Landor's Cottage," with its New York setting and its comfortable domesticity, confirms that Poe no longer feels the antipathy between the "ideal" and the "everyday" that is implicit in his verse and explicit in his aesthetic theory. Even a work centered in a hermetic consciousness, such as "Berenice," pays its dues to the real world. Indeed, it is because Poe allows the world to enter, in the person of the servant, that we have a norm by which to judge the aberrations of Egaeus.

In the tales Poe grapples more openly with space and time, filling his pages with chambers, houses, apartments, vaults, boats, clocks, writing instruments, torture devices, and sundry other mechanisms, and describing the sensations of mind and body when they are subject to duration, expectation, and the thought of death. It is not that Poe ceases to portray the anxieties a man feels when threatened by the "other": interest in this type of fear is a constant of his fiction as of his verse. What happens, rather, is that he widens the field. He is now able to show that man victimizes himself equally through the manmade environment, which represents an alienated human power still human enough to resent its alienation and powerful enough to seek its revenge. He is able also to suggest that the agonies he portrays, as in "The Pit and the Pendulum," say something fundamental about the human condition. He tried of course to say something fundamental in the poems as well. The difference between the poems and the tales is that the latter, while showing the same interest in radical existential states, show a much greater interest in the world, and take on thereby a quality of fullness that Poe did not achieve in his verse because he did not seek it.

This expanding process is accompanied by an increase in consciousness, or at least in the overtly conscious treatment of earlier patterns. In the verse, terror and guilt, for example, are intensely felt but rarely described in detail and rarely analyzed. By contrast, tales like "The Fall of the House of Usher" and "The Black Cat" give such feeling an ample embodiment; if everything about them is not "explained," we have at least a fuller context from which to draw hermeneutic inferences, hints, and clues. Thus the close attention to peculiarities of physical constitution, such as Usher's hypersensitivity; thus the attempt, in "The Black Cat," to trace uncanny phenomena back to chemical causes, and to analyze the psychological origins of delusion. The problem of "interpretation" itself undergoes a similar evolution. In "The Raven" or "Ulalume" a man stakes his centeredness on his ability to interpret some strange thing that seems to hold great meaning for him. So, of course, do Pym and Peters, who must decide whether certain earthworks embody a signifying intention, or the male lovers, who must solve the mystery of a woman's identity. But interpretation also assumes in the tales a conscious and pragmatic form. The hero of "The Gold-Bug" offers what amounts to an essay on cryptography, and applies his interpretative powers to a search for buried treasure. Dupin offers fully developed guidelines for interpreting the intentions, motives, and behavior of other human beings. The first-person of "The Black Cat" interprets his own behavior in the light of an elaborate philosophy of perverseness.

"The intellect of man is forced to choose, as Yeats said, and Poe chose to perfect the work as well as he could."[68] Although Stephen Mooney is speaking here of the individual work, the same applies to groups or series of works and to the canon as a whole. Once Poe has done a thing it is likely that he will do it again, wholly or in part. As a result we find recurring types of stories and recurring patterns within them. It is also likely that he will try to do the thing better, in which case the result is not necessarily improvement so much as a kind of purification or heightening, testifying to Poe's persistent quest for the ideal. Let us examine this pattern now in

[68] "Poe's Gothic Wasteland," p. 282.

a broad selection of tales, beginning with "Berenice." This tale sets a pattern for the love relations in other tales and offers a portrait of a human being unnaturally preoccupied with himself. The trouble with the story was not merely that it was too gruesome, as Poe said, but that it tended to affirm the reality of death: Berenice expires and does not come back. In the subsequent tales about women, Poe makes up for this by having the women return from death, thus confirming the indestructibility of life. This is not to say that the later works are mere correctives to the first. It is to say that Poe wanted to make a more affirmative and fuller statement than he had managed to do in the earlier tale; it is also to say that he discovered, after his first effort at this class of narrative, that much remained to be done if he was to develop the type to its full potential.

In the detective tales we find more people and more plot; we also find, if not more conscious experience, at least more conscious use of reason and imagination. The desire for greater fullness and for greater ideality is seen in "The Mystery of Marie Rogêt," which, as an explicit sequel to "The Murders in the Rue Morgue," is longer than the earlier work, and is to be thought of as implying a parallel between its earthly events and some "ideal series of events" in a realm above the human. If Dupin is drawn forward by the unfolding of the design of human events, Poe's metaphysical voyagers are drawn forward as by some preternatural undertow to whose force they half-consciously surrender. Here the goal is not conscious knowledge but something more instinctual and primal, a kind of divine but material vision that can be quite indeterminate, as in "MS. Found in a Bottle," or literally embodied, as in *Pym*.

The metaphysical voyager faces an open-ended time, a future he cannot know because it has never been. The Ushers, by contrast, face a future that is also, strangely, the past, for they can only become, in a manner of speaking, what they already were. Prisoners of time, they are equally prisoners of space; in this work the hermetic space of the chamber is expanded into an entire house and its environs. More fully embodied than other living-spaces in Poe, the House is also more human (it shares its being with its occupants) and more self-sufficient (it is a complete microcosmic world with its own laws). William Wilson, too, is determined by the past, although in his case fate takes longer to fulfill itself: thus the story assumes, uniquely, the form of a complete biography or "life." Wilson's problem is too much self. What is unusual about him is his tendency to think, if belatedly, in moral terms. In "The Black Cat" Poe portrays a miscreant who matches Wilson for cruelty but surpasses him, through his philosophy of perverseness, in the theory of evil, while in "The Tell-Tale Heart" he portrays an egotist whose experience carries further the aural dimension contained in the typical confessional narrative. Meanwhile, another egotist, Prince Prospero, tries in vain to create an entire, self-contained world, only to see it claimed by a power higher than his own.

Whereas these protagonists are victimized by their own desires, the hero of "The Pit and the Pendulum" is victimized —and rescued—by something outside himself, the fact that he escapes testifying to Poe's yearning for an affirmative outcome, even at the expense of a hurried ending for which there is no preparation. The hero of "The Premature Burial" suffers a different and in a way a greater bondage, being the victim of his own excessive fears. His physical constitution, moreover, makes him eminently eligible for the worst of all terrors. Yet his will to affirmation is such that he escapes by effecting his own permanent cure. By conquering the terror within, he is able truthfully to say that "out of Evil proceeded Good" (v, 273).

In the landscape tales the good has even greater scope. It spreads before our eyes and stretches beneath our feet: it is the extended embodiment of the ideal. Woman is an embodiment, too; the advantage of the landscape is that here man, the artist, is in control of the design. In landscape, therefore, there is no antagonism or threat, but harmony, plenitude, repose. Landscape, as the embodiment of harmonious creative design, is greater than woman, with the result that such female presence as we see in these tales is reduced and literally contained. Where other protagonists build walls between themselves and their women, the lord of the landscape merely keeps his indoors.

It may be that Poe's desire for fullness and ideality is not always realized. Such is the case, perhaps, with "The Mystery of Marie Rogêt," or *The Journal of Julius Rodman*, neither of which, for all its breadth, breaks much new ground. A standard remark would be that Poe was feeling the pressures of a market that he could accommodate only by exploiting what had already proved to be a good thing. To be sure, one should never underestimate the influence on an author's work of financial need and contemporary taste. But it could also be argued that the works in a group represent different stages of an effort to fulfill all the possibilities of a given aesthetic type—an effort that could well produce an impression of redundancy or mere elaboration.

To refer to the master of design as a lord, as I have done, is to suggest that there is something godlike about conceiving and carrying out, in earth, one's original designs. Poe implies as much himself. It is evident, furthermore, that he was fascinated by power relations that tended toward the hierarchical (master and slave, sovereign and subject, victimizer and victim). When we consider that these relations in Poe are arbitrary and absolute, we recognize that there *is* an important sense in which Poe tries to get God, or a god-figure, or a godly power, into his stories. In a recent article Robert Daniel sees such a figure in the person of Dupin, whose ratiocinative feats amount to "miracles."[69] But the detective corresponds, it seems to me, to a fourth type, the seer or enlightened one who is elevated to a sacred place by those who lack his vision. His function is certainly different from that of the master of design. The latter increases the order in the material world, creating beauty where none exists, adding to it where it does.

[69] "Poe's Detective God" (see n. 21 above).

The master of design is forward-tending. He looks ahead to new horizons, both literally and figuratively, and projects his vision across the land toward them. The detective, on the other hand, is an interpreter who reveals a design that already exists. He neither makes nor alters. Least of all does he devote himself to the improvement of the countryside. The detective accepts the existing order, and, when it is threatened, as by the actions of a lawbreaker, he does what he can to set it right again. His method is to work backwards, retracing in time and space the design of human movements and motives. The designer, in summary, is a creator whose medium is the material world, while the detective is an interpreter whose medium is the social world.

"Supreme irony," says Karl Solger, "reigns in the conduct of God as he creates man and the life of men. In earthly art Irony has this meaning—conduct similar to God's."[70] The Poe characters who undertake a conduct similar to God's are the egotists like Prospero or the murderer in "The Tell-Tale Heart," who seek to become (to borrow from a discussion above) the absolutes of their own fiction. In his own eyes this pseudo-God is masterly, rational, omnipotent, a superior being who rises above the ordinary world and its denizens. But the reader, standing apart from him, sees him ironically. To us he is simply brutal, bizarre, or mad. We perceive, furthermore, that such a being, for all his show, is in the grip of some force greater than himself.

The victimizer-god is revealed to be an extreme form of the being who cannot love enough. The innocence of his victim merely heightens the guilt for which, through the power of words, he punishes himself. Poe's "detective god" is not so culpable. He is guilty, at worst, of the more conventional degree of failure that according to Poe's moral theology characterizes man by virtue of his being man. Even this failure (which takes the form of disdain) may be the necessary complement of his superiority to other men. The limitation

[70] Quoted in G. G. Sedgewick, *Of Irony, Especially in Drama*, 2nd ed. (Toronto, 1948), p. 17.

of such an interpreter is that he must necessarily perform after the fact: he has no gift of prophecy, save in the restricted sense that he can see now what other men will see slightly later. What is therefore still lacking in Poe's system up to this point (and what he eventually provides) is an interpreter who speaks to others, as it were, *while there is still time.* How Poe meets this need will be seen in the chapter that follows.

A second form of transcendental being in the tales is embodied in the female presence at the end of "Ligeia," "Morella," and "Eleonora," or the numinous figure at the end of *Pym.* In this relation the god-figure is presented through the eyes of the lowly. It is contemplated, in other words, much as God or an image of God is contemplated by a believer in real life. In the landscape tales the godliness is more diffused, embodied now in the female presence (Annie, the Fay, the portraits of ladies), now in the master of design and his theories, now in the earth itself. If these works represent an "advance" on the others, it is because they manage to bring man, world, and God closer together. They suggest that the creativity of God and the creativity of man are somehow parallel, and that man is most godlike when he is most fully himself.

The final and most obvious "conduct like God's" is of course that of the author himself. His is the power of the creator and the lawgiver, his the supreme authority and the supreme responsibility. In the end there is no absolute within a fiction that can compare to the power that shapes it from without. To exist within a fiction is to exist by grace of that creative consciousness which alone determines the design of the work and the forms of being it bodies forth.

The romantic philosophy to which Poe subscribed considered that "the artist is the man who goes out into the empty space between man and god and takes the enormous risk of attempting to create in that vacancy a new fabric of connections between man and the divine power. . . . The new type of man is the romantic artist, the man who in the absence of a given world must create his own. The central assumption of romanticism is the idea that the isolated individual, through poetry, can accomplish the 'unheard of work,' that is, create through his own efforts, a marvellous harmony of words which will integrate man, nature, and God."[71]

Ellison was one example of such artist; Edgar Allan Poe was another.

[71] Miller, *The Disappearance of God*, pp. 13-14.

5

THE DIALOGUES AND *EUREKA*

In a space beyond earthly space, in a time beyond earthly time, two beings speak. One is already an inhabitant of this transcendent realm of novelty called Aidenn (iv, 2, 8); the other has just arrived. The dialogue starts at this point because the moment initiates, literally, a new beginning. If the tales take place on this side of the gulf beyond, the "metaphysical dialogues," as Ransome aptly terms them, take place on the other side—in a site that is beyond the gulf beyond.[1]

Being situated beyond even the extreme limits of human experience does not presuppose discontinuity with that experience. On the contrary, anyone who comes to Aidenn knows perfectly well how he got there. The realm to which I ascend after seeming annihilation may be novel, but I am not. I remember the lesson of "The Pit and the Pendulum" or "Morella," for I bring with me both consciousness and continuous identity. My predecessor in the realm of novelty also retains his ties to earthly experience. He continues to speak the language of that planet, and he continues to care about its fate. Indeed, one of the striking features of the dialogues, especially the earlier ones, is the concern with the terrestrial past. In "The Conversation of Eiros and Charmion," Charmion asks the newly arrived Eiros to explain the catastrophe that devoured mankind; in "The Colloquy of Monos and Una," Monos recounts his experience of passing through the gulf; in "The Power of Words," Agathos tells Oinos how he came to create the planetary orb they are both contemplating; in "Mesmeric Revelation," Vankirk, the mesmeric subject, places man in the context of creation that he elucidates.

"The Conversation of Eiros and Charmion"

The interstellar confrontation that Eiros depicts is victimization on a colossal scale. As in "Al Aaraaf" the denizens

[1] *Edgar Allan Poe: A Critical Study*, p. 184.

of earth witness the advent "of a *new* comet" (IV, 4) that hovers above them, moves closer, and eventually destroys them through combustion. One difference between this victimization and those in, for example, "The Pit and the Pendulum" or "The Tell-Tale Heart," is that here the victim has been collectivized. In the crowd Eiros describes there are many faces but, as it were, a single identity. There are no intersubjective relations, but rather a convergence-in-one; mankind becomes, in effect, a single body: "We gasped in the rapid modification of the air. The red blood bounded tumultuously through its strict channels" (IV, 8). Another difference is that the force that overpowers has a supernal origin, relevant parallels in this case being, among others, "MS. Found in a Bottle," *Pym*, and such poems as "Tamerlane," "Al Aaraaf," and "Annabel Lee." The punishing force acts upon the inhabitants of earth even more gratuitously than in "Al Aaraaf," where mankind has sinned by creating a false model of God's infinity. By contrast, man sins, in "The Conversation of Eiros and Charmion," through a pervasive ignorance. His faulty knowledge causes him to misread the holy prophecies predicting annihilation by fire. Faced with a presence that throws their powerlessness into relief, the people of earth yearn for that true knowledge which they have heretofore neglected: "The learned *now* gave their intellect—their soul—to no such points as the allaying of fear, or to the sustenance of loved theory. They sought—they panted for right views. They groaned for perfected knowledge. *Truth* arose in the purity of her strength and exceeding majesty, and the wise bowed down and adored" (IV, 5). The piety comes, inevitably, too late. In "Tamerlane" the man who failed to give a portion of his willing soul to God lost the natural world in that he could no longer experience it directly. In "The Conversation of Eiros and Charmion," the failing is universal, and so too is the loss: "For a moment there was a wild lurid light alone, visiting and penetrating all things. Then let us bow down, Charmion, before the excessive majesty of the great God!—and then, there came a shouting and pervading sound, as if from the mouth itself of HIM: while the whole incumbent mass of ether in which we existed, burst at once into a species of intense flame, for whose surpassing brilliancy and all-fervid heat even the angels in the high Heaven of pure knowledge have no name. Thus ended all" (IV, 8).

The punishment for failure is a consummate victimization. From the viewpoint of "beyond," however, disaster is never disastrous: all of these dialogues involve the *survivors* of catastrophes, both collective and individual. The victimization becomes what is called in "Mesmeric Revelation" "a painful metamorphosis." It is, in a word, the process through which the truant spirit is saved. One can experience the saving victimization through the woman, who overpowers her lover, then stands before him in transcendence: this occurs in the poems to women that we have examined above. But ultimate salvation comes about, not unexpectedly, through ultimate victimization: the destruction of man himself by God Himself; or rather, the apparent destruction, for if the earth ceases, *life* goes on. *The disappearance of the world reveals the presence of the universe.* The victim finds himself in a new time that has its complement in an equally new space. In this most consistent and continuous of universal systems death is the mediation through which being encounters ever new manifestations of itself.

"The Colloquy of Monos and Una"

Una. "Born again?"
Monos. Yes, fairest and best-beloved Una, "born again." These were the words upon whose mystical meaning I had so long pondered, rejecting the explanations of the priesthood, until Death himself resolved for me the secret. (IV, 200)

What could be newer, what could be more full of life, than rebirth? Yet it is only through the agency of death, which terminates one phase of existence, that another and higher phase can come about. Death is at once an ontological and a heuristic process. It is both the means through which we become something new, and the means through which we come to know this becoming. The philosophical dialogue, more than any other literary form, is the genre of coming-to-know. This does not mean that the participants in the dialogue advance through a series of evenly balanced dialectical exchanges. Here as in the Socratic dialogues the direction of the argument is determined by one whose knowledge is superior. The dialogue form, despite its "round-table" quality, often conceals a hierarchical principle: to this extent it presents the appearance of a static, vertical structure. But the dialogue is also a process, a leading-forward to new understanding, the effect of which is to raise the less-advanced toward a higher level. This tendency is evident in all of Poe's dialogues: Eiros enlightens Charmion, Monos enlightens Una, Agathos enlightens Oinos, and Vankirk enlightens his mesmerist. In every case except the first the senior spirit guides the junior. But the apparent exception merely underlines the extent to which all the dialogues are oriented toward the past. Charmion is "burning with anxiety to hear the details of that stupendous event which threw you among us" (IV, 2), while Una declares, "I burn to know the incidents of your own passage through the dark Valley and Shadow" (IV, 201). The recitation of these events and incidents provides so much narrative interest that the dialogue moves toward the tale. One might also say that the dialogue tends to become a monologue. The common feature in these two formulations is that one speaker is, to borrow Orwell's phrase, more equal than the other. Like the narrators of the tales, such a speaker is the teller of his own story, and the story is his own because of the irreducibility of individual consciousness and identity. Whatever happens, happens to *me*—this unique, discrete, conscious and continuous being. That is why, even in the collectivity I try to portray, there are no intersubjective relationships, but a single subjectivity housed in a plural pronoun. Consciousness and identity are by definition that which cannot be lost. If I am to survive I must survive in the form of "myself, knowing." This necessity is all the more important in "The Colloquy of Monos and Una," which becomes, after less than two pages of exchange, and with only one subsequent interposition by Una, Monos' first-person narrative of his own death and regeneration.

A second reason for the narrative component in the dialogues is that knowing is oriented toward the past. In Aidenn one learns about things that transpired in an historical past (catastrophes, individual death, and rebirth), and about things that have always been (the creation). Despite the fact that the dialogues take place, as the Sophoclean epigraph to "The Colloquy" indicates, in a future time, knowing cannot look indefinitely forward, for it is finite, limited—a kind of enclosed space with boundaries that cannot be surpassed. Mankind is condemned in "The Colloquy" precisely for its failure to recognize this limitation: "Occasionally the poetic intellect—that intellect which we now feel to have been the most exalted of all—since those truths which to us were of the most enduring importance could only be reached by that *analogy* which speaks in proof-tones to the imagination alone, and to the unaided reason bears no weight—occasionally did this poetic intellect proceed a step farther in the evolving of the vague idea of the philosophic, and find in the mystic parable that tells of the tree of knowledge, and of its forbidden fruit, death-producing, a distinct intimation that knowledge was not meet for man in the infant condition of his soul" (IV, 202). Having invoked the Christian myth of virtue-through-incapacity, Monos goes on to explain the specific consequences of man's transgression. If powerlessness is good, power must be evil. Through power man enchains himself—becomes, like Tamerlane, a bondsman to his own praxis: "Art—the Arts—arose supreme, and, once enthroned, cast chains upon the intellect which had elevated them to power. Man, because he could not but acknowledge the majesty of Nature, fell into childish exultation at his acquired and still-increasing dominion over her elements. Even while he stalked a God in his own fancy, an infantine imbecility came over him" (IV, 203). Here as in "Al Aaraaf" the supplanting of deity can never be reversed. The "arts" man creates turn against him in the same way as that other creation, technology: "Meantime huge smoking cities arose, innumerable. Green leaves shrank before the hot breath of furnaces. The fair face of Nature was deformed as with the ravages of some loathsome disease" (IV, 203).[2]

The consequence of these distortions, according to the theory developed by Monos, is general annihilation followed by general rebirth. Monos reaches this conclusion, or rather the conclusion comes to him, in a familiar way: "I had imbibed a prescience of our Fate from comparison of China the simple and enduring, with Assyria the architect, with Egypt the astrologer, with Nubia, more crafty than either, the turbulent mother of all Arts. In history of these regions I met with a ray from the Future" (IV, 204-205). The imbibing recalls Tamerlane. So does the perception of the future-revealing and therefore prophetic ray. Furthermore, the perception comes late, as both men near the end of their earthly term. But lateness is a relative concept, and has a different meaning for the two men. By the time Tamerlane sees his existence in relation to a higher order, a beyond, that existence has already been lived. The rays of truth, though they come from

[2] The wanderer in "The Elk" dreams "of the 'good old days' when the Demon of the Engine was not, when pic-nics were undreamt of, when 'water privileges' were neither bought nor sold, and when the red man trod alone, with the elk, upon the ridges that now towered above" (V, 161). In an article written for the *Columbia Spy* (1844) and reprinted by Jacob E. Spannuth and T. O. Mabbott in their *Doings of Gotham* (Pottsville, Penn., 1929), pp. 25-26, Poe complains that the old mansions of east Manhattan "are doomed. The spirit of Improvement has withered them with its acrid breath. Streets are already 'mapped' through them, and they are no longer suburban residences but 'town-lots.' In some thirty years every noble cliff will be a pier, and the whole island will be densely desecrated by buildings of brick. . . ." The diatribe in "The Philosophy of Furniture" against the "Benthams" is of course written in the same spirit. Cf. Ernest Marchand, "Poe as a Social Critic," *American Literature*, 6 (1934), pp. 28-43.

the future, are meaningful only in relation to his past; he sees himself now in a larger context that has always obtained but that he has been unable to perceive: his future, being merely the aftermath of his past, is essentially closed. Monos's future, on the other hand, is open. The ray he perceives draws him forward. It is literally a guiding light, and his own role, consequently, is passive, a condition enforced by Poe's footnote in which the word "history," from the last sentence just quoted, is traced etymologically to the Greek infinitive, *to contemplate*. In sum Tamerlane comes to know "too late," while Monos comes to know "just in time."

Premature burial terrifies by imprisoning the victim in a situation from which there is no possible escape. For someone who has been prematurely buried there is no beyond; the burial vault is all the "universe" he has. But the beyond that is denied to the prematurely buried is precisely what Monos possesses: the universe itself. Against that ultimate background death presents a very different silhouette: "The individual artificialites of the three latter [Assyria, Egypt, Nubia] were local diseases of the Earth, and in their individual overthrows we had seen local remedies applied; but for the infected world at large I could anticipate no regeneration save in death. That man, as a race, should not become extinct, I saw that he must be '*born again*' " (IV, 205).

Monos becomes the test case of his own theory through the most passive of acts: he merely succumbs to a fever that is one feature of "the general turmoil and decay" (IV, 206). The helpless posture to which he is reduced is not that of the bad victimization but of the good, or saving, victimization. He becomes, in a word, the sleeper: "My condition did not deprive me of sentience. It appeared to me not greatly dissimilar to the extreme quiescence of him, who, having slumbered long and profoundly, lying motionless and fully prostrate in a midsummer noon, begins to steal slowly back into consciousness, through the mere sufficiency of his sleep, and without being awakened by external disturbances" (IV, 206). To know the condition in its fullness one must, as Monos does, live it inwardly; that is not to say that annihilation is interior, but only that it is experienced through interiority. Death, like life, is unitary, an experience of mind and body, at once external and inward: "Philosophers, medical men and natural scientists concerned with the mind-body problem converge more and more toward a unified conception. It is one and the same life which, in its being for others, has a physical structure."[3]

The passage of Monos through death to new life confirms the ultimate continuity of being in two ways. First, by stressing the perdurance of materiality: "Thus the pressure of your sweet fingers upon my eyelids . . . filled my whole being with a sensual delight immeasurable. I say with a sensual delight. *All* my perceptions were purely sensual" (IV, 207). The continuity of being is confirmed, secondly, by that very indestructibility of consciousness on which the victim of "The Pit and the Pendulum" insisted:

"All of what man has termed sense was merged in the sole consciousness of entity, and in the one abiding sentiment of duration. The mortal body had been at length stricken with the hand of the deadly *Decay*.

"Yet had not all sentience departed; for the consciousness and the sentiment remaining supplied some of its functions by a lethargic intuition. I appreciated the direful change now in operation upon the flesh. . . . So, too, when the noon of the second day came, I was not unconscious of those movements which displaced you from my side, which confined me within the coffin . . . and which thus left me, in blackness and corruption, to my sad and solemn slumbers with the worm." (IV, 210-211)

This is not the ordinary matter that we perceive, in earthly life, as something distinct from spirit, but a matter attenuated, merged: it is as close to spirit as matter can get without ceasing to be matter. The process matter undergoes is essentially one of abstraction. Little by little the thing is

[3] Max Scheler, *Man's Place in Nature*, trans. Hans Meyerhoff (Boston, 1961), p. 73.

purged in such a way that in the end it exists primarily in our idea of it: "The consciousness of *being* had grown hourly more indistinct, and that of mere *locality* had, in great measure, usurped its position. The idea of entity was becoming merged in that of *place*. The narrow space immediately surrounding what had been the body, was now growing to be the body itself" (IV, 211).

The problem, for Monos, is how to represent something that cannot be expressed. It is neither true that being is any longer material in the usual sense, nor that being is solely spiritual. It is neither true that Monos has ceased to be what he was, nor that he is yet what he will finally become: the state Monos experiences at the end of the story is precisely intermediate. His situation, in relation to the earth, is a beyond; yet there is another beyond—a still higher sphere of existence—beyond his situation. Monos is being saved, yet his condition is still, in a measure, one of victimization: "The sense of being had at length utterly departed, and there reigned in its stead—instead of all things—dominant and perpetual—the autocrats *Place* and *Time*. For *that* which *was not*—for that which had no form—for that which had no thought—for that which had no sentience—for that which was soulless, yet of which matter formed no portion—for all this nothingness, yet for all this immortality, the grave was still a home, and the corrosive hours, co-mates" (IV, 211-212).

"Mesmeric Revelation"

Through the "condition" or "state" (V, 241, 244, 250) created by the mesmeric trance the illuminations of the afterlife are glimpsed from this side of the gulf beyond. In the relationship established between the mesmeric subject, Vankirk, and the practitioner who converses with him, Vankirk is essentially a mediator. Unlike Monos, who reports the process of annihilation from beginning to end, Vankirk reports everything up to the point at which annihilation begins, any actual passage through the gulf being incommunicable, except from the perspective of the afterlife. His revelation is a speculative anticipation of the kinds of knowledge to which he will have full access only with the attainment of the angelic state.

The primary revelation is the essential unity of life and the nullity of death: "There are two bodies—the rudimental and the complete; corresponding with the two conditions of the worm and the butterfly. What we call 'death,' is but the painful metamorphosis. Our present incarnation is progressive, preparatory, temporary. Our future is perfected, ultimate, immortal. The ultimate life is the full design" (v, 250). If the angels know more than men it is not because the angels have a "higher" vision, but because they enjoy what Geoffrey Hartman would call "unmediated vision": "When I say that [the mesmeric state] resembles death, I mean that it resembles the ultimate life; for when I am entranced the senses of my rudimental life are in abeyance, and I perceive external things directly, without organs, through a medium which I shall employ in the ultimate, unorganized life" (v, 250).

The ultimate life does not differ from the rudimental in kind, but only in degree. Continuity, the governing principle of the universe, requires that the two phases of life operate in basically the same way. Accordingly, the kind of perception one finds in the rudimental phase is identical with the kind of perception one finds in the ultimate. In both, the external world is the active agent, and perception is passive. Perception in the rudimental life originates in the vibrations that a luminous body imparts to the surrounding ether. These vibrations cause corresponding vibrations in the retina of the perceiver; the retina causes still more vibrations in the optic nerve; the optic nerve evokes the same response in the brain that in its turn initiates more vibrations in "the unparticled matter which permeates it" (v, 251). In the ultimate life the perceiver, again, is passive while the external world is active; the only difference is in the nature of the mediating phenomena, which are simplified: "the external world reaches the whole body . . . with no other intervention than that of an infinitely rarer ether than even the luminiferous; and to this ether—in unison with it—the whole body vibrates, setting in motion the unparticled matter which permeates it" (v, 251).

Life exists, not on earth alone, but throughout the universe. Even the "nebulae, planets, suns, and other bodies" are "tenanted by a distinct variety of organic, rudimental, thinking creatures" (v, 252). For these beings, too, life is continuous and thus endless; when death comes they merely enter a new phase of being: "At death, or metamorphosis, these creatures, enjoying the ultimate life—immortality—and cognizant of all secrets but *the one*, act all things and pass everywhere by mere volition:—indwelling, not the stars, which to us seem the sole palpabilities . . . but that SPACE itself—that infinity of which the truly substantive vastness swallows up the star-shadows—blotting them out as non-entities from the perception of the angels" (v, 252). Through this destruction is revealed the underlying continuity that unites the angelic with the earthly state: the angels themselves are limited in their ability to know, just as man is limited; the only difference, again, is in degree.

What distinguishes, then, an angel's powers from a man's? If an angel knows more than a man (though neither knows all), what is the consequence? It is to these questions that the last of the dialogues provides at least partial replies.

"The Power of Words"

Oinos. Pardon, Agathos, the weakness of a spirit newfledged with immortality!

Agathos. You have spoken nothing, my Oinos, for which pardon is to be demanded. Not even here is knowledge a thing of intuition. For wisdom ask of the angels freely, that it may be given!

> *Oinos.* But in this existence, I dreamed that I should be at once cognizant of all things, and thus at once happy in being cognizant of all.
>
> *Agathos.* Ah, not in knowledge is happiness, but in the acquisition of knowledge! In for ever knowing, we are for ever blessed; but to know all were the curse of a fiend. (VI, 139)

The highest happiness in Aidenn is thus a coming-to-know that cannot end. There is nothing Faustian about this quest; the inquisitive mind is empowered neither to generate new conceptual worlds nor to acquire knowledge directly from phenomena. The denial of intuition establishes all knowing as knowing-by-mediation. That is why, as I have already suggested, each dialogue involves a guide and a follower—a mediator and a questioner. The mediator enjoys no innate superiority over the questioner. He occupies a higher position in this hierarchy of two merely because of his priority in time—he knows more because he has been there longer. The sole hierarchy based on innate differences is the overarching one extending from God down through the occupants of Aidenn collectively and down again to the populations of other planetary bodies, such as earth, as long as they shall exist.

Agathos tries to demonstrate that coming-to-know cannot end by pointing out that the universe is, in effect, nothing more than a great chamber: "Look down into the abysmal distances!—attempt to force the gaze down the multitudinous vistas of the stars, as we sweep slowly through them thus—and thus—and thus! Even the spiritual vision, is it not at all points arrested by the continuous golden walls of the universe?—the walls of the myriads of the shining bodies that mere number has appeared to blend into unity?" (VI, 139). What reveals the unlimited nature of coming-to-know? The very fact that man's capacity to know is limited. Agathos explains that infinite matter was created in order to allay the soul's thirst for knowledge. When Oinos asks whether

God Himself does not know all, Agathos replies: "*That* (since he is The Most Happy) must be still the *one* thing unknown even to HIM" (VI, 139). The infinity of matter thus relates primarily to the feelings of the knower—it is an assuagement that placates a drive that, in the nature of things, can never be fully satisfied (VI, 140).

In his new existence on Aidenn, Oinos (who may be identical with the Oinos of "Shadow. A Parable") learns that creation itself is, like knowledge, mediate: "In the beginning *only*, [God] created. The seeming creatures which are now, throughout the universe, so perpetually springing into being, can only be considered as the mediate or indirect, not as the direct or immediate results of the Divine creative power" (VI, 140). Such a theory takes God out of present creation—the creation of which one is capable on earth or on Aidenn. But if present creating is only secondary, then at the same time it removes real creativity from human or angelic beings, throwing them back again on the creativity of a God who has ceased to create. The paradox, which is extreme, arises from the inescapable tendency to "alienate." One looks for the true creativity only to find it in a vague "somewhere" that, as soon as it is found, immediately dissolves. Original creation was, and is no more. But if it was the origin of all subsequent creation, then it still is. Yet where exactly *is* it? It is not here. Here there is only a mediate phenomenon "which has all the *appearance* of creation" (VI, 141). Thus creation is nowhere—yet I am myself constantly creating. Agathos declares:

"You are well aware that, as no thought can perish, so no act is without infinite result. We moved our hands, for example, when we were dwellers on the earth, and, in so doing, we gave vibration to the atmosphere which engirdled it. This vibration was indefinitely extended, till it gave impulse to every particle of the earth's air, which thenceforward, *and for ever*, was actuated by the one movement of the hand." (VI, 141)

The description recalls Pascal, who observed that:

"The slightest movement affects the whole of nature; a stone cast into the sea changes the whole face of it. So, in the realm of Grace the smallest act affects the whole by its results. Therefore everything has its importance.

"In every action we must consider, besides the act itself, our present, past, and future conditions, and others whom it touches, and must see the connections of it all. And so we shall keep ourselves well in check."

As Allen Tate points out, it almost seems as if Poe had gone directly from reading the *Pensées* to composing "The Power of Words," and by ignoring "the moral responsibility, the *check* upon human power, enjoined in the last sentence . . . had concentrated upon Pascal's physical analogy for divine grace. . . ."[4] What Tate does not point out is that this emphasis is in keeping with Poe's pervasive and conscious materialism, as exemplified in Ellison's pursuit of purely physical loveliness. It is also in keeping with his interest in beings who wield ungoverned power without regard for the feelings of others or the laws of society. What links these beings with Agathos is the fact that the power they use is never really theirs. It is a borrowed thing, something channelled *through* them. The particular dilemma of the angel is that he "expresses" a creative power he neither originates nor controls. Agathos cannot help creating, any more than an ordinary mortal can help breathing, or any more than the being in "The Haunted Palace" can prevent his utterance from flowing out of him. It is the words, and not the speaker, that have the power. If Agathos moves a muscle, some new thing springs into life and stays to haunt him:

Oinos. "But why, Agathos, do you weep?—and why—oh why do your wings droop as we hover above this fair star—which is the greenest and yet most terrible of all we have encountered in our flight? Its brilliant flowers look like a fairy dream—but its fierce volcanoes like the passions of a turbulent heart.

[4] "The Angelic Imagination," p. 127.

Agathos. They *are*!—they *are*! This wild star—it is now three centuries since with clasped hands, and with streaming eyes, at the feet of my beloved—I spoke it—with a few passionate sentences—into birth. Its brilliant flowers *are* the dearest of unfulfilled dreams, and its raging volcanoes *are* the passions of the most turbulent and unhallowed of hearts." (VI, 143-144)

If we compare this confrontation with the one in "MS. Found in a Bottle," we discern a similarity as well as a difference. The similarity is that in both cases the "utterance" is unplanned; it is something that just happens. The difference is that the word the voyager paints is just a word, whereas the word the angel speaks is a creative force that makes an already full Creation even fuller. To contribute to plenitude in this way is not, however, a painless task. Agathos declares, I cannot stop creating. Yet nothing I create is really created by me, through my own volition. Every move I make, every word I say, derives ultimately from God, the prime mover. The trouble is that every time some new thing issues from me it takes some of me with it. It is as though I had accidentally spilled a little of my being into space and cannot now get it back. The moment of separation, the moment this bit of matter starts living on its own, marks the beginning of an interminable confrontation. Henceforth I must face this "other" who is still strangely, in some sense, "me." What my creative power amounts to, in the end, is a capacity for creating *separation*, for *extending* myself in such a way as to *confront* myself.

Agathos is unquestionably nearer to God than an ordinary mortal could hope to be: not even a landscape designer can speak things into instantaneous being. "Agathos' doctrine," Tate therefore concludes, "transcends the ideal of mere angelic knowledge: it is superangelism. Man is not only an angel, he is God in his aspect of creativity."[5] But this is to accelerate Poe's timetable. Not until *Eureka* will Poe presume

[5] *Ibid.*, p. 128.

to elevate man to so lofty an eminence. The setting of the dialogues, we must remember, is an intermediate realm above the earthly but beneath the divine; a realm in which one creates like a god but suffers like a man. The ontological structure of this realm, like the structure of the dialogue itself, is implicitly hierarchical. The relation of angel to God remains a transcendent relation, the relation of the Most High to one who is not yet high enough.

EUREKA: A PROSE POEM

"Eureka, eureka" was the cry Archimedes uttered on making his great discovery. That Poe should owe his title to a man of science and geometry is fitting, since Poe was convinced of the scientific validity of his own "findings," and since many of his leading terms—circle, sphere, body, point—are geometric in origin. By adding the subtitle, "A Prose Poem," Poe warns that he does not advance the work, however, on this basis alone. *Eureka* is to be a work of art, a book that is beautiful partly, at least, because it is also true. The dual claim is taken up in the preface, where Poe, speaking in his own person above the initials E. A. P., announces, "I offer this Book of Truths, not in its character of Truth-Teller, but for the Beauty that abounds in its Truth; constituting it true. To these I present the composition as an Art-Product along:—let us say as a Romance; or, if I be not urging too lofty a claim, as a Poem." The statement is highly compressed. Beauty and truth, which Poe had never been keen to reconcile, are brought together in a stroke. With scarcely a pause he then tells us that, within the general category of artwork, his composition may be thought of as belonging to the first, and equally the second, of two genres. The advantage of the first of these genres is that it allows the author, in Hawthorne's words, "a certain latitude." The romance permits a man, says James, to deal with "experience liberated, so to speak; experience disengaged, disembroiled, disencumbered, exempt from the conditions that we usually know to attach to it and, if we wish so to put the matter, drag upon it, and operating in a medium which relieves it, in a particular interest, of the inconvenience of a *related*, a measured state, a state subject to all our vulgar communities." In the words of a recent critic, "romance, being absorbed with the ideal, always has an element of prophecy. It remakes the world in the image of desire."[6] Ideality and prophecy being central features in his poetic theory, it is not surprising that Poe should round things off by putting *Eureka* forward "as a Poem," or that he should do so in a way that leaves its status as a romance intact. In a critic such telescoping, such blurring of types and blending of claims, would show "want of keeping." But Poe is not speaking as a critic. He is speaking as a man who has seen the light. His relatively simple aim is to express in an intense oral way his own feelings of excitement and awe, and to suggest that there is nothing contradictory in a work that is at once imaginary and scientific, at once romance and poem.

The remaining paragraphs, while equally compressed, are more intense and also more personal:

"*What I here propound is true*:—therefore it cannot die: —or if by any means it be now trodden down so that it die, it will 'rise again to the Life Everlasting.'

"Nevertheless it is as a Poem only that I wish this work to be judged after I am dead."

The note of urgency that will run throughout *Eureka* is already audible here. Poe wants passionately to be heard and believed, for, as becomes increasingly clear, the missing element in his system is to be supplied by the author himself: Poe is the interpreter who speaks while there is still time. It is Poe who will say truly and beautifully what must be and what must be known. It is Poe who will reveal the universe

[6] Gillian Beer, *The Romance* (London, 1970), p. 179. The Hawthorne and James quotations are discussed in the first chapter of Richard Chase's influential *The American Novel and Its Tradition* (New York, 1957), pp. 1-28.

through the power of words. "That little piece of prose," says Ransome, "has always seemed to me a very moving embodiment of a great man's hesitation. It is hope almost throttled by fear and for that very reason raising its voice to an unnatural pitch."[7] We shall examine below the consequences of this vocal intensity. Here we need only recognize that Poe is staking his centeredness on the gamble that his interpretation will be as viable as it is true. In this context the final sentence, in which he looks beyond the shadow of his own death, acquires a poignance that is not common in prefaces, or for that matter in Poe.

While there is reason in all this, there is also emotion. The reader, as a result, is ready to sympathize with the author even if he is not yet ready to agree with him. In the words of Pascal, quoted by Monos in "The Colloquy of Monos and Una," "*tout notre raisonnement se réduit à céder au sentiment*" (IV, 204). This is not to suggest any lack of rationality in the preface; it is merely to point out the superfluity of feeling.

There is a similar affective plenitude in the opening lines of the main body of the text, and a similar concern with "sentiment":

"It is with humility really unassumed—it is with a sentiment even of awe—that I pen the opening sentence of this work: for of all conceivable subjects I approach the reader with the most solemn—the most comprehensive—the most difficult—the most august.

"What terms shall I find sufficiently simple in their sublimity—sufficiently sublime in their simplicity—for the mere enunciation of my theme?" (XVI, 185).

Marshall McLuhan would explain such statements by reference to Poe's Southern background, in particular the Ciceronian tradition with its "ideal of a rational man reaching his noblest attainment in the expression of an eloquent wisdom."[8]

[7] *Edgar Allan Poe: A Critical Study*, p. 175. Cf. D. E. S. Maxwell, *American Fiction: the Intellectual Background* (London, 1963), p. 71.

[8] "Edgar Poe's Tradition," *Sewanee Review*, 52 (1944), pp. 24-33.

Poe would doubtless have been pleased to be credited with rationality, eloquence, and wisdom. But he would have wanted to be credited as well with reverence and piety. The knowledge he would impart is not the cool sort; it is full of divine heat, and the words he uses are instinct with an imparted warmth. What he offers is not an eloquent wisdom but a passionate knowledge, something of which he is privately sure and of which he may therefore publicly speak. The author of *Eureka*, in short, is a man who would employ his sovereign reason in behalf of his sovereign belief.

That Poe is aware of all this is suggested by his consciousness of himself as speaker and author: thus his use of words like "enunciation" and "pen," and thus his attention in the opening sentence to his relationship with his audience. Little by little the speaker-author emerges as the guide who will lead the auditor-reader to higher knowledge just as the experienced angel leads the fledgling: ". . . I propose to take such a survey of the Universe that the mind may be able really to receive and to perceive an individual impression" (XVI, 186). The pairing "receive-perceive" recalls the theory of perception advanced in "The Power of Words," while the emphasis on a universal context recalls the setting of all the dialogues. From the supply of techniques provided by other earlier works the author draws the device of the borrowed voice (XVI, 187 ff.). Although the voice is recorded in a letter found in a bottle, it is not "MS. Found in a Bottle" that anticipates the argument it advances, but such satirical pieces as "Mellonta Tauta" and "The Thousand-and-Second Tale of Scheherezade," which exploit the discrepancy between the actual nature of the things being viewed and the alienated perspective that views them. Those who object that the letter-writer does not belong in a work of this kind forget that the cosmogony is an omnibus form that, like the anatomy to which Northrop Frye has attracted new critical attention, is omnivorous. The cosmogonist, as Thomas Wolfe would say, is a "putter-inner" rather than a "leaver-outer." Through the borrowed voice, moreover, one can slay the *bête noire* of scientific rationalism by proxy, thereby avoiding the rough-and-tumble of the arena and preserving the reigning tone of chaste intensity and sublimity.

The vortex-velocity motif that appears in this section of *Eureka* is also familiar, but with a difference: "Only by a rapid whirling on his heel could he hope to comprehend the panorama in the sublimity of its *oneness.* But as, on the summit of Aetna, *no* man has thought of whirling on his heel, so no man has ever taken into his brain the full uniqueness of the prospect . . ." (XVI, 186). The combination of spinning and great speed that produced terror in the tales takes on, in the universal context, a positive quality.[9] This is not merely because the combination is experienced by a "he," but because the process expresses an intention and is controlled by a volition. This third-person wants to achieve a simultaneity of view, and has the power to achieve it through a means at his exclusive disposal. The situation thus reverses the relationship between motion and stasis that prevails, as we have seen, in so many of the poems and tales. Whereas in those victimizing situations I am helplessly immobile in relation to a motion around or toward me, in this situation it is I who move and the environment that remains still. The man who surveys the universe is literally surrounded and enclosed. His equivalent in the tales is the character afflicted by impinging walls. But here there is no impingement because there is no antagonism. This circumscribed space does not retaliate against man, for man did not create it. Space, like man, is the creation of God, and is inalienable from man. Subsequently, we shall see this lack of alienation turning into a broad theory of identity embracing all created phenomena.

A rapid spin-about might produce a sense of simultaneity for the spinner, but it is no help in explaining the process by which the surrounding creation came into being. Such an explanation must be serial, for words must follow each other in time, as in space. The author goes a step further, making the

[9] The comic version of the vertiginous spin is the pirouette ("A Predicament. The Scythe of Time," II, 292; "Loss of Breath," II, 152).

explanation into a narrative: "But the diffusive energy being withdrawn, and the rëaction having commenced in furtherance of the ultimate design—*that of the utmost possible Relation*—this design is now in danger of being frustrated, in detail, by reason of that very tendency to return which is to effect its accomplishment in general" (XVI, 210). But of course there is no point at which the design is really in danger. The universe *is* its design, which is complete and perfect in every phase, and the theory of *Eureka* fully accounts for this. The danger arises because the state of the universe is being made into a story. In the actual creation, everything is already given, as the theory will eventually make clear: on the one hand is attraction, and on the other repulsion; and so on. But the author is pretending here that repulsion does not yet exist—that the universe faces a crisis that can be saved only by some thrilling intervention. When in the following paragraph suspense is broken by the sudden appearance of the needed repulsion, the universe is saved much as the victim of "The Pit and the Pendulum" is saved, at the last moment, by the arrival of General La Salle.

The practice of turning theory into story is a corollary of the thoroughgoing parallelism in *Eureka* between aesthetic creation and the creation that is the universe: "In the construction of *plot* . . . in fictitious literature, we should aim at so arranging the incidents that we shall not be able to determine, of any one of them, whether it depends from any one other or upholds it. In this sense, of course, *perfection* of *plot* is really, or practically, unattainable—but only because it is a finite intelligence that constructs. The plots of God are perfect. The Universe is a plot of God" (XVI, 292).

Such a plot derives its unity from the perfection of design, which, like plot itself, can be either human or divine. Design can be a verb through which I express my intention: "I design to speak of the *Physical, Metaphysical and Mathematical—of the Material and Spiritual Universe:—of its Essence, its Origin, its Creation, its Present Condition and its Destiny*" (XVI, 185). Design is also a noun, expressive of an overarching plan that is already given: "Now, distinctness—intelligibility, at all points, is a primary feature in my general design" (XVI, 199). As designer I perform on the creatural level a version of the divine act of creation, God himself being the great designer: if the thinking man cannot solve a problem, "he perceives that the Deity has not *designed* it to be solved" (XVI, 204).

In order to determine the underlying pattern of the divine designer: if the thinking man cannot solve a problem, "he interprets his texts, or as Dupin interprets a train of circumstances. The successful design of the universe depends upon the same kind of unity as the design of fiction: "As the novel cannot be read at one sitting, it cannot avail itself of the immense benefit of *totality*. Worldly interests, intervening during the pauses of perusal, modify, counteract and annul the impressions intended. But simple cessation in reading would, of itself, be sufficient to destroy the true unity. In the brief tale, however, the author is enabled to carry out his full design without interruption" (XIII, 153). What applies to the existence of the literary creation applies with even greater force to the universal creation of which the literary is a part. In the words of "Mesmeric Revelation," "Our present incarnation is progressive, preparatory, temporary. Our future is perfected, ultimate, immortal. The ultimate life is the full design" (V, 250). The existence of a full design for the universe as a whole does not deny discreteness to individual beings any more than the full design of an author's canon denies discreteness to individual works. Within the full design, there are many smaller ones: "That every work of Divine conception must cöexist and cöexpire with its particular design, seems to me especially obvious . . ." (XVI, 309).

If one is to interpret the full design, one must find a way of situating oneself in the universe and of distinguishing the elements of which that universe is composed. One accomplishes this purpose by reference to *points*. The point is a spot when it designates a location in space: "Neither is the Sun absolutely the centre of the system; for this Sun itself, with all the planets, revolves about a perpetually shifting point of space, which is the system's general centre of gravity. . . . [The paths through which the spheroids move] are, in fact, *ellipses—one of the foci being the point about which the revolution is made*" (XVI, 277). So thorough is the unity of the universal system that one also moves, physically, in relation to a point. In order to see creation in its true universal context, "we require something like a mental gyration on the heel. We need so rapid a revolution of all things about the central point of sight that, while the minutiae vanish altogether, even the more conspicuous objects become blended into one" (XVI, 187). The point provides orientation; it is that in relation to which some other phenomenon may be judged or revealed. Wherever this definition applies, the relevance of the point lies not in itself but in something it helps to illuminate. But there are also immanent points—aspects or features that, far from existing outside of the phenomenon, are contained within it. Such points heighten the effect of unity. As Poe explains in his review of De la Motte-Fouqué's *Undine*, "Its unity is absolute—its keeping unbroken. Yet every minute point of the picture fills and satisfies the eye. Everything is attended to, and nothing is out of time or out of place" (X, 37). The proliferation of points can result in a "want of keeping" that is no more acceptable to the author of an essay on Alexander von Humboldt than to the author of "The Philosophy of Furniture": "But however admirable be the succinctness with which he has treated each particular point of his topic, the mere multiplicity of these points occasions, necessarily, an amount of detail, and thus an involution of idea, which preclude all *individuality* of impression" (XVI, 187).

Points are to be found in the natural world, in the man-made environment, and in man himself. Thus, in "The Domain of Arnheim," the term is applied to the landscape, to the roof of Ellison's house and his boat, and to Ellison's mind. The highest function of this all-purpose phenomenon, in whatever sphere, is to facilitate the attainment of plenitude.

Ellison's friend, for example, considers that "the primitive intention of nature would have so arranged the earth's surface as to have fulfilled at all points man's sense of perfection in the beautiful, the sublime, or the picturesque . . ." (VI, 184). Although this intention has not yet been realized, as he at first supposes, the narrator is right about the relation of point and plenitude: "The truthfulness, the indispensable truthfulness of the drama, has reference only to the fidelity with which it should depict nature, so far as regards her points, first, and secondly, her general intention. Her arrangement or combination of points may be improved—that is to say, a greater number of striking points than are ever seen closely conjoined in reality, may, for artistical purposes be gathered into the action of a drama—provided always that there be no absolute controversion of nature's general intention" (XIII, 113).

The concept of points enables the interpreter of design to suggest the wholeness of that design while preserving the integrity of its many individual parts. A phrase like "at all points" thus acquires a resonance in *Eureka*, as in the criticism, which is missing from casual use of those words.

"Now, distinctness—intelligibility, at all points, is a primary feature in my general design." (XVI, 199)

". . . we shall be warranted in conceiving continual differences at all points from the uniquity and simplicity of the origin." (XVI, 208)

"In a word, not because the atoms were, at some remote epoch of time, even *more than together*—is it not because originally, and therefore normally, they were *One*—that now, in all circumstances—at all points—in all directions—by all modes of approach—in all relations and through all conditions—they struggle *back* to this absolutely, this irrelatively, this unconditionally *one*?" (XVI, 219)

The point makes it possible to discuss, in almost spatial terms, something that has no spatial fixity, such as a starting point (XVI, 205) or the place in an argument when the writer pauses (XVI, 292, 308), or, as in Ellison's usage (VI, 184), point of view. When applied to time, the point specifies a juncture at which a new phenomenon arises or comes into prominence: "No thinking being lives who, at some luminous point of his life of thought, has not felt himself lost amid the surges of futile efforts at understanding, or believing, that anything exists *greater than his own soul*" (XVI, 312). If the point is crucial in the development of an individual, it is no less crucial in designating junctures of plots, whether literary or divine. In his effort to reach Dickens' "original design" in *Barnaby Rudge*, Poe quotes a passage in which the word "point" is used in a distinctly temporal sense, then comments: "Here the design is to call the reader's attention to a *point* in the tale . . ." (XI, 55), a usage of the word that adds to the time sense an overtone of wider significance, suggesting that the juncture arrived at is a place in which certain meanings peak or culminate. The points that the critic traces in his scrutiny of a text are exactly like the points traced by the interpreter of the universe: they are links in a chain, or perhaps better, steps on a journey. They are also the limits of the journey—the "spot of time," as it were, beyond which the divine restrictions on knowledge will not allow the human explorer to go:

"In the effort to entertain [the idea of infinity], we proceed step beyond step—we fancy point still beyond point; and so long as we *continue* the effort, it may be said, in fact, that we are *tending* to the formation of the idea designed. . . . But it is in the act of discontinuing the endeavor—of fulfilling (as we think) the idea . . . that we overthrow at once the whole fabric of our fancy by resting upon some one ultimate and therefore definite point. This fact, however, we fail to perceive, on account of the absolute coincidence, in time, between the settling down upon the ultimate point and the action of cessation in thinking." (XVI, 203)

The emphasis on points has its dangers, as the interpreter realizes, for in speaking of a point one cannot help suggesting the presence of an actual entity that in fact does not exist: "It is not to any *point* that the atoms are allied. It is not any *locality*, either in the concrete or in the abstract, to which I suppose them bound. Nothing like *location* was conceived as their origin. Their source lies in the principle, *Unity*" (XVI, 220). The literary interpreter finds the same tendency to unity in the text he examines: ". . . the plot of 'Night and Morning' is decidedly excellent. . . . This the author has evidently designed to make it. For this purpose he has taxed his powers to the utmost. Every page bears marks of excessive elaboration, all tending to one point—a perfect adaptation of the very numerous atoms of a very unusually involute story" (X, 117). The interpreter of the universe has the task of explaining the same process in the physical world without relying too heavily upon physicality. He turns accordingly, as the reviewer turned, to a metaphorical way of speaking, his chief image of convergence and unity being the "centre." The problem is that the centre carries with it the notion of a merely material entity, while the theory insists that matter is essentially a mediation through which an indestructible unity returns upon itself: "For, in fact, the tendency to the general centre is not to a centre as such, but because of its being a point in tending towards which each atom tends most directly to its real and essential centre, *Unity*—the absolute and final Union of all" (XVI, 233). The interpreter thus establishes "point" as the more neutral descriptive term, and consequently the superior term from a heuristic point of view. But the point itself does not survive for long, for everything that is built up in *Eureka* is torn down. Accretion, first, then reduction: here is the method of the book. Once the centre has served its purpose, it is dispensed with; then the point, too becomes expendable: "It is merely the *condition*, and not the point or locality at which this condition took its rise, that these atoms seek to re-establish;—it is merely *that condition which is their normality*, that they desire. 'But they seek a centre,' it will be said, 'and a centre is a point.' True; but they seek this point not in its character of point . . . but because it so happens . . . that only *through* the point in question—the sphere's centre—they can attain their true object, Unity" (xvi, 235).

What creates and maintains the condition of the universe, urging it back to original unity? Force. What draws the interpreter forward, from insight to insight, to a correct understanding of the full design? Again, force: ". . . I now assert—that an intuition altogether irresistible, although inexpressible, forces me to the conclusion that what God originally created—that that Matter which, by dint of his Volition, he first made from his Spirit, or from Nihility, *could* have been nothing but Matter in its utmost conceivable state of—what? —of *Simplicity*?" (xvi, 206).[10] The interpreter's relation to that all-powerful force resembles the victim's relation to the victimizing agency in the poems and tales, but lacks precisely the sense of victimization. The sole force that does not oppress is the one of which I am a part—the force of divine creativity. This force cannot oppose me because it made me, and because no created thing is every entirely separate from its creator. Rather, this force works *through* me, as interpreter, toward the unfolding of the full design, by presenting me with perceptions too forceful to be resisted: "Unless we are to conceive that the appetite for Unity among the atoms is doomed to be satisfied *never*;—unless we are to conceive that what had a beginning is to have no end . . . we are forced to conclude that the repulsive influence imagined, will, finally —under pressure of the *Uni-tendency collectively* applied . . . yield to a force which, at that ultimate epoch, shall be the superior force precisely to the extent required . . ." (xvi, 211). The identical quality informs literary creation. Of the poetry of Elizabeth Barrett Browning, Poe can say: "There is an Homeric force here—a vivid picturesqueness which all

[10] In "The Purloined Letter" it is the very simplicity of the problem that baffles the police, though not, of course, Dupin (vi, 29). Similarly, it is the sheer simplicity of the matter that enables Poe to explain the nature of poetry in a few pages where others, living in "the cloudland of metaphysics," have wasted many pages ("The Rationale of Verse," xiv 209-210).

men will appreciate and admire" (XII, 10). The flexibility of the term "force" is demonstrated in the discussion, later in the same essay, of her meters: "In imitating the rhythm of 'Locksley Hall,' the poetess has preserved with accuracy . . . the forcible line of seven trochees with a final caesura. The 'double rhymes' have only the force of a single long syllable—a caesura; but the natural rhythmical division, occurring at the close of the fourth trochee, should never be forced to occur, as Miss Barrett constantly forces it, in the middle of a word, or of an indivisible phrase" (XII, 27-28). It is perhaps this flexibility which accounts, at least in part, for the preference in *Eureka* of "force" over "power," while in the criticism (where both words are ubiquitous) the reverse is the case. As both noun and verb, force denotes a real entity—something "out there" in the world that I can perceive—and at the same time the *way* that perception comes to me. A force exists that in the nature of things I am forced to recognize and interpret.

Force is not something confined to the experience of the interpreting I. Every man has it, or rather, it operates within every man, human consciousness being nothing but a site in which, as in the universe itself, one force vies with another: "Not less eccentric [than the orbit of the comet] is the orbit of the human mind. If, as some have supposed, the comet in its upward flight is drawn away by the attraction of some other sun . . . the analogy will be more perfect. For while man is ever seen rushing with uncontrollable violence toward one or the other of his opposite extremes, fanaticism and irreligion—at each of these we find placed an attractive force identical in its nature and in many of its effects" (VIII, 267).

The stabilizing effect produced by the balancing of the attractive and repulsive forces—which function in *Eureka* just as they do in the essay, edited by Poe, from which I have just quoted—produces unity. Indeed, force and unity are virtually synonymous terms: "Thus, in the contemplation of a statue, or of an individual painting of merit, the pleasure derivable from the comments of a bystander is easily and keenly appreciable, while these comments interfere in no perceptible degree, with the force or the unity of our own comprehension" (xi, 9). Had the author of another work avoided conflict of thought, the passage being examined "would have derived that force, from unity, which it does not at present possess" (x, 75). In a similar way a prose narrative loses, when it is too long, "the immense force derivable from totality" (xi, 107), this totality arising in turn from a firmness of authorial control (xi, 108) precisely analogous, in the sphere of divine creation, with the volition of God, and from "one pre-established design" (xi, 108) comparable to the full design of the universe. The unity of effect insisted on in "The Philosophy of Composition" cannot be dissociated from the kinds of force through which unity is severally bodied-forth:

"As commonly used, the *refrain*, or burden, not only is limited to lyric verse, but depends for its impression upon the force of monotone—both in sound and thought." (xiv, 199)

"About the middle of the poem, also, I have availed myself of the force of contrast, with a view of deepening the ultimate impression." (xiv, 205)

"The next point to be considered was the mode of bringing together the lover and the Raven—and the first branch of this consideration was the *locale*. For this the most natural suggestion might seem to be a forest, or the fields—but it has always appeared to me that a close circumscription of space is absolutely necessary to the effect of insulated incident:—it has the force of a frame to a picture. It has an indisputable moral power in keeping concentrated the attention, and, of course, must not be confounded with mere unity of place." (xiv, 204)

In the literary work as in the physical universe, unity is the animus, force the expression. When the interpreter of the universe completes his "retrograde" analysis he discovers not so much the dominance of force as its subservience. The expansion and contraction of the universe are less a dynamic process of development than the means by which a state becomes once again what it was. The polar forces of attraction operate reciprocally so as to arrive, at the pre-established time, at the original point of ontological departure. But they are always phenomena *within* a state that is realizing itself—being wholly in the power of the unity into which they will themselves disappear. The expansion and contraction of the universe are simply the exertion of a force followed by its withdrawal. "Now a certain exertion of the diffusive power (presumed to be the Divine Volition)—in other words, a certain *force* . . . emits, by irradiation, this certain number of atoms; forcing them in all directions outwardly from the centre . . ." (XVI, 230). The reverse process comes about through a mere cessation of the same force: "Upon withdrawal of the force, the tendency [to return to unity] acts. . . . We may say that Rëaction is the return from the condition of *as it is and ought not to be* into the condition of *as it was, originally, and therefore ought to be*:—and let me add here that the *absolute* force of Rëaction would no doubt be always found in direct proportion with the reality . . . if ever it were possible to measure this latter:—and, consequently, the greatest of all conceivable rëactions must be that produced by the tendency which we now discuss—the tendency to return into the *absolutely original*—into the *supremely* primitive. Gravity, then, *must be the strongest of forces* . . . " (XVI, 234).

Italics and dashes, always more frequent in Poe than in any comparable American writer of his time, are myriad in *Eureka.* There is no central passage without its strong—indeed, its forceful—italic emphases. While such a practice makes one aspect of an argument more prominent than another, it has some corollary effects that are equally important. When combined with countless rhetorical emphases and a general repetitiveness, it indicates an intensity on the part of the author that we do not find in the critical essays or the marginalia. This interpreter of the universe is not merely arguing; he is arguing with great feeling. As befits an essay that is, in effect, a treatise on the sublime, there is a pervasive sense of awe. There is also a pervasive sense of will. The italics, the dashes, and the repetitions all suggest a mind bearing down with all the force of its volition, and, at the same time, a peculiarly insistent voice. The interpreter conducts his argument like a speaker keeping part of his attention on the evolution of his argument and another part on the audience, which can follow him only if he provides clear cues and signals, strong emphases and pauses, careful recapitulations and conspicuous transitions. To this extent, the art practiced here resembles that of the lyceum-speaker or the elocutionist,[11] while the manner, with its intensities and vocal pressures, recalls some of the more exercised protagonists in the tales. I am not arguing that our interpreter suffers from hysteria or even "nerves." He is eminently in control; but the control comes about through a strenuous exertion that differs from the efforts of the characters in the tales more in degree than in kind. The interpreter wants to convince—*must* convince—and accordingly, like the nervous characters in the tales, he sometimes "protests too much." This quality emerges through the use of the dash, which serves in part as a type of breath control, now relieving pressure and now building it up; in part as a way of suggesting that the argument is being presented one dramatic step at a time, and that the reader, by pausing along with the interpreter and then jumping forward with him, can live the expansion and contraction of the universe as it is theoretically unfolded; and in part, finally, as an expression of force:

"Without entering now into the *why*, let me observe that the printer may always ascertain when the dash of the MS. is properly and when improperly employed, by bearing in mind that this point represents *a second thought—an emendation.* In using it just above I have exemplified its use. The words 'an emendation' are, speaking with reference to gram-

[11] Poe read *Eureka* as a lecture on Feb. 3, 1848, at the Society Library in New York before an audience that apparently had no difficulty in following the argument. See Arthur Hobson Quinn, *Edgar Allan Poe: A Critical Biography*, p. 539; *The Letters of Edgar Allan Poe*, pp. 358, 359; and Fagin, *The Histrionic Mr. Poe*, pp. 52-58.

matical construction, put in *ap*position [sic] with the words 'a second thought.' Having written these latter words, I reflected whether it would not be possible to render their meaning more distinct by certain other words. Now, instead of erasing the phrase 'a second thought,' which is of *some* use—which *partially* conveys the idea intended—which advances me *a step toward* my full purpose—I suffer it to remain, and merely put a dash between it and the phrase 'an emendation.' The dash gives the reader a choice between two, or among three or more expressions, one of which may be more forcible than another, but all of which help out the idea. It stands, in general, for these words—'*or, to make my meaning more distinct.*' This force *it has*—and this force no other point can have; since all other points have well-understood uses quite different from this. Therefore, the dash *cannot* be dispensed with." (XVI, 131-132)

Although "The Philosophy of Composition" most fully exemplifies the kind of authorial self-consciousness displayed here, *Eureka*, too, is a self-conscious work. This is because, as already indicated, the interpreter wants to bring his audience along with him as his theory dramatically and rather breathlessly unfolds, and also because awareness is a positive feature of the productive mind. Only "a mind not thoroughly self-conscious—not accustomed to the introspective analysis of its own operations," can fall into the naive error of supposing that it can imagine infinity (XVI, 202). For "the finest quality of Thought is its self-cognizance . . ." (XVI, 204).

To cognize in this way is not to exalt, but to recognize. The self-conscious mind appreciates the nature and the limitations of its own functions; it knows what it can and cannot do. To be self-conscious is to recognize the indispensable, imperfect human element. Inevitably, despite the cool abstractness of much of the theorizing, *Eureka* becomes increasingly a human-centered work: the physics of the universe leads to God, who leads in turn to man in whom God is immanent. The Creation is, in a word, a kind of family. The source of the atoms which are returning to unity "lies in the principle, *Unity. This* is their lost parent." (XVI, 220)

"Having shrunk, however, so far as to fill only the orbit of our Earth, the parent sphere whirled from itself still one other body—the Earth . . ." (XVI, 251).

"The fact is, that, in regard to the distance of the fixed stars—of any one of the myriads of suns glistening on the farther side of that awful chasm which separates our system from its brothers in the cluster to which it belongs—astronomical science, until very lately, could speak only with a negative certainty." (XVI, 287-288)

The secret of existence lies in the origin of existence—not in the period of human generation but of the great universal creation of which human generation is a part. Consequently, the child, as in Wordsworth, is "closer" to the secret. But the child is eventually overpowered by that same reason which the angelic dialogues strive to repudiate: "But now comes the period at which a conventional World-Reason awakens us from the truth of our dream. Doubt, Surprise and Incomprehensibility arrive at the same moment. They say:—'You live and the time was when you lived not. You have been created. An intelligence exists greater than your own; and it is only through this Intelligence you live at all' " (XVI, 312). Against these false voices the interpreter raises the truth that only memory, being oriented in the direction of original unity, can preserve: "that nothing is, or can be, superior to any one soul—that each soul is, in part, its own God—its own Creator:—in a word, that God—the material *and* spiritual God—*now* exists solely in the diffused Matter and Spirit of the Universe; and that the regathering of this diffused Matter and Spirit will be but the re-constitution of the *purely* Spiritual and Individual God" (XVI, 313).

Eureka tears down what it builds, takes away what it gives. The universe gradually expands in preparation for its gradual contraction and return to unity, and the entire process—or rather, the living out of the condition—is material, as is God

Himself. Yet the attainment of that unity which is the fate of the expansion and contraction is, for all purposes, immaterial: ". . . when, I say, Matter, finally, expelling the Ether, shall have returned into absolute Unity,—it will then . . . be Matter without Attraction and without Repulsion—in other words, Matter without Matter—in other words, *Matter no more*" (XVI, 310-311).

At this point of ultimate contraction, when being as we know it disappears, the interpreter of the universe emulates Monos, who, nearing the term of earthly existence, hit upon the saving idea of new genesis:

"Guiding our imaginations by that omniprevalent law of laws, the law of periodicity, are we not, indeed, more than justified in entertaining a belief—let us say, rather, in indulging a hope—that the processes we have here ventured to contemplate will be renewed forever, and forever, and forever; a novel Universe swelling into existence, and then subsiding into nothingness, at every throb of the Heart Divine?

"And now—this Heart Divine—what is it? *It is our own.*" (XVI, 311)

The rhythm of *Eureka,* with its repetitions and reversals, its dashes and its pauses, is the rhythm of breathing, the life-sustaining process central to so many of the tales, and indissociable from the beating of the heart that, here and in "The Tell-Tale Heart," is the seat of life. The heart, ordinarily, is within a body, much as the occupant of a house is in a chamber and in the house itself. Indeed, *Eureka* presents a hyphenated phenomenon that is at once a wall-chamber-heart-man-universe-God. In this condition of being-within-something-larger there is no feeling of claustration, however, precisely because the hyphenated phenomena are ultimately identical. The walls or the chamber oppress me, when I am a victim in the tales, because they oppose my identity, my consciousness, my continuity of being. The universe can never oppress, by contrast, because the universe is God and God is man. This climactic "point" in the argument of *Eureka*

—the most daring feature of the theory by any standard—is not expressed directly by the interpreter himself, but by the voices of memory. In this relationship to these voices the interpreter resembles, superficially, the victims of the tales and poems, the helpless being who can only stand and listen as he is confronted by words created by a power other than his own. The difference is that here the message is immanent. The memories who speak are in the interpreter and in every man. In listening to the memories he is listening to himself and to Himself:

". . . just as it *is* in your power to expand or to concentrate your pleasures . . . so did and does a similar capability appertain to this Divine Being. . . . What you call The Universe is but his present expansive existence. He now feels his life through an infinity of imperfect pleasures—the partial and pain-intertangled pleasures of those inconceivably numerous things which you designate as his creatures, but which are really but infinite individualizations of Himself. . . . These creatures are all, too, more or less conscious Intelligences; conscious, first, of a proper identity; conscious, secondly and by faint indeterminate glimpses, of an identity with the Divine Being of whom we speak—of an identity with God." (XVI, 314)

Through the borrowed voices the interpreter brings to bear that most overtly forceful of tenses, the imperative. He becomes at the same time a prophet, a being whose access to the unity of the past reveals to him the unity of the future: "Think that the sense of individual identity will be gradually merged in the general consciousness—that Man, for example, ceasing imperceptibly to feel himself Man, will at length attain that awfully triumphant epoch when he shall recognize his existence as that of Jehovah. In the meantime bear in mind that all is Life—Life—Life within Life—the less within the greater, and all within the *Spirit Divine*." (XVI, 314-315)

Man is no longer, as in Pascal, a being of *disproportion*, caught between the *deux infinis*. If the infinite exists, says

Poe, it exists humanly, in man-who-is-God. Through the power of words the interpreter thus anticipates the state he will experience once he has finished his passage through the gulf beyond. Through himself the interpreter speaks through Himself.

6

CONCLUSION

Isaiah Berlin called his study of Tolstoy *The Hedgehog and the Fox*, drawing on a distinction made by Archilochus. According to Archilochus, the fox knows many things, the hedgehog one big thing. There are at least two ways in which the maxim may be applied, heuristically, to literature. One way is to decide which authors fall into which classification. The hedgehog family might include, for example, St. John of the Cross, Blake, Nerval, Hart Crane, Rilke, and a number of mystics. The foxes might be, among others, Chaucer, Montaigne, Shakespeare, Jane Austen, Stendhal. Applied in this way, the distinction provides an overview that, even if it is later abandoned, may serve to point out certain patterns in an author's work. Another way to use the distinction is to consider that there are hedgehog elements and fox elements in every writer. That is to say that the writings of any author are at once monistic and pluralistic—a unity in which everything converges in a single pattern, and in a variety of discrete phenomena having their own interest and identity. This use of the distinction is more dialectically productive than the other, because it encourages us to see how the two tendencies in an author's work relate to one another, and obliges us, as interpreters, to do justice to both.

I have tried to do justice in this study by taking each of Poe's works as it comes; by reading this work closely; and by comparing it with works that are like it or different from it. I have tried to recapture the sense of the individual work as process—as an unfolding activity of consciousness—without forgetting that, for all its uniqueness and "flow," it presents certain constant features. I have tried to show, finally, that Poe's imaginative writings constitute an overarching unity or whole—that Baudelaire was right when he observed that Poe, like Balzac, was absorbed in creating a "system." The recurring features in this system include power struggles between beings over who shall survive and on what terms; confrontations between an isolated individual and another human being, or between an individual and the material world, or, in cases where he externalizes something that reacts against him, between an individual and himself; a fascination with states or conditions of being; a concern with the way phenomena in the universe fit within one another, as container and contained; polarities and reversals, whereby one phenomenon calls into appearance its dialectical "counterpart" (Sartre's "metastable" structure); the continuity of consciousness and identity; the reciprocity of body and soul; the need for plenitude and affirmation; the indestructibility of being; and the supremacy of God.

Samuel Beckett's Molloy complains—or boasts—that all he knows is what the words know. If we look back at all the tales individually, all we know is what the fox knows, for we limit ourselves to the horizon of the given work. But if we look back at the long steady march of works, if we view them against a horizon that includes *Eureka*, if we see them, in short, from the standpoint of the hedgehog, then we know one big thing: the unity and eternality of being. Poe's "saving" myth is the deliverance of being from apparent destruction. Deliverance is facilitated, in turn, by the theory of unity, which exists as a critical principle, is embodied in each work, and forms the basis of the cosmogony. The theory of unity is itself, finally, an expression of the underlying principle of the universe, which is literally synonymous with God and virtually synonymous with man. This principle is physical, aesthetic, religious, and even, though we do not often use the word in relation to Poe, moral:

"We are now prepared to discover, at the symbolic hub of Poe's works, an ethical structure. Poe's holy war upon the didactic in art notwithstanding, this pattern of values controls his critical, philosophical, and imaginative writings. The highest value, Unity, is the characteristic of both death and art. Hence, all that conduces to Unity—to blissful completion whether in imagination or direct experience—is a 'good'; and all that perpetuates diversity is 'evil.' Yet, since the intensification of separateness provokes violent reactions like the urge to kill, even division can be understood as instrumental to goodness. Disease, decay, mental 'alienation'—all the apparent antitheses to the state of harmonious rest—are, in this view, the threshold to Unity."[1]

If Poe insists, in his theory, on the plenitude of being, it is partly to compensate for the fact that often, in his fiction, there is too little being to go around. Thus the deep, recurrent fear of being deprived of breath, or of losing consciousness, through which personal identity is continued and known. This scarcity is the corollary of that material scarcity (*rareté*) which more than any other factor, according to Sartre, influences the direction of history. Scarcity—the fact that neither you nor I have enough of a thing—is what causes me to negate you. That is why individual men have conflicts, and why countries have wars. Poe's characters live this scarcity, not in economic terms, but in terms that are at once physical, emotional, and ontological. They behave violently toward one another for the same reason. "Violence is not merely an exterior act—it can be an act no doubt—but it is also interiorized scarcity, or that by which everyone sees in everyone else the Other and the principle of Evil."[2] There may be a similar lack in consciousness itself. "Consciousness," in Sartre's definition, "is a being, the nature of which is to be conscious of the nothingness of its being."[3] Poe would reply: "Consciousness is a being, the nature of which is to suspect the nothingness of its being, but to insist on its plenitude." Poe's cosmogony tries to overcome this suspicion by establishing plenitude as the principle of the universe and of God Himself. Again Sartre provides a useful vantage point by emphasizing "one of the most fundamental tendencies of human reality—the tendency to fill. . . . A good part of our

[1] Moldenhauer, "Murder as a Fine Art," p. 296.

[2] Wilfred Desan, *The Marxism of Jean-Paul Sartre* (New York, 1965), p. 94.

[3] *Being and Nothingness*, p. 47.

life is passed in plugging up holes, in filling empty places, in realizing and symbolically establishing a plenitude. The child recognizes as the results of his first experiences that he himself has holes. When he puts his fingers in his mouth, he tries to wall up the holes in his face . . . he seeks again the density, the uniform and spherical plenitude of Parmenidean being. . . ."[4]

Poe's tendency to situate experiences "within"—to put one phenomenon inside another—belongs to the same pattern. Poe's created world is a series of containers, each of which is itself contained in a container, and so on, through an expanding series to the universe itself. One can trace the sequence upward from the heart and breath within the individual being, who is within walls (chamber, coffin, ship's hold, house, school, palace) that are located in a region of earth located in a planetary system contained, in turn, within the universe itself. There the expansion ends. But at this point it is no longer expansion. The container and the contained theory tacitly recognizes discreteness, scale, separation; for each container is in some sense higher than what it contains, and consequently different. But *Eureka* changes all that. *Eureka* transcends difference by affirming identity. By the end of the cosmogony, it is no longer possible to say that lower forms of existence are contained within higher. Not even the universe is "in" God; rather, the universe *is* God. There are at least two implicit, related archetypes in this system, the monad and the circle. We have seen Poe's interest in what Peirce called "the monadic state of feeling," and we have seen the closeness in substance and feeling between Poe's ideas and certain ideas of Leibniz. Poe's ubiquitous chamber—indeed, any enclosure in Poe—is monadic, as is consciousness itself. Moreover, Poe tends to make each work a little world in itself, the better to reflect the universe of which they are a part; and supports the tendency with a theory that makes unity a function of the circumscription of space. But the monad, as Georges Poulet has shown, is closely associated

[4] *Ibid.*, p. 613.

with the circle. According to three basic medieval definitions, "God is a monad which engenders a monad and reflects in Himself His own ardor," "a sphere of which the center is everywhere, and the circumference nowhere," and an entity "entirely complete in every part of Himself."[5] The definitions accord with Poe's aesthetic practice, his view of being and consciousness, his critical theories, and his ideas about the universe and God. One metamorphosis of the circle in Poe's work, as we saw earlier, is the vortex, which is a kind of downward-moving, inward-turning circle in motion. The point, on the other hand, is the circle in its immobile, centralized aspect: "In the divine sphere, which has no circumference, every point is identical with every other point, every moment is identical with every other moment. God is wholly Himself in whatever part of His Being or His existence that one may consider; or more precisely, there is in God no division of parts, no succession of moments in time, but an absolute simplicity and an absolute simultaneity. One can therefore say that in God the immensity of the circumference can be found again in the unity of the central point. . . ."[6] With this recognition Poe's system folds in on itself. Having expanded all the way out to the divine, it then contracts to the human; the existence throughout the universe of perfect, unbroken continuity and perfect, unbroken identity is affirmed: man himself becomes God.

Paul Ricoeur warns that "There does not exist, in fact, any act of signifying that is equal to its aim. . . . it is always with something that plays the role of analogon as starting point that the symbol symbolizes; the multiplicity of the symbols is the immediate consequence of their subservience to a stock of analoga, which altogether are necessarily limited in extension and individually are equally limited in comprehension."[7] The analogon of *Eureka* is man—his materiality, his desire for unity, the very rhythm of his breathing—despite

[5] *Metamorphoses of the Circle*, p. xi.
[6] *Ibid.*
[7] *The Symbolism of Evil*, p. 168.

the fact that the mode of being to which man ultimately belongs is in reality suprahuman and spiritual. The analoga in the other works are many: the house, the pit, the vortex, the beautiful woman, the star. In each case, it can be argued, the act of signifying falls short through a scarcity of means: like any human act, the act of signifying can never directly attain the ideal. But if we look toward the cosmogony from the perspective of the other works, we see that these works are themselves analoga of the meaning *Eureka* strives to express. They are analoga because each is, like the universe itself, a complete creation with a unity of its own. This is not to refute the argument of Ricoeur, who has raised a fundamental question about communication that only a book much longer and more ambitious than mine could hope to explore. Heidegger goes further than Ricoeur by suggesting that the act of writing establishes a horizon that it then cannot reach. Every poet thus speaks parts of a poem that he can never complete. The interpreter's job, therefore, is not merely to read the actual poem but to explore the one that was never written. I have pursued a more modest aim, first, because I do not feel capable, at this time, of going as far as Heidegger wants to go; and, second, because it seems to me that Poe's last major work *is*, for Poe, the unwriteable poem. So, to a lesser degree, are the other works that wholly (as in the dialogues) or in part (as in some of the poems and tales) anticipate the final, cosmic vision of *Eureka.* What is unique about the cosmogony is that it attempts not only to elucidate the unity it argues for, but to *be* it. Whereas the tales and poems are generally about man, *Eureka* is about God in man. Tamerlane is not sure, at first, that he can hope. Even when he decides that he can, hope depends entirely upon the will of God. Thus, in Poe's earliest major work, the first-person stands apart from a third-person God. In *Eureka,* the last major work, there is no separation because the first-person has become the First-Person. The full design, at last, is truly full.

INDEX